Conflict in Myanmar

The **ISEAS – Yusof Ishak Institute** (formerly Institute of Southeast Asian Studies) was established as an autonomous organization in 1968. It is a regional centre dedicated to the study of socio-political, security and economic trends and developments in Southeast Asia and its wider geostrategic and economic environment. The Institute's research programmes are the Regional Economic Studies (RES, including ASEAN and APEC), Regional Strategic and Political Studies (RSPS), and Regional Social and Cultural Studies (RSCS).

ISEAS Publishing, an established academic press, has issued more than 2,000 books and journals. It is the largest scholarly publisher of research about Southeast Asia from within the region. ISEAS Publishing works with many other academic and trade publishers and distributors to disseminate important research and analyses from and about Southeast Asia to the rest of the world.

Myanmar Update Series

Conflict in Myanmar

War, Politics, Religion

EDITED BY
**NICK CHEESMAN
NICHOLAS FARRELLY**

First published in Singapore in 2016 by
ISEAS Publishing
30 Heng Mui Keng Terrace
Singapore 119614

E-mail: publish@iseas.edu.sg
Website: http://bookshop.iseas.edu.sg

All rights reserved. No part of this publication may be reproduced, translated, stored in a retrieval system, or transmitted in any form or by any means, electronic, mechanical, photocopying, recording or otherwise, without the prior permission of the ISEAS – Yusof Ishak Institute.

© 2016 ISEAS – Yusof Ishak Institute, Singapore

The responsibility for facts and opinions in this publication rests exclusively with the authors and their interpretations do not necessarily reflect the views or the policy of the Institute or its supporters.

ISEAS Library Cataloguing-in-Publication Data

Conflict in Myanmar : War, Politics, Religion / edited by Nick Cheesman and Nicholas Farrelly.
  Papers originally presented to the Myanmar/Burma Update Conference 2015 held at the Australian National University, Canberra, from 5 to 6 June 2015.
  1. Burma—Politics and government—21st century—Congresses.
  2. Social conflict—Burma—Congresses.
  3. Ethnic conflict—Burma—Congresses.
  4. Civil war—Burma—Congresses.
  5. Religion and politics—Burma—Congresses.
  I. Cheesman, Nick.
  II. Farrelly, Nicholas.
  III. Australian National University.
  IV. Myanmar/Burma Update Conference (2015 : Canberra, Australia)
DS530.4 B972 2015   2016

ISBN 978-981-4695-84-8 (soft cover)
ISBN 978-981-4695-86-2 (hard cover)
ISBN 978-981-4695-87-9 (e-book, PDF)

Cover photo: Children clutching the flags of ethnic minority groups welcome a convoy of soldiers arriving in Laiza, Kachin State, for a gathering of non-state armed forces in 2013.
Photograph by 'Boothee' Thaik Htun.

Typeset by Allison Ley
Printed in Singapore by Markono Print Media Pte Ltd

CONTENTS

List of Maps	viii
List of Tables	viii
List of Figures	ix
Acknowledgements	xi
Contributors and Editors	xiii

Part I Introduction

1. Myanmar's conflicted politics 3
   Nicholas Farrelly

Part II War and Order

2. The politics of policymaking in transitional government: A case study of the ethnic peace process in Myanmar 25
   Su Mon Thazin Aung

3. Reexamining the centrality of ethnic identity to the Kachin conflict 47
   Costas Laoutides and Anthony Ware

4. A feminist political economy analysis of insecurity and violence in Kachin State 67
   Jenny Hedström

5. Pacifying the margins: The Pa-O Self-Administered Zone and the political order in southern Shan State 91
Ricky Yue

6. Landmines as a form of community protection in eastern Myanmar 121
Gregory S. Cathcart

Part III   Elections and After

7. The 2015 elections and conflict dynamics in Myanmar 139
Michael Lidauer

8. Institutions in Myanmar's 2015 election: The election commission, international agencies, and the military 163
Chaw Chaw Sein

9. Ethnicity and Buddhist nationalism in the 2015 Rakhine State election results 177
Than Tun

10. The Hluttaw and conflicts in Myanmar 199
Chit Win

11. Legislating reform? Law and conflict in Myanmar 221
Melissa Crouch

Part IV   Us and Them

12. Making sense of reactions to communal violence in Myanmar 245
Tamas Wells

13. Public perceptions of a divided Myanmar: Findings from the 2015 Myanmar Asian Barometer Survey 261
Bridget Welsh and Kai-Ping Huang

14. On Islamophobes and Holocaust deniers: Making sense of
violence, in Myanmar and elsewhere 285
Matt Schissler

15. Buddhist welfare and the limits of big 'P' politics in
provincial Myanmar 313
Gerard McCarthy

16. Threat perceptions in the Myanmar–Bangladesh borderlands 333
Helal Mohammed Khan

Part V Conclusion

17. Myanmar and the promise of the political 353
Nick Cheesman

Abbreviations and Key Terms 367

Index 371

LIST OF MAPS

5.1	The locations of the main ceasefire groups in Shan State	96
16.1	Security forces' combing operations: Bandarban (Bangladesh) 2015	342

LIST OF TABLES

4.1	Female representation in local- and national-level governance, 2014	70
4.2	Reports of conflict-related gender-based violence in Kachin State	74
4.3	Gender equality indicators, Kachin State	76
5.1	The pro-establishment camp versus pro-democracy camp, southern Shan State	101
9.1	Percentage votes for main parties for Pyithu Hluttaw in Rakhine State	192
9.2	Percentage votes for main parties for Amyotha Hluttaw in Rakhine State	193
9.3	Percentage votes for main parties for the State Hluttaw in Rakhine State	194
16.1	Major conflicts along the Myanmar–Bangladesh border (1978–2014)	340

LIST OF FIGURES

5.1	The evolution of the PNO and the PNLO	98
5.2	The political order in Pa-O areas before 2010	104
5.3	A different political economy driving power from the bottom	105
5.4	The political landscape in the southern Shan State	107
10.1	Non-partisan legislature, 2011–14	210
10.2	Questions and motions, 2011–14 (per session, per legislature)	212
13.1	Views of conflict (% agree) cross-national comparison	266
13.2	Ethnic backgrounds	267
13.3	Equal treatment between ethnic communities (% agree)	268
13.4	Economic vulnerability	269
13.5	Income distribution unfair (% agree)	270
13.6	Support autonomy (% agree)	271
13.7	Self-identity	272
13.8	Traditional values	274
13.9	Equal treatment between religious communities (% agree)	275
13.10	Partisanship and religion	276
13.11	Government responsiveness (% agree)	277
13.12	Military involvement in politics (% agree)	277
13.13	Support for systemic change	278
13.14	Use force for a cause	279

ACKNOWLEDGEMENTS

The June 2015 Myanmar/Burma Update conference at the Australian National University (ANU) was the most significant event of its kind since the Update series began in 1999. Commencing with a keynote address by the then-Speaker of the Upper House of the Myanmar legislature, U Khin Aung Myint, it brought together academics, researchers, policymakers and politicians from Myanmar and abroad for two full days of intense discussion and debate at a time of unprecedented political and economic change in Myanmar.

To the great credit of the ANU, the Update was supported almost entirely by funding from within the University. The conference convenors, who are also the editors of *Conflict in Myanmar*, are tremendously grateful to the ANU College of Asia and the Pacific, the Coral Bell School of Asia Pacific Affairs, and the Research School of Asia and the Pacific for their generous financial support for the conference, as well as to Veronica Taylor, the College Dean, and Michael Wesley, the Bell School Director, for their personal commitment to making the event a success.

The 2015 Update rested heavily on the organising skills of the Bell School events team, among whom Kerrie Hogan and Trish Sullivan deserve special mention for their tireless efforts and leadership. Sandy Hawke, the ANU VIP visits coordinator, ably guided the organisers through the mysteries of protocol. James Giggacher, the editor of the New Mandala website, handled media inquiries and podcasting with finesse. Luke Hambly put together the conference photo exhibit. The newly established ANU Myanmar Students' Association was actively involved throughout, organising a roundtable and hosting a friendly Myanmar language session at the end of the first day. The convenors and editors look forward to the Association's continued participation in future conferences and thank its members for their enthusiasm. They also especially acknowledge the conference advisory panelists: Justine Chambers, Violet Cho, Charlotte Galloway, Chit Win, David Gilbert, Khin Khin Mra, Khin Maung Yin, Gerard McCarthy, Myint Zaw, Naing Ko Ko, Pyone Myat Thu, Janelle Saffin, Andrew Selth and Trevor Wilson.

This edited volume, and the series in which it is the latest installment, has been made possible only with the cooperation of many persons. Above all, the editors wish to thank Allison Ley for her dedicated work in laying out the text. They also are grateful to Belinda Henwood for copyediting and Sherrey Quinn for indexing, which the ANU Myanmar Research Centre funded, again with generous support from the College of Asia and the Pacific. The Department of Political and Social Change provided its staff all the time and resources necessary to ensure the book's prompt and high quality completion. We thank Greg Fealy, the Head of Department, for his encouragement, and for the Department's ongoing commitment to the conference series.

Last but by no means least the editors are very grateful to Ng Kok Kiong and Rahilah Yusuf at ISEAS – Yusof Ishak Institute (formerly Institute of Southeast Asian Studies) in Singapore for their interest in the ANU's work on Myanmar, and for their professionalism, thanks to which the ISEAS Myanmar Update Series has gone from strength to strength. The current volume is the largest and most ambitious to date, and we look forward to working closely with our colleagues at ISEAS towards even greater things in years ahead.

CONTRIBUTORS AND EDITORS

Gregory S. Cathcart is an international development consultant specializing in community responses to landmine usage in Southeast Asia.

Chaw Chaw Sein is a Professor and Head of the Department of International Relations, University of Yangon.

Nick Cheesman is a Fellow in the Department of Political and Social Change, Australian National University, and convenor of the 2015 Myanmar/Burma Update.

Chit Win is a doctoral candidate in the Department of Political and Social Change, Australian National University.

Melissa Crouch is a Lecturer in the Faculty of Law, University of New South Wales.

Nicholas Farrelly is a Fellow in the Coral Bell School of Asia Pacific Affairs, Australian National University, and Director of the ANU Myanmar Research Centre.

Jenny Hedström is a doctoral candidate in politics and international relations at Monash University.

Kai-Ping Huang is a postdoctoral fellow in the Center for East Asia Democratic Studies, National Taiwan University.

Helal Mohammed Khan is the Director, International Research Initiative Bangladesh and a Chevening scholar at the Univerity of Edinburgh.

Costas Laoutides is a Lecturer in International Relations at Deakin University.

Michael Lidauer is the Senior Elections and Conflict Advisor in Myanmar for the International Foundation for Electoral Systems.

Gerard McCarthy is a doctoral candidate in the Department of Political and Social Change, Australian National University, and Visiting Fellow in the Department of International Relations, University of Yangon.

Matt Schissler is a doctoral student in anthropology at the University of Michigan.

Su Mon Thazin Aung is a doctoral candidate in the Department of Politics and Public Administration, University of Hong Kong.

Than Tun is an Honorary Lecturer in the Department of Political and Social Change, Australian National University.

Anthony Ware is a Senior Lecturer in International and Community Development at Deakin University.

Tamas Wells is a doctoral candidate in politics at the University of Melbourne.

Bridget Welsh is a Professor of Political Science at Ipek University, a Senior Research Associate in the Center for East Asia Democratic Studies, National Taiwan University, and a member of the Asian Barometer Survey.

Ricky Yue is a doctoral candidate in the Department of Politics, Languages and International Studies, University of Bath.

I
Introduction

1

MYANMAR'S CONFLICTED POLITICS

Nicholas Farrelly

BROKEN LIVES, BITTER HOPES

One of the sad facts about the long history of conflict in Myanmar is that nobody knows how many people have died, how many lives have been broken. Perhaps a million? Maybe more? In the civil wars, some of which have raged since the 1940s, the mountains and valleys have echoed with gunfire and artillery blasts, with shouted commands, and with the screams of the people as they have fled for their lives. Damage still pockmarks the landscape, landmines often lie unmapped, a hazard to everyone, and vast territories remain locked in standoffs between the government and its remaining opponents. Round after round of negotiations between these ethnic armed groups and the central government have enjoyed only mixed success. In some areas, central authorities have accepted local governance arrangements that see armed ethnic groups control substantial economies. They levy local fees and taxes, determine what gets taught at school, and inculcate society with their values of resistance and ethnic pride. These arrangements have often proved unstable, with ceasefires teetering, held together only by economic largesse and grim appreciation that the costs of war are immense. Where compromise cannot be found, Myanmar's people suffer through long-running jousts, which can sometimes escalate into full-blown battles, forcing thousands from their homes. During the past half-decade — even as life in Myanmar improved for tens of millions of people — difficult conditions have remained in parts of the Shan, Kachin and Rakhine States. In certain areas, ethnic armed forces have battled hard against the central government, unwilling to concede ground to what they consider occupying forces.

In the past, there was in fact no clear distinction between Myanmar's armed forces, often known by their Burmese name, the Tatmadaw, and the central government. Under the State Peace and Development Council (SPDC) that ruled until 2011, Myanmar's military high command and executive leadership were one-and-the-same (see Seekins 1999; Rogers 2009; Farrelly 2013). In practice, this system gave army officers, whatever their rank, dual responsibilities as both administrators and war-fighters. For instance, the head of Myanmar's Northern Command, usually a major general based in the Kachin State capital, Myitkyina, also served as the chairman of the Kachin State Peace and Development Council. This parallel structure disciplined civilian bureaucrats to the expectations of their military superiors. The SPDC mandated strict limits on all public spheres, and there was relatively severe scrutiny of information flows, publications and artistic expression (Brooten 2006; Carlson 2016; also Brooten 2013). The education system and the media were strangled so that only officially endorsed perspectives were circulated openly (Han Tin 2008, pp. 121–123). Dissenters were rounded up and subjected to long periods of incarceration (see Cheesman 2015). Many decided that survival under the military regime was impossible and fled abroad for a better chance at a livelihood and happiness. Thailand ended up absorbing millions of Myanmar exiles and migrants; thousands more ventured to Malaysia, Singapore, India and China (Farrelly 2012a; Meyer et al 2015). Significant numbers were also resettled in the western democracies that, with varying degrees of assertiveness, kept up pressure on the military regime.

What is remarkable is just how much has changed since the formal end of the SPDC era in 2011. The first step was the transition to a semi-civilian regime, where former senior military officers, including top brass from the SPDC, managed the new constitutional government (Egreteau 2014). President Thein Sein, who had been the fourth ranking officer in the SPDC, was the head of state from 2011 through to 2016. Shwe Mann and Khin Aung Myint, who served the transitional government in pivotal roles as speakers of the Union Assembly, also had backgrounds as top commanders in the military regime (Chit Win, this volume). Their civilian reincarnation was accompanied by important changes to the country's security agencies (see Selth 2014) and to the range of opportunities for popular participation in the political process (Lall and Hla Hla Win 2013). During this phase of democratic development, the Union Solidarity and Development Party (USDP) dominated the legislature in Naypyitaw and also held large majorities in the fourteen states and regions. They learned to work with a range of ethnic and democratic political parties, and also with their uniformed military peers. Over time, the USDP became fractious, with dueling powerbrokers in the legislature and the executive vying for control. Among the democratic forces, Aung San Suu Kyi's National League for Democracy (NLD), which had boycotted the 2010 election, ended up winning seats at the 2012 by-election. With elected representatives serving in the country's legislatures, Myanmar's iconic opposition movement quietly went about the business of re-establishing a vibrant nationwide network of campaigners.

During these transitional years, progress towards economic, political and social reform was inconsistent. While the government confidently adjusted some critical policies and benefited from renewed foreign interest, those who had anticipated a more thorough transformation of society were immensely frustrated. For any progress, the Thein Sein government needed to coordinate with the armed forces, and with reluctant elements among the USDP (Maung Aung Myoe 2014). Thein Sein's civilianised administration did enough, however, to enjoy a partially rehabilitated international image (see Tin Maung Maung Than 2012, pp. 75–76). Welcoming the NLD into the formal political arrangement was crucial in this regard. In mid-2013 the World Economic Forum put on a grand investment summit, before Myanmar hosted the Southeast Asian Games (for details on the games see Creak 2014) and then, in 2014, the country chaired the Association of Southeast Asian Nations for the first time. The ASEAN and East Asia Summits held toward the end of 2014 were an opportunity to showcase the increasing vibrancy of Myanmar society. Attention then turned to preparations for the 2015 general election. While the floods of mid-2015 affected many people, the elections ended up running smoothly and were judged reasonably free and fair by independent observers. In the final tally, the NLD was triumphant, going on to hold over sixty per cent of seats in the Union Assembly (see Min Zin

2016). It also performed very strongly in the elections for the State and Region legislatures, with the striking exceptions of the Rakhine and Shan States.

In Rakhine State, Myanmar's reforms have yet to have much positive impact, mostly because of ongoing tension between Muslim and Buddhist communities. In 2012, a wave of violence across northern Rakhine State saw 140,000 people, the majority of them Muslims, displaced from their homes. Many villages and neighbourhoods were burned to the ground in this anti-Muslim pogrom. Retaliatory attacks on Buddhist villages tore at the fabric of multi-religious local life, with unreconciled claims of indigeneity providing fuel for the communal antagonism (Thawnghmung 2016a). After the smoke had cleared, Myanmar was faced with an emboldened Buddhist chauvinist movement seeking to stamp its values on the national story. Politicians retreated in the face of support for these bigoted politics, which were made famous by the sermons of monks around the country (Walton and Hayward 2014). Wirathu, a preacher from Mandalay, became the most outspoken advocate for the nationalist cause, cloaking himself in ideas about the defence of race and religion. In the lead-up to the 2015 vote, people wondered about the potential influence of nationalist rhetoric on the election outcome. As it happened, the nationalist anti-NLD mobilisation failed to sway enough voters to influence the final result.

With its post-election majority in the Union Assembly, the NLD's Htin Kyaw, one of Aung San Suu Kyi's close confidants, was elevated to the presidency while Henry Van Thio, an ethnic Chin, became vice-president. The military's nominee for vice-president, Myint Swe, a retired general who previously served as chief minister of Yangon Region, took the other senior post. Htin Kyaw's cabinet also blends elements of the old and the new, seeking to strike a balance between experience, technical competence, and democratic orientation. The difficulty for the NLD is that so few of its senior figures have any substantial experience of government decision-making. And now that they have a greater say in national affairs there are difficulties aplenty. For a start, the separation between the military and the government has the potential to introduce tension at the heart of the Naypyitaw decision-making apparatus. There are few obvious mechanisms apart from trust building and personal connections that will avoid future showdowns between alienated elements of the NLD and military.

As Myanmar's political system continues to evolve, *Conflict in Myanmar* takes the time to consider conflict in its military, political and religious dimensions. The story of these enduring problems needs extra attention at a time when Myanmar's newly elected leaders are seeking to find better mechanisms for resolving old grievances. Aung San Suu Kyi talks of a twenty-first century Panglong Conference that draws its strength from the 1947 deal between her father, General Aung San, and the leaders of three major ethnic minorities. With this in mind, an historical sensibility is the basic foundation for any serious consideration of conflict in Myanmar today. As a response to contemporary conflict situations, this volume is structured around three key themes: war, politics and religion. To help introduce the volume, this chapter explains the historical and political context for each of these issues, starting with war.

WAR

In Myanmar, like in other countries defined by civil conflict, families and communities have been torn apart by their divided loyalties. These battles go back to the 1940s when, in the aftermath of the Second World War, the central government struggled to control secessionists at the margins (Smith 2007). Battles over political ideology and ethnic identity eventually left vast areas of the country relatively ungoverned, with Tatmadaw units bunkered down in well-fortified garrisons. In the early years of conflict, the consequences for local people varied immensely, with many welcoming the fresh ambition of communist or ethnic armies that operated in their areas. Through the 1960s and 1970s, under the socialist government of General Ne Win, conflict shaped all aspects of life, especially in the ethnic majority States (see Nakanishi 2013). Rebels established fixed bases and exerted influence over large proportions of the country. It was only in the late 1980s that the Communist Party of Burma imploded, splintering into ethnic militias, such as the powerful United Wa State Army (UWSA). Some of these groups agreed to ceasefires with the central government, which, after its own change of top-level leadership, was enthusiastic about a self-proclaimed mission to restore "law and order".

The 1990s then witnessed erratic progress towards what the military government described as "peace and development". Some of the ceasefires, like the one agreed with the Kachin Independence Army (KIA) in 1993, benefited from sophisticated local deal-making that enriched Myanmar military commanders and their counterparts in ethnic military, political and business groups (see Farrelly 2012b). Consolidating these agreements helped to develop the political prowess of all sides; they learned to work together even when their long-term interests diverged. The government allowed ethnic armed groups to manage designated "special regions" which offered a chance to imagine autonomous cultural and economic policies. Under these often-temperamental conditions, the negotiation of ceasefires was an ongoing process, vulnerable to the whims of new leaders and their commercial associates. In some localities, day-to-day skirmishes have been the pattern for as long as anyone can remember.

The most significant new war of recent years was in northernmost Myanmar, where the old antagonisms between the KIA and the central government reignited. This war, which started in its modern form in 1961, paused under the ceasefire from 1993 to 2011 (for a fuller history see Sadan 2013). Those years of ceasefire created new wealth, in particular among those who controlled the region's extractive industries. Jade, gold and timber offered untold profits for the businesses that exported to China's hungry markets. The ceasefire was made possible by the enmeshment of commercial, political and cultural interests. But nobody was greatly surprised when the ceasefire ended. Years of negotiation about the future of the KIA, and its potential transformation into a so-called Border Guard Force, had left all sides questioning the sincerity of their opponents. When in June 2011 the KIA challenged Myanmar government troops, the escalation came quickly. Within weeks, a tempo of guerrilla ambushes, infantry surges, and hit-and-run attacks had forced 10,000s of people to flee their homes. Soon, more than 100,000 internally displaced people sought refuge from the violence, many huddled against the Chinese border (Cook 2014).

This explosion of conflict generated considerable doubt about the overall trajectory of Myanmar's political changes. It showed that the armed forces remained willing to strike against perceived enemies, including with air power and heavy artillery. Questions about the military's chain of command fueled suspicion about the extent to which it had surrendered power at all. Under the 2008 Constitution, defence, security and border issues remained the preserve of the armed forces, with the commander-in-chief, by this stage Min Aung Hlaing, empowered to appoint uniformed officers to the relevant ministerial posts. In day-to-day operational matters, it was still the regional commands and the Bureau of Special Operations that played the central roles. For Northern Myanmar, it was Bureau of Special Operations No. 1. Its most important subordinate command, Northern Command, is headquartered at Myitkyina, the bustling riverside capital of Kachin State.

As the war continued, Myitkyina's ordinary business — trade, education, bureaucracy and transport — started to wilt. Munitions and personnel from elsewhere were originally brought in by rail until trains were attacked and the tracks sabotaged. Then boats were used, but they too were vulnerable to audacious KIA raids. Eventually, supplies and reinforcements were brought in by air.

The consequences of this war were felt deeply by the people of Kachin State and adjacent areas of northern Shan State, as explained by Hedström in this volume. While older people had direct memories of the effects of such conflict, an entire generation of local youth, including young women, had been raised under the relatively benign conditions of the ceasefire. They may have learned to resent central government impositions — the learning of the Burmese language in schools, the prominence of Buddhist ceremony in national life, the perception that their opportunities were limited by their ethnicity — and yet most had also enjoyed the benefits of a booming local economy. Myitkyina before the war was a key hub for education, business and cultural initiatives. It also enjoyed increasingly strong links with other areas of northern Myanmar, especially as better roads were constantly under construction, and new areas opened up for mining, logging and hydro-electricity projects. These routes served multiple purposes, especially for the many companies trading with counterparts in China (see Egreteau 2012).

China figured in the wartime calculations in other ways. Under the ceasefire, the KIA reinforced its fixed bases along the Chinese border, setting up relatively independent governance. Under the auspices of what was called "Kachin State Special Region 2", the KIA-controlled territories administered their own affairs and cultivated close ties with authorities across the border in China, including at the political level. They established casinos as one means of earning revenue, while the KIA also levied taxes on passing cross-border trade. When the war erupted, this access to China proved more valuable than ever, offering a way for the KIA to interact with the rest of the world. While the Chinese government is wary of any perception that it actively supports Myanmar's ethnic armed groups, it has also worked assiduously to ensure these groups are not overwhelmed by Tatmadaw firepower. China's double game is a significant factor along the entire length of this mountainous frontier.

That double game is also apparent in the Kokang Region in northern Shan State, where outbreaks of violence in 2009 and 2015 have shifted the terms of local government. The Kokang, whose armed group is more formally known as the Myanmar National Democratic Alliance Army, were the first to agree to a ceasefire when the Communist Party of Burma imploded in the late 1980s. Their "Shan State Special Region 1" is centered on the borderlands town of Laukkai. Like the KIA-controlled territories in Kachin State, it prospered under the unusual economic and political conditions of ceasefire. The Kokang maintained a reputation as a group with strong links to the regional narcotics business, especially opium cultivation and amphetamine production. The Myanmar government, while sometimes active in its efforts to stop the drug trade, also tolerated the Kokang presence. Part of the explanation for this cosy arrangement is the Chinese government's support for the ethnic-Chinese Kokang. While designated as one of Myanmar's "national races", the Kokang continue to speak Chinese and maintain a wide range of cross-border connections, as seen when the Myanmar government launched offensives against the MNDAA in recent years. Kokang refugees fleeing to China received support not made available to other ethnic groups in similarly desperate circumstances.

The most complicated situation in Myanmar's borderlands still relates to the United Wa State Army, which may have around 20,000 fighters (Ei Ei Toe Lwin and Htoo Thant 2015; Ferguson 2010). It is the best-provisioned ethnic armed group in the country, with a level of technical and industrial capacity that challenges even the Myanmar government itself. For that reason, the Wa are persistently problematic for the central authorities. While open warfare has been rare, the tentative ceasefire that holds in their areas of Shan State is among the country's most fragile. Chinese support for the UWSA is one reason that Sino-Myanmar relations are a challenge for both sides. The Wa are also alleged contributors to the production of narcotics and the United States sanctions their top leaders for running a "narco-army". Indeed their business allegedly ranges from ordinary consumer goods and raw materials through to the illicit flows of weapons, people, and drugs (Chin 2009; Lintner 1994). Making this formidable strategic and commercial force fit the needs of Myanmar's centralising government is a long-term political and military headache.

Careful management of rebellious groups is apparent further south, where some ethnic armed forces continue to antagonise the government from their bases along the Thai border. Since the late 1940s this "buffer" region has proved beyond the comprehensive control of central governments from either side of the frontier. Such a complicated strategic dynamic has encouraged discreet Thai support for insurgent groups that fight the

Myanmar government, among them the Mon, Kayin, Kayah and Shan ethnic groups. Hundreds of thousands of refugees and migrants from these groups have also sought sanctuary in Thailand. They tend to do low-paid jobs in the Thai economy, often under parlous conditions. This workforce is especially evident in borderland provinces where people who once lived in Myanmar provide much of the labour for manufacturing, agriculture and fishing. Myanmar's long history of displacement has created a new underclass in Thai society, ripe for exploitation by callous economic and political interests.

A different type of manipulation on the Myanmar side has kept these border wars in a perpetually unfinished state. Since the ceasefire agreements first emerged, particularly during the spurt of enthusiastic negotiations in the 1980s and 1990s, the country has endured stop-start progress towards final peace agreements. It does not help that trust in the government is patchy, as explained by Welsh and Huang in this volume. Nonetheless, when the Thein Sein government took power in 2011 it redoubled official peace-making efforts under the guise of the Myanmar Peace Center (MPC). Its mandate, to further diminish the level of conflict around the country, was entrusted to Aung Min, a government minister, who became the preferred negotiator (for details see Su Mon Thazin Aung, this volume). Aung Min worked closely with MPC staff to create conditions for a nationwide ceasefire agreement. While similar initiatives in the 1990s had failed, there was hope that the MPC could generate a more comprehensive and long-lasting peace deal. Negotiations with the different armed groups were slow and, in the end, the agreement signed in October 2015 only included a fraction of the country's major fighting forces. The key point of contention was reluctance to accept a resolution to conflict in the absence of a durable political structure that would offer sufficient autonomy to ethnic groups. The UWSA and KIA were among the major groups that decided to stay out of the deal. They were no doubt motivated not to participate by the idea that, before long, they would be negotiating with a different government entirely.

POLITICS

The NLD won a resounding victory at the 8 November 2015 general election (Thawngmung 2016b; Chaw Chaw Sein, this volume). Its win changes the equation for conflict in Myanmar in many ways. For a start, the new government does not have a track record on which it is possible to assess its long-term intentions or its potential success in implementing complex policies. In her initial statements, party chair Aung San Suu Kyi has insisted that resolving ethnic conflict remains a high priority. The difficulty for her team is that they will need to negotiate with both their own armed forces headed by Min Aung Hlaing and with the ethnic armed groups, under dozens of different commanders, to secure any long-term peace agreement. With Aung San Suu Kyi serving as State Counsellor, the ethnic armed groups are positioning themselves to demand a genuinely federal union where local rights merit utmost consideration. Some of the issues on the agenda include ethnic language education policy (South and Lall 2016), resource royalty distribution (Thet Aung Lynn and Oye 2014), land tenure (Kramer 2015), and the devolution of greater powers to State legislatures (Walaiporn and Pritchard 2016). At the same time, for ethnic armed groups themselves, the most pressing issues concern their future status after a peace deal. Many have resisted calls for disarmament and eventual demobilisation. Any disarmament, they fear, puts their people at the mercy of future Myanmar governments and they may not be able to rely on central government forces for protection. The fact that ethnic Bamar make up the majority of government troops, and that Bamar, Rakhine, and Mon are the only groups well represented in the officer ranks, is a further cause for concern. Discussion of a "union army" that draws its strength from all ethnic groups has yet to progress.

Nonetheless other political changes, especially elections, have already shifted the basis for interaction. At the start of the transition, the 7 November 2010 general election was held under deliberately constrained circumstances (see Lidauer 2012). The USDP, which emerged from the mass membership organisation created by the former military regime, needed to ensure it won the majority of seats. Along with the twenty-five per cent allocation for uniformed military personnel, this would guarantee it controlled a handbrake on radical political change. When the NLD decided to boycott the election, the USDP's position strengthened significantly. In the end, the USDP won nearly eighty per cent of seats at the union level, and also seized control of the fourteen State and Region legislatures. Its dominance of politics after the election suggested continuity with the dictatorial period. When Thein Sein appointed his first cabinet, former senior military officers held almost all of the key positions. Over time, some technocratic ministers came to take important posts. These changes did not shift the overall sense that the Myanmar government functioned with the support of the military rather than the people. At the same time, active elected ethnic representations from the Rakhine, Mon, Shan, Chin and Kachin States made their presence felt (Farrelly 2014).

The next phase of political reconfiguration followed the by-election held on 1 April 2012. By this stage, the National League for Democracy had agreed to participate in politics under the 2008 Constitution. Aung San Suu Kyi and forty members of her NLD team were elected to the Union Assembly. While they remained a modest force in Naypyitaw, the NLD could get familiar with how the system worked from the inside. Under these conditions, Aung San Suu Kyi had regular opportunities to interact with senior members of the USDP, particularly the speakers of the Union Assembly, Shwe Mann, and Khin Aung Myint. As retired senior military officers and loyal servants of the SPDC regime, they welcomed her presence in the legislature. The NLD representatives tended to keep quiet, only occasionally attacking government policies or querying the direction of the reform process. Their lack of law-making experience was telling even among an almost entirely novice contingent of USDP legislators.

After much waiting, and while there was some doubt about the potential for a free and fair vote, the 2015 general election offered the Myanmar people a chance to have their say. At the ballot box, voters rushed to endorse NLD candidates even though most were not well-known figures. This trend carried into ethnic areas where narrowly focused ethnic political advocates struggled to receive enough votes to win in the unforgiving first-past-the-post system. This result also revealed the changing demographics of many ethnic regions. They have become genuinely multi-ethnic, especially in urban townships that have drawn migrants from across the country. For now, the hard electoral mathematics seems to favour those parties that can create a genuinely national story of inclusion and change.

But the NLD's strong election result does not imply that political contention has disappeared. Religious politics remains a specific concern, especially among Buddhist communities anxious about the direction of social change. For now, no Muslims sit in the legislatures or hold any senior government positions. Other political interests that are not well represented in the new political system include young people, women, LGBTI communities, and the peasant and labouring classes. Politics in Myanmar remains an elite activity, where Aung San Suu Kyi, the daughter of the country's independence hero, exemplifies the distance between most voters and the politicians who take their seats in Naypyitaw: her comfort with international audiences contrasts with what are sometimes erratic performances on the local stage. The NLD makes no apology for this elitism or the advanced age of its senior decision-makers (for context see Farrelly 2016). They are the product of a long-running struggle for greater democratic participation in politics. The harsh reality, for these top leaders, is that their recent electoral success has revealed just how much work still needs to be done.

RELIGION

Perhaps the most demanding challenge in Myanmar today is the social faultline between Muslims and Buddhists. Muslims make up at least four per cent of the population although some guess that the actual proportion is nowadays much higher (see discussion in Crouch 2016, pp. 10–12). Such are the sensitivities around religious adherence that the government has proved reluctant to release the relevant parts of the 2014 census. The unspoken fear is that an accurate count of Myanmar's Muslims will further inflame the simmering resentments felt by many Buddhists. While there is a treasured local tradition of tolerance for different faiths, anti-Muslim sentiments also have a long history (Kipgen 2013). Under the Thein Sein government, the situation deteriorated greatly, particularly in northern Rakhine State, home to the persecuted Rohingya. Anti-Muslim violence in 2012 entrenched the divisions between Myanmar's two largest faith communities, and focused attention on the spiteful rhetoric of nationalist politicians and monks. In this volume, both Wells and Schissler look at the resulting challenges. In the years since that spike in violence, Muslims have struggled to protect their previous status and many Rohingya have been forced to live hand-to-mouth in informal settlements. Others have sought sanctuary across the border in Bangladesh, as explored in this volume's chapter by Khan.

Under these conditions, even the term "Rohingya" is contested. Those who seek to extinguish its usage on Myanmar soil claim that the designation hides illegal immigrants from Bangladesh who should be expelled from Myanmar territory. Myanmar's own official scheme of categorisation, which encompasses 135 ethnicities, includes one group that is predominately Muslim, the Kaman. They also live in Rakhine State and have been caught up in the recent religious conflicts. By the end of 2012, the violence had displaced over 140,000 Muslims, including Rohingya and Kaman. This population of displaced people joined the more than 400,000 Rohingya who already live in camps and informal settlements on the Bangladesh side of the border. The international community expressed deep concern about this explosion of communal animosity. Protests from the Muslim world were particularly strident. In the aftermath, there were claims of crimes against humanity and even genocide (Maung Zarni and Cowley 2014; Bauer 2015; also Southwick 2015).

Elsewhere in Myanmar, there was concern that the violence might spread. Cities like Yangon and Mandalay, and countless other towns across the country, have large and well-established Muslim populations. The perception that the Muslim community is large and growing adds to the popular anxieties that are inflamed by hardline Buddhist chauvinist rhetoric. Around the country, the symbols of the 969 movement and of the Committee for the Protection of Race and Religion (commonly known by its Burmese acronym "MaBaTha") are very common. Through 2013 there was more violence, with significant episodes in Meiktila, in central Myanmar, and at Lashio in the Shan State. Even though the level of violence has dropped since 2014, animosity towards Muslims remains a significant factor in local and national political relations. The NLD and USDP did not endorse Muslim candidates at the 2015 election. And many Muslim voters who were eligible to cast a vote in 2010 found themselves disenfranchised by new rules about voter eligibility.

Other religious minorities face different challenges. Most of Myanmar's Christian communities are found in the Kayin, Kachin and Chin States where ethnic identity has, for many people, been fused to their Christian faith. Strong Baptist and Catholic congregations exert influence on local politics, often in defiance of the expectations of Myanmar's Bamar Buddhist majority. Religion and politics are still fused in many minds, especially across the borderlands. The other religious minorities — such as Hindus, Sikhs and Jews — have relatively small populations, around which there tend to be fewer political skirmishes. Nonetheless any consideration of religious conflict still involves these visible minorities, who may also feel alienated from Myanmar's Buddhist majority culture and the powerful interests that it relies on for support.

THE MYANMAR UPDATE SERIES AND THIS VOLUME

The first Myanmar Update conference was held at the ANU in 1990. Since 2004 the conferences have been organized on a regular, biannual schedule. Over this period, the conferences have become the most significant events of their kind, drawing practitioners, analysts, and academics from around Australia, from Myanmar, and from across the world. The 2015 event was particularly notable. Khin Aung Myint, the speaker of the Union Assembly's House of Nationalities from 2011 to 2016, delivered the keynote address. For him, it was a very rare speech in English and an opportunity to explain the challenges of the transition from military rule. Years earlier it would have been inconceivable that such a senior retired military figure could even travel to Australia, let along participate in an academic event that prides itself on free expression and open debate. To his credit, Khin Aung Myint relished the chance to present his views and take questions from all-comers. We hope that future events will be similarly open to high-level political figures from among Myanmar's changing group of leaders.

In 2015, the Myanmar Update grappled directly with the dynamics of ongoing conflict and contention. The Buddhist–Muslim faultline was the subject of sustained and sometimes heated discussion. The issue of Muslim refugees taking to the Andaman Sea in search of safer harbour ensured the audience left with a strong impression of the real world implications of academic debate. The Myanmar Update conference series has long sought to engage with Myanmar's difficult political, economic and social conditions with a keen eye to practical consequences. This tradition now offers a rising generation of scholars, analysts and practitioners a chance to test their ideas and to seek out the most effective solutions to prevailing problems. Focusing attention on Myanmar's conflict dynamics is yet another way of showcasing our consistent attention to the most pressing political concerns.

Over the past decade each conference has been followed by academic publications, usually in the form of an edited volume. We are delighted that this volume includes a wide range of authors, drawn from across generations, national backgrounds and political perspectives. Taken together, the authors showcase the value of considered academic reflection on contemporary events and the need for creative responses to entrenched issues. The grim reality is that, for generations to come, Myanmar's development will feel the reverberations of conflict. Even when peace is finally proclaimed it will be necessary to keep revisiting the history of conflict as efforts to put society back together continue. There is no easy answer after so many years of strife and trauma. To help reconcile this history with Myanmar's current situation, the book is divided into three parts in addition to this introduction and the conclusion: 'war and order', 'elections and after', and 'us and them'.

The book's examination of war in contemporary Myanmar begins, in Chapter 2, with Su Mon Thazin Aung's discussion of the peace process that unfolded under Thein Sein. Her chapter offers a crucial foundation for assessment of conflict in Myanmar during this fragile stage of political transition. Next, in Chapter 3, Costas Laoutides and Anthony Ware re-examine the relevance of ethnic identity to the Kachin conflict, drawing on research undertaken since the resumption of hostilities in 2011. Given the level of violence suffered in Kachin areas in recent years, it is important that Jenny Hedström, in Chapter 4, explores the gendered aspects of insecurity in Kachin State. Taken together these Kachin-focused chapters offer a strong overview of the unresolved wars that have made life so difficult in Myanmar's borderlands. Ricky Yue then looks, in Chapter 5, at the Pa-O Self-Administered Zone in southern Shan State. This is an important case study for thinking about how marginal areas have been incorporated into the Myanmar nation-building project. It is followed, in Chapter 6, by Gregory S. Cathcart's discussion of landmines as a form of community protection in eastern Myanmar.

In the next part, writers turn their attention to the political process and the elections. This section begins with Chapter 7, which is by Michael Lidauer. It explains the results of the 2015 general election in terms of evolving conflict dynamics. This is followed by Chaw Chaw Sein's Chapter 8, on the role of various institutions in Myanmar's 2015 election. She looks particularly closely at the election commission, international agencies, and the military. Next is an essay by Than Tun on the challenging context of religion and ethnicity in Rakhine State. He considers the role of Buddhist nationalism in the 2015 election result. Chapter 10 by Chit Win then explores the changing role of the legislature in managing conflict during Myanmar's fragile transition from direct military rule. It offers lessons on the unexpected potential of the Union Assembly to deal with some of the country's most difficult issues. This chapter is followed by Melissa Crouch's interrogation of legislative practice during the reform period, with a specific focus on the various ways that conflict has been managed.

The subsequent part contains five chapters on religious and communal disquiet in a context where hatreds have been mobilised around potent notions of 'us' and 'them'. In Chapter 12 Tamas Wells explains how we might want to sensitively and cautiously appreciate reactions to communal conflict. His chapter is followed by a quantitative analysis, authored by Bridget Welsh and Kai-Ping Huang, of public perceptions of social division based on the 2015 Myanmar Asian Barometer Survey. Matt Schissler then offers, in Chapter 14, an appreciation of Islamaphobia and holocaust denial in an effort to make sense of anti-Muslim violence. That essays leads to Gerard McCarthy's analysis of Buddhist charitable organisations in provincial areas and their role in supporting the social safety net. Then, in Chapter 16, Helal Mohammed Khan considers the profound difficulties of jointly managing the Myanmar–Bangladesh borderlands, the site of so much of the region's recent heartache.

In the concluding chapter, my co-editor, Nick Cheesman, explains the variety of ways that we should think about political activity. His critique offers guidance on some of the further developments that may emerge in social scientific analysis of conflict and politics in Myanmar. As his intervention suggests, there is no sense in which any of these observations on recent history are the final word. Life in Myanmar continues to change rapidly, and the NLD-led government that took power in 2016 is now forced into a novel set of negotiations with the remnants of the former military regime. The military itself — for so long a principal actor in war, politics, and religion — is adjusting to the contested political landscape. For once, there is hope that deft policy-making and implementation will bring Myanmar's sad history of violent conflict to a close. If that proves a sustainable result, the country's political institutions will have changed in many ways. The chapters in this volume identify both the lingering problems and the enticing possibilities of a more peaceful tomorrow.

References

Bauer, Amie. "Reviews – The Hidden Genocide: Humanizing the Struggle of the Muslim Rohingya of Myanmar". *Children's Legal Rights Journal* 35, no. 1 (2015): 79–81.

Brooten, Lisa. "Political Violence and Journalism in a Multiethnic State: A Case Study of Burma (Myanmar)". *Journal of Communication Inquiry* 30, no. 4 (2006): 354–373.

———. "The Problem with Human Rights Discourse and 'Freedom' Indicators:

The Case of Burma/Myanmar Media". *International Journal of Communication* 7 (2013): 681–700.

Carlson, Melissa. "Painting as Cipher: Censorship of the Visual Arts in Post-1988 Myanmar". *SOJOURN: Journal of Social Issues in Southeast Asia* 31, no. 1 (2016): 116–172.

Chaw Chaw Sein. "Institutions in Myanmar's 2015 Election: The Election Commission, International Agencies, and the Military". In Cheesman and Farrelly, eds.

Cheesman, Nick. *Opposing the Rule of Law: How Myanmar's Courts Make Law and Order*. Cambridge: Cambridge University Press, 2015.

Cheesman, Nick and Nicholas Farrelly, eds. *Conflict in Myanmar: War, Politics, Religion*. Singapore: Institute of Southeast Asian Studies, 2016.

Chin, Ko-Lin. *The Golden Triangle: Inside Southeast Asia's Drug Trade*. Ithaca & London: Cornell University Press, 2009.

Chit Win. "The Hluttaw and Conflicts in Myanmar". In Cheesman and Farrelly, eds.

Cook, Alistair D.B. "Civilian Protection and the Politics of Humanitarian Action in the Kachin Conflict". In *Law, Society and Transition in Myanmar* edited by Melissa Crouch and Tim Lindsey. Oxford: Hart Publishing, 2014.

Creak, Simon. "National Restoration, Regional Prestige: The Southeast Asian Games in Myanmar, 2013". *The Journal of Asian Studies* 73, no. 4 (2014): 853–877.

Crouch, Melissa. "Myanmar's Muslim Mosaic and the Politics of Belonging". In *Islam and the State in Myanmar: Muslim–Buddhist Relations and the Politics Belonging*, edited by Melissa Crouch. New Delhi: Oxford University Press, 2016.

Egreteau, Renaud. "The Burmese Jade Trail: Transnational Networks, China and the (Relative) Impact of International Sanctions on Myanmar's Gems". *Myanmar's Transition: Openings, Obstacles and Opportunities*, edited by Nick Cheesman, Monique Skidmore and Trevor Wilson. Singapore: Institute of Southeast Asian Studies, 2012.

———. "The Continuing Political Salience of the Military in Post-SPDC Myanmar". In *Debating Democratization in Myanmar*, edited by Nick Cheesman, Nicholas Farrelly and Trevor Wilson. Singapore: Institute of Southeast Asian Studies, 2014.

Ei Ei Toe Lwin and Htoo Thant. "Military Rule Descends on Kokang". *The Myanmar Times*. 23 February 2015.

Farrelly, Nicholas. "Exploitation and Escape: Journeys Across the Burma–Thailand Frontier". In *Labour Migration and Human Trafficking in Southeast Asia: Critical Perspectives*, edited by Michele Ford, Lenore Lyons and Willem van Schendel. Oxford: Routledge, 2012a.

———. "Ceasing Ceasefire? Kachin Politics Beyond the Stalemates". In *Myanmar's Transition: Openings, Obstacles and Opportunities*, edited by Nick Cheesman, Monique Skidmore and Trevor Wilson. Singapore: Institute of Southeast Asian Studies, 2012b.

———. "Discipline without Democracy: Military Dominance in Post-colonial Burma". *Australian Journal of International Affairs* 67, no. 3 (2013): 312–326.
———. "Cooperation, Contestation, Conflict: Ethnic Political Interests in Myanmar Today". *South East Asia Research* 22, no. 2 (2014): 251–266.
———. "The NLD's Iron-fisted Gerontocracy". *The Myanmar Times*. 1 February 2016.
Ferguson, Jane. "Sovereignty in the Shan State: A Case Study of the United Wa State Army". In *Ruling Myanmar: From Cyclone Nargis to National Elections*, edited by Nick Cheesman, Monique Skidmore and Trevor Wilson. Singapore: Institute of Southeast Asian Studies, 2010.
Han Tin. "Myanmar Education: Challenges, Prospects and Options". In *Dictatorship, Disorder and Decline in Myanmar*, edited by Monique Skidmore and Trevor Wilson. Canberra: ANU Press, 2008.
Hedström, Jenny. "A Feminist Political Economy Analysis of Insecurity and Violence in Kachin State". In Cheesman and Farrelly, eds.
Khan, Helal Mohammed. "Threat Perceptions in the Myanmar–Bangladesh Borderlands". In Cheesman and Farrelly, eds.
Kipgen, Nehginpao. "Conflict in Rakhine State in Myanmar: Rohingya Muslims' Conundrum". *Journal of Muslim Minority Affairs* 33, no. 2 (2013): 298–310.
Kramer, Tom. "Ethnic Conflict and Lands Rights in Myanmar". *Social Research: An International Quarterly* 82, no. 2 (2015): 355–374.
Lall, Marie, and Hla Hla Win. "Myanmar: The 2011 Elections and Political Participation". *Journal of Burma Studies* 17, no. 1 (2013): 181–220.
Lidauer, Michael. "Democratic Dawn? Civil Society and Elections in Myanmar 2010–2012". *Journal of Current Southeast Asian Affairs* 31, no. 2 (2012): 87–114.
Lintner, Bertil. *Burma in Revolt: Opium and Insurgency since 1948*. Chiang Mai: Silkworm Books, 1994.
Maung Aung Myoe. "The Soldier and the State: The Tatmadaw and Political Liberalization in Myanmar since 2011". *South East Asia Research* 22, no. 2 (2014): 233–249.
Maung Zarni and Alice Cowley. "The Slow-Burning Genocide of Myanmar's Rohingya". *Pacific Rim Law & Policy Journal* 23 (2014): 683–754.
Meyer, Sarah R., W. Courtland Robinson, Nada Abshir, Aye Aye Mar and Michele R. Decker. "Trafficking, Exploitation and Migration on the Thailand–Burma Border: A Qualitative Study". *International Migration* 53, no. 4 (2015): 37–50.
Min Zin. "Burma Votes for Change: The New Configuration of Power". *Journal of Democracy* 27, no. 2 (2016): 116–131.
Nakanishi, Yoshihiro. *Strong Soldiers, Failed Revolution: The State and Military in Burma, 1962–88*. Singapore: NUS Press, 2013.
Rogers, Benedict. *Than Shwe: Unmasking Burma's Tyrant*. Chiang Mai: Silkworm Books, 2010.

Sadan, Mandy. *Being and Becoming Kachin: Histories Beyond the State in the Borderworlds of Burma*. Oxford: Oxford University Press, 2013.

Schissler, Matt. "On Islamophobes and Holocaust Deniers: Making Sense of Violence, in Myanmar and Elsewhere". In Cheesman and Farrelly, eds.

Seekins, Donald M. "Burma in 1998: Little to Celebrate". *Asian Survey* 39, no. 1 (1999): 12–19.

Selth, Andrew. "Police Reform and the 'Civilianisation' of Security in Myanmar". In *Law, Society and Transition in Myanmar*, edited by Melissa Crouch and Tim Lindsey. Oxford: Hart Publishing, 2014.

Smith, Martin. *State of Strife: The Dynamics of Ethnic Conflict in Burma*. Policy Studies, No. 36. Washington, D.C.: East-West Center, 2007.

South, Ashley, and Marie Lall. "Language, Education and the Peace Process in Myanmar". *Contemporary Southeast Asia: A Journal of International and Strategic Affairs* 38, no. 1 (2016): 128–153.

Southwick, Katherine. "Preventing Mass Atrocities against the Stateless Rohingya in Myanmar: A Call for Solutions". *Columbia Journal of International Affairs* 68, no. 2 (2015): 137–156.

Thawnghmung, Ardeth Maung. "The Politics of Indigeneity in Myanmar: Competing Narratives in Rakhine State". *Asian Ethnicity* (2016a): 1–21.

———. "The Myanmar Elections 2015: Why the National League for Democracy Won a Landslide Victory". *Critical Asian Studies* 48, no. 1 (2016b): 132–142.

Thet Aung Lynn and Mari Oye. *Natural Resources and Subnational Governments in Myanmar: Key Considerations for Wealth Sharing*. Subnational Governance in Myanmar Discussion Series, No. 4. Yangon: Asia Foundation, 2014.

Tin Maung Maung Than. "Myanmar". In *Regional Outlook: Southeast Asia, 2012–2013*. Singapore: Institute of Southeast Asian Studies, 2012.

Walton, Matthew J., and Susan Hayward. *Contesting Buddhist Narratives: Democratization, Nationalism, and Communal Violence in Myanmar*. Policy Studies 71. Washington, D.C.: East-West Center, 2014.

Walaiporn Tantikanangkul and Ashley Pritchard, eds. *Politics of Autonomy and Sustainability in Myanmar: Change for New Hope... New Life?* Singapore: Springer, 2016.

Wells, Tamas. "Making Sense of Reactions to Communal Violence in Myanmar". In Cheesman and Farrelly, eds.

Welsh, Bridget and Kai-Ping Huang. "Public Perceptions of a Divided Myanmar: Findings from the 2015 Myanmar Asian Barometer Survey". In Cheesman and Farrelly, eds.

II
War and Order

2

THE POLITICS OF POLICYMAKING IN TRANSITIONAL GOVERNMENT

A Case Study of the Ethnic Peace Process in Myanmar

Su Mon Thazin Aung

In a country such as Myanmar, which has long been in a constant state of civil war, there is no better reform agenda for a new government than negotiations with armed opponents. Given the long history of military rule in Myanmar, where fighting regularly breaks out between the Burman-dominated armed forces (Tatmadaw) and ethnic armed groups (EAGs), ethnic reconciliation has been one of the challenging tasks for successive governments. After the Tatmadaw's withdrawal from direct political rule in March 2011, the new quasi-civilian government placed persistent attention on the ethnic negotiation issue by bringing ethnic leaders to the table for peace talks. Unlike in the past, where the Tatmadaw (on behalf of both the military government and the armed forces) made ceasefire deals with the EAGs directly, the new peace process in Myanmar put the government and the Tatmadaw in different roles. The quasi-civilian government acted as a negotiating institution between two key stakeholders of the peace process: the Tatmadaw and the EAGs.

Coming during a political transition, the peace talks have been fragile. The talks have sometimes produced promising deals between the Tatmadaw and the EAGs. At other times, disputes between the Tatmadaw and ethnic leaders pertaining to political and security issues have seriously impeded talks. Such political and security issues range from the country's internal domestic affairs — such as heated discussions of "federalism", and "demobilize, disarm, reintegration" (DDR) — to the country's diplomatic affairs, such as different preferences between the military and EAGs on choices of international observers as foreign witnesses to sign a nationwide ceasefire agreement.

Nevertheless, to the surprise of many scholars and political observers, the Thein Sein government continued to manage its hold on the fragile peace process until the end of its administration in 2015. As a major milestone of the process, the government signed a ceasefire deal with the Tatmadaw and eight EAGs just a month prior to the November 2015 general election, while inviting seven other EAGs, which did not sign at this time, to continue joining the process.

How did the Myanmar transitional government sustain the peace process despite political and security constraints? Analysts have offered different explanations. Attention has been paid to both the characteristics of leaders and of institutions. Some analysts and intermediaries closer to the president's office, for instance Government Chief Negotiator Aung Min (2015) and Aung Naing Oo (2014), describe the current peace negotiations as a result of the agency determinant, focusing on the abilities of the leadership. Aung Naing Oo (2014, p.1) argues that the political leadership provided by President Then Sein at the political opening served as "a turning point" for the current peace process to become successful. However, this assessment fails to account for variations in the president's personal influence over the Tatmadaw.

On the other hand, Ashley South (2014, p. 1) argues that any future government would be less likely "to accord the same degree of privilege and credibility to ethnic armed groups as the current military-backed regime has done". South's explanation focuses on institutional determinants, noting the existence of the Thein Sein government backed by the military. South implies that being a military-backed regime, the Thein Sein government enjoyed the support from the Tatmadaw, which allowed it to grant more privileges to EAGs and have more credibility than a future government would. This argument does not fully recognize the fluctuations in the Tatmadaw's support toward the government peace agenda throughout the peace process.

This chapter acknowledges the importance of the aforementioned explanations in assessing the prospects of the ongoing peace process. However, they are insufficient by themselves to answer the question of how the government managed to keep both the Tatmadaw and the EAGs adhering to the peace process despite political and security constraints.

This chapter is descriptive rather than explanatory in most of its content. Throughout, the focus is on institutional determinants: the roles of the civilian technical team, the Myanmar Peace Center (MPC), and its coping strategy with respect to the peace process. I will denote the MPC as the centre of a peace "political community" — the core group of interrelated policy actors pursuing a matter of public policy important to them for instrumental reasons (Miller and Demir 2007, p. 137). The specific research puzzles I intend to address are: (i) is there a policy community centred on the MPC substantial enough to have been responsible for the sustained peace process; and (ii) if so, how did it manage to shape the dynamic of the peace negotiations in Myanmar in recent years such that it produced this sustained peace process?

In my explanation, I will argue that the role of the MPC as the centre of peace policy community and its approaches particularly shaped the dynamic of the peace process in Myanmar. Despite political and security constraints, the centre of the policy community, the MPC, was vital in sustaining the peace process throughout the Thein Sein administration. It has been employing a piecemeal approach in its dealings with the Tatmadaw and the EAGs through formal and informal binding mechanisms. This approach has helped the major stakeholders stick to their respective commitments during the ongoing process.

There are four sections in this chapter. Firstly, the research design is explained. Secondly, the empirical foundations of the state's approaches to President Thein Sein's peace project are discussed. Thirdly, my central argument is presented in two parts: I analyse the institutional trajectory of the centre of the peace policy community — the MPC — and examine its piecemeal approach to the ethnic peace process. My explanation uses two case studies to analyse formal and informal binding of the piecemeal approach. Finally, the conclusions are presented.

RESEARCH DESIGN

Definitions

Following the definition provided by Miller and Demir (2007), "policy community" in this chapter means a special type of interconnected social formation between policy actors, sharing the same policy objective, wherein communication and influence may flow in non-hierarchical patterns. The "centre of policy community" means the core group formed within such a community, and is considered as the heart of the policy community. A "piecemeal approach" denotes a coping strategy employed by the core group of the policy community in dealing with issues incrementally, with one problem and one goal at one time.

Research strategy

How do we assess the role of the technical team as the centre of a new peace policy community? How do we analyse the influence of the peace technical team and its piecemeal approach in sustaining the peace process under constraints? In order to examine the characteristics of the peace technical team as the centre of a peace policy community, we must first observe its institutional trajectory and characteristics. Next, we need to analyse the coping strategy employed for the peace process. For this chapter, the patterns of its negotiation approaches were observed in terms of "vision" and "practice" on peace policy, which can shape and redefine the entire process. Evidence throwing light on the negotiation approach by the peace technical team is presented through two significant cases: (i) federal vision as formally binding; and (ii) facilitation of ethnic summits as informally binding.[1]

To appreciate the implications of the evidence concerning why the piecemeal approach has helped sustain the peace process, this chapter adopts a causal observation process (Brady and Collier 2010). Particular attention is given to short-run problems with short-run feedback (Miller and Friesen 1982). The chapter draws on three types of evidence, namely: (i) in-depth and focused interviews; (ii) reports and personal notes; and (iii) published information. It covers the period June 2011 until December 2015, three months prior to the end of the tenure of the Thein Sein administration.

THE POST-2011 PEACE PROJECT

Background

After taking office in March 2011, President Thein Sein sought to break from the former military government by resolving the country's biggest challenge, the decades-long fight between the government and the EAGs. The ethnic policy under President Thein Sein was historically unprecedented in ideological, strategic, and operational terms. Ideologically, unlike ceasefire truces under previous military governments, which did not seek political dialogue with EAGs, a "federal union" became the vision of the new ethnic policy (Tun Tun Thein 2014). Strategically, the government now held peace talks of a collective nature that accepted ethnic political alliance groups as dialogue partners when the ceasefire talks reached the union level. This was contradictory to the previous military regime's ceasefire arrangements, where deals were made with individual EAGs. Lastly and importantly, the new operational style for policy implementation was clearly unorthodox. The new government relied on a resourceful technical institution made up of civilian experts to implement its peace policy agenda, whereas previously the military was solely in charge of ceasefire arrangements. This peace technical team served as the main political outreach of President Thein Sein to implement his policy initiatives on the ethnic conflict.

Resumption of conflict in north and northeast Myanmar became a major disadvantage for the new government. The president framed and identified the issue of armed clashes as a problem for "national unity" in light of the political transition towards democratization. Therefore, the government sought to move beyond mere ceasefire arrangements with the EAGs. The government officially aimed to bring all the EAGs into mainstream politics through political dialogue. On 18 August 2011, President Thein Sein announced his official invitation to all ethnic groups to peace talks by dropping the demand that they first convert to the Border Guard Force (BGF).[2] He offered two-tier peace talks — initially, to implement a preliminary peace program with state/regional-level governments, and then hold union-level peace discussions with the union government's peace team (New Light Of Myanmar 2011).[3] This was the first official nationwide announcement to all ethnic groups in decades.[4] It contained a commitment of the new government to pursue internal peace and regional development.

To implement the state's peace policy agenda with the EAGs, President Thein Sein assigned two peace teams, Team A and Team B, at the beginning of the peace process (Min Zaw Oo 2014). Team A was formed by powerful lawmakers from the ruling party, Aung Thaung and his close ally Thein Zaw (who was also a retired general and had a reputation as a moderate when dealing with Kachin ethnic groups under the previous government) (Aung Naing Oo 2014). According to internal sources, the initial slow reactions of the EAGs to the president's peace offer prompted the government to look for other alternatives that might produce dramatic changes in the ongoing peace discussions. Around that period, the president and his top executives began to re-engage the country with the international community, especially with Scandinavian countries, and individual policy advocates from non-governmental institutions, such as Myanmar Egress and the Vahu Development Institute.

By the end of 2011, on the president's verbal instruction, Union Minister Aung Min (then Minister for Railways) initiated peace discussions with some of the EAGs, taking assistance from Harn Yawnghwe, a powerful political exile and director of the Euro-Burma Office. Yawnghwe acted as a go-between for the government peace team and some ethnic armed groups with whom he had long-established personal networks. Consequently, Team B was formed at the end of 2011 with Aung Min as its leader. Soon after its formation, the team gained momentum. Several armed groups, including one of the largest armed groups, the Karen National Union (KNU), signed a ceasefire agreement with the government. Thereafter, Team A slowly became inactive after the first quarter of 2012.

With the initial success of Team B, the president began to groom it by granting a higher executive mandate to the leader and creating a technical team to support its work on the peace process. He created a "super cabinet", effectively promoting and transferring Aung Min to the president's office in August 2012 to oversee the running of the ministries, together with Industry Minister Soe Thein (another powerful minister in the cabinet) (Callahan 2012). Aung Min thereafter enjoyed the highest executive mandate, to be in charge of the government peace team and executive authority on supervising ministerial affairs related to foreign policy, security, peace, and the rule of law (personal note from senior staff of the President's Office, 2014). To institutionalize Minister Aung Min's peace initiatives, President Thein Sein formed union-level peace teams in May 2012, namely the Union Peacemaking Central Committee (UPCC) and the Union Peacemaking Working Committee (UPWC) (Myanmar Peace Monitor 2015). The UPCC was formally the highest authority in the peace process, having among its members constitutionally powerful decision-makers, such as the president, the army chief, heads from both houses of parliament, and numbers of ministers responsible for security-related ministries (Tin Maung Maung Than 2014). The UPWC held the highest mandate for peace policy implementation, being accountable to the central committee. Vice President Dr Sai Mauk Kham chaired the UPWC, while Aung Min from Team A, Thein Zaw from Team B, and the army commander were deputy chairmen. It consisted of fifty-two members in total, including union ministers, regional and state chief ministers, regional commanders, and ethnic lawmakers.

Challenges and continuity

The peace process has not been smooth sailing. At times, disagreements between the Tatmadaw and the EAGs brought the process to a standstill (Tin Maung Maung Than 2014, p. 113). Conflicts arose on several fronts. The contents of the peace discussions sporadically sparked tensions between the military and ethnic counterparts. Establishment of a federal army and topics under the DDR policy have been especially sensitive. Likewise, armed clashes on the ground occasionally have halted peace talks. For instance, fighting erupted between the Tatmadaw and ethnic armies, such as the KIA, Ta'ang National Liberation Army (TNLA), and the Myanmar National Democratic Alliance Army (MNDAA) in late 2014 and the first quarter of 2015, delaying the peace talks.

Under the military government, there was no official "negotiating institution" for making ceasefire deals with the EAGs. With the current peace process, the government peace team attempted to act as a third party negotiator and often managed to secure promising deals with the Tatmadaw and the EAGs. Instances include the agreements on a federal system of government in August 2014, deeds of commitment in February 2015, the Nationwide Ceasefire Agreement (NCA) draft of April 2015, signing of the NCA with eight EAGs in October 2015, and the framework for political dialogue developed in December 2015.

In order to understand the dynamics of the peace policymaking process, it is necessary to explain further who has been involved in it and how decisions have been made. In the following section, I will first discuss the institutional trajectory of the peace technical team as the centre of a new peace policy community under the Thein Sein administration. Next, its piecemeal approach will be examined.

PEACE TECHNICAL TEAM AS THE CENTRE OF A PEACE POLICY COMMUNITY

The term "policy community" refers to the interactions of a group of individuals, beyond or outside the formal processes of government, that occur in the interstices between and among government agencies, interest groups, corporations, industry associations, elected officials, and other institutions and individuals (Miller and Demir 2007). Throughout this new ethnic peace process in Myanmar under the Thein Sein administration, the peace technical team, the MPC, became the heart of the peace policy community. It was formed in November 2012 with strong international assistance received with regard to technical and financial matters, especially from the European Union (Seng Maw Lahpai 2014, p. 296).

The MPC was set up to provide substantial technical assistance to the government peace team, the UPWC; and to serve as a bridge between government officials, donor governments, and INGOs for the purpose of initiating peace activities. Being formed as a mediating organization for peace initiatives, the MPC does not have executive power, but it can influence administrative decision-making through its organizational position as "a secretariat for the Myanmar Peace Committee" and enjoys direct access to decision-making on the part of the president (Burma News International 2013).

The role of the MPC is more than that of a technical team. Being a part of the government's peace committee, it serves as one of the most influential groups in providing policy input to the president. In the five years of President Thein Sein's administration, the MPC supported the president as loyalists dealing with various stakeholders for major policy-making projects in addition to peace policy, such as media reform, and foreign direct investment law reform.

The MPC was the main force behind the state-initiated peace process.

Although the UPWC was the officially designated institution for peace policy implementation, some members of the UPWC, including the chairman and most of its ethnic lawmaker members, were not actively involved in the overall peace process. Behind the scenes, there was a considerable amount of political maneuvering by key members of the MPC on peace negotiations between the Tatmadaw and the EAGs. Their crucial roles ranged from setting the strategic agenda of the state-initiated peace policy, implementing them, and reshaping directions of the policy process when needed, to supporting the day-to-day activities of the UPWC. Under the formal structure, the UPWC had the highest authority for policy implementation. However, it appears that the overall direction of the peace process was set through MPC policy devices: (i) membership; and (ii) shared goals and its coordination with key stakeholders.

Membership

One of the special characteristics of the MPC under the Thein Sein administration was its membership. The MPC mainly consisted of civilian exile-returned policy advocates headed by several powerful ministers. Aung Min himself was the chairman of the MPC, run by President Office Minister Soe Thein and Khin Yi, Minister for Population and Immigration. Its civilian technocrats included individual policy advocates from think tanks, such as Hla Maung Swe, Tin Maung Than, and returned exiled academics Dr Kyaw Yin Hlaing, Dr Min Zaw Oo, and Dr Salai Ngun Cung Lian. However, among all members, it appears that Aung Min held the highest mandate from the president for implementation of the government's overall peace plan from the beginning of the peace negotiation process.[5] Most of the other members have personal networks with some ethnic leaders and could provide technical assistance and detailed information on the peace project. Throughout the peace process, exchange of resources — executive power, personal networks with ethnic stakeholders, technical capacity, and information advantage — among members created privileged relationships. On the other hand, Team A, in which all individual members were soldiers-turned-lawmakers and executives, did not have such a distinctive membership apparatus with which to implement the peace policy. After Team A was dissolved in mid-2012, the peace process slowly turned into a non-bureaucratic affair driven by civilian technocrats (Transnational Institute 2015).

More than serving as a "secretariat office", the exchange of resources among distinctive members explains the pervasive informal institutional power of the MPC. However, it is a matter of dispute whether the growing informal power of the MPC was a good or bad thing. The tight networks with self-contained agenda often provoked other stakeholders' discontent. Those disappointed included some working committee members who felt excluded from membership, especially the members of parliament, some associated departments from the administration, and the non-state owned media (interviews with three parliamentarians, 2014; with members of UPWC, 2014; and with a senior executive from the Ministry of National Planning, 2015). The MPC's practices during the peace process were often criticized for their exclusionary nature. Some critics from the local media and lawmakers were attentive to its "out-of-the-public-eye gatherings" with some ethnic leaders, including some leaders from the KNU, and spending donor money on individual institutional projects in the hope of redirecting policy attention towards the implementation of a narrowly focused private agenda.[6]

Shared goals and coordination with key stakeholders

Individuals within the MPC under the Thein Sein government shared explicit and implicit goals. Key members integrated as a tight and small group at the centre of the peace policy community in order to address officially declared objectives: (i) ceasefire negotiations; and (ii) political dialogue with the EAGs (interviews with the members of the UPWC and the MPC, 2015). Cognizant of the ups and downs in the peace process in recent years, the MPC members were aware that to have all EAGs sign the NCA would take time. The key members of the MPC were concerned that the process would collapse before the end of the Thein Sein administration. Therefore, the sustainability of the peace process toward the next administration from early on was a pragmatic objective of the MPC (interviews with senior members of the MPC, 2015).

To sustain the peace process, it was vital for the MPC to coordinate effectively and efficiently with key stakeholders, while dealing with constraints. It had to make sure key policy actors would stick to the peace project without giving up. The MPC itself was a brainchild of the Thein Sein government, the major stakeholder in the peace process and also the negotiating institution between the Tatmadaw and the EAGs. Throughout the peace process under Thein Sein's administration, the MPC enjoyed direct access and held an influential position in executive decision-making through its individual members, some of whom were ministers, political advisors to the president, and technocrats. Therefore, it could provide political input to the president in making strategic decisions and secure his unwavering support throughout the peace process.

The two major political actors (institutions) on which the MPC placed primary focus in this project were the Tatmadaw and the EAGs. But having strong support from the government did not imply that the MPC received consistent support from the Tatmadaw, because the government peace team's objectives could not entirely reflect those of the Tatmadaw. The former was concerned to sustain the peace process for political reasons, and the latter seemed to place threats to national security at the forefront of the ethnic negotiation project. The Tatmadaw was often reluctant to commit to ethnic peace negotiations. Its hesitancy in following President Thein Sein's orders in December 2011 and January 2012 to halt offensive operations against the Kachin Independence Army (KIA) revealed its basic indisposition to implement President Thein Sein's instructions immediately.

Although the president is the head of the government constitutionally, the real power of President Thein Sein — a former army general himself — over the Tatmadaw was arguable. According to the 2008 Constitution of Myanmar, the Tatmadaw stands as an authoritative institution under the executive, and also constitutes a separate bloc in the parliament.[7] Furthermore, it has six out of eleven influential members in the constitutionally highest decision-making institution, the National Defence and Security Council (NDSC).[8] One of the MPC's major responsibilities therefore was to make sure of the constitutionally powerful Tatmadaw's support for President Thein Sein's peace agenda.

On the other hand, more than twenty individual EAG groups were engaged in the peace talks as members of two ethnic alliance groups, namely the Nationwide Ceasefire Coordination Team (NCCT) and the United Nationalities Federal Council (UNFC). The establishment of a common position among them during collective bargaining has often been problematic. Some have occasionally raised their demands, based on their strategic calculations. For instance, one of the largest armed ethnic armies, the United Wa State Army, asked for a separate state when the Tatmadaw was heavily engaged in conflict with the MNDAA in their region. That demand cast doubt on the feasibility of signing a ceasefire agreement prior to political dialogue (Radio Free Asia 2015). Therefore, continuation of the peace process depended heavily on whether the peace technical team could encourage the Tatmadaw and the EAGs to continue with peace talks despite disputes. The next section explains how the approach of the MPC helped sustain the peace process to the end of 2015.

A PIECEMEAL APPROACH

This section examines the second part of my argument: that the MPC as the centre of the peace policy community employed a piecemeal approach in dealing with the Tatmadaw and EAGs. This piecemeal approach allowed the Tatmadaw and the EAGs to affirm their commitments incrementally, and to adhere to the peace process. The question of whether such a piecemeal approach influenced the decisions of the Tatmadaw and the ethnic leaders in committing to the process is analysed from two perspectives: (i) formal binding; and (ii) informal binding.

Formal binding

Binding decisions formally offer assurance to policy actors. These formal bindings are legitimate products of the negotiations made either through the inclusion and (possible) participation of the full set of legitimate decision-makers, or by recourse to a formally restricted area. As Christiansen and Neuhold (2012) highlight, negotiations made outside formal settings are crucial, but they require legitimation through formalization. The decision-makers' formal commitments represent their positions as authorities of organizations.

In the Myanmar ethnic peace process, formal binding was crucial. It made the MPC's piecemeal actions legitimate through authoritative guarantees established by policy actors representing their institutions, and encouraged the Tatmadaw and the EAGs to remain attached to peace talks despite constraints. The peace policy's federal vision is an instance of how formal binding worked through the MPC's piecemeal approach.

The federal vision as formally binding: One of the principal demands of the EAGs was discussion about federalism, including the establishment of a federal system followed by a federal army (Kuok 2014). But the Tatmadaw did not agree to discuss the issue in official meetings until three years into the negotiation process. On 15 August 2014, the peace technical team managed to secure the Tatmadaw's official agreement to discuss a possible federal system of government in peace talks. But the federal army issue has been left to settle in future discussions.

From a formal perspective, the agreement on talks over a federal system of government made during official meetings is legitimate. But a more thorny issue, the discussion of a federal army, has been left for the future. Therefore, it captures the features of a piecemeal approach where policy actors handle complex issues incrementally, that is, without taking a holistic view.

It can be argued that the peace technical team binds the Tatmadaw through its official commitment to the peace process while reducing possible risks associated with making commitments. It is obvious that an agreement on a federal system involves ideological and security risks for the Tatmadaw. In the past, the Tatmadaw had considered the term "federalism" as a threat to national unity (Collin and Martin 2012, p. 283). It strongly rejected any moves toward the idea, treating them as a prelude for the break up of the country. Therefore, the federalism issue has become one of the most pressing obstacles between the Tatmadaw and the EAGs over the last sixty years of successive military regimes.

Although the peace policy community and the EAGs had been discussing a federal system of government during their bilateral talks, the Tatmadaw initially appeared to be against the federal concept as a whole (both the federal system and federal army ideas) during the first two years of the negotiation process. The Tatmadaw refused to use the term "federal" in the single-text agreement draft, a combination document of a separate proposal from the Myanmar government and EAGs, before making a nationwide ceasefire agreement (Tun Tun Thein 2014). This became the major barrier for the continuation of peace talks in that period. Moreover, the military commander-in-chief took a position against the establishment of a federal army by stating that the union army already existed, referring to the Myanmar military. Consequently, when the EAGs pressed the federal issue in peace discussions, the Tatmadaw showed strong resistance to cooperating with the government team or the EAGs (interview with senior members of the UPWC, 2015).

After rounds of meetings, Aung Min managed to secure the president's agreement and NDSC decisions for federal system discussions at peace talks. The key point raised by the chief negotiator to the president and to NDSC members was "to accept the 'federal union' idea first; while leaving the federal army issue aside" (interview with NDSC member, 14 August 2014). If not, this issue would remain the major obstacle and would stall the peace talks. With endorsement from the NDSC, the Tatmadaw pledged to discuss the issue ahead of a nationwide ceasefire agreement, without compromising its position on the federal army demand. It was the first time in the history of the Tatmadaw that it officially agreed to discuss a federal system with the EAGs.

Although the peace technical team was unable to settle the debate on federalism, it dealt with the need for discussions on a federal system of government. Resolving one issue at a time, it formally bound key stakeholders to the peace process. The piecemeal agreement allowed the Tatmadaw to commit to the peace process while providing opportunities to remedy grievances if necessary. It therefore reduced the Tatmadaw's concerns over possible significant losses from far-reaching decisions, which are harder to alter in future. On the other hand, a formal commitment by the government and Tatmadaw reduced strains on EAGs over their long-standing demands for a federal system, although the "federal army" issue was not solved at the same time. For the EAGs, the agreement has been a remarkable achievement for their participation in the state-initiated peace process. Therefore, both the Tatmadaw and the EAGs adhered to the peace process despite its constraints.

Informal binding

Although formal binding is essential for legitimate negotiations, informal binding should not be underestimated in complex negotiations. To deal with complex issues, which fall under formally restricted areas, policy actors engage in self-enforcing binding activities. These sometimes require them to work outside formal boundaries. Christiansen and Neuhold (2012) explain that establishing informal binding increases efficiency as it could ease decision-making or facilitate negotiations. It serves as a mechanism to cope with obstacles to the complex policy process gradually, especially in a situation where formal binding is not likely to be achieved. Decision-making under an informal approach is "responsive to the requirements of the situation" (Christiansen et al 2003, p.10).

Informal binding efforts make a piecemeal approach more efficient. They incrementally increase the chance of reaching an agreement between key stakeholders in a situation where reaching formal arrangements is cumbersome. After a decades-long conflict, Myanmar's peace process is complex and opaque. Some issues are almost impossible to deal with in a formal setting. In such cases, the peace technical team employs informal binding in order to remove immediate obstacles while aiming to solve underlying causes in the future. The second case study, on facilitation of ethnic summits, examines the piecemeal approach when combined with informal binding.

Facilitation of ethnic summits as informal binding: Under the previous military government, the 1908 Unlawful Associations Act, commonly known as 17(1) (in reference to its section assigning penalties for offences under the law), was used to detain those people associated with EAGs. Under this law, individuals contacting an unlawful organization can be imprisoned for a period of between two and three years. Ethnic leaders, lawmakers, and party leaders did not forget the 17(1) issue throughout the process. The peace technical team was often questioned about the possibility of the government's annulment of the law (Hlaing Kyaw Soe 2014). Although the government has been engaging the EAGs under the peace negotiation process, as of 2015 this act remains in force.

In this respect, the peace technical team's actions associated with the EAGs over the peace process have clearly been informal. The team has kept the underlying issue, the legalization of the EAGs, to be settled in the future. Therefore its approach to the 17(1) issue has become piecemeal in nature.

Despite 17(1), the peace technical team has bound the EAGs to the peace process by offering help for their on-the-ground needs associated with legal and formal constraints. The peace technical team not only helped form the ethnic alliance group, the NCCT, on 2 November 2013, but also facilitated ethnic summits for NCCT leaders in their regions. The EAGs' conferences were held in the Kachin Independence Organisation (KIO)'s capital Laiza, the Karen National Union (KNU)-controlled Lawkhila, and the Wa headquarters at Pang Sang from 2013 to 2015 respectively. These meetings were intended to consolidate the ethnic groups' positions in relation to the nationwide ceasefire agreement.

The logistical arrangements of these conferences were a major concern to EAG members, who are spread all over the country, and some of whom do not have legal status. The peace technical team made it possible for the groups to meet by obtaining the government's endorsement and helping the EAGs with transportation of the ethnic leaders to the meeting destinations (Sai Wansai 2015). The team's facilitation of ethnic summits helped build trust in the government's commitment to the peace project and to bind the EAGs informally. On the other hand, the peace technical team left the 17(1) issue to be resolved in the future, specifically under the ceasefire agreement setting. Although the on-the-ground needs of the EAGs were fulfilled incrementally, they were still labelled as unlawful associations.

The peace technical team may have decided to defer the 17(1) issue because the underlying aspects of the problem are too big to be resolved within a short time frame or have some unwanted implications. During the negotiation meetings, the MPC suggested that it might address the 17(1) issue under the draft of a full NCA. According to a provision in Chapter 6 of the NCA document, all the EAGs signing the agreement would be removed from the list of unlawful associations (Nationwide Ceasefire Agreement 2015, p. 10). In order to gain legitimate status inside the country, it was imperative for the EAGs to get their organizations' names removed from the list, so the peace technical team could present this issue to the EAGs as one of the major driving forces to sign the NCA as soon as possible (Hlaing Kyaw Soe 2014). In fact, just a few days prior to the signing of the NCA on 15 October 2015, the government removed the groups signing from the list of unlawful associations. Therefore, interim agreements offered incentives to ethnic leaders to adhere to the negotiation process.

On the other hand, the peace technical team still managed to facilitate the EAGs' summits without intervening in formal aspects related to the 17(1) issue, leaving room for the Tatmadaw to exercise its power in ethnic politics. In practice, the Tatmadaw still leveraged the 17(1) provision in its relations with some EAGs fighting against it. It issued a warning to the NCCT concerning its Pang Sang conference invitation sent to three ethnic groups, namely the MNDAA, TNLA, and Arakan Army. It also warned media outlets over their association with the Kokang armed group,

MNDAA, while the EAGs' conference in Pang Sang was in progress. The letter from the Tatmadaw to the Myanmar Press Council (Interim) stated that, "if the media broadcast or publish statements of the MNDAA, they will face action under the law" (Ye Mon and Lun Min Mang 2015). This suggests that the peace technical team's facilitation of ethnic summits did not diminish the Tatmadaw's exercise of power on the EAGs, making it willing to continue to adhere to the peace process.

CONCLUSION

In this chapter I have explained how the Thein Sein government was able to sustain the peace process in Myanmar despite many constraints. Throughout the chapter, I have focused on the institutional role of the peace technical team, the MPC, and its strategy for sustaining the ongoing peace process. A fairly detailed examination followed of how the peace process obtained continuing participation from the Tatmadaw and EAGs although there have been several altercations between them. One way to analyse the work of the peace technical team is through case studies, throwing light on their coping strategies in terms of policy vision and practice, to arrive at several key observations and conclusions.

My findings offer two major contributions to the understanding of the peace policymaking process in Myanmar. First, the role of the MPC has been more than that of a formal secretariat. The emergence of the MPC under the transitional government changed the nature of the peace policy process. Although the UPWC officially kept the highest policy implementation under its authority, the directions to be pursued in the peace process from 2012 to 2015 came almost entirely under the purview of the MPC and non-ministerial affairs. Individuals in the government's peace team who were completely in charge of policy formulation under Team A found their influence diminishing with time. As Team A kept losing its power, the MPC secured better control over the peace process in terms of agenda setting and implementation.

Membership of the core group is critical in any policy community focusing on interactions with other policy actors through personal attributes. Limited numbers of participants make the MPC a resourceful centre of the "policy community". Local media often raised attention to the discriminatory nature of peace operations whenever the MPC acted in a consciously exclusive manner. Moreover, the negative connotations associated with the peace technical team were pronounced in its arrangements for 'out-of-the-public-eye gatherings', and spending of donor money on individual institutional projects. Nevertheless, the role of the team remained indispensable for sustaining the peace process throughout the tenure of the transitional government.

Secondly, my study has produced evidence that the MPC has been adopting piecemeal approaches with formal and informal binding in order to encourage the Tatmadaw and the EAGs to continue with the peace process. Although the government has adopted a three-phrase peace plan and certain ceasefire guidelines on paper, in terms of policy vision and practice, strategic negotiations are continuing under the piecemeal approach. The incremental approach allows the Tatmadaw and the EAGs to make small changes independently without taking much risk.

The piecemeal approach of the peace technical team enabled the government to sustain the peace process through formal and informal mechanisms. In my case study on "federal vision", if the Tatmadaw had to make dramatic changes by officially accommodating demands of the EAGs for a federal system and federal army at the same time, it is doubtful it would have been as willing to compromise. Likewise, informal binding with the EAGs on the 17(1) issue promoted trust in the government's commitment to the peace project. The facilitation of ethnic summits may not have helped the EAGs by resolving their long-awaited concerns, for example, being recognized as legitimate organizations, but the peace technical team's on-the-ground assistance to the EAGs helped earn their trust and bind them informally to the peace process. It further offered them incentives for a future settlement plan, encouraging adherence of the EAGs to the peace process. If the peace technical team had attempted to get the Unlawful Associations Act revoked, it could have posed a threat to the Tatmadaw by undermining its influence over the EAGs. In such a situation, it is unlikely that the Tatmadaw would have persisted with the peace process. All in all, despite the many political and security constraints, the role of the technical team as a policy apparatus along with its piecemeal approaches helped sustain the peace process until the end of the Thein Sein administration.

Notes

I wish to thank Nick Cheesman, Gerry van Klinken, Allen Hicken, and Min Zin who provided me with insightful comments on drafts of this chapter, and Ian Holliday for his valuable suggestions on my presentation prepared for the 2015 Myanmar Update conference at the ANU.

This article is a part of larger project in which I intend to address "why did quasi-civilian government manage to pursue bold reform policies despite policy disengagement among ruling elites?" I want to express my gratitude to individuals who provided me the opportunity to meet them and share their valuable analyses about the ongoing peace process based on available information during my course of study. These key individuals include, but are not limited to, the Speaker of the Upper House, Khin Aung Myint; Ministers for the President's Office, Soe Thane, Aung Min, and Tin Naing Thein; the late Union Auditor General, Thein Htike; Deputy Minister for Information Ye Htut (subsequently Minister for Information); Deputy Minister for Social Welfare, Relief and Resettlement, Phone Swe; the former Attorney General, Aye Maung; Deputy Attorney General Tun Tun Oo; retired minister Aung Kyi; Sumlut Gun Maw from the KIO; the president's political advisor Ko Ko Hlaing; Lower House lawmakers Thura Aung Ko, Dwe Bu, Hkyet Hting Nan, and Saw Tun Mya Aung; Directors of the MPC, Hla Maung Shwe, Dr Min Zaw Oo, and Dr Salai Ngun Cung Lian; Directors of the President's Office, Zaw Htay and Htet Aung; the International Labour Organization's liaison officer in Myanmar, Steve Marshall; International Crisis Group consultant Richard Horsey; and journalists, including executive editor of *Daily Eleven* Nay Tun Naing, freelancer Sai Aung Tun Lwin, and stringer for the *New York Times* Wai Moe.

1   There are two possible limitations to the chapter: (i) confirmation bias in relation to other stakeholders' strategies; and (ii) cherry-picking risk on case selection. Firstly, if it is true that the peace technical team had resolved its problems largely by taking into account how each group of policy actors would respond, then we must accept that both the Tatmadaw and EAGs have been equally strategic in their actions towards the peace process. There may have been other factors influencing the strategic choices made by the Tatmadaw and the EAGs with regard to whether or not to keep up with the process. Secondly, the chapter is confined to the study of two very difficult cases of the vision and practice of the peace process, omitting from consideration other important cases relating to the piecemeal approach followed by the MPC. Omitted cases may have yielded different results. Further research is needed to address both possible limitations, and therefore the findings presented here are provisional.

2   The previous military government set up the BGF to absorb the ceasefire ethnic armies into the command of the Tatmadaw. It resulted in the collapse of a seventeen-year ceasefire in April 2009 when armed groups refused to comply with orders to convert to the BGF.
3   Announcement No. 1/2011 by the Government of the Republic of the Union of Myanmar.
4   In 1963, General Ne Win made a similar announcement, initiating peace talks with ethnic insurgent groups. However, it was mainly for discussion of terms to surrender. See Min Zaw Oo (2014) and South (2013).
5   When the federal decision was made by NDSC, there seems to have been some disputes between Aung Min, his peace team, and the military generals. Internal sources confirmed that these were mainly related to promises made by Aung Min to ethnic groups at the peace discussions which the military found unacceptable. Therefore it appears that the mandate of Aung Min began to dissolve in the later days of the Thein Sein government.
6   Since the beginning of 2013, party leaders and lawmakers began to critique the opaque operational style of the government peace team supported by the MPC. The Speaker of the Lower House of Parliament, Thura Shwe Mann, raised concerns about the need for the parliamentarians to understand the ongoing peace process, and possibly prohibit concessions granted to the EAGs by Aung Min's executive power, and the UPWC's use of foreign grants in the peace project (see Burma News International 2014).
7   Under the executive branch, the Tatmadaw has authority over three security-related ministries, namely, defence, home affairs, and border affairs. The military also holds twenty-five per cent of seats in the union parliament and all regional and state parliaments. For discussion, see Chit Win, this volume.
8   Chapter XI of the 2008 Constitution allows the NDSC to impose martial law, disband parliament, and rule directly if a state of emergency is declared, and to exercise the powers of the legislature, executive, and judiciary before parliaments are formed.

References

Atkinson, Michael M., and William D. Coleman. "Policy Networks, Policy Communities and the Problems of Governance". *Governance* 5, no. 2 (1992): 154–80.

Aung Min. "Seize the Moment for Peace". *Foreign Policy*, 26 June 2015.

Aung Naing Oo. "Myanmar and the 'Ripe Moment'". *Myanmar Times*, 10 April 2014. <http://www.mmtimes.com/index.php/opinion/10143-myanmar-and-the-ripe-moment.html>. Accessed 20 April 2015.

Brady, Henry E., and David Collier, *Rethinking Social Inquiry: Diverse Tools, Shared Standards*. Lanham, MD: Rowman and Littlefield, 2010.

Burma News International. "Deciphering Myanmar's Peace Process: A Reference Guide 2013". Chiang Mai: Chiang Mai University, Wanida Press, 2013.

———. "Deciphering Myanmar's Peace Process: A Reference Guide 2014". Chiang Mai: Chiang Mai University, AIPP Printing Press, 2014.

Callahan, Mary. "The Generals Loosen Their Grip". *Journal of Democracy* 23, no. 4 (2012): 120–31.

Christiansen, Thomas, Andreas Føllesdal and Simona Piattoni. "Informal Governance in the European Union: An Introduction". In *Informal Governance in the European Union*, edited by Thomas Christiansen and Christine Neuhold, Cheltenham, UK and Northampton, MA, USA: Edward Elgar, 2003.

Christiansen, Thomas and Christine Neuhold (eds). *International Handbook on Informal Governance*. Cheltenham, UK: Edward Elgar Publishing, 2012.

Collin, Richard Oliver and Pamela L. Martin, *An Introduction to World Politics: Conflict and Consensus on a Small Planet*. Lanham, MD: Rowman and Littlefield, 2012.

Government of the Republic of the Union of Myanmar. *The Nationwide Ceasefire Agreement*, 2015. <http://mmpeacemonitor.org/images/2015/oct/nca%20contract%20eng.pdf.>. Accessed 25 December 2015.

Hlaing Kyaw Soe. "Calls Grow for End to Unlawful Association Act". *Myanmar Times*, 27 November 2014.

Kuok, Lynn. "Promoting Peace in Myanmar: US Interests and Role". Washington DC: Centre For Strategic And International Studies, 1 May 2014. <http://csis.org/publication/promoting-peace-myanmar>. Accessed 20 April 2015.

Miller, Danny and Peter H. Friesen. "Structural Change and Performance: Quantum Versus Piecemeal-Incremental Approaches". *Academy of Management Journal* 25, no. 4 (1982): 867–92.

Miller, Hugh T., and Tansu Demir. "Policy Communities". In *Handbook of Public Policy Analysis: Theory, Politics, and Methods*, edited by Frank Fischer, Gerald J. Miller and Mara S. Sidney, Boca Raton, FL: CRC Press, 2007.

Min Zaw Oo. "Understanding Myanmar's Peace Process: Ceasefire Agreements". Yangon: Swisspeace, *Catalyzing Reflection*, no. 2 (2014).

Myanmar Peace Monitor. "Government Peace Plan". <http://www.mmpeacemonitor.org/peace-process/government-peace-plan>. Accessed 20 April 2015.

New Light of Myanmar. "Union Government Offers Olive Branch to National Race Armed Groups: Invitation to Peace Talks". *New Light Of Myanmar*, 19 August 2011.

Radio Free Asia. "Myanmar Army Offensives Could Threaten Peace Deal with Armed Ethnic Groups". 4 May 2015. <http://www.rfa.org/english/news/myanmar/army-offensives-could-threaten-peace-deal-05042015171749.html>. Accessed 20 May 2015.

Sai Wansai. "Panghsang Meet to Foster Understanding Not to Decide on Nationwide Ceasefire Agreement". 1 May 2015. <http://mizzima.com/news-opinion/panghsang-meet-foster-understanding-not-decide-nationwide-ceasefire-agreement >. Accessed 2 June 2015.

Seng Maw Lahpai. "State Terrorism and International Compliance: The Kachin Armed Struggle for Political Self-Determination". In *Debating Democratization in Myanmar*, edited by Nick Cheesman, Nicholas Farrelly and Trevor Wilson. Singapore: ISEAS, 2014.

South, Ashley. *Mon Nationalism and Civil War in Burma: The Golden Sheldrake*. London: Routledge, 2013.

———. "Prospects for Peace in Myanmar: Opportunities and Threats". Oslo: Peace Research Institute Oslo (PRIO), 2012.

———. "Where Next in Burma's Peace Process?" *The Irrawaddy*, 8 December 2014. <http://www.irrawaddy.com/contributor/next-burmas-peace-process.html>. Accessed 20 April 2014.

Tin Maung Maung Than. "Ethnic Insurgencies and Peacemaking in Myanmar". In *ISEAS Perspective: Selections 2012-2013*. Singapore: ISEAS, 2014.

Transnational Institute. "Political Reform and Ethnic Peace in Burma/Myanmar: The Need for Clarity and Achievement". In *Myanmar Policy Briefing Series*, no. 14, April (2015).

Tun Tun Thein. "Burmese Govt Agrees, in Principle, to a Federal Union". *Democratic Voice of Burma*, 16 August 2014. <http://www.dvb.no/news/burmese-govt-agrees-in-principle-to-a-federal-union-burma-myanmar/43310>. Accessed 20 April 2014.

Vignat, Ella. "Shan State in Myanmar's Problematic Nation-Building and Regional Integration Conflict and Development". *Transnational Dynamics in Southeast Asia: The Greater Mekong Subregion and Malacca Straits Economic Corridors*, 2014.

Ye Mon and Lun Min Mang. "Army Warns Media Off Kokang". *Myanmar Times*, 4 May 2015. <http://www.mmtimes.com/index.php/national-news/14262-army-warns-media-off-kokang.html>. Accessed 25 May 2015.

3

REEXAMINING THE CENTRALITY OF ETHNIC IDENTITY TO THE KACHIN CONFLICT

Costas Laoutides and Anthony Ware

Myanmar has been plagued by armed conflict since independence. Kachin armed resistance, the focus of this chapter, has challenged the state since 1962, now more than half a century. Initial independence claims have been revised to demands for a federal union, but recourse to armed resistance to secure full or partial autonomy constitutes an explicit or implicit separatist claim. The conventional characterization of separatist conflicts in Myanmar, including the Kachin conflict, has focused on centre-periphery ethno-nationalist politics (for example, Egreteau 2012; Smith 1991, 1997, 2007; South 2008). The idea that 'ethnic' identity is primary has largely been taken for granted, and analysis has predominantly focused on the structure and patterns of inequality in inter-ethnic relations. This chapter reframes that presupposition.

For all its faults, the previous military government achieved some form of ceasefire deal with forty armed groups between 1998 and 2010 (Min Zaw Oo 2014). One of the most significant of these was the 1994 ceasefire with the Kachin Independence Organisation (KIO) and its armed wing, the Kachin Independence Army (KIA). The KIO/A are one of the larger, better organized and more formidable of the non-state armed groups, with a presence spread across a significant part of Kachin and northern Shan States, and while the other ceasefire deals were unwritten 'gentlemen's agreements', the Kachin ceasefire was the only one with a signed document (although the signed document was kept secret for a decade). For most of its seventeen years, the Kachin ceasefire also appeared among the most stable and led to a wealth of state-led, civil society and commercial development activity, including the rapid expansion of resource extraction.

Since the return to armed conflict by the KIO/A in June 2011, and their recalcitrant stance in national ceasefire negotiations, analysis has begun to emphasize the growing role of resource exploitation, and it has been tempting to characterize this as a resource-driven conflict. Certainly, almost all violent clashes between the Tatmadaw and the KIA since 2011 have centred around the control of resources and resource trade corridors, suggesting it is pertinent to once again re-examine the causes and characteristics of the Kachin conflict.

This chapter presents analysis of field research conducted by the authors in late 2014, using responses of key informants to discuss the key theoretical ideas employed in most discussions of this conflict: namely, 'ethnicity', 'identity', 'territory', and 'resources'. It seeks to make sense of the contemporary Kachin conflict through critical analysis of the expressions of proximal and root causes given by key actors against history and the literature, to illuminate the framing and drivers of the conflict and derive implications for achieving sustainable peace in the upcoming political dialogue. The field research involved key informant interviews with senior state officials, representatives from the non-state armed and civil groups, negotiators and advisors to the peace process, and key personnel from CSOs, multilateral agencies, donors, and INGOs.

There has been a long academic debate about the causes of conflict, particularly between 'grievance' and 'greed' theories. 'Ethnic' conflict is almost always perceived as a form of 'grievance' (for example, Geertz 1973; Horowitz 1985; Huntington 1996). Since Collier and Hoeffler (1998, 2002), debate about the causes of conflict have been focused mainly between 'grievance' and 'greed' theories. Rejection of ethnic-based 'grievance' as a driver of conflict has therefore often been used to categorize conflict as driven by 'greed', such as contestation over resource control and elite enrichment. This chapter challenges this dichotomy, questioning ethnicity as a framework for understanding the Kachin conflict, but without adopting simplistic greed-based alternative explanations.

Nationalist movements and counter-movements in Myanmar employ 'ethnic identity' as the key means of framing identification and political mobilization, but this chapter finds that conceptually these rigid categories are detrimental to peace processes — observations in tune with previous findings about the Moldovan conflict in Transnistria (Laoutides 2008). Recent comparative literature on 'ethnic conflict' suggests the flattening of conflict into an 'ethnic' label implicates all members of a given collectivity in the conflict and interpolates elements into a unified whole, erasing or ignoring distinctions and difference (Murer 2012). This chapter departs from a treatment of social groups in the Kachin conflict as distinct social categories, refocusing attention on how power is framed and contested in relation to processes of identification (Malešević 2006). It concludes that 'ethnicity' has become the outward manifestation of a conflict far more deeply underpinned by issues of political rights and distribution, state power versus decentralization, the quest for equality and freedom, and the question of who constitutes the demos in Myanmar's future democracy. Control over territory is seen to be both instrumental and strongly symbolic, a powerful tool for building a nationalistic sense of identity and a sine qua non condition for survival in the global international political context of sovereign states (Bartelson 2014). As such, this chapter concludes that engagement with the peace process needs to move beyond focus on the 'ethnicity' and 'ethnic dialogue' framework to address these underlying drivers of conflict.

The chapter consists of a series of theoretical discussions based on key observations made during our 2014 fieldwork. It is divided into seven sections. The first explores the problematic practice of framing conflict in Myanmar around ethnicity. The second considers the instrumental adoption of historical narratives in the construction of this nationalism. The third section explores the widely accepted primary cause of inequality, while the fourth uses this framework to analyse whether the root cause of the conflict is more about identity or ideology. The fifth and sixth sections then apply this analysis to the roles of territory and resources respectively, and to the return to conflict by the KIO/A in 2011. A concluding section explores the implications of this analysis for sustainable peace to be able to emerge from the political dialogue process.

FRAMING OF THE CONFLICT: MOVING BEYOND THE CANON OF ETHNIC IDENTITY

One of the starkest observations made during our research was that all local informants and a majority of international analysts framed their responses in terms of 'ethnic conflict', even though we carefully avoided such terminology during the research so as not to prejudice responses and analysis. Informants who identified as Kachin exclusively framed the conflict as ethnic, regularly adopting terms such as 'the Kachin', Bamar, and Tatmadaw as if distinct, homogenous, and exclusive parties. Most of the literature on conflicts in Myanmar, including the Kachin conflict, frames them in terms of ethnic identity and race in a similar manner.

Recent scholarship has heavily criticized the oversimplification of conflict as 'ethnic', suggesting that such portrayals largely fail to recognize the diversity of actors and identities, and tends to consider identities as distinct, binary, and enduring social categories. The 'ethnic' assumption for the study of conflict in Myanmar is in tune with an established analytical framework for the study of internal conflict and civil wars along identity lines, with the tendency to encompass all members of an 'ethnic' group as parts of the conflict (Cordell and Wolff 2010; Esman 2004; Gurr and Harff 1994; Wolff 2006). This line of analysis starts with a presupposition that 'ethnic identities' exist as distinct social categories, and that tensions caused by differences in identities constitute the primary source of collective violence and conflict. Analysis thus attempts to unveil the exact types and nature of ethnic identities, and the structure and patterns which lead to inequality and conflict.

Ethnic identities and nationalisms do not exist in a vacuum, but emerge in response to particular and dynamic sociopolitical contexts. Lived ethnic identity and sociocultural tradition is inherently fluid, diverse, and riven by division. The danger is, however, that the polarizing narratives used to mobilize nationalism mean that using the term in relation to conflict almost inevitably implies an inelasticity and staticism of internally homogenous and externally bounded groups that does not reflect the realities of the social world (Malešević 2004). Conflation of conflict into an 'ethnic' label also tends to engage all members of collectivities as part of the conflict, when in reality only a segment may be involved, and may interpolate elements into a unified whole, erasing or ignoring distinctions and difference (Gilley 2004; Murer 2012).

Kramer (2010), Smith (1991, 1999, 2007), South (2008), and others do offer more nuanced and detailed research into conflicts in Myanmar. While still seeing them through an 'ethnic lens', their treatment illustrates the point that 'ethnicities' should not be seen in terms of static, binary social categories, but as complex social realities. As Brubaker (1998, 2004) argues, ethnicity is not about distinct social groupings but dynamic social relationships and sets of historically framed processes. We argue that it is more useful to think about 'ethnicity without groups', or about nation-ness as a set of contingencies, discursive frames, political projects, or organizational routines than as groups of people. Static definitions of ethnicity that categorize individuals and groups not only reify group and individual relations, but also become a form of oppression, caging individuals into involuntary associations and groups into unmalleable identities (Malešević 2004). It is important to treat 'ethnicities' as categories of social practice, not discrete and static entities with clearly defined membership.

There has been a long academic debate about the causes and characteristics of conflict. 'Ethnic' conflict, as the conflicts in Myanmar have long been framed, is almost always perceived as a form of 'grievance', around issues such as ethnic structural violence (Geertz 1973; Horowitz 1985), incompatible cultural values (Huntington 1996), or loss of identity (Sen 2006). Since the influential work of Collier and Hoeffler (1998, 2002), rejection of ethnicity as a driver has often been used as a means to categorize conflict as driven by 'greed' motives, such as competition over scarce resources (Homer-Dixon 1994), or contestation of the control of economic opportunity (Collier et al. 2003), including the 'resource curse' (Le Billon 2001). However, our questioning of the 'ethnic' categorization of the Kachin conflict does not inherently constitute an argument for 'greed' motives around resources, but a plea to look beyond simplistic, binary categorization.

Our recent research confirms that most Kachin (and most others) discussing the conflict do so in terms of 'ethnicity' and identity. There is thus a need to explore the historically framed processes and ideological underpinnings of this framing as social practice, where ideology is seen as a process that incorporates thinking and action in order to produce cognitive maps that influence human behaviour (Williams 1988). Exploration of the historical and ideological narratives employed in legitimization and mobilization is a practical way to do so. As the contents of ideological discourses are informed by imagined ideal social orders that invoke collective ethical claims, interests, and emotions, or claims of superior knowledge, most ideologies avoid testability by surpassing everyday experience (Mann 2005). Ideological discourses are efficient in justifying a particular course of social action and in legitimizing or contesting existing power relations, thus it is important to focus on the ideological processes through which 'ethnic identity' is naturalized as the self-evident, legitimate point of reference to make sense of the world we try to understand (Malešević 2013). Rather than focusing on 'ethnic identity', the key issue in Myanmar appears to be how power is framed and contested in relation to processes of identification (Malešević 2006). What is at stake is the ideological question of managing political power that is "inherently territorial, authoritative and monopolistic" (Mann 2005, p. 53).

IMPORTANCE OF HISTORICAL NARRATIVES: PANGLONG

During our fieldwork, the main point of reference vis-à-vis the Kachin conflict — almost universally raised by respondents — was the narrative of the 1947 Panglong Agreement and the processes around independence. This is the dominant narrative used to articulate contemporary Kachin claims (see also Seng Maw Lahpai 2013; Walton 2008). It combines historical memory with a degree of mythology, as nationalist narratives do, and its centrality to contemporary claims demonstrates its centrality to the process of 'ethnic' mobilization. The creation of a shared sense of historical identity is central to the construction of nationalism, and is used to articulate and legitimize particular claims (Halbwachs 1992 in Walton 2008).

The narrative argues that, before British colonialism, the Kachin hills were never significantly or consistently brought under the control of the Burmese kingdoms, and this degree of separation was perpetuated by the British administration through the separate administration of the 'Frontier Areas'. As independence was being discussed, the Kachin's initial hope was for a future independent of the Burman state — despite strong Kachin representation in the national army, police, and civil service. The narrative continues that the agreement to create the 'Union' of Burma at the Second Panglong Conference, signed by Kachin, Shan, Chin, and Burman representatives on 12 February 1947 (with Karen observers present), was largely based on trust in the Burman leader Aung San, the architect of independence, with minimal text in the signed document and much of the other discussion either a gentleman's agreement or still undetermined (see also Walton 2008). It was therefore a voluntary agreement by the Kachin leaders to bring their land and people into a federal union between equal negotiating partners, to create something along the lines of the Shan federation or Malay federal states. After Aung San's assassination, the narrative argues, Kachin brigades in the army remained loyal to the state during the post-independence civil war while Kachin politicians worked within the system to address discriminatory economic, social, and political practices — until it became patently clear that the spirit of Panglong would never be willingly implemented. Eventually, and reluctantly, 'the Kachin' had no other recourse but to take up arms to reclaim their territory and protect their people and culture.

This narrative is well known, and will not be new to most readers. There is a great deal of truth in it, despite its mythological aspects (as Walton 2008 describes). Smith (1999) and South (2008) both agree that most of the area incorporated into the Frontier Areas on the central plains of Burma had been little affected by precolonial governments (see ICG 2013). There is consensus, *contra* to some Burman narratives of a precolonial unified kingdom, that there were frequent wars between nominally independent kingdoms prior to the colonial period (Lieberman 1978; Renard 1988; Smith 1999). The British then ruled most non-Burman areas via local leaders under the Frontier Areas Office, perpetuating separation to such an extent that at one time Burmans even needed a visa to travel to Kachin territory. It is thus not surprising that proposals involving independent statehood for the Frontier Areas were promoted prior to independence. Walton (2008) documents the Stevenson plan presented at the 1946 first Panglong conference, and a key Kachin informant pointed to a 1945 Churchill plan. Both proposals give currency to the idea that Kachin territory was not automatically being considered nor was considering itself part of Burma during the early independence negotiations. The Panglong Agreement's objective was to speed the process of independence rather than determine the details of the post-independence union (Sadan 2013), again concurring with contemporary Kachin narratives. In one sense, then, the historic and contemporary conflict has been over two competing narratives of the form of independence agreed at Panglong: a voluntary federal agreement between equals, or a commitment to union as the means to defend against subjugation now being undermined by separatism (Walton 2008).

Returning to our previous analysis, the Panglong narrative constitutes a 'process of identification' for the Kachin, used since the KIO/A took up arms to articulate claims and mobilize nationalism. Its political effectiveness has strengthened a sense of shared 'ethnic identity', while at the same time laying claim to control central tenets of that Kachin ethnicity. It could be argued that this Kachin nationalism was a response to the growth of Burman nationalism in the push for independence, as well as the way the Burmese-dominated state employed identity difference as a means to distribute public goods and allocate privileges after independence (Walton 2013). This historical narrative, however, reinforces and solidifies Kachin identity politics as the vehicle through which a legitimate political alternative can be pursued. The danger is that using this historical narrative as a tool of political legitimation and mobilization reifies spheres of inclusivity and exclusivity, overlooks the complexity and diversity of the Kachin, and obfuscates the deeper issues peace processes and political dialogue need to address into a simplistic focus on federal power sharing.

EXPRESSION OF PROXIMAL CAUSE: INEQUALITY

The most common issue we heard from the Kachin we spoke with was a perception of having been systematically dismissed, suppressed, and sidelined. As Sadan (2013) notes, most Kachin feel they experience economic, social, and political discrimination, which they believe to be the result of deep-seated antagonism and hostility toward them by 'the Burman elite'. The government has never disputed that Kachin are citizens, but most — even the state officials and negotiators interviewed — agree that there has been institutionalized discrimination against all minorities, including the Kachin. This is corroborated by the 2015 Asian Barometer Survey results (see Welsh and Huang, this volume); also Welsh (2015) found fifty-nine per cent of those who identify as being from an 'ethnic minority' report discrimination, with much higher figures for respondents from non-Buddhist minorities. Even Kachin living in Yangon and urban centres expressed concern in our interviews that they are not treated as equal members of Myanmar society, and are discriminated against unless they hide their identity. Burman informants noted that even the country's ambassadors are all Burman, with none from ethnic minorities.

Numerous respondents expressed a fear that was encapsulated by a civil society leader who commented, "If we are not allowed to practice our culture, educate in our language, and express our religion, one day we will no longer be Kachin." Both civil society and non-state Kachin leaders interviewed said that 'the Burman elite' and military are trying to homogenize identity to achieve the ideological ideal of a strong nation-state. As a Kachin civil society leader said, "The Tatmadaw are fighting for what they believe is nation-building, but in so doing they become a predatory force."

If individual Kachin citizens and civil society representatives express concerns about discrimination and denial of equal citizenship rights, the Kachin non-state actors we interviewed all articulated their contemporary grievances in terms of Panglong, as discussed above. One was particularly strident, suggesting that Panglong offered them a place in a union between equal partners, but that they have been treated as subjects ever since. Seng Maw Lahpai (2013, p. 298) elaborates this grievance as being denied self-determination in terms of control over the administration of their region (systems of governance, population, and territory), including the resources that could provide independent revenue streams, thus limiting financial dependency on Naypyitaw and maximizing their ability to deliver development opportunities to the Kachin people.

The intense passion about their inability to exercise governance over what they consider to be 'their' communities and territory is very strong. As a KIO spokesman said:

> We continue to emphasize Panglong because that was where we signed a formal agreement with the Burmans. We invested our land to build this nation. We are here with our own land. When they breached the Panglong agreement, they tried to occupy our land and dominate and control us. We are still asking for Panglong to be honoured, but if they do not recognize Panglong, the land should revert to pre-Panglong terms, which did not put the land automatically into the Union.

Or put another way by a foreign consultant:

> The Burman elite adopted the role of big brother, taking on the responsibility and burdens of the minorities in a patron-client sort of relationship to help them develop. The Burmans invited the minorities to come under their umbrella, and they are meant to be pleased with this — but the ethnic minority leaders want to be patrons in their own right! The Kachin elite's grievance about inequality is not so much regarding inequalities in citizenship or development, as in position and roles in governance.

The process of identification of 'the Kachin' as an identity group appears primarily the result of a clash of different worldviews about the nature of the political community, and of an effective, appropriate, and equitable distribution of power and sociopolitical rights. But is that in fact the case?

EXPRESSION OF ROOT CAUSE: CLASH OF IDENTITIES OR IDEOLOGIES?

When we asked informants about causes of grievances, all the Kachin civil society and non-state leaders as well as most international observers and some Burman elite referred to deep-seated paternalistic and chauvinistic attitudes by most Burmans towards the 'ethnic' minorities. Most suggested that particularly the Burman military and ex-military ruling elite express these attitudes.

Concerns over Burman paternalism and chauvinism are widespread, and are not new. As a Kachin civil society leader said, "All Burmans are somewhat chauvinistic, and only since [the crackdown on dissent after] '88 have the Burmans begun to see themselves as victims too — which has led to some increase in empathy and feeling of a shared struggle against authoritarianism and an increased recognition of the way minorities have been treated." Another minority civil society leader noted that ordinary Burmans suffered under military rule too, but argued strongly that they never had to face the chauvinistic discrimination felt by the ethnic minorities. There is concern that the Burman majority don't see themselves as an 'ethnic' group; they are 'the Bamar', the rest are 'ethnic minority races', implying a subordinate and dependent status. So in some ways the conflict is not only about ethnic identity, but a ruling elite employing ideas about identity to control political power, both over Burmans but particularly over minorities.

Several Kachin leaders and KIO representatives went further in the interviews, however, arguing for a clash of deep-seated ideologies about sociopolitical organization, claiming a fundamental difference between Kachin and Burman ideals about the proper order of political power and the social contract. This is an interesting narrative, particularly in light of the significant historic role the Communist Party of Burma (CPB) played in the conflicts in the eastern borderlands of Kachin and Shan States.

Quite a few Kachin informants argued at length that the Tatmadaw officers see themselves as guardians of the legacy of the great Burmese conquering kings, and that their nationalistic duty is to perpetuate this historic vision of an expansionist centre subduing competing kingdoms and other minority peoples. This model of political organization, they argue, has been compounded by the motivation of all post-independence Burman rulers (civilian and military) to restore Burmese prestige and international reputation, and has led most Burmans to still be bound by traditional Burmese social hierarchical thinking. By contrast, these informants argued, Kachin social ideals are far more egalitarian. The Kachin civil society and non-state leaders interviewed co-opt the historic, documented Kachin distinction between *gumlao* (egalitarian-democratic-republican) ideals and *gumsa* (feudal hierarchy with ranked lineages and hereditary privilege) practice (Leach 1970 [1954]).

This is a fascinating narrative for contemporary Kachin leaders and KIO representatives to articulate. The CPB long sought to unify opposition to the Ne Win government along non-ethnic lines, which brought out a heated debate in all groups on the role of ethnicity and ethno-nationalism (Lintner 1990; Smith 1991). The KIO/A gave little support to the CPB's political class analysis and their all-Burman leadership, highlighting that self-determination and addressing Burman chauvinism were their central priorities. The appeal of this sort of narrative, though, as a tool for nationalistic political legitimation and mobilization is obvious, as it suggests that the visible clash of identities is the epiphenomenon of a deeper ideological clash, where ideology is understood as a (universal) process through which human actors articulate their actions and beliefs — making sense of the world around them and how to intervene in it. This narrative lays claim to a fundamental ideological difference between 'Kachin' and 'Burman', and there is clearly some support for such a notion. As one foreign consultant noted, there is a surprising level of symbolic sympathy for the armed groups across the country, particularly the KIO/A, even from those who are critical of their leadership and rent-seeking, and disavow the use of violence. This narrative effectively argues that even if Kachin and KIO/A leadership show some authoritarian and elite rent-seeking behaviour, they in fact remain closer to their people than the Tatmadaw or Burman elite, in both practice and in principle.

It would be unwise to suggest there is only one ideological process of identification (*gumlao* vs *gumsa*) in the Kachin conflict. That would imply yet another homogenizing narrative substituting 'ethnic identity' as a cause of the conflict. Rather, the complexity of the conflict and the number of diverse actors suggest numerous opposing ways that power is framed and contested. For example, the political contests in the KIO/A and among civil society groups call for different processes of articulating actions and beliefs, while actors who have benefitted from the Kachin ceasefire (businessmen, militias, empowered local leaders) and the militia groups that have become de facto government forces have blurred the ethno-nationalist divisions.

Further examination of the emergence of a Kachin sense of identity as 'an ethnic group' will need to be the subject of another paper. The Kachin have a very strong sense of collective identity, which is surprising given their diverse subgroups, some only distantly related and sometimes with their own internal tensions. The collective experience of systematic discrimination and chauvinistic paternalism, however, bolsters the legitimacy of the separatist argument. This narrative of a clash of ideology does point to the issue of political rights and the distribution of power as fundamental and the quest for equality and freedom — only not solely along narrowly constructed 'ethnic' lines.

THE ROLE OF TERRITORY AND RESOURCES

If the Kachin conflict is fundamentally about processes of identification, with issues of political rights and the distribution of power perhaps fundamental, this raises the question of the role of territory and resources in the conflict. As noted in the introduction, the conflict has clearly morphed in recent years, with almost all violent clashes between the Tatmadaw and the KIA since 2011 now centred around the control of resources and resource trade corridors.

Territory is very significant to the Kachin we interviewed: even in Yangon many spoke passionately about the land and identify with Kachin State. The ideas of territory and nationalist identity were strongly connected, not as a mystical attachment to the land but based on cultural survival. As one diaspora academic said, "The idea of land and territory expresses life, the life of the people." Continuity of identity is seen to be linked to control of territory, making the value of territory mostly the ability to sustain cultural identity, through self-government and control over the resources required to sustain and develop Kachin society (Seng Maw Lahpai 2013).

Territory exercises a hegemonic influence in global political organization, due to the strength and priority of the notion of the nation-state. At the symbolic level, effective control of territory is a sine qua non condition for survival in international politics (Buzan 1991; Toft 2006). The structure of global politics requires communities to exercise effective control over territory as supreme authorities (demonstrate state-sovereignty, or something equivalent for de facto states), both as proof of their ability to rule themselves and as a means of visibly claiming a place in the world of sovereign communities. The strong presence of territory as the spatial manifestation of the presence and survival of political communities is inherent to this idea. Ethnicity and nationalistic identity are often employed as the main narratives for survival in such international relations, which invest their claim to territory with legitimizing moral value and make the cause imperative and non-negotiable (Laoutides and Kingsbury 2015). In this context ethnic and national conceptions of identity seem to be the only collective identities able to qualify for citizenship and participation in a territorially demarcated and organized global political society. Beyond affective and cultural attachment, therefore, territory is instrumentally important for the material aspect of Kachin community survival. It is a means to ensure self-government, economic survival, and the survival of cultural identity.

Recent scholarship has stressed that violent action against the state requires economic and political opportunity. Collier and Hoeffler (1998, 2002) link armed resistance with the availability of both financing (particularly abundant natural resources) and potential recruits (individuals with reduced prospects of material advancement through peaceful activity). There is a growing consensus that insurgent access to resource revenues prolongs armed conflicts and presents significant hurdles to peace, although in Kachin State the issue is potentially as much one of the perceived protection of natural resources from exploitation by the state or state-sanctioned international investors. Many Kachin actors and international advisors pointed out that the Kachin take issue with the 2008 Constitution, which declares that all natural resources belong to the central state, not states and regions, and fear that the Tatmadaw is waging war against them to gain control over vast resources wealth, hence loss of control and identity.

The scramble for the control of resources in the Kachin area thus appears to be a symptom rather than the cause of the conflict. Resources and rent-seeking have certainly shifted conflict dynamics and most agree that some leaders are fighting for resources, but that is not what drives recruitment and tribute to the KIO/A, which has quite strong (although not uncritical) popular support. While Kachin civil society leaders express concerns that many high-ranking Kachin officers have become very rich from their positions due to resource extraction, they blame government tactics during the ceasefire. Recruitment, community mobilization, and payment of taxes or tribute still appear to be primarily driven by the desire not to be governed by the Burmese state, or subject to its chauvinistic control and cultural assimilation.

UNDERSTANDING THE RETURN TO ARMED CONFLICT IN 2011

Detailed analysis of the return to conflict by the KIO/A in June 2011, as the political transition to a new semi-civilian government commenced, will need to be the subject of another paper, but brief consideration is due here. The Kachin civil society leaders interviewed observed that the KIO/A lost a great deal of political capital during the seventeen-year ceasefire (1994–2011), as promises were not delivered (see also ICG 2013). The KIO/A took the initiative to open negotiations with the government in 1994 (ICG 2013), aiming for a nationwide ceasefire on behalf of all armed groups to be followed by political dialogue, but this initiative was not well received by other groups or the military. The KIO/A proposal to transform their education, health, police, and other civil departments into a state government was also rejected by the government, and KIO education, health, police, and other civil officers asking for transfer to state institutions were consistently rejected. Thus the ceasefire did not lead to a comprehensive agreement that would address the political self-determination rights and ideological clashes vis-à-vis the distribution of political power at the heart of 'processes of identification' examined in this chapter. Civil society activists argue that the central problem was the government's elite-led approach to transform the armed organization, by giving the elite commanders economic opportunities in a deliberate and explicit strategy of 'ceasefire capitalism' (see also Woods 2011). In place of the promised negotiation about political rights, power distribution, and equitable development, therefore, the concessions created evolving governance regimes and rendered new mechanisms through which the Burmese military–state was able to increase its hold of contested territory.

The Kachin leaders interviewed all bemoaned having little to show for the seventeen-year accord, apart from being sidelined, discriminated against, and subject to rights abuses. The resumption of violence highlighted the incomplete nature of the ceasefire, which did not lead to renegotiation of the deep-seated ideological question of how sociopolitical power would be distributed to address systemic discrimination and disparity. They argued that Kachin participation in the flawed National Convention process and commitment to working within the system failed to produce an opportunity for genuine political dialogue. This would make the military government's denial of KIO registration to compete in the 2010 elections the real trigger for the resumption of violence in 2011. The regime's ultimatum — contravening previous assurances — that the Kachin troops must become border guards under partial control of the Tatmadaw prior to participation in the 2010 election, and thus prior to political dialogue, was central. From a Kachin perspective, this ultimatum invalidated the ceasefire and delegitimized armed non-state actors prior to the elections, diminishing KIO/A ability to negotiate for self-determination in any political dialogue, making a return to conflict almost inevitable.

CONCLUSION

Reframing 'ethnicity' in the Kachin conflict from a category of social analysis to a form of social relationships, or a dynamic set of historical narratives around how power is framed and contested in relation to processes of identification, leads us to conclude that the fundamental issues in the Kachin conflict are not resources, territory, or even discrimination based on cultural and religious difference. Rather, the key issues of the conflict are the politicized manifestations of competing ideological beliefs about the framing, distribution, and management of political power. Thus while personal vested economic interests have emerged, complicating pathways to peace, control of territory and resources remains both instrumental and symbolic: instrumental to providing the space and resources for communal survival and expression of identity, and symbolic in creating international legitimacy in the global political context of established state-sovereignty norms, as well as strengthening that nationalistic sense of identity.

The first step to lasting peace is ensuring a successful cessation of hostilities and constituting a national political dialogue. The seventeen-year-old ceasefire between the KIO/A and the Tatmadaw ended in June 2011, just as the Karen National Union and many other insurgent groups signed individual ceasefire agreements with the government in early 2012. The KIO/A have maintained demands for agreement about political dialogue before they will agree again to a ceasefire, based on their inability to get to dialogue during their last ceasefire. They signed a tentative and fragile Kachin accord in 2013, a ceasefire in all but name, and were part of the drafting of the Nationwide Ceasefire Agreement (NCA) signed by eight armed groups on 15 October 2015. However, subsequent Tatmadaw attacks on KIA positions, and the KIO/A boycott on signing the NCA even after the commencement of a political dialogue convention on 12 January 2016, are significant. Political dialogue will be a long road, posing great difficulty.

Based on our analysis of interview data and the literature, it seems clear that the KIO/A and many Kachin are not yet convinced the government is committed to addressing what they see as central issues: political rights, power distribution, state power versus decentralized authority, and the quest for equality and freedom. Many Kachin need their equal citizenship rights affirmed and to see agreement over decentralization and power sharing before they can let go of their ethno-nationalist agenda and regard themselves as citizens of Myanmar who are of Kachin cultural identity. In essence, what is required is a redefinition of the concept of citizenship in Myanmar beyond the nationalist/ethno-nationalist rhetoric that generates spheres of exclusion from the political process for a significant part of the population. It is a call for a clear and inclusive answer to the question of who the demos are in Myanmar's future democracy. This will undoubtedly involve constitutional change, something the government has been reticent to consider to this point.

This analysis leads us to conclude with two challenges for the peace process in Myanmar. Firstly, the next round of political dialogue will need to genuinely address these fundamental issues, which will not be easy. The danger perceived by KIO/A leadership and many Kachin appears to be that if political dialogue fails to address these underlying issues, further state encroachment into Kachin State through service delivery, development activities, and resource exploitation will undermine any chance of later renegotiation. There appears to be truth in this, although the KIA continues to lose ground militarily too, so this may be the only opportunity either way. The required trust and goodwill have not been evident in the process to date. Secondly, continuing to frame these conflicts as being about 'ethnic' minorities risks undermining the breadth and depth of social and political change required for lasting peace. Most Burmans want greater political rights and decentralization of power too. Conflating multiple conflict dynamics and fault lines into a simplistic 'ethnic' label poses the danger that any renegotiation of political rights, power distribution, and decentralization will not address the demands and aspirations of the diversity of people involved. A long-term solution to both authoritarianism and conflict in Myanmar may require resolving questions of political rights, power distribution, and decentralized authority across the whole country, not just in 'ethnic' states, for example. There is thus a real danger that focus on this being a political dialogue with 'ethnic minorities' around ethnic nationalism, federalism, and a peace process could be counter-productive to the broader constitutional reform required.

References

Bartelson, Jens. *Sovereignty as Symbolic Form*. London and New York: Routledge, 2014.
Brubaker, Rogers. "Myths and Misconceptions in the Study of Nationalism". In *The State of the Nation: Ernest Gellner and the Theory of Nationalism*, edited by John Hall. Cambridge: Cambridge University Press, 1998.
———. *Ethnicity Without Groups*. Cambridge, MA: Harvard University Press, 2004.
Buzan, Barry. *People, States and Fear*. London: Harvester Wheatsheaf, 1991.
Collier, Paul and Anke Hoeffler. "On Economic Causes of Civil War". *Oxford Economic Papers* 50 (1998): 563–73.
———. "Special Issue on Understanding Civil War". *Journal of Conflict Resolution* 46, no. 1 (2002): 3–12.
Collier, Paul, Lani Elliott, Håvard Hegre, Anke Hoeffler, Marta Reynal-Querol and Nicholas Sambanis. *Breaking the Conflict Trap: Civil War and Development Policy*. Washington, DC: World Bank and Oxford University Press, 2003.
Cordell, Karl and Steffan Wolff. *Ethnic Conflict: Causes, Consequences, Responses*. Cambridge: Polity Press, 2010.
Egreteau, Renaud. "Assessing Recent Ethnic Peace Talks in Myanmar". *Asian Ethnicity* 13, no. 3 (2012): 311–13.
Esman, Milton. *An Introduction to Ethnic Conflict*. Cambridge: Polity Press, 2004.
Geertz, Clifford. *The Interpretation of Cultures*. New York: Basic Books, 1973.
Gilley, Bruce. "Against the Concept of Ethnic Conflict". *Third World Quarterly* 25, no. 6 (2004): 1155–66.

Gurr, Ted Robert and Barbara Harff. *Ethnic Conflict in World Politics*. Boulder, CO: Westview Press, 1994.
Halbwachs, Maurice. *On Collective Memory*. Chicago: University of Chicago Press, 1992.
Harvey, Godfrey Eric. *History of Burma from the Earliest Times to 10 March 1824, the Beginning of the English Conquest*. London: Longmans, Green and Co., 1925.
Homer-Dixon, Thomas. "Environmental Scarcities and Violent Conflict". *International Security* 19, no.1 (1994): 5–40.
Horowitz, Donald. *Ethnic Groups in Conflict*. Berkeley, CA: University of California Press, 1985.
Huntington, Samuel. *The Clash of Civilizations and the Remaking of World Order*. New York: Simon & Schuster, 1996.
International Crisis Group (ICG). *A Tentative Peace in Myanmar's Kachin Conflict*, Asia Briefing no. 140. Yangon/Jakarta/Brussels: International Crisis Group, 7 May 2013 <http://www.crisisgroup.org>. Accessed 15 September 2013.
Kramer, Tom. "Ethnic Conflict in Burma: The Challenge of Unity in a Divided Country". In *Burma or Myanmar? The Struggle for National Identity*, edited by Lowell Dittmer. Singapore: World Scientific Publishing, 2010.
Laoutides, Costas. "The Role of Hegemony in Secessionist Movements: The Case Study of Moldovan Republic of Transnistria". *Science and Society* 20 (2008): 143–69.
Laoutides, Costas and Damien Kingsbury. "Introduction: Territorial Separatism in Context". In *Territorial Separatism in Global Politics: Causes, Outcomes and Resolution*, edited by Costas Laoutides and Damien Kingsbury, London and New York: Routledge, 2015.
Le Billon, Philippe. "The Political Ecology of War: Natural Resources and Armed Conflict", *Political Geography* 20, no. 5 (2001): 561–84.
Leach, Edmund. *Political Systems of Highland Burma: A Study of Kachin Social Structure*. London: Athlone Press, 1970 [1954].
Lieberman, Victor. "Ethnic Politics in Eighteenth-Century Burma". *Modern Asian Studies* 12, no. 3 (1978): 455–82.
Lintner, Bertil. *The Rise and Fall of the Communist Party of Burma (CPB)*. Cornell University Press, Southeast Asia Program Publications, 1990.
Malešević, Siniša. *The Sociology of Ethnicity*. London: Sage Publications, 2004.
———. Identity as Ideology: Understanding Ethnicity and Nationalism. Houndmills: Palgrave Macmillan, 2006.
———. *Nation-States and Nationalism: Organization, Ideology and Solidarity*. Cambridge: Polity Press, 2013.
Mann, Michael. *The Dark Side of Democracy*. Cambridge: Cambridge University Press, 2005.
Mayall, James. *Nationalism and International Society*. Cambridge: Cambridge University Press, 1990.
Min Zaw Oo. *Understanding Myanmar's Peace Process: Ceasefire Agreements*. Bern: Swiss Peace, 2014.

Murer, Jeffrey. "Ethnic Conflict: An Overview of Analyzing and Framing Communal Conflicts from Comparative Perspectives". *Terrorism and Political Violence* 24, no. 4 (2012): 561–80.

Renard, Ronald. "Minorities in Burmese History". In *Ethnic Conflict in Buddhist Societies*, edited by Kingsley de Silva. London: Pinter, 1988.

Sadan, Mandy. *Being and Becoming Kachin: Histories Beyond the State in the Borderworlds of Burma*. Oxford: Oxford University Press, 2013.

Sen, Amartya. *Identity and Violence*. New York: Norton, 2006.

Seng Maw Lahpai. "State Terrorism and International Compliance: The Kachin Armed Struggle for Political Self-Determination". In *Debating Democratization in Myanmar*, edited by Nick Cheesman, Nicholas Farrelly and Trevor Wilson. Singapore: Institute of South East Asian Studies, 2013.

Smith, Martin. *Burma: Insurgency and the Politics of Ethnicity*. London: Zed Books, 1991.

———. "Ethnic Conflict and the Challenge of Civil Society in Burma". In *Strengthening Civil Society in Burma: Possibilities and Dilemmas for International NGOs*, 2nd edn. Royal Tropical Institute, Amsterdam: TransNational Institute (TNI) and the Burma Centrum Nederland, 1997.

———. *Burma: Insurgency and the Politics of Ethnicity*, 2nd edn. London: Zed Books, 1999.

———. "Ethnic Conflicts in Burma: From Separatism to Federalism". In *A Handbook of Terrorism and Insurgency in Southeast Asia*, edited by A. T. H. Tan. Cheltenham, UK: Edward Elgar, 2007.

South, Ashley. *Ethnic Politics in Burma: States of Conflict*. London and New York: Routledge, 2008.

Toft, Monica. *The Geography of Ethnic Violence*. Princeton, NJ: Princeton University Press, 2006.

Walton, Matthew J. "Ethnicity, Conflict and History in Burma: The Myths of Panglong". *Asian Survey* 48, no. 6 (2008): 889–910.

———. "The 'Wages of Burman-ness:' Ethnicity and Burman Privilege in Contemporary Myanmar". *Journal of Contemporary Asia* 43, no. 1 (2013): 1–27.

Welsh, Bridget. Presentation for Feedback for Final Report, Myanmar Political Aspirations, Yangon: 2015 Asian Barometer Survey. <http://www.asianbarometer.org>.

Williams, Howard. *Concepts of Ideology*. New York: St. Martin's Press, 1988.

Wolff, Steffan. *Ethnic Conflict: A Global Perspective*. Oxford: Oxford University Press, 2006.

Woods, Kevin. "Ceasefire Capitalism: Military–private Partnerships, Resource Concessions and Military–state Building in the Burma–China Borderlands". *The Journal of Peasant Studies* 38, no. 4 (2011): 747–70.

4

A FEMINIST POLITICAL ECONOMY ANALYSIS OF INSECURITY AND VIOLENCE IN KACHIN STATE

Jenny Hedström

The drama and tragedy that began to unfold in June 2011 after a military attack on Kachin army outposts in the north of Myanmar is usually explained in terms relating to military conflict, power struggles, and the failure of the Myanmar state to include and respect the rights of minority groups (International Crisis Group 2013; Lintner 1990; Smith 2007). The relationship between gender and conflict rarely enters the discussion, unless (Kachin) women are portrayed as victims of (state) violence. Women's experiences of and responses to the conflict that do not fit with the dominant image of woman-as-victim are then typically silenced.[1]

This chapter challenges that dominant narrative by critically investigating women's conception of and involvement in the Kachin Independence Army (KIA).[2] It provides a new lens to understand the conflict between the Myanmar state and the Kachin minority group by exploring the circumstances that lead women to join or support the armed struggle in Kachin State, asking why and how women are involved in the conflict. Using theoretical insights provided by feminist political economy, it analyses the material basis for women's support for and involvement in the KIO/KIA.

Recent research (Henshaw 2015; Mazurana 2013; Shekhawat 2015) suggests that women — like men — join armies for ideological and political reasons related to their position as members of a marginalized ethnic and religious group. However, a more careful gender analysis will reveal that women's decisions to participate in or support armed struggle stem from gender-specific experiences of insecurity and oppression. In Kachin State, these gender differences are visible in the high number of female-headed households compared to other areas of Myanmar (Union of Myanmar 2015b); the inability of women to inherit property (KWAT 2014, p. 26); and the deliberate targeting of minority women by Myanmar armed forces, or Tatmadaw, officers and soldiers (Human Rights Watch 2012).

It is important to note that women's exposure to gender-based violence in Myanmar is related to their exclusion from positions of power and influence. This exclusion reflects a gendered division of labour that holds men as the representatives of the collective, as evidenced by the acute lack of women in leadership positions within both the local and the national polity (Minoletti 2014). Oppression based on ethnicity and religion is then experienced through gender identities. It is precisely their gender-specific experiences of physical and material insecurity, including poverty, gender-based violence, and discrimination, which lead women to support or participate in the armed struggle. A feminist political economy analysis renders visible these underlying gendered patterns of conflict, thereby enhancing the prospects for sustainable peace by paying attention to the needs and objectives of Kachin women in general, and female soldiers in particular.

This research was informed by a set of questions aimed at understanding the relationship between gendered insecurity and Kachin women's participation in and support of the military struggle. Believing that women have been silenced in much research on Myanmar, intentionally the majority of the interviewees were women. In total, twenty-five women and one man currently or previously working in key Kachin resistance or civil society organizations were interviewed. These organizations included the Kachin Independence Organisation (KIO), the KIA, the Kachin Women's Association (KWA), the Kachin Women's Association Thailand (KWAT), and the Kachin Women's Union (KWU). In seventeen of the twenty-five cases, those interviewed were former or current soldiers or reservists. In addition, interviews were also conducted with twenty-three women and three men who were active in Kachin religious associations, multi-ethnic civil society organizations, and peace missions, as well as with external human rights groups and other non-state armed groups not associated with the KIO. The interviews took place during three field trips to the US, Myanmar, and Thailand in 2013 and 2014, each trip lasting about two to three weeks. Three translators were used for the majority of the interviews undertaken in Myanmar, two women and one man.[3] The information garnered during these relatively short research trips was studied in relation to existing literature on gender, women, and conflict, area studies on Myanmar, and previous research and work undertaken in the same area by the author.

Insecurity is important because it informs women's involvement in and relationship to political violence, which here is defined as violent acts carried out by groups and institutions with a political mandate, including non-state armed groups and governments (Davies and True 2015, p. 3). Insecurity in this context does not only relate to physical insecurity, such as the occurrence of gender-based violence, but includes broader notions of legal justice and voice, participation in decision-making structures, and socio-economic status and rights. This notion of insecurity stems from a feminist political economy approach, which understands violence as rooted in gendered inequalities (Cockburn 2004; Tickner 1992; True 2012). Such an approach is important because it allows the researcher to explore the connection between political participation, legal representation, and gendered divisions of labour as contributing to women's insecurity (True 2012, p. 30).

Insecurity informs women's participation in and support of political violence in Kachin State. This is because the outbreak and sustainment of conflict are linked to overarching structural inequalities that contribute to minority communities' exclusion from political decision-making and their relative poverty vis-à-vis dominant communities. This discrimination is even more pronounced for minority women who lack representation in the community (see Table 4.1), do not enjoy equal rights to land and household ownership (Faxon, Furlong and Sabe Phyu 2015), and report lower levels of income compared to men (MPC 2015). By paying attention to the relationship between gendered insecurity and the sustainment of conflict, I am able to analyse multiple levels of gendered socio-economic and political links that contribute to the conflict. This method allows me to identify the underlying gendered drivers of conflict, in order to envision strategies for how to end it (see Pugh, Goodhand, and Cooper 2004).

Table 4.1. Female representation in local- and national-level governance, 2014

Body	% women	no. of women	total no.
Lower House (MPs & military appointees)	5.79	25	432
Upper House (MPs & military appointees)	1.79	4	224
Upper and Lower House (MPs & military appointees)	4.42	29	656
State and Region (MPs)	2.83	25	883
State and Region (Ministers)	2,37	4	169
Townships Administrators	0	0	330
Ward/Village Tract Administrators	0,11	19	16,743

Source: Minoletti 2014

This chapter begins with a brief overview of the literature on Myanmar and civil war, noting an absence of gender analysis of war and insecurity. I will here argue that the lack of scholarly attention to the relationship between gender, minority communities, and conflict limits our understanding of the gendered drivers of conflict and therefore also limits possible solutions to it. I will then define feminist political economy, showing how a gendered analysis of the division of labour from the level of the household to the level of the state produces the setting for Kachin women's support of and participation in political violence. Here I will outline a method drawing on the work of Jacqui True (2010, 2012), and apply it to the conflict in Kachin State, through analysis of the divisions of labour at the level of the family, the army, and the community, political marginalization on a national and local scale, and socio-economic inequality. This method will allow me to link different levels of political economy that impact gendered insecurity, and explore the relationship between political violence and experiences of gendered insecurity. Throughout this section, this method will be employed to analyse women's motivations to participate in and support political violence in Kachin State, showing the connection between gendered experiences of insecurity and armed conflict.

GENDERING MYANMAR STUDIES

In the scholarly literature on Myanmar, women's experiences of and responses to the conflict are commonly overlooked in favour of research situating ethnicity (Holliday 2010; Smith 2007) or the military (Callahan 2003) as the primary lens through which to understand political developments in the country. In this way, conflict is typically identified as being the result of differential colonial treatments of ethnic groups (Harriden 2002, p. 87; Holliday 2010, p. 117; Smith 2007, p. 15). This is problematic, as the focus on ethnicity and armed groups means that the roles and experiences of women in these conflicts have been largely left out of the picture, even though gender norms are critical for sustaining the war(s) practically and ideologically.

According to feminist scholars, gender roles are at the heart of the making of national collectives and thus, ethnic conflict. Yuval-Davis and Anthias (1989) have identified five ways that women have distinct roles in supporting and upholding ethnic nationalism. These include biological, cultural, and symbolic reproduction, as well as active participation in armed and national struggles, and as signifiers of collective difference (Yuval-Davis and Anthias 1989, p. 7).

Understanding nationalism as inherently gendered renders visible the importance of the gender order in the outbreak and sustainment of political upheaval and conflict in Myanmar. For example, a gender analysis would reveal how the Tatmadaw, in situating itself as the 'guardian' and 'protector' of the country (Callahan 2012; Walton 2012), uses a gendered script where it inhabits the paternal role to help justify its military rule. Understanding nationalism as inherently gendered would also explain the Tatmadaw's deliberate targeting of minority women for sexual violence because women are positioned as signifiers of the ethnic collective and because crimes committed in conflict areas enjoy impunity. A gender analysis would further demonstrate how women's exposure to sexual and gender-based violence depends on a gendered division of labour that results in women's exclusion from positions of power.

Understanding nationalism as inherently gendered highlights how conflict relies on narratives built around traditional notions of masculinity and femininity, where men are seen as the protectors and the warriors, and women as innocent and in need of protection (Elshtain 1987; Hansen 2001; Shepherd 2006). The construction of the gender order, then, plays a fundamental part in the outbreak and sustainment of political conflict and war by motivating (good) men to fight in order to protect (innocent) women, and by situating women as symbols and signifiers of the ethnic nation-state (Elshtain 1987). A gender analysis would reveal how this results in Kachin women experiencing and responding to the conflict in ways that are gender-specific and that have implications for political violence.

Despite a paucity of work in Myanmar studies incorporating a gender perspective, there are some notable exceptions. Mi Mi Khaing's early work on the family and the status of Burmese women was one of the first such accounts to be published in English (1946, 1984), highlighting the role of women in education, employment, politics, religion, and society at large. Her books are largely descriptive and do not employ feminist theories to explore gender roles. However, she does note that women's pervasive exclusion from political office is often "disguised as protectiveness" (1984, p. 150), a point still significant today. Historian Chie Ikeya's study (2011) on how women's bodies were used in colonial Myanmar to signify resistance to or support of nationalism have informed this chapter's argument that the construction of femininity is important for understanding conflict and nation-making narratives. Of particular interest is her analysis of how the notion of Burmese women's 'high status' has been manipulated by political elites to masquerade for the continued exclusion of women from leadership roles (Ikeya 2005, p. 51; also see Than 2014).

The centrality of gender for the British colonial project has similarly been emphasized by scholars Jonathan Saha (2010, 2013), and Nick Cheesman (2013). They both show how constructions of femininity and masculinity were filtered through lenses of race and ethnicity and used by colonial officials to rationalize and justify decisions taken, such as for meting out justice and enforcing concepts of social order. For example, Saha shows how women, from the very commencement of the colonial project, were seen as symbolizing both the colonial and the colonized collective (see also Yuval-Davis and Anthias 1989). Therefore, norms regarding gender and sexuality, framed as related to women's positioning in relation to 'their' ethnic group, served to inform court rulings on gender-based violence (Saha 2010). These ideas still hold relevance today, not least in narratives of sexual violence, which are similarly filtered through ethnic lenses and prevalent in discussions on the Kachin conflict. Finally, Jessica Harriden's (2012) account of the relationship between conceptualizations of power and gender in Myanmar as explaining the lack of female representation in the public sphere has influenced this article's thesis that gendered identities are used in particular ways to provide legitimacy and support for political narratives.

These are all critical contributions to academic discussions on Myanmar, but as they are primarily focused on the gender relations within Burman, as opposed to minority communities, there is a lack of scholarly attention on the impact of gender relations within minority communities in Myanmar. As a result, they are blind to the gendered roots of political violence in Kachin State, and this is limiting our understanding of conflict and possible solutions to it. This chapter, then, aims to add to the body of knowledge in Myanmar studies by bringing a new analysis to the debate on intrastate conflicts by considering the impact of gender and political economy on the war in Kachin State.

ANALYSING THE KACHIN CONFLICT WITH A FEMINIST POLITICAL ECONOMY METHOD

In order to understand the relationship between poverty and violence, Jacqui True's recent work on the political economy of violence against women is important. True has put forward a convincing thesis that draws out the relationship between materiality and insecurity by examining the connection between women's access to productive resources, power and justice, and gender-based violence (2010, 2012). This framework renders 'strategic sites' visible, where the nexus of political and economic processes coalesce towards "heightening the conditions for and increasing the extent of violence against women" (True 2012, p. 19).

True argues that all forms of violence have a material basis (2010, p. 30), meaning that violence against women must be contextualized in gendered structures of poverty and political exclusion. In other words, it is not poverty per se that determines women's levels of insecurity, but their relative level of inequality vis-à-vis men in their community (True 2012, p. 18). This means that socio-economic and political inequality as experienced by Kachin women, in both times of conflict and peace, detrimentally impacts their access to justice, and economic and political opportunities, resulting in these women being unable to effectively challenge or question discrimination, and thus, making them more vulnerable to abuse.

Although this framework needs to be taken further in certain areas to be applicable to the Kachin context, the identification of 'strategic sites' is helpful for providing a method for the examination of the connection between women's access to productive resources, gender-based inequality in socio-economic and political spheres, and gender-based violence. In the context of Kachin State, this helps to highlight the relationship between women's vulnerability to violence and macro-level poverty in conflict-affected areas. For instance, increased material insecurity as a result of the conflict has been accompanied by a rise in the level of women trafficked abroad and by the number of rape cases reported (see Table 4.2). According to local women's groups, in the first two months of the renewed conflict, thirty-seven women and young girls were sexually abused; thirteen of these were killed (KWAT 2013a). Thus, this method allows analysis of the relationship between a gendered division of labour and experiences of gendered insecurities to contextualize women's motivations to join or support the KIO/KIA.

Table 4.2. Reports of conflict-related gender-based violence in Kachin State

Type	Source	Year	Reports
Sexual violence	Kachin Women's Association Thailand 2011	2011	37
Sexual violence	Quintana 2011	2011	18
Sexual violence	Women's League of Burma 2014	2011–14	59
Trafficking	Kachin Women Association Thailand 2013	2011–13	24
Sexual violence	Ban 2012	2011	32
Sexual violence	Lee 2015a, 2015b	2015	2

It is to these sites that I will now turn, analysing them in the context of political and macroeconomic processes that not only detrimentally impact women's insecurity, but also sustain the conflict. In particular, I will highlight four strategic sites of relevance to Kachin State: the relationship between poverty, political participation, and gender-based violence in conflict areas, and in internally displaced persons communities; the relationship between gender insecurity, participation in social reproduction, and political activities in the army; and the relationship between gender insecurity and sexual and gender-based violence within the state.

GENDERED INSECURITY AND GENDERED RELATIONS AT THE STATE LEVEL

A feminist analysis of socio-economic relations reveals a link between gender inequality and gender insecurity. This is because inequality in accessing power, justice, and resources provides the conditions that enable the use of gender-based violence (Davies and True 2015). For example, recent research has shown a significant correlation between the systematic occurrence of sexual violence and the absence of laws relating to domestic violence; acceptance of domestic violence; and poor or limited access to public space, property, resources, and entitlements for women (Davies and True 2015, p. 10). In this way, women's inequality in accessing property, employment, and political decision-making provides an important strategic site for analysing the relationship between gendered insecurity and violence.

As will be elaborated in more detail below, Kachin women, often situated as single heads of households during conflict times, report lower levels of income compared to men in their community (see Table 4.3), and face serious barriers in accessing both public spaces and justice mechanisms. For example, in areas under KIO control, issues related to women's physical insecurity are often delegated to customary authorities or, if the matter involves KIA soldiers, are dealt with by a military court (Kamler 2015). Kachin women's groups maintain that neither of these authorities takes issues of sexual violence or domestic violence seriously enough. At the national level, women in Myanmar lack legal protection given the absence of laws penalizing domestic violence and marital rape (Gender Equality Network 2013a).[4] In addition, the current constitution includes a clause that effectively absolves the state military of any responsibility for crimes committed against women during conflict.[5] This culture of impunity heightens women's exposure to gender-based violence. The low level of women in public office arguably also exacerbates this, as women lack access to levers of legislative power. The violence that women experience in Kachin State is thus directly connected to their inequality in social and economic status, and the lack of legal avenues to address this. In other words, gender inequality ensures that the marginalization of women from public decision-making processes is maintained. This in turn contributes to exacerbating women's insecurity.

Gender insecurity, either experienced directly by women or by other women in their community, motivates women to join or support the KIO/KIA. Female soldiers believe the organization will provide them, and their community, with protection:[6]

> Sometimes I had to go to the village to find supplies. But even though I have a pistol, I felt unsafe and very nervous about the enemy ... I feel unsafe for a long time. Only when I can turn back to liberated areas and I am sure I am inside the territory controlled by our troops, I feel relief.[7]

Table 4.3. Gender equality indicators, Kachin State

2015	Myanmar Census, Kachin State data [8]	Male literary rate	94.1%
		Female literacy rate	89.4 %
		Male labour force participation (15+)	83.6 %
		Female labour force participation (15+)	43.5 %
		Female-headed households	27.3 %
		Infant mortality rate	53 (per 1000 live births)
		Under five mortality rate	61 (per 1000 live births)
		Percentage of households with access to tap water	5.2 %
		Percentage of households using firewood for cooking	72.8 %

Source: Union of Myanmar (2015a)

Research has found a significant link between gender equality and peace, showing that countries where women are experiencing high levels of violence are more likely to engage in conflict and war (both within and between countries) compared to countries with low levels of violence against women (Hudson et al. 2008). Countries where women have greater equality and greater political representation are also less likely to become involved in wars. There is then a relationship between marginalization, gender inequality, and conflict (Caprioli 2005; Hudson 2005). As shown below, a climate of gendered insecurity motivates women to support the armed forces. However, as women's experiences of insecurity are heightened by their unequal status within the KIO/KIA, the relationship between women's inequality in accessing resources, access, and power, and their participation in political violence is more complex than assumed.

GENDERED INSECURITY AND GENDERED RELATIONS WITHIN THE ARMY

> Many times we were starving; we didn't have enough food and we didn't have enough clothes. ... It was very cold, and we have to take clothes from the dead Burmese soldier because we couldn't afford new clothes, and it was also very difficult to find military colors for the uniforms. We used to dye white fabric with forest leafs to make it green, but the color would not last in the rainy season so when it rained, our bodies became stained.[9]

Despite the hard work endured by women to support the uprising, women's participation in the armed struggle in Myanmar is depoliticized by a gendered narrative that frames women's duties as domestic (for example, nursing, cooking), thereby relegating women's support of and involvement in political violence to the private sphere (Ferguson 2013; Hedström 2015b; Tharaphi Than 2014). In this way, dominant gendered divisions of labour are reproduced in the armed conflict. This public/private dichotomy then serves to rationalize the exclusion of women from public decision-making roles in the country. For example, with only a few notable exceptions, women have not been invited to participate in the ceasefire talks that began in 2011 (Hedström 2013). Similarly, within the KIO/KIA, women's inclusion is circumscribed by gendered norms: women are prevented from participating in combat, despite the fact that every woman interviewed for this research expressed a wish to fight on the frontlines alongside male soldiers:[10]

> I want to be a very brilliant fighter in combat, but as a woman I cannot go ... When I was in the [Defence Academy] the other woman cadets and me demanded 'let us go to the battlefield' because a lot of our school mates, the male soldiers, went to the battlefield but we were left behind at the school.[11]

By excluding women from combat, traditional family values are maintained. These values see women as the cultural and biological reproducers of the nation, but not as able to represent or protect the nation per se. Men are instead positioned as the primary defenders and protectors of both women and the community. Women's involvement is structured around feminized duties, such as cooking, sewing, and nursing, a gendered division of labour that serves to depoliticize women's involvement by placing it in the private sphere and trivializing the fact that the armed struggle is dependent on women's labour and participation. This is reinforced by the idea that women serving in the KIA should retire on marriage in order to fulfil their duty to have children and take care of their home (see Jacoby 2010). Importantly, as extensive military experience, including official combat experience, is a de facto prerequisite for high-ranking political positions, women are in effect banned from reaching high-level positions in either the civilian or the military administration:

> They say women are not qualified enough ... [but] after they get married, mostly the [women] have to quit their job, so how can they get many years' experience? Right? Because first they have to take care of their family, they have to take care of their kids so they will get no more chance to be a leader or a [high-ranking] leader in the military. Only men. Why do these men not quit their job?[12]

Women's roles in conflict are then reflective of gendered divisions of labour, from the household to the state. As Parashar shows with regards to the Maoist conflict in India, alternative shadow economies centred on the household provide non-state armed groups with important supplies and support (2013, p. 43). Similarly, in Kachin State, interviews reveal how normative gendered roles centred on the household are essential for the effective running of the war machinery: mothers and wives fulfil feminized duties for the army, such as sewing uniforms for the troops, sending food to the frontlines, and nursing wounded soldiers.

The reproduction of dominant gendered divisions of labour in the army means that women's inclusion in the KIA/KIO does not actually upset the gendered status quo in any meaningful way. As women are largely prevented from participating in decision-making processes, opportunities to address women's marginalization are limited. In other words, by excluding women, normative gendered identities and structures are preserved, leaving little room for redress or transformation to take place.

GENDERED INSECURITY AND GENDERED RELATIONS IN THE COMMUNITY

As of 2014, no women were employed in decision-making positions at the township level in Myanmar, including in Kachin State (Minoletti 2014, p. 10). The three seats reserved for members of the Kachin army's women's wing, the KWA, in the KIO's governing body were empty. How do we explain this systematic exclusion of Kachin women from positions of influence and power? In addition to the gendered division of labour, as discussed above, part of the answer can also be found in the use or even the threat to use gender-based violence. Violence undermines women's ability to participate effectively in peace- and state-building activities as do other forms of gender-based violence that go unaddressed. In concert with actual threats to security, male invocation of a gender discourse where women are "in need of protection" ensures the continuation of men's privilege and power over women and access to resources. An example of how this narrative is used to prohibit women from participating in political activities is aptly captured in the following quote from a Kachin woman who sought to participate in peace negotiations as part of a government team:

> I requested Minister U Aung Min to include me as a member of the negotiation team for the talks with KIO. But he told me that the road to the place where the talk would be held is so bad and it is not easy for women to travel. Actually, the place where the talk would be held is not an unfamiliar place for me. It is really nonsense that a responsible woman for her own people was not allowed to go there. The reason was so meaningless.[13]

Gendered insecurity (real or imagined) is important for understanding women's exclusion from political decision-making and helps to contextualise women's response to the conflict as community-wide experiences of gender-based violence propels women to support the KIO/KIA. In other words, forms of gender-based violence, such as trafficking or rape, perpetrated by people outside the Kachin community have been discursively positioned as evidence of discrimination and threat to the Kachin people, and thus as a key factor for conflict. Consequently, violence against women in Myanmar is being filtered and made sense of through ethnic and religious lenses, which has resulted in making largely invisible violence perpetrated against women *within* Kachin communities (see Roy 2012, p. 129). As one community activist says: "I have never heard of [violence] happening within Kachin liberated areas. But in Burmese areas I hear that it is likely to happen."[14]

There is then a hierarchy of violence, in which gender, religion, and ethnicity play key roles. A recent study on civilian women and men's views in the peace process noted a significant statistical relationship between self-identified Kachin Christian women and feelings of physical insecurity compared to men and women of other ethnic and religious identities living in Kachin State (MPC 2015, pp. 100–1). Insecurity is gendered, and women are responding to the insecurity they experience by, for example, supporting the KIO/KIA.

Accounts of discrimination during both the ceasefire period and the conflict were frequently used to explain motivations sparking women's involvement in or support for the conflict. This oppression is felt in both the public and the private sphere, and encompasses a range of interconnected areas including the labour market, education, health, justice, and infrastructure development. A feminist political economy analysis holds that these experiences are gendered and rooted in overarching social-economic and political inequalities. All female soldiers interviewed explained their participation in the army as contributing to the survival and struggle for Kachin nationhood on an equal footing to men. Most framed their involvement as related to nationalism and the national duty, and positioned women as protectors of their community. In this way, women's decisions to join or support the army are related to the insecurity that these women and their communities experience. As one KIA officer put it:

> The existence of KIO means that we can defend us against severe suppression from the government. Also, there are many parts in Kachin State where the government didn't take care of, but the KIO take care of the people and the land, also in the very remote areas, for education and health care. ... Without the KIO the life of the people will be very difficult. KIO protects the people.[15]

GENDERED INSECURITY AND GENDERED RELATIONS IN IDP CAMPS

Within IDP camp communities, expectations of women to fulfil their gendered roles as caretakers of near and extended families are heightened. Women are expected to provide welfare for their families, but as resources are more limited, women's reproductive duties become strained. In addition to the responsibilities they hold for their families, women undertake unpaid labour in the camps, such as cleaning the camp compounds and building houses, which has a negative impact on their household income (Gender Equality Network 2013b, p. 11). These unpaid duties result in women having less time to participate in decision-making processes in the community and, as a consequence, women have not been able to influence decisions taken by camp committees in any substantial way. This is unfortunate, as the application of the male experience for designing the camps and social services available in them has had a negative impact on women's security.

A report on the status of women living in seventeen IDP camps shows that the major overriding concern noted by women was women's and girl's heightened risk of suffering violence within their community due to the poor design of the camps. In particular, water, sanitation, and hygiene facilities and sleeping areas were identified as key areas of security concern. The types of violence identified by the women and girls interviewed for the report included rape, sexual harassment, domestic violence, and forced marriage (Gender Equality Network 2013b). Worryingly, the report noted an absence of justice mechanisms available for women living within the camps:

> At some camps, men from the camps are given responsibility for security. Sometimes, those men entered women's rooms making security as a reason and they slept there. Though women would like to report these cases, they cannot, as the camp administration people are men too.[16]

As this quote suggests, without women represented on camp committees, perpetrators of gender-based violence are neither identified nor punished. This creates a climate of impunity for such crimes, where the woman is typically blamed for the violence she experiences:

> The men said that wives are the only reason and the source of the family problems because they do not behave well. That they should understand well about the situation of men serving the country by putting their lives at risk, that women are guilty.[17]

In addition to the security concerns experienced by women in the camps, women face security threats linked to their gendered role and socio-economic position outside the camp areas. For instance, women and men may be given the same rations of water and food in the camps, but because of gender-based expectations women are responsible for the welfare of extended families and frequently leave the camps to seek resources. However, in leaving the camps they are put at risk of being attacked by soldiers, or stepping on landmines (Htoi Gender and Development Foundation 2014).

The lack of income in the IDP camps and other conflict-affected communities causes women to cross the border to neighbouring China to find work, exposing them to exploitation by traffickers involved in the war economy. Reports by local women's groups have found an increase of trafficking in women to China as brides or bonded labourers (KWAT 2011, 2013b). This increase in trafficking is closely linked to women's socio-economic position, which exacerbates their marginalized gender and minority identities (Kamler 2015, p. 221). In other words, gender-based violence experienced by Kachin women stems from poverty at the level of the household, which in turn is tied to broader socio-economic structures, such as organized crime. Trafficking networks are embedded in the shadow economy, as is the regional trade in logging, precious stones, and drugs, all of which have resulted in an increase in female-headed households (KWAT 2014).

There is then a clear link between material insecurity at the level of the household, political marginalization within the IDP camps, and gender-based violence. Importantly, female soldiers' decisions to join or support the army are related to the insecurity these women and their communities experience, inside and outside the IDP camps, as one interviewee noted:

> When the conflict broke out again, my family fled to this area to live in the IDP camps. I was not involved in political activities before this. My father joined the local militia troops but he was killed in action. KIO and KIA are very important for us, very important part of our lives, because in the serious situation like this, almost every Kachin family has to serve at least one or two family members because we need to protect and defend our motherland.[18]

GENDERED INSECURITY AND GENDERED RELATIONS IN THE HOUSEHOLD

A feminist political economy approach highlights the importance of analysing gender relations at the level of the household for understanding women's experiences of insecurity and access to justice, political decision-making, and power. This approach renders the structural causes of insecurity visible, as it understands gender relations as being produced within a framework of political and economic power. In particular, it allows for a focus on household intra-bargaining dynamics in shaping women's ability to challenge gender norms both within the home and in the public sphere (Agarwal 1997). A feminist political economy approach then helps to make visible the relationship between women's ability to negotiate gender norms, and their experiences of material and physical insecurity: for example, taking responsibility for the wellbeing of households' impact on women's access to power, resources, and justice. The number of female-headed households in Kachin State ranks third in the country, with more than a quarter of all homes headed by a woman

(Union of Myanmar 2015c, p. 48). This number is probably under-reported, however, as it does not take into account families living in KIO-controlled areas, where many families have male soldiers based away for most of the year:

> Mostly, the husband will go to the frontline so usually the woman has to take care of the family. This is a big problem. The family could neither stay in the village nor run to other places. If we have to move to other place, faraway place, it costs a lot of money, so women have to do the work, have to find more money for transportation, and so on. Because women are now the breadwinners for the family, they have more responsibilities.[19]

In this way, conscription plays an important role in determining not only household but community dynamics, as the critical role played by the household in sustaining the war effort, both in terms of providing essential goods and as a unit of recruitment, helps to sustain the conflict. All Kachin families living in KIA/KIO areas are pressured to support the organization, which results in a high number of female-headed households. Being responsible for the survival of near and extended families means that women often lack the time and income to participate in public decision-making processes, as the quote above aptly captures. However, in not participating, women's ability to influence these processes is constrained. In other words, household support for the KIA/KIO results in exacerbating gender inequality.

Gender inequality, and the insecurity it produces, provides the context for women's support for the KIO/KIA. This is because the ways women experience insecurity inform their reactions to the conflict, and to the armed uprising. For example, the interviews show how the renewal of the conflict itself and the suffering imposed on the household have informed Kachin women's motivations for joining the army. The majority of soldiers raised the issue of female-headed households, seen as linked to an increase in poverty, and poverty was understood as increasing young women's susceptibility to trafficking:

> In my town youths were exploited; boys became drug addicts, girls were exploited [trafficked], and the Kachin people, don't have job opportunities. ... We don't have good education in our region. We didn't have anything in our houses, because the Burmans, they just take as much as they want.[20]

However, the ways women are included in the armed uprising, whether as soldiers or as members of households, ensure women's inclusion preserves rather than upsets the very gendered insecurities they set out to challenge.

CONCLUSION

This chapter has shown how gender roles, and the insecurities that emanate from them, provide community-wide support and labour for the conflict in Kachin State. The insecurity that women experience during and after conflict is co-constitutive of gender-based inequalities rooted in economic and political systems of power. These, ironically, propel women to support political violence in ways that ensure their inclusion preserves rather than upsets the very gendered insecurities they set out to challenge.

Using a feminist political economy approach has helped to highlight the crucial role the household plays in providing labour and support for the conflict. As this chapter has argued, gendered norms position women as the primary caretakers of near and extended families. This means women often lack the time and income to participate in public decision-making processes, and are relegated to lower-level support roles in the army. Exclusion from participation in political decision-making processes impacts women's ability to have voice and leaves little room for redress. This systematic marginalization and devaluation of their rights as equal citizens increases their insecurity. The insecurity women face is then directly related to their gendered status, and exacerbated by their ethnic and religious minority identity. Importantly, it is precisely their gender-specific experiences of physical and material insecurity, including poverty, rape, and discrimination, which provides the context for women's support of and participation in political violence.

Mainstream research and policy interventions on the conflict in Kachin State tend to treat the state or military actors as both the objects and subjects of security and, as such, fail to take into consideration people's gendered experiences of insecurity. By failing to consider this dimension, they fail to address how insecurity and marginalization, and by association, conflict, might be prevented in the long term. In focusing on the themes of insecurity and violence as expressed by Kachin women involved in military organizations, this chapter has offered a new perspective, encouraging scholars and researchers of Myanmar to think more broadly about insecurity in relation to gender, political representation, and socio-economic status and rights in Kachin State. By exploring the ways Kachin women have developed strategies to combat insecurity, this chapter has shown how women from marginalized communities are stakeholders in both conflict and peace building, and must be recognized as such.

Notes

I would like to thank Professor Jacqui True, Dr. Nick Cheesman, David Baulk and an anonymous reviewer for their very helpful feedback on earlier versions of this paper.

1 Exceptions to this are typically reasoned in discourses that highlight the workings of gender, ethnicity and class in situating particular women as anomalies to the rule, and as such confirm rather than subvert the exclusion of women from public dialogues and processes. These inscribe women with masculine characteristics: for example, Olive Yang, whose command over ethnic Kokang rebel forces in the 1950s was understood to have been made possible precisely because of her 'male' attributes, or discourses that emphasize women's royal and/or political male connections, for example, Aung San Suu Kyi and Nang Hern Kham (one of the founders of the Shan State Army) (Ferguson 2013).
2 This chapter draws on select publications, including Hedström (2015a).
3 For more information about the research process, see Hedström (2015a).
4 Marital rape is only criminalized if the wife is younger than fourteen. See Gender Equality Network (2013).
5 Article 445 of the 2008 Constitution of Myanmar states that, "No proceeding shall be instituted against the said [previously ruling] Councils or any member thereof or any member of the Government, in respect of any act done in the execution of their respective duties." Article 381 states that "[e]xcept in the following situations and time, no citizen shall be denied redress by due process of law for grievances entitled under law: (a) in time of foreign invasion; (b) in time of insurrection; (c) in time of emergency." Article 382 states that "[i]n order to carry out their duties fully and to maintain the discipline by the Defence Forces personnel or members of the armed forces responsible [for ensuring] peace and security, the rights given in this Chapter [Citizen, Fundamental Rights and Duties of the Citizens] shall be restricted or revoked through enactment [of] law".
6 Similarly, a report published in 2014 highlights how female soldiers felt that civilian women do not have security in Kachin State. These soldiers then went on to discuss the importance of the KIA, and the bearing of arms to defend oneself and one's community (Centre for Peace and Conflict Studies 2014).
7 Corporal, KIA, Kachin State, Myanmar, 12 October 2013. All quotes are translated from Burmese unless otherwise indicated and have been transcribed verbatim.
8 The 2015 Census was not carried out in KIO-controlled areas of Kachin State, therefore the results are estimates.
9 Soldier, KIA, Kachin State, Myanmar, 11 October 2013.
10 This holds true also for the Tatmadaw where women were until recently banned

from working in any positions other than as nurses. Recently positions have been opened for women to join the Tatmadaw, although they cannot go to combat and must be single and (presumably) childless, indicating that women's primary duties are as mothers and wives.

11 Second Lieutenant, KIA (quoted in Hedström 2015a, p. 73).
12 Community Activist (quoted in Hedström, 2015a, p. 69). Original statement in English.
13 Daw Doi Bu (quoted in Khen and Nyoi 2014, p. 25).
14 Community Activist (quoted in Project Maje, 1995, p. 18).
15 Captain, KIA, Kachin State, Myanmar, 10 October 2013.
16 Field Volunteer (quoted in Gender Equality Network 2013b, p. 15).
17 Field Volunteer (quoted in Gender Equality Network 2013b, p. 15).
18 Second Lieutenant, KIA, Kachin State, Myanmar, 10 October 2013.
19 Lieutenant, KIA, Kachin State, Myanmar, 10 October 2013.
20 Captain, KIA, Kachin State, Myanmar, 10 October 2013.

References

Agarwal, Bina. "'Bargaining' and Gender Relations: Within and Beyond the Household". *Feminist Economics* 3, no. 1 (1997): 1–51.

Asian Development Bank. *Interim Country Partnership Strategy: Myanmar 2012 – 2014*, Asian Development Bank, 2012. <http://www.adb.org/documents/myanmar-interim-country-partnership-strategy-2012-2014>. Accessed 10 March 2015.

Ban Ki-moon. *Conflict Related Sexual Violence*. New York: United Nations General Assembly, 2012. <http://www.refworld.org/pdfid/4fbf5b382.pdf>. Accessed 5 March 2015.

Callahan, Mary. *Making Enemies: War and State Building in Burma*. Ithaca, NY: Cornell University Press, 2003.

———. "The Generals Loosen Their Grip". *Journal of Democracy* 23, no. 4 (2012): 120–31.

Caprioli, Mary. "Primed for Violence: The Role of Gender Inequality in Predicting Internal Conflict". *International Studies Quarterly* 49, no. 2 (2005): 161–78.

Cheesman, Nick. "Bodies on the Line in Burma's Law Reports, 1892–1922". In *Law, Society and Transition in Myanmar*, edited by Melissa Crouch and Tim Lindsey. Oxford: Hart Publishing, 2013.

Cockburn, Cynthia. "The Continuum of Violence: A Gender Perspective on War and Peace". In *Sites of Violence: Gender and Conflict Zones*, edited by Wenona Giles and Jennifer Hyndman. Los Angeles: University of California Press, 2004.

Davies, Sara and Jacqui True. "Reframing Conflict-Related Sexual and Gender-Based Violence: Bringing Gender Analysis Back In". *Security Dialogue* 46, no. 6 (2015): 1–18.

Elshtain, Jean Bethke. *Women and War*. New York: Basic Books, 1987.

Faxon, Hilary, Roisin Furlong and May Sabe Phyu. "Reinvigorating Resilience: Violence against Women, Land Rights, and the Women's Peace Movement in Myanmar". *Gender and Development* 23, no 3 (2015): 463–79.

Ferguson, Jane. "Is the Pen Mightier than the AK-47 ? Tracking Shan Women's Militancy Within and Beyond". *Intersections: Gender and Sexuality in Asia and the Pacific*, no. 33 (2013): 1–12.

Gender Equality Network. *Myanmar Laws and CEDAW: The Case for Anti-Violence Against Women Laws*, Yangon: Gender Equality Network, 2013a.

———. *Women's Needs Assessment in IDP Camps, Kachin State*. Yangon: Gender Equality Network, 2013b.

Hansen, Lene. "Gender, Nation, Rape: Bosnia and the Construction of Security". *International Feminist Journal of Politics* 3, no. 1 (2001): 55–75.

Harriden, Jessica. "'Making a Name for Themselves:': Karen Identity and the Politicization of Ethnicity in Burma". *Journal of Burma Studies* 7, no. 1 (2002): 84–144.

———. *The Authority of Influence: Women and Power in Burmese History*. Copenhagen: NIAS Press, 2012.

Hedström, Jenny. *Where Are the Women? Negotiations for Peace in Burma*, Stockholm: Swedish Burma Committee, 2013.

———. "Myanmar". In *Women In Conflict and Peace*, edited by Jenny Hedström and Thiyumi Senarathna. Stockholm: International IDEA, 2015.

———. "We Did Not Realize about the Gender Issues. So, We Thought It Was a Good Idea". *International Feminist Journal of Politics*, March (2015): 1–19.

Henshaw, Alexis Leanna. "Where Women Rebel". *International Feminist Journal of Politics*, April (2015): 1–22.

Holliday, Ian. "Ethnicity and Democratization in Myanmar". *Asian Journal of Political Science* 18, no. 2 (2010): 111–28.

Hudson, Heidi. "'Doing' Security As Though Humans Matter: A Feminist Perspective on Gender and the Politics of Human Security". *Security Dialogue* 36, no. 2 (2005): 155–74.

Hudson, Valerie M, Mary Caprioli, Bonnie Ballif-spanvill, Rose Mcdermott and Chad Emmett. "The Heart of the Matter: The Security of Women the Security of States". *International Security* 33, no. 3 (2008): 7–45.

Human Rights Watch. "Untold Miseries": Wartime Abuses and Forced Displacement in Kachin State. New York: Human Rights Watch, 2012.

Ikeya, Chie. "The 'Traditional' High Status of Women in Burma: A Historical Reconsideration". *Journal of Burma Studies* 10, no. 1 (2005): 51–81.

———. *Refiguring Women, Colonialism, and Modernity in Burma*. Honolulu: University of Hawai'i Press, 2011.

International Crisis Group. A Tentative Peace in Myanmar's Kachin Conflict, International Crisis Group. 12 June 2013, Asia Briefing N°140, 2013. <http://www.crisisgroup.org/~/media/Files/asia/south-east-asia/burma-myanmar/b140-

a-tentative-peace-in-myanmars-kachin-conflict.pdf>. Accessed 2 March 2015.
Kachin Women Association Thailand (KWAT). *Burma's Covered Up War: Atrocities Against the Kachin People*, Chiang Mai: Kachin Women Association Thailand, 2011
———. *Pushed to the Brink: Conflict and Human Trafficking on the Kachin-China Border*, Chiang Mai: Kachin Women Association Thailand, 2013a.
———. *State Terror in the Kachin Hills*, Chiang Mai: Kachin Women Association Thailand, 2013b.
———. "Undermining the Peace Process: Burmese Army Atrocities against Civilians in Putao, Northern Kachin State," Chiang Mai: Kachin Women Association Thailand, 2013c.
———. *Silent Offensive: How Burma Army Strategies Are Fuelling the Kachin Drug Crisis*. Chiang Mai: Kachin Women Association Thailand, 2014.
Kamler, Erin "Women of the Kachin Conflict: Trafficking and Militarized Femininity on the Burma-China Border". *Journal of Human Trafficking* 1, no. 3 (2015): 209–34.
Khen, Salai Isaac, and Muk Yin Haung Nyoi. *Looking at the Current Peace Process in Myanmar through a Gender Lens*. Catalyzing Reflection Series. Bern, Switzerland: Swiss Peace, 2014.
Lee, Yanghee. *End of Mission Statement Special Rapporteur on the Situation of Human Rights in Myanmar*, 2015a. <http://www.ohchr.org/EN/NewsEvents/Pages/DisplayNews.aspx?NewsID=16309andLangD=E>. Accessed 20 September 2015.
———. *Report by the Special Rapporteur on Myanmar*. New York: United Nations General Assembly, 2015b. <http://reliefweb.int/report/myanmar/report-special-rapporteur-situation-human-rights-myanmar-yanghee-lee-ahrc2872>. Accessed 20 September 2015.
Lintner, Bertil. *Land of Jade: A Journey through Insurgent Burma*. Bangkok: Orchid Press, 1990.
Mazurana, Dyan. "Women, Girls, and Non-State Armed Opposition Groups". In *Women and Wars*, edited by Carol Cohn. Cambridge: Polity Press, 2013.
Mi Mi Khaing. *Burmese Family*. Bloomington, Indiana University Press, 1946.
———. *The World of Burmese Women*. London, Zed Press, 1984.
Minoletti, Paul. *Women's Participation in the Subnational Governance of Myanmar*, Discussion Paper no. 3 in Subnational Governance in Myanmar Discussion Paper Series, 2014. <https://asiafoundation.org/resources/pdfs/WomensParticipationintheSubnationalGovernanceofMyanmar.pdf>. Accessed 12 July 2015.
Parashar, Swati. "Armed Resistance, Economic (In)security and the Household: A Case Study of the Maoist Insurgency in India". In *The Global Political Economy of the Household in Asia*, edited by Juanita Elias and Samanthi Gunawardana. London: Palgrave Macmillan, 2013.
Pugh, Michael, Neil Cooper and Jonathan Goodhand. *War Economies in a Regional Context. Challenges for Transformation*. London: Lynne Rienner, 2004.

Quintana, Tomás Ojea. *Report of the Secretary-General on the Situation of Human Rights in Myanmar.* New York: United Nations General Assembly, 2011.

Roy, Srila. *Remembering Revolution: Gender, Violence and Subjectivity in India's Naxalbari Movement.* Dehli: Oxford University Press, 2012.

Saha, Jonathan. "The Male State: Colonialism, Corruption and Rape Investigations in the Irrawaddy Delta C. 1900". *Indian Economic and Social History Review* 47, no. 3 (2010): 343–76.

———. "Madness and the Making of a Colonial Order in Burma". *Modern Asian Studies* 47, no. 2 (2013): 1–30.

Shekhawat, Seema. *Female Combatants in Conflict and Peace: Challenging Gender in Violence and Post-Conflict Reintegration,* edited by Seema Shekhawat. New York: Palgrave Macmillan, 2015.

Shepherd, Laura J. "Veiled References: Constructions of Gender in the Bush Administration Discourse on the Attacks on Afghanistan Post-9/11". *International Feminist Journal of Politics* 8, no. 1 (2006): 19–41.

Smith, Martin. *State of Strife: The Dynamics of Ethnic Conflict in Burma*, Policy Studies, Washington, DC: East-West Center Washington, 2007.

Tharaphi Than. "Introduction". In *Women of Modern Burma.* London: Routledge, 2014.

Tickner, J. Ann. *Gender in International Relations: Feminist Perspectives on Achieving Global Security.* New York: Columbia University Press, 1992.

True, Jacqui. "The Political Economy of Violence Against Women: A Feminist International Relations Perspective". *Australian Feminist Law Journal* 32 (2010): 30–59.

———. *The Political Economy of Violence Against Women.* Oxford: Oxford University Press, 2012.

Union of Myanmar. *The 2014 Myanmar Population and Housing Census.* Ministry of Immigration and Population, Naypyitaw: Union of Myanmar, 2015a.

———. *The 2014 Myanmar Population and Housing Census: Highlights of the Main Results.* Ministry of Immigration and Population, Naypyitaw: Union of Myanmar, 2015b.

———. *The 2014 Myanmar Population and Housing Census: Kachin State.* Ministry of Immigration and Population, Naypyitaw: Union of Myanmar, 2015c.

Walton, Matthew J. "The 'Wages of Burman-Ness:' Ethnicity and Burman Privilege in Contemporary Myanmar". *Journal of Contemporary Asia* 43, no. 1 (2012): 1–27.

Women's League of Burma. *"If They Had Hope, They Would Speak": The Ongoing Use of State-Sponsored Sexual Violence in Burma's Ethnic Communities,* Chiang Mai: Women's League of Burma, 2014.

Yuval-Davis, Nira and Floya Anthias. *Woman-Nation-State.* London: Macmillan, 1989.

5

PACIFYING THE MARGINS

The Pa-O Self-Administered Zone and the Political Order in Southern Shan State

Ricky Yue

On 28 August 2014, a lieutenant colonel of the Restoration Council of Shan State/Shan State Army — South (RCSS/SSA-S) inspected land on top of a mountain he bought less than a year before for about US$10,000. The land has a commanding view of Taunggyi and Lake Inle. He said with excitement that a general in Yangon recently bought a similar plot adjacent to his for US$150,000. He added that once he had sufficient money, he would develop the site into a hotel. On the way back to Taunggyi town centre, his Toyota four-wheel drive was stopped by traffic police at an ad hoc checkpoint. He lowered the tinted glass and the police immediately recognized him. After exchanging a few words, the police made an apologetic gesture and waved the car on. The lieutenant colonel explained that they were stopping cars to fine those without the necessary permit. They stopped him because they did not know he had changed his car.

The lieutenant colonel is well known in town because he helped broker a ceasefire agreement between the RCSS/SSA-S and the central government. Before signing the agreement in 2011, the RCSS/SSA-S was one of the major ethnic armed groups in the country (Keenan 2012). In April 1988 the officer was a summer school teacher in Taunggyi and only planned to stay there until the end of classes. However, he was caught up in the student protests and arrested, according to him, simply because he was in the wrong place at the wrong time. He was released after three months in prison. While there he began to understand the struggles of the ethnic minorities and was sympathetic to them. After his release, he joined the SSA together with five other teachers who had been arrested at the same time. He fought in the jungles and eventually rose to the rank of lieutenant colonel. In 2005 he was seriously ill, so he left the SSA and went to China for treatment. He returned to Taunggyi after he recovered. In 2010 when the RCSS/SSA-S began ceasefire talks with the government, his former superior called him to lead the negotiation team, probably because he was the most educated person they could trust. In barely three years, the lieutenant colonel had undergone a dramatic identity transformation, from being an enemy of the state to becoming a landowner and developer.

The story of the lieutenant colonel is not unique in Myanmar. Many of the country's wealthy elite were drug lords or enemies of the state before they became successful entrepreneurs. The country's largest conglomerate, Asia World, was formed by the 'godfather of heroin' Lo Hsing Han. Likewise, Nay Win Tun, a former general of the Pa-O National Army (PNA), owns the Ruby Dragon group of companies, which operates lucrative jade mines in Kachin State. These former enemies of the state were co-opted with economic incentives.

The RCSS/SSA-S signing the ceasefire agreement and the lieutenant colonel's increase in fortune constitute a form of ceasefire capitalism — a term coined by Kevin Woods (2011) to describe the production of capital that relies on a specially constructed political economy conducive to state control. While this specially formed political economy is itself a subject of interest, how a ceasefire agreement translates into furthering state control requires clarification.

Moreover, the story of the lieutenant colonel is interesting on two counts. First, it appears the ceasefire dividends not only benefited the top brass, but also trickled down to lower levels of the armed opposition. This officer had been absent from RCSS/SSA-S operations for almost five years. Indeed, according to his own admission, he thought he had left the SSA after becoming ill and was surprised by the call up in 2010.[1] There was no indication he would directly benefit from the ceasefire agreement, yet he became a well-recognized landowner after it was signed. Therefore, there appear to be layers of beneficiaries, but their roles in the state-building project require substantiation. Second, the ad hoc vehicle police check to collect fines is an instance of Myanmar's informal economy, itself a by-product of the local political economy, which plays an important role in absorbing the deficiency in the allocation of state resources and helps maintain order at the local level. To what extent this informal economy helps sustain local order also requires clarification.

When placed together, the changing role of the lieutenant colonel, the emergence of a political economy binding warlords with the state, and a political order built on corruption and extortion are all part and parcel of a project to pacify conflict areas in Myanmar through co-optation of local armed groups. Plenty of literature discusses the political outcomes of ceasefire agreements (for example, Bray 1995; Egreteau 2012; Sakhong and Keenan 2014; Zaw Oo and Win Min 2007), political economy (for example, Brown 1999; Meehan 2011; Myanmar Peace Monitor 2013; Smith 2007; Tin Maung Maung Than 2007; Woods 2011), and state policy (for example, Kramer 2010; Kyaw Yin Hlaing 2012). Instead of repeating the arguments in existing work, this chapter adopts a different perspective, viewing the political order in the southern Shan State and the Pa-O Self-Administered Zone (SAZ) as a frontier of the state.

Benedikt Korf and Timothy Raeymaekers (2013) draw a very important distinction between a border and frontier. Although a border is often epitomized by cross-border trade, immigration (legal or otherwise), smuggling, and corruption, a borderland nonetheless is inherently central to the state because it performs the function of economic redistribution through the flows of people, capital, goods, and services. By contrast, frontiers are "not necessarily boundaries, but rather political spaces with distinct spatialities of rule and sovereign power" (Korf and Raeymaekers 2013, pp. 9–10). Frontiers are at the margins of state power (Donnan and Wilson 2001). Veena Das and Deborah Poole (2004) describe margins as the areas where the state apparatus is replaced by less organized practices that allow for the formation of a unique political economy that is different from the state. Pierre-Yves Le Muer (2006) calls it an institutional and moral vacuum. In essence, the difference between a border and a frontier is that a border needs to be controlled by the state. Its law and order is determined by the state, and the sovereignty of the state in terms of the monopoly on the use of force is indisputable. By contrast, the political order of the frontier can be mutually constituted between the state and locals, and therefore is more flexible. This difference in terms of the level of state control has important bearing on the development of the political order in a border and a frontier.

In his study of post-colonial statecraft in the Philippines, Wong Pak Nun (2013) suggests that frontier strongmen should not be seen as a threat to the state, but could be co-opted in the state-building process to bridge the development and resistance dichotomy. Essentially, Wong argues that decentralization of state management to local strongmen could help to pacify the frontier. The tools that facilitate the decentralization are networking, identity switching, and brokering (Wong 2013, p. 94). In short, through a process of co-optation the frontier is treated as separate from the state but is made to work for the state by bringing local strongmen into a client-patron relationship.

To understand the Pa-O SAZ as a frontier requires identification of the key political actors in the area who need to be co-opted by the state, and consideration of how they are co-opted. Accordingly, this chapter is divided into several sections. The first section sketches the political, economic, and social landscape of the southern Shan State, drawing attention in particular to the rivalry between the two major ethnic groups in the area: the Shan and Pa-O. This leads to a descriptive section on the main political actors in the area, who are divided into three categories: actors from the Pa-O community; actors from the Shan community; and actors from the international community. The next section examines the co-optation mechanism, who gets co-opted and why, and what sort of political order is established as a result. The subsequent section examines the effectiveness of the political order in terms of augmenting state control in the area by using the 2015 election result as the reference point. Finally, the analysis concludes that ceasefire capitalism can help to transform warlords to state builders; however, show of force still determines the political order in a frontier.

BACKGROUND TO THE ETHNIC STRUGGLE IN THE SOUTHERN SHAN STATE

The main inhabitants in the southern Shan State are Shan and Pa-O (Christensen and Sann Kyaw 2006; Risser et al. 2003). Their relationship has not been cordial, sometimes even hostile. Shan traditionally operated a system of hereditary leadership under rulers known in Shan as *saopha*. Pa-O were mainly farmers who lived under the shadow of their powerful neighbours. They had to pay the Shan lords taxes, hence the resentment against them (Yawnghwe 2013, pp. 93–94). Pa-O are commonly regarded as a sub-group of Karen (Christensen and Sann Kyaw 2006, p. 27; Hackett 1953, p. 27). Before independence, General Aung San and the leaders of Shan, Kachin, and Chin ethnic groups signed the Panglong Agreement in February 1947. The Karen sent U Hla Pe, a Pa-O leader in Thaton, to represent them as an observer at the conference (Christensen and Sann Kyaw 2006, pp. 17–18). To institutionalize their own freedom movement, U Hla Pe, U Aung Sa, and U Kyaw Sein formed the Pa-O National Organization (PNO) in 1947 (Christensen and Sann Kyaw 2006, p. 17). Initially, the PNO was only fighting against the Shan elites. Indeed, Samara Yawnghwe (2013, p. 175), whose grandfather was a Shan *saopha* and acted as the first president of the Union of Burma, has noted that the Burmese government did not see Pa-O as a threat to their authority in the early days. Pa-O began their struggle against the central government after the parliamentary government was seized by the military in the 1962 coup.

Shortly after crushing the democracy movement in 1988, the newly formed State Law and Order Restoration Council (SLORC) introduced the Program for the Progress of the Border Areas and National Races Development, or Border Areas Development (BAD) for short, to pacify the country's frontier areas (Lambrecht 2004). However, following the collapse of the Communist Party of Burma (CPB) in 1989, many CPB members escaped to the frontier areas either by joining local ethnic armed groups or by forming their own groups (Lintner 1990; Lintner and Black 2009). As a result, the BAD initiative was in tatters (ICG 2004). The military regime was proactive on ceasefire diplomacy with local armed groups, desperately needing more positive news to support its legitimacy to govern and to prevent further escalation of ethnic uprisings due to reinforcement from ex-CPB members.

Between 1989 and 1995, a total of sixteen ceasefire agreements were reached, nine with armed groups in Shan State. In the southern Shan State, the Shan State Army (SSA), PNO, and Shan State Nationalities People's Liberation Organization (SSNPLO) reached ceasefire agreements with the regime in 1989, 1991, and 1994 respectively. The ceasefire areas were demarcated: SSA was allotted Shan State Special Region 3, and the PNO was confined to Shan State Special Region 6. SSNPLO did not get a special region but had to share territories with the PNO in Hsihseng and Mawkmai townships; however, their areas of control extended all the way to the Thai border (Map 5.1).

Map 5.1. The locations of the main ceasefire groups in Shan State

Source: Adapted from CartoGIS, College of Asia and the Pacific, The Australian National University

It is important to note that although the SSA was confined to Special Region 3 in the northern Shan State, its footprint and sphere of influence covered much of the Shan area, at least until 1996 when the Shan State Army – South (SSA-South) split from the group. Although the main ethnic armed groups in the southern Shan State had come to terms with the central government, the region was far from being pacified because rivalry among the SSA, PNO, and SSNPLO never truly subsided due in part to history and ideology, but more importantly due to overlapping economic interests. The three armed groups were practically narcotics armies in those days. They fought over trade routes and shares of the narcotics business. According to Lambrecht (2004 p. 172), BAD did nothing to develop the frontier areas other than helping the regime to tighten its grip on the periphery, and amass billions of dollars from natural resource extraction in the process.

POLITICAL ACTORS IN THE SOUTHERN SHAN STATE

There are three things to bear in mind when examining the political actors in the southern Shan State. First, the transition from narcotics armies to political actors is an evolutionary process. It has taken time, and some have been more adaptable to the changing environment than others. It also allows for the emergence of new political actors. Therefore, some of the actors discussed in this section underwent changes in stages, and may go on evolving. There are also new actors that did not exist before 1989, but which today have significant implications for the political order in the area. Second, because the ethnic composition in the region is not homogeneous, political actors often find themselves having to face at least two fronts. Pa-O have to deal with the state and Shan, and vice versa for Shan, while the state can play Shan and Pa-O off against each other. Third, internal divisions within Pa-O and Shan groups play into the hands of government divide-and-rule tactics.

Accordingly, this section will first identify the political actors in the Pa-O community, followed by the political actors in the Shan community, and finally, international actors who are increasingly having a significant impact on the local community.

The actors in the Pa-O community

Despite organizational name changes, the Pa-O national movement remained united until 1973 when the Shanland Nationalities Liberation Front (SNLF) separated from the main group, which at that time was called the Shan State Nationalities Liberation Organization (SSNLO), because the latter was increasingly influenced by communist ideology. Through several more splits and amalgamations, the SNLF eventually became PNO as it is known today (the nationalist Pa-O), and SSNLO became today's Pa-O National Liberation Organization (PNLO) (the communist Pa-O) (Callahan 2007; Charney 2009; Christensen and Sann Kyaw 2006; Keenan 2012; Lintner 1999; Sakhong and Keenan 2014; Smith 1999) (for details and stages of change, see Figure 5. 1).

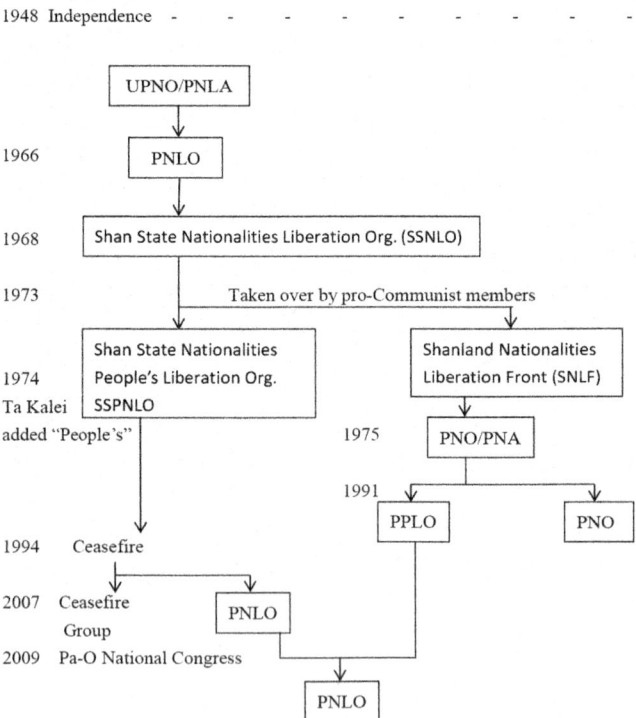

Figure 5.1. The evolution of the PNO and the PNLO

Although both the PNO and PNLO claim to represent Pa-O people, the rift between the two is not simply caused by ideological differences, but also has been encouraged by divide-and-rule tactics. The SSNPLO tried to reconcile with the PNO after the CPB broke up, however, the PNO refused reconciliation as many of its leaders were assassinated during the two decades of intra-Pa-O fighting (Christensen and Sann Kyaw 2006; Smith 1999). In 2010, the PNO registered as a political party and won all the seats in Special Region 6. In contrast, even though the PNLO also signed a ceasefire agreement, it has remained as a ceasefire armed group and has no other legal status.[2]

Under the more pluralistic political environment in Myanmar since 2011, the Union Pa-O National Organization (UPNO) registered as a political party in 2013 on the claim that the PNO is corrupt and working for the government.[3] However, the party lacks financial resources and cannot seriously challenge the PNO's position. In 2015 it failed to win any of the ten seats it contested at the national election.

Along with a new political party came a revival of community sector organizations (CSOs). Most have mandates to promote democracy and build capacity among Pa-O people, which puts them in direct confrontation with the PNO. The Kaung Rwai Social Action Network (KRSAN) runs a centre to teach Pa-O youth English, and is actively involved in pro-democracy campaigns. The Democracy for Ethnic Minorities Organization (DEMO) has a similar agenda. The Pa-O Youth Organization (PYO) acts as a claim-maker to raise social and environmental issues. As a damage-control strategy, the PNO set up the Parami Development Network (PDN) in 2012 to fund the renovation of pagodas, and to build roads and schools. Pa-O villagers who benefited from the renovations appear to appreciate these projects.[4]

The actors in the Shan community

The political actors in the southern Shan State come from more diverse backgrounds than in the Pa-O community. The most obvious actors are state representatives and Shan ethnic political actors. However, because of the importance of its location, the area also attracts political actors and activists from other parts of the country.

Shan ethnic armed groups resisted state authority in the southern Shan State after independence. In the beginning, the resistance was fragmented. Then the military coup by Ne Win in 1962 helped to unify the resistance. As a result, the SSA was formed by the amalgamation of the Shan National United Front and Shan State Independence Army in 1964 (Chao Tzang Yawnghwe 2010; Sai Aung Tun 2009; Yawnghwe 2013). Yet, it is too simplistic to brand the SSA as anti-state. In fact, the state and the SSA had a common interest in defeating the CPB (Lintner 1999; Lintner and Black 2009).

Despite official denouncement of the cultivation of opium, all armed groups in Shan State took advantage of the easy rent-seeking opportunities, which put the SSA, PNO, and PNLO into direct confrontation. In 1989, after the SSA signed a ceasefire agreement with SLORC, a breakaway group led by drug lord Khun Sa formed the Mong Tai Army and the political unit known as the Shan State Restoration Council to protect their opium interests, and continued fighting against the state. Khun Sa eventually surrendered in 1996, but Lieutenant General Sao Yawd Serk led another breakaway group to establish the SSA-S and formed the RCSS as its political wing. The RCSS/SSA-S signed its ceasefire agreement with the government in 2011. As a result of overlapping interests in the smuggling trade routes between southern Shan State and Thailand, conflicts between the RCSS/SSA-S and PNLO constantly flare up, with the central government playing a role in flaming the hostilities between the two.

The 2008 Constitution turned a new chapter in Myanmar's political history, as it paved the way for the first general election in twenty years, in 2010. The election reactivated political party activities, as ethnic Shan parties and national parties began to contest one another to represent the ethnic minorities in the southern Shan State. Among them was the Shan Nationalities League for Democracy (SNLD), which was founded in 1989, around the same time as the NLD. The party boycotted the 2010 election, but registered again as a political party to contest the 2015 election. In its stead, the Shan Nationalities Democratic Party (SNDP) was formed in 2010 to represent Shan in the election that year. Also known as the White Tiger Party or the Tiger Head, the party was considered pro-regime.

Despite reports the SNLD would cooperate with the SNDP in the 2015 election, both parties ran their own election campaigns and contested seats in the same constituencies.[5] The SNDP lost all upper and lower house seats in 2015, whereas the SNLD won three seats in the Amyotha Hluttaw, twelve seats in the Pyithu Hluttaw, and twenty-five seats in the State and Regional Hluttaws.[6] While the SNLD does not have any direct conflict of interest with the Pa-O, the party is sympathetic to Shan armed groups and enjoys a good relationship with the RCSS/SSA-S.

The southern Shan State is also the host to some influential political actors such as the NLD and the 88 Generation Group, which are closely linked to the CSOs in the Pa-O community. The military-established USDP has a presence too.[7] Also in the mix are non-state actors such as Myanmar Egress and MPC. Although holding the banner of promoting peace, not everyone in the pro-democracy camp trusts these groups.[8]

It is apparent that some of the political actors in Pa-O and southern Shan State have firm agendas opposed to the state. Therefore, in terms of pacifying the frontier by decentralization as Wong discusses in relation to the Philippines, those groups that were more pragmatic and showed less concern for democracy were co-opted. In the Pa-O community, the PNO and PNLO were not really championing democracy, they just demanded self-determination, and therefore, potentially both could be co-optation candidates. However, since the PNLO had a communist background, the regime favoured the PNO.[9] The situation in the southern Shan State is much more complicated. Since the SNLD was one of the victims in the 1990 election renunciation, it was obviously not on the regime's co-optation list. However, the RCSS/SSA-S was not a suitable candidate either. Despite reaching a ceasefire agreement, fighting continued in the northern Shan State because both sides wanted to maintain their control of vital border areas. Therefore, the regime did not find a suitable local partner until the SNDP was established in 2010.

As a quick summary, most of the actors in Pa-O areas and southern Shan State can be divided into two camps, the pre-2011 pro-regime camp, which after the election might be called the pro-establishment camp, and the pro-democracy camp (Table 5.1).[10]

Table 5.1. The pro-establishment camp versus pro-democracy camp, southern Shan State

	pro-establishment	pro-democracy
Pa-O Community	PNO	UPNO
	PDN	KRSAN; DEMO; PYO
	PNLO	
Southern Shan State	SNDP; USDP	NLD; SNLD; 88 Group
	Myanmar Egress; Myanmar Peace Center	

International actors

The mushrooming of CSOs in southern Shan State is one of the most prominent features of the post-2010 political landscape. While these CSOs may have different objectives, they share several similarities. First, they receive financial support from international donors. The main patron of KRSAN is the National Endowment for Democracy (NED), an INGO funded by the United States Congress. Its three-storey office costs US$250 a month to rent, which is underwritten by the NED.[11] DEMO is also funded by the NED. In October 2014, the American Center in Yangon invited a senior officer in charge of DEMO to participate in a capacity-building workshop in New York for three weeks. The PYO is funded by the Open Society Foundation, an INGO backed by the famous financier George Soros. It also receives financial assistance from the Burma Relief Center, based in Thailand, and Volunteer Service Overseas.[12]

With foreign patrons, the CSOs do not need to rely on the Shan State political economy. Their leaders are very young, mostly under thirty. They are well educated, speak fluent English, are ideologically oriented towards democracy, and more importantly, they are politically mobilized. These young leaders' achievements motivate other youths to follow their causes. Working for CSOs has become an attractive alternative to being farmers in villages where job opportunities are few. This has inspired many young people to take English lessons at the KRSAN centre and to participate in activities organized by these CSOs. The involvement of the NED and Open Society invites speculation that these foreign donors are sowing the seeds for an Arab Spring-style uprising in Myanmar should the democratic transition falter, but in the short term at least, these international actors have empowered the pro-democracy actors in the Pa-O community to resist the state and its pro-establishment affiliates.

CO-OPTATION AND THE POLITICAL ORDER IN PA-O AREAS AND SOUTHERN SHAN STATE

The purpose of identifying the key political actors at the local, state, and international levels is to reveal how the political order in Pa-O areas and the southern Shan State is constructed and resisted. In a frontier area, the state needs to balance decentralization of authority and maintaining state control. From an authoritarian perspective, success in pacifying a frontier is measured by who has been co-opted, and whether they can deliver on the state's agenda. Therefore, this section's three parts focus on the selection of candidates for co-optation. The first part examines the construction of the political order in the Pa-O SAZ through the state-sponsored political economy that ties the PNO to the regime, while at the same time highlighting the divide-and-rule tactics that keep the PNLO in check. The second part examines how local CSOs are resisting the political order in the southern Shan State. Finally, a template integrates the political order in the entire southern Shan State for subsequent evaluation of the effectiveness of the regime's frontier pacification project.

Overview of the political order in Pa-O areas

The PNO was among the first batch of ethnic armed groups to sign a ceasefire agreement with SLORC in 1991. Consistent with the finding by Wong (2013) in the Philippines, the regime recruited local strongman Nay Win Tun, an ex-PNA general, as the anchor for the frontier pacification project. By giving away substantial business concessions, the regime transformed Nay Win Tun from a state enemy into a successful entrepreneur (Callahan 2007, pp. 46–47; South 2008, pp. 124–25). His company, Ruby Dragon, was granted exclusive precious stones mining concessions in Hpakant, Kachin State. The company is the country's largest producer of gems and jade.[13] He also owns Kyauk Sein Nagar (Gems) Limited, a jewellery retail operation in Yangon, which means he is vertically integrated in the upstream mining and downstream retailing operations. Helped by a good relationship forged with the government, Nay Win Tun's business empire also stretches to construction, property development, and tourism. Under the Golden Island Hotel Group, the PNO operates the Nangang Hotel (opened in 1996) and the Golden Island Cottages, Thale U (opened in 1999), in the prime tourist hotspot of Lake Inle.[14] In 2004, he started the Ruby Winery Factory in Nyaung Shwe in southern Shan State. In 2005, amid controversies of land grabbing and pollution, Nay Win Tun invested in the Dragon Cement Factory, on a 728-acre site in Tigyit. In 2007, he opened the Ruby Jade Hotel Resort and Spa in Yangon. In return for favourable business concessions, Nay Win Tun uses part of the group's profit to fund the PNO, which in turn helps to promote the state political agenda.[15]

In contrast, the PNLO was offered very little when it signed a ceasefire agreement with SLORC in 1994. Unlike the PNO, the PNLO was not offered any specific territory. Instead, it was only given fifteen car permits worth US$50,000 each, and thirty car permits with sixty per cent of tax waived.[16] Given the PNO's income source is recurrent, and the PNLO only received a one-off gain, the ceasefire agreement clearly favoured the PNO and reflects the regime's divide-and-rule strategy (Figure 5.2).

Figure 5.2. The political order in Pa-O areas before 2010

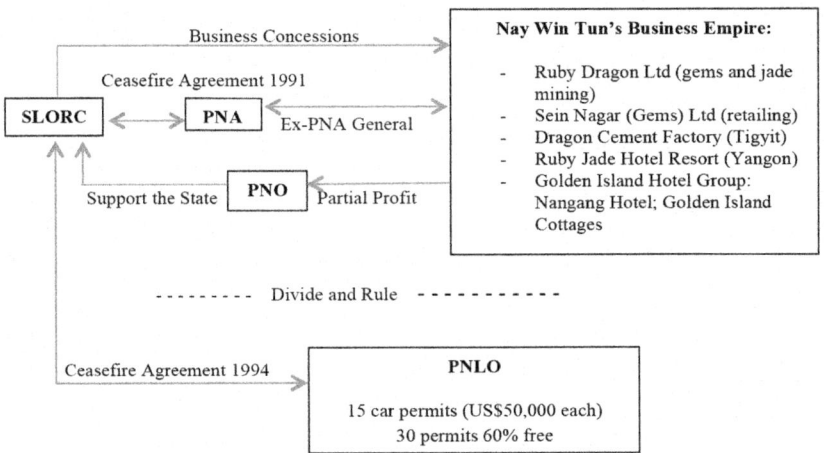

CSOs and the political order after 2010

The emergent CSOs can be seen as political socialization agents trying to reinforce, or even impose, a certain political culture on the Pa-O youth community. Political culture is the learning of political attitudes and behaviours (Kourvetaris 1997, p. 101). This is not a normal knowledge acquisition process, but a conscious, deliberate, sometimes manipulative form of learning. Whereas political culture is "a product of the history of the political system and the individual members of the system" (Dowse and Hughes 1986, p. 227), in the case of Pa-O, these CSOs are cultivating a political culture that is not indigenous, but rather, is based on Western values.

The political socialization process in the Pa-O community takes two forms; the first is via learning, and the second is through reaffirmation of values. To give an example of the first form, KRSAN holds regular English reading classes for Pa-O youth in their centre. On one occasion, a group of ten Pa-O youth aged between twelve and sixteen attended the English reading class. Later, they were shown a video called *Vote for Me*, which was about how to choose a class representative in school.¹⁷

The new political culture is also being constantly reaffirmed through cross-fertilization. Ceremonies marking the anniversary of the 1988 democracy movement are a case in point. At the 2014 occasion, KRSAN led a group of Pa-O youth to attend the event, and during the ceremony, they led the delegates in singing songs about democracy. At the end, they boarded two trucks and headed towards Taunggyi town centre to continue singing about democracy. From the activities of KRSAN and other CSOs, it appears that grassroots resistance to the political order in southern Shan State has emerged from the sponsorship of international actors. This movement's political economy is independent from the state, and therefore they are able to claim the moral high ground. International actors are linked to the local political order by providing the impetus to undermine the authority of the pro-establishment camp, thereby indirectly reinforcing other pro-democracy actors outside the Pa-O to form a united front to challenge the agents of the state (Figure 5.3). Therefore, it comes as no surprise that the PNO declared KRSAN as an "enemy of the party" during its general meeting on 14 December 2014.¹⁸

Figure 5.3. A different political economy driving power from the bottom

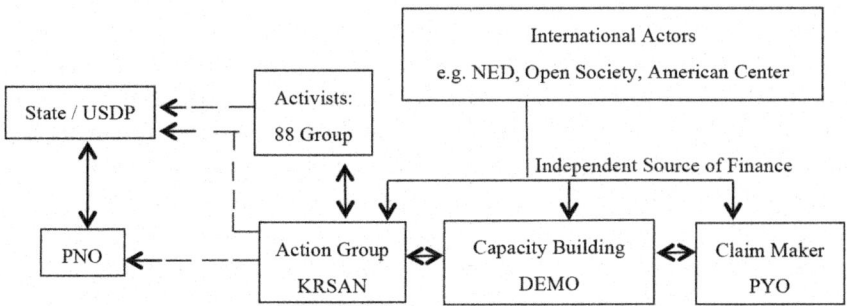

Overview of the political landscape in southern Shan State

Lacking a clear candidate for co-optation, the political order in the southern Shan State presents a mixed picture made up of triangular interactions among Pa-O and Shan actors and the state. Conflict between Shan and Pa-O armed groups flare up regularly. For instance, in September 2014 the SSA fought with the PNLO. The SSA was accused of burning down new facilities built by the PNLO in Maukmae. As mentioned previously, the PNLO has no fixed territory, but the main population of Maukmae are Pa-O and the PNLO considers itself the "administrator" of the town. The PNLO obtained permission from the central government to build two complexes in the town for administrative purposes. In return, the PNLO allowed the government to use part of the buildings. The RCSS/SSA-S felt the presence of government officials was too close for comfort, so it burned the buildings down when they were around ninety per cent complete. Fighting between PNLO and SSA ensued, and only stopped when the government threatened to send in its own troops.[19]

The CSO activities are also causing tension. The USDP has been particularly annoyed by KRSAN; the group frequently holds gatherings outside the university, hospitals, and in public areas of Taunggyi to sing about democracy. It has called in the police to evict them on several occasions.[20] Likewise, a CSO report on land-grabbing and pollution caused by the Tigyit coal and power project brought considerable embarrassment to the pro-establishment camp (Pa-Oh Youth Organization and Kyoju Action Network 2011).[21]

Figure 5.4 shows the relationships between political actors in the southern Shan State, with solid lines representing a supportive relationship and dotted lines depicting conflicts. Patronage works in the Pa-O community because the PNO is the dominant actor, helped by the regime's divide-and-rule strategy. However, the same tactic has not been effective in the southern Shan State because there are no dominant actors to co-opt. Meanwhile, hostility remains both within and between groups. The PNO and PNLO are not on speaking terms, the PNLO is still fighting with the RCSS/SSA-S, and CSOs and political activists such as the 88 Generation Group are trying to undermine central authority.

Figure 5.4. The political landscape in the southern Shan State

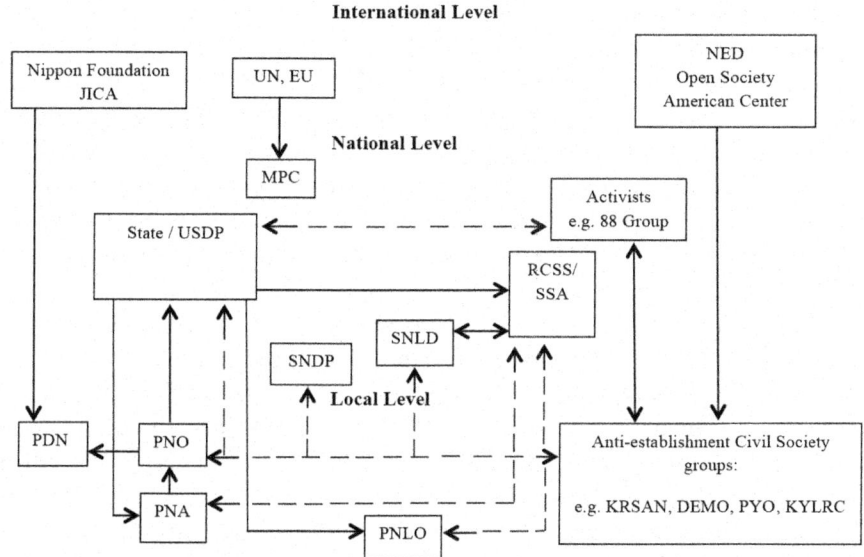

ASSESSING THE EFFECTIVENESS OF CO-OPTATION ON THE FRONTIER

In the frontier pacification project, the state has used co-optation at the macro level to secure loyalty and control. At the micro level however, while patronage matters, finding the right broker to deliver political objectives is equally important, as Aspinall and As'ad show in their study of elections in Indonesia. They conclude "what gave the victor his winning edge were state-centred forms of patronage and assiduous networking with a group we have described ... as state brokers" (Aspinall and As'ad 2015, p. 191). Following their logic, the success of the government frontier policy in southern Shan State depends on the effectiveness of the brokers employed.

As a well-rewarded broker, Nay Win Tun needs to deliver on the political objective of securing control in the area. This can be determined by examining the PNO's performance in the 2010 and 2015 elections. In the 2010 election, the PNO won all the seats available for Pa-O Special Region 6. This result should not come as a surprise, as voting irregularities marred the election, and the PNO had no competitor locally at that time. However, the PNO managed to retain all its seats in the 2015 election; it was the only pro-establishment ethnic political party nationwide that managed to do so, which comes as a big surprise and warrants closer scrutiny.[22]

It is important to point out that the 2015 win came on the back of three negative developments as far as the PNO is concerned. First, the PNO had two challengers in the shape of the NLD and UPNO. Second, villagers were more aware of their rights and the purpose of the election due to better voter education organized by CSOs. Third, voting irregularities were at a minimum under the watchful eyes of international observers. How did the PNO manage the win amid the challenging circumstances? Finding the answer will reveal how power is asserted at the micro level in the Pa-O SAZ.

The conventional administrative structure that links village with township is the village tract system. Villages are grouped into village tracts. The number of villages in a tract depends on the size of the villages, and sometimes can be more than twenty. Each village has a headman, and each village tract also has a leader, who serves to co-ordinate the village headmen and acts as the main conduit between the villages and township. The township administrator appoints the village tract leader, who is not necessarily a village headman within the tract.

The authority of village headmen has been culturally embedded in Burma's rural society (Hackett 1953; Leach 1954, pp. 159–71), therefore, they naturally become the targets for political control by outside forces. But instead of forming a patron-client relationship with the villagers, the PNO controls them in two ways. First, it holds the power to appoint the village tract leader, who uses his authority to command villagers. Second, the PNO instils fear into villagers with the threat of violence, because it has enjoyed a monopoly on use of force in Special Region 6 (and subsequently the Pa-O SAZ) since signing its ceasefire agreement.

Referring to the 2010 election, the chairman of UPNO explained the technique the PNO uses to control votes:

> Each village has a village head, and four to six villages combine to have one representative, referred to as the 'executive head'.[23] The PNO appoint the executive head. During the 2010 election, the SNDP wanted to talk to the villagers. However, the PNO told the villagers not to go because it would not be safe. Instead, they asked the villagers to send the executive village heads to attend. In the election, the executive village heads all voted for the PNO, and the villagers followed.[24]

He did not mention why it was not safe or where the danger would come from, but the following examples illustrate how the PNO's control and use of fear manifested in Pa-O villages.

During a field trip to Thathanshwe, a Pa-O village about one-and-a-half hour's drive from Taunggyi, the research team was forced to make a detour as part of the main road was closed for reasons unknown.[25] The car passed a village, and the team decided to pull over to interview some villagers about their views on development. This part of the fieldwork was therefore unscheduled, and the village selected was by chance. The villagers were asked to complete a questionnaire, which had been translated into Burmese and Pa-O. Initially, two villagers immediately agreed to complete the questionnaire and volunteered to ask more villagers to participate. They asked us to wait at the general store opposite while they gathered more villagers. While waiting, a large man in his forties introduced himself as the owner of the general store and offered the team drinks. In subsequent conversation, it transpired that he was the PNO-appointed village tract leader. After explaining the purpose of the stop over, he became uneasy and said he would not complete the questionnaire as it might be "unfair to other villages", and he refused to continue with the interview. By this time the two villagers who volunteered to recruit more people had returned with about seven villagers. The village tract leader said a few words to them and they all refused to do the questionnaire. The first two villagers had expressions of reluctance and fear on their faces.

Fieldwork conducted between June 2014 and March 2015 covered nine Pa-O villages. In all nine villages, the village headmen shared one thing in common: they all owned the general store. In the case of a larger village where there is more than one general store, the village head ran the biggest. During the fieldwork three village tract leaders were also encountered and they all had cars, which distinguishes them as local elites, because ordinary villagers have to walk for hours on rugged dusty roads to go to the market. Where did the village tract leaders find the money to buy cars? Under the Ward and Village Tract Administration Law the tract leaders are entitled to token remuneration, but it is definitely not sufficient to maintain, let alone buy, a car.

A clue may lie in the answer one village tract leader gave when asked about whether village headmen were paid for their jobs. According to him, the village headman was paid if he helped to settle issues. He gave two examples. If a thief is caught in a village, depending on the value of the stolen item, the village head could get between several hundred and 2,000 kyats. The other example involved buying and selling land, where the village headman would get a percentage as "witness" fees.[26] If the village headman receives money for trivial jobs, how much would a village tract leader get if he helped to settle land disputes? This is the informal economy that helps sustain order at the micro level.

It is not known whether the village tract leaders were already part of the elite in their respective areas before their appointment by the PNO, however, their power over the villagers is clear. Backed by the PNO and the armed soldiers of the PNA, they imposed themselves as the supreme authority in the village tract. Village headmen settle everyday disputes, such as petty thefts or marital problems. More complicated issues, such as land grabbing, are referred to the village tract leader, and if the issue is still not resolved, then the PNO/PNA will ensure the case is settled by the use of force.[27]

Village headmen are not appointed by the PNO. Villagers nominate them in what seems to be quite a democratic manner. However, in the nine villages studied, five headmen said they were reluctant to assume the role because they did not get paid. Moreover, they often found themselves having to deal with villagers' grievances because the village tract leader failed to respond to their requests. A headman of a village in Ho Pong township is a case in point. The village is located about 1.5 kilometres from the main road, but the surface of the existing path is full of potholes, which makes the village almost inaccessible during rainy seasons. For three years the villagers had been asking the village headman to raise the issue of paving a road to the village with the village tract leader. The village headman explained the procedure as follows. First, he has to discuss it with the village tract leader. If the leader agrees, he will prepare a proposal including a cost estimate and submit the application to the PNO at township level for authorization. Despite numerous meetings with the village tract leader, nothing has been done. However, villagers found out that a new road had been built in a nearby village in 2015. The first village's headman explained that the neighbouring village got its road because the village grew opium and paid the PNO and the villagers bribed the village tract leader, but the villagers still blamed him for not doing his job. It seems that the village headman has no power and has very little incentive to work for the villagers. On the other hand, the village tract leader has the means to get things done but the villagers aren't his concern because they do not nominate him. Therefore, even though in terms of line management the village tract leader and village headman should be working closely together, they are in fact loosely linked because the village tract leader serves the interests of the PNO, whereas the village headman serves the villagers.

The advantage in having both a carrot and stick to control villagers serves to explain why the PNO retained its seats in 2015 despite challenges from the NLD and UPNO. The regime seems to have appointed the right brokers to help it deliver political objectives, and in the process helped maintain order in the frontier area by decentralizing power without losing control.

The regime also tried to recruit brokers in the southern Shan State. Since the SNLD was pro-democracy, the SNDP became the regime's next best choice. The party's major source of income is the Top White Tiger Company owned by the party chairman and party directors. The company obtained a gypsum-mining concession from the regime, and an application for a copper mining concession is in progress.[28] But the links between the regime and the party in the political economy were not as strong as between the regime and the PNO, and unlike the PNO, the SNDP has no armed force to back it.

In the 2010 election, the SNDP won three seats in the Amyotha Hluttaw, eighteen seats in the Pyithu Hluttaw, and thirty-six seats in the State/Regional Hluttaw. The positive result could be attributed to two factors. First, the NLD and SNLD did not participate in the election. Second, the USDP collaborated with SNDP by not contesting in the constituencies where the SNDP was strong. In an interview with its chairman in the party's Taunggyi office the day before the election in 2015, he was confident that his party would retain all its seats and could even be the kingmaker if the USDP and NLD tied. As it turned out, the election was almost a complete whitewash for the party — it lost all its seats in the Amyotha and Pyithu Hluttaws and managed to get only one seat in the State/Regional Assembly.

In contrast, in 2015 the SNLD — which boycotted the election in 2010 — won twelve seats in the Pyithu Hluttaw, three seats in the Amyotha Hluttaw, and twenty-five seats in the State/Regional Hluttaw. Its election victory to an extent reflected the Shan people's genuine desire for self-determination and democracy, and their contempt for the SNDP. However, could the party have achieved that number of seats without some muscle at its back? The SNLD is close to the RCSS/SSA-S and has backed the latter in the past.[29] Close scrutiny of where the SNLD got its seats reveals an interesting pattern: the seats won by the SNLD are concentrated in the north, where the SSA-North is based, and to the east of southern Shan State, where the RCSS/SSA-S is strong. In southern Shan State, the SNLD did not have the advantage and the NLD won most of the seats (with the exception of the area controlled by the PNO and a pocket won by the USDP). This pattern requires an explanation.

As observed in the Pa-O areas, the PNO is the dominant actor, the political economy that feeds the party is very well established, and the spoils from ceasefire capitalism trickle down to the village tract leaders who have direct authority over the villagers. However, the benefit chain broke down in the southern Shan State. The SNDP did not receive strong financial support from the regime and it lacked the influence to force the issue at the village level. While the SNLD is close to the RCSS/SSA-S, the benefit and power chains broke down at the micro level. The ceasefire dividend did trickle down to the lieutenant colonel, but then he became a property developer. Moreover, the SNLD does not have soft power at its disposal. Its appeal is self-determination and democracy, but the NLD shares much the same values and it has soft power in democracy icon Aung San Suu Kyi. This explains why the SNLD could only get seats in the north and east, and failed in the tussle with the NLD in the west of the state.

CONCLUSION

What are the contributions and implications of the analysis for the study of the political order in Pa-O areas and southern Shan State? Drawing a distinction between the frontier and border to examine the political order allows the focus to shift from the state onto local political actors. In the frontier, devolution of power to local warlords is tolerated, and through them some form of order can be restored in areas where there was previously conflict. The analysis also links the co-optation process at the macro level with the implementation and maintenance of order at the micro level to establish how ceasefire capitalism advances state control in the frontier.

The PNO experience in retaining its seats in the 2015 election demonstrates that ceasefire capitalism could indeed be used to consolidate state control in the frontier; however, the SNDP experience is the opposite. What accounts for the different outcomes? At first glance, there is an obvious difference in terms of the substance of the political economy formed with the PNO and SNDP respectively. The gypsum concession obtained by the SNDP is nothing compared to Nay Win Tun's jade mine. However, this is not the only reason why ceasefire capitalism did not work in southern Shan State. The role of the beneficiaries at different levels of the power chain and the structure of the informal economy also made a difference. In the Pa-O areas, the PNO controls villagers through village tract leaders, and village tract leaders are rewarded for settling disputes and they receive bribes. There is a coherent formal structure and informal arrangements for an authoritarian political order. By contrast, the SNDP does not enjoy the luxury of having an army to back its cause, and the layer of beneficiaries is not there to deliver political objectives at the micro level. These findings lend support to the claim by Aspinall and As'ad that partnering with the right broker is essential in delivering political objectives, and substantiate the suggestion by Wong that frontier strongmen can be co-opted into the state's project.

However, this line of analysis, which tends to emphasize the importance of patronage and authority, may be too simplistic and ignores the significance of soft power. If patronage, power, and finding the right broker are all that matter, why can the model not be replicated in other parts of the country? Why was the PNO the only pro-establishment ethnic political party that managed to retain all its seats in 2015? The PNO victory cannot be boiled down to authority over villagers. Better voter education and the presence of international observers reduced the scope for electoral manipulation. One cannot dismiss the possibility that some Pa-O people voted wholeheartedly for the PNO instead of the UPNO and NLD.

This brings the local CSOs into the debate. The analysis presented in the chapter places CSOs as "enemies" of the state. Their advocacy for self-determination and democracy appealed to many young Pa-O voters. However, what tangible benefits have these CSOs actually brought to the Pa-O community as a whole? In response to the challenge by these CSOs, the PNO set up PDN in 2012 to repair pagodas, and build roads and schools. Many old villagers said that before 1991 they had to pay tax to the government but after the PNO became the administrator of their areas, they did not have to.[30] These are tangible benefits that Pa-O villagers appreciate. PNO candidates conducting their election campaigns in monasteries speaks volumes about their relationship with monks, who are highly respected by Pa-O people.[31] This soft power that the PNO has cannot be matched by the UPNO and NLD. In sum, arms are still relevant to party politics in a frontier where the state has withdrawn its monopoly on the use of violence. However, the PNO case shows that soft power could also come in handy.

The political order of the frontier is not fixed, but is constantly being constituted by the interactions of different actors. The PNLO was one of the signatories in the Nationwide Ceasefire Agreement in October 2015. The significance of this development is that the PNLO has been removed from the unlawful associations list and it can now enjoy full legal status and conduct formal business, or engage with INGOs to improve the living standards of Pa-O people. This development will inevitably undermine the PNO's authority, and even challenge its legitimacy to rule the Pa-O. While the PNLO has no immediate intention to form a political party, it does not rule out the possibility of working with the UPNO.[32] If the argument is valid that the SNDP's loss and the PNO's victory was partly because the latter had an army, would the alliance of the UPNO, a political party with a strong ethnic background, and the PNLO, a ceasefire armed group with teeth, be a game changer and serve as a platform to challenge the PNO? And if the alliance does materialize, what is the edge (soft power) that could tilt the balance to its favour? Or will the area return to conflict? It will be interesting to see what further changes occur in the southern Shan State in the coming years, and what changes to the region a parliament under the NLD will bring.

Notes

1   Interview, 28 August 2014 in Taunggyi.
2   Interview with a PNLO Central Committee member on 6 November 2015.
3   Interview with UPNO leader on 15 January 2015.
4   Interview with villagers near Kakku, where the PNO helped to repair the monastery, 7 November 2014. On the relationship between social welfare networks and politics in Myanmar more generally, see McCarthy, this volume.
5   There were even talks of a merger of the two parties, see "Biggest Shan Political Parties to Consider Merger" *The Irrawaddy*, 1 April 2014 <http://www.irrawaddy.org/burma/biggest-shan-political-parties-consider-merger.html>. Accessed 24 March 2015.
6   Union Election Commission, Announcement 92/2015 and 93/2015.
7   In 1993, SLORC formed the Union Solidarity and Development Association

(USDA) to alter the image of military control of the state and with a view to it functioning as a ruling political party (Taylor 2009, pp. 446–47). In 2010, the regime disbanded the USDA and transferred its members and assets to a newly registered political party, the USDP, which contested and won the general election later that year in the absence of the NLD. The USDP is therefore the incarnation of the regime after 2010 without the military uniform.

8 According to KRSAN staff, Pa-O youth who attended the capacity-building programme organized by Myanmar Egress usually returned believing the government would gradually move towards democracy (interview, 10 August 2014). Similarly, one 88 Generation leader said that Egress "accepts the 2008 Constitution when other democratic parties (are) against" it (interview, 10 August 2014). For more on the MPC, see Su Mon Thazin Aung, this volume.

9 The UPNO arrived late on the scene and is pro-democracy, hence it is not a suitable candidate for co-optation.

10 The PNLO is classified as neutral because it is neither pro-regime nor pro-democracy. Likewise, Myanmar Egress and the MPC have been classified as neutral, although they have been criticized as pro-regime due to having senior government officials on their boards of directors.

11 Interview, 8 August 2014.

12 The group appears to be very well funded, as they have nine full time staff occupying two detached houses.

13 The mine unearthed the world's largest jade boulder in 2001. Nay Win Tun donated the find to the military.

14 In 1995 when representing the Myanmar Fund, which had just completed a deal to build the Traders Hotel (name changed to Shangri-la in 2014) in Yangon, I was told by the Director General of the Directorate of Hotels and Tourism Lieutenant Colonel Khin Maung Latt that it was impossible to get a permit to build hotels at Lake Inle because of an issue concerning the land there. This was the time when Western sanctions were in full swing and the country badly needed foreign investment. Despite the Shangri-la group being much more qualified for a hotel project at Lake Inle, the PNO obtained permission to build hotels instead. The land issue was an excuse, because according to the person in charge of the Golden Island, the government owned all the land in the lake area (interview, 9 January 2015, Yangon).

15 Interview with the chairman of the PNO, Khun San Lwin, 27 August 2014.

16 Interview with a director of the PNLO, 8 August 2014.

17 I was a participant observer in the class on 10 August 2014.

18 Interview with KRSAN, 14 January 2015.

19 Interview with PNLO, 24 March 2015. The incident was reported in *The Irrawaddy*, 11 September 2014 <http://www.irrawaddy.org/burma/pa-o-shan-rebels-meet-clash-territory.html>. Accessed 26 April, 2015.

20 Interview with KRSAN staff, 14 January 2015.
21 Interview with PYO members, 14 January 2015.
22 The Pa-O SAZ consists of three townships, Hopong, Hsihseng, and Pinlaung, and is formed under article 56(c) of the 2008 Constitution. The PNO won all the ten Pa-O SAZ seats, which included three lower house township seats, one upper house seat (Shan-9) and six Shan State assembly seats for these three townships.
23 The correct term should be 'village tract leader' but the quote is as per the term used.
24 Interview 7 January 2015.
25 On 24 March 2015, the team consisted of the author, an informant who also acted as translator, and a driver.
26 Interview, 7 November 2015.
27 The NLD leader of Taunggyi revealed that in early 2014 a member of the NLD was murdered in the middle of the night after he helped a villager with a land dispute case. The spouse of the deceased man claimed men in uniform dragged her husband to an open field in the middle of the night and shot him dead. According to a petition submitted to the Shan State Court, the perpetrators were PNA soldiers. Interview, 8 August 2014.
28 The chief executive claimed that the PNO would have easily obtained the permit because they would bribe the officials.
29 In May 2014, a leader of the SNLD from Namlinmau village was arrested by the Tatmadaw. He was accused of possessing firearms supplied by the RCSS/SSA-S. The SNLD issued a statement on 15 May 2014 denying the accusation and demanding the release of the party member. The statement did not deny the SNLD member was in possession of a gun supplied by RCSS/SSA-S, and interestingly it even went on to defend the RCSS/SSA-S by saying, "such kind of incident will not only affect [the] ceasefire agreement and peace process which [the] Union Peace-making Work Committee and RCSS/SSA-S [are] committing to implement but also will cause ethnic armed groups not to trust the government". Statement of SNLD, 15 May 2014 <http://www.burmapartnership.org/tag/shan-nationalities-league-for-democracy>. Accessed on 26 April 2015.
30 Interview with villagers, 7 November 2015.
31 When asked about what disadvantage they faced in their election campaign, the chief officer of the UPNO said the PNO were allowed to conduct their campaigns in local monasteries, which helped to convince the villagers that the PNO were good because they respect the monks. Interview, 6 November 2015.
32 Interview with the director of the PNLO, 6 November 2015.

References

Aspinall, Edward and Muhammad Uhaib As'ad. "The Patronage Patchwork". *Bijdragen tot de taal-, land- en volkenkunde* [Journal of the Humanities and Social Sciences of Southeast Asia] 171, no. 2–3 (2015): 165–95.
Bray, John. *Burma: The Politics of Constructive Engagement*. London: The Royal Institute of International Affairs, 1995.
Brown, Catherine. "Burma: The Political Economy of Violence". *Disasters* 23, no. 3 (1999): 234–56.
Callahan, Mary P. *Political Authority in Burma's Ethnic Minority States: Devolution, Occupation, and Coexistence*. Washington: East-West Center, 2007.
Chao Tzang Yawnghwe. *The Shan of Burma*. Singapore: ISEAS, 2010.
Charney, Michael W. *A History of Modern Burma*. Cambridge: Cambridge University Press, 2009.
Christensen, Russ and Sann Kyaw. *The Pa-O: Rebels and Refugees*. Chiang Mai: Silkworm Books, 2006.
Das, Veena and Deborah Poole, eds. *Anthropology in the Margins of the State*. Santa Fe: School of American Research Press, 2004.
Donnan, Hastings and Thomas M. Wilson. *Borders: Frontiers of Identity, Nation and State*. Oxford: Berg, 2001.
Dowse, Robert E and John A. Hughes. *Political Sociology*, 2nd edn. Chichester: John Wiley & Sons, 1986.
Egreteau, Renaud. "Reflection: Assessing Recent Ethnic Peace Talks in Myanmar". *Asian Ethnicity* 13, no. 3 (2012), 311–13.
Hackett, Wilson D. "The Pa-O People of the Shan State Union of Burma: A Sociological and Ethnographic Study of the Pa-O (Taungthu) People". Ph.D. dissertation, Cornell University, 1953.
International Crisis Group (ICG). "Myanmar: Aid to the Border Areas". *Asia Report*. Yangon: International Crisis Group, 2004.
Keenan, Paul. *By Force of Arms: Armed Ethnic Groups in Burma*. Delhi: Vij Books, 2012.
Korf, Benedikt and Timothy Raeymaekers, eds. *Violence on the Margins: States, Conflict, and Borderlands*. New York: Palgrave Macmillan, 2013.
Kourvetaris, George A. *Political Sociology: Structure and Process*. Needham Heights: Allyn & Bacon, 1997.
Kramer, Tom. "Ethnic Conflict in Burma: The Challenge of Unity in a Divided Country". In *Burma or Myanmar? The Struggle for National Identity*, edited by Lowell Dittmer. Singapore: World Scientific Publishing, 2010.
Kyaw Yin Hlaing. "Understanding Recent Political Changes in Myanmar". *Contemporary Southeast Asia* 34, no. 2 (2012): 197-216.
Lambrecht, Curtis W. "Oxymoronic Development: The Military as Benefactor in the Border Regions of Burma". In *Civilizing the Margins: Southeast Asian Government*

Policies for the Development of Minorities, edited by Christopher R. Duncan. New York: Cornell University Press, 2004.

Le Meur, Pierre-Yves. "State Making and the Politics of the Frontier in Central Benin". *Development and Change* 37, no. 4 (2006): 871–900.

Leach, Edmund R. *Political Systems of Highland Burma: A Study of Kachin Social Structure*. Great Britain: Fletcher & Son, 1954.

Lintner, Bertil. *The Rise and Fall of the Communist Party of Burma (CPB)*. Ithaca, NY: Southeast Asia Program Publications, 1990.

———. *Burma in Revolt: Opium and Insurgency Since 1948*. Chiang Mai: Silkworm Books, 1999.

Lintner, Bertil and Michael Black. *Merchants of Madness: The Methamphetamine Explosion in the Golden Triangle*. Chiang Mai: Silkworm Books, 2009.

Meehan, Patrick. "Drugs, Insurgency and State-building in Burma: Why the Drugs Trade is Central to Burma's Changing Political Order". *Journal of Southeast Asian Studies* 42, no. 3 (2011): 376–404.

Myanmar Peace Monitor. *Economics of Peace and Conflict*. Chiang Mai: Burma News International, 2013.

Pa-Oh Youth Organization and Kyoju Action Network. *Poison Clouds: Lessons from Burma's Largest Coal Project at Tigyit*. Yangon: Pa-Oh Youth Organization and Kyoju Action Network, 2011.

Risser, Gary, Oum Kher, and Sein Htun. *Running the Gauntlet: The Impact of Internal Displacement in Southern Shan State*. Bangkok: Asian Research Center for Migration, Chulalongkorn University, 2003.

Sai Aung Tun. *History of the Shan State: From its Origins to 1962*. Chiang Mai: Silkworm Books, 2009.

Sakhong, Lian H. and Paul Keenan. *Ending Ethnic Armed Conflict in Burma: A Complicated Peace Process (A Collection of BCES Analysis and Briefing Papers)*. Chiang Mai: Wanida Press, 2014.

Smith, Martin. *Burma: Insurgency and the Politics of Ethnicity*. New York: Zed Books, 1999.

———. *State of Strife: The Dynamics of Ethnic Conflict in Burma*. Washington: East-West Center, 2007.

South, Ashley. *Ethnic Politics in Burma*. Oxon: Routledge, 2008.

Taylor, Robert H. *The State in Myanmar*. London: Hurst Publishers Ltd, 2009.

Tin Maung Maung Than. *State Dominance in Myanmar: The Political Economy of Industrialization*. Singapore: ISEAS, 2007.

Wong, Pak Nung. *Post-Colonial Statecraft in South East Asia: Sovereignty, State Building and the Chinese in the Philippines*. London: I.B. Tauris, 2013.

Woods, Kevin. "Ceasefire Capitalism: Military-private Partnerships, Resource Concessions and Military-state Building in the Burma-China Borderlands". *Journal of Peasant Studies* 38, no. 4 (2011): 747–70.

Yawnghwe, Samara. *Maintaining the Union of Burma 1946-1962: The Role of the Ethnic Nationalities in a Shan Perspective*. Bangkok: Institute of Asian Studies, Chulalongkorn University, 2013.

Zaw Oo and Win Min. *Assessing Burma's Ceasefire Accords*. Washington: East-West Center, 2007.

6

LANDMINES AS A FORM OF COMMUNITY PROTECTION IN EASTERN MYANMAR

Gregory S. Cathcart

> "Some people want to remove landmines. Some want to keep [them] for security and protection." — Church leader, Tanintharyi[1]

Myanmar currently ranks third internationally in the number of accidents and deaths from landmines, after Afghanistan and Columbia.[2] While the use of landmines in Myanmar's myriad conflicts has been documented (Geneva Call 2011; Moser-Puangsuwan 2000a; Selth 2000a), the factors determining their inclusion as a form of community protection have been less researched (South 2012).

To better understand the role of landmine use in Myanmar, this chapter uses civilian self-protection frameworks put forward by South, Perhult, and Carstensen (2010) and Jose and Medie (2015) to outline how several historical and cultural factors, including a culture of militarization and the arbitrary role of patron-client relations, have together with the "four-cuts" counterinsurgent strategy created an environment of "chronic emergency"

(Duffield 2008, pp. 8–10) for populations living in conflict-affected areas. Concomitantly, it points to a shift of landmine use away from primary military objectives to the targeting and protection of infrastructure, private assets, and community spaces.

This chapter argues that communities have adopted the military use of landmines to establish an element of control within an "emerging political complex" (Duffield 2014, p. 231), posing an immutable choice between the protection of their community and possible causation of physical and psychological trauma of the same local population.

In some circumstances, landmine use can be a form of community agency, not only to deal with insecurity but also to assess risks on the community's own terms (Bottomley 2001; KHRG 2008). Often communities are left with an immutable decision between the dangers of landmine use or exposure to other threats. They undertake risk assessments that weigh the risk of landmine use against other threats.

These findings are derived from research gathered as part of two Knowledge, Attitude, and Practices (KAP) surveys, the first representative of a population of 110,000 people across east Bago and Tanintharyi Regions, and Mon, Kayin, and Kayah States who have been directly impacted by landmine accidents. The second was on a population of 100,000 internally displaced persons residing in various locations across northern Shan and Kachin States. The surveys included a series of extensive coordination meetings and interviews with stakeholders, from senior and junior officials in government, ethnic armed groups (EAGs), and CSOs, as well as participant observation of interactions among these groups. A total of seventy semi-structured key informant interviews were conducted, together with 922 interviews with heads of households, and 390 separate and specific interviews with children, aged eight to eighteen (MRE WG 2014, 2015). The Department of Social Welfare, Ministry Social Welfare Relief and Resettlement coordinated the survey on behalf of working group members, with technical input from UNICEF and DanChurchAid.[3]

The chapter also aligns its findings with outcomes from two national processes, the union government reforms since 2011 and the post-Nationwide Ceasefire Agreement (NCA) process, to illustrate how international responses to landmine use in Myanmar have occurred primarily within the frame of a "security-development nexus" (Jacob 2014, p. 393). This has limited current intervention on landmines to technical discussions centred on 'de-mining' and behavioural change.

In order for sustainable changes in the use of landmines to occur, this chapter argues broader engagement at local levels will be necessary. Those seeking to engage conflict-affected communities will achieve more with approaches that acknowledge chronic insecurity and recognize the agency present in Myanmar's conflict-affected communities, including the capacity for a community's own militarized responses to prevailing conditions. In so doing, the promotion of non-military strategies will be critical to draw communities, armed actors, and local power brokers together. Promoting trust in interim governance institutions under the NCA that can build physical, psychological, and environmental security will be critical to successful behavioural change. Such an approach can produce not only a reduction in landmine use, but can build further legitimacy in local governance reforms.

INTERNATIONAL LAW AND DE-MINING IN MYANMAR

While the government of Myanmar is not a signatory to the tripartite conventions on conventional weapons, landmines and cluster munitions, the United Nations Committee on the Rights of the Child requested it take appropriate actions to protect children from the dangers of landmines (UN CRC 2012, p. 2). In response, the Department of Social Welfare established a Mine Risk Education Working Group (MRE WG) as a cross-ministerial body together with representatives from international and local organizations, yet with little representation from EAGs. For reasons explained below, this body has had limited impact in engaging parties in bilateral and national ceasefire processes on the issue of landmines, remaining focused on a core mandate of risk education and behavioural change.

Currently, five ceasefires, including two with the Karen National Union (KNU), state and Union level, have included de-mining or the consideration of broader mine action within their texts (Min Zaw Oo 2014).[4] However, EAGs in Myanmar are ineligible to ratify international laws. Nevertheless, they are often interested in bringing focus on their efforts to protect the rights of populations living within their administration areas. One initiative from Geneva Call, an INGO working specifically with non-state actors, is deeds of commitment. As discussed below, these provide EAGs with the opportunity to highlight their recognition of humanitarian norms on the use of landmines, as well as the protection of children and women in conflict.[5]

MPC FORMATION AND APPROACHES TO DE-MINING

In November 2012, the MPC was formed as a "national focal point for coordination, political negotiations, mine action and outreach" (MPC 2015; see Su Mon Thazin Aung, this volume), with mine action coordinated by the Myanmar Mine Action Centre operating under the auspices of the MPC. This brought a burst of international activity in mine action, mostly promoting de-mining efforts and mine risk education (LRC 2013; NPA 2013). The discussion of landmines focused on technical inputs for de-mining, including survey and risk education to enable greater access for humanitarian and development responses, for example, as part of durable solutions in Kachin State (HCT 2014).

These approaches, enacted before the NCA was signed, conjoined landmine removal with military and humanitarian security issues, and overlooked political imperatives at local levels. As Jacob (2014, p. 393) shows, such approaches reinforce a "security–development nexus" that prevents understanding of broader political contestations. They narrow the 'protection' of populations to a question of de-mining. The strong emphasis on de-mining unwittingly brought more attention to the military and strategic value of landmines for Myanmar's armed actors, leading to the view that ceasefires needed to be well in place before work on their removal begins (Myanmar Times 2014).

These approaches also overlooked crucial trust-building efforts needed to work with EAGs and their local populations (see Myanmar Peace Support Initiative 2013, p. 27). The situation was exacerbated by a perception among some EAGs that international organizations operating predominately from government areas into those administered by EAGs were being used as government proxies to reduce their administrative and military control over their own regions.[6] Landmine use by EAGs and communities could be said to prevent this from occurring. As a result, humanitarian mine action has been limited to risk education to raise awareness of the dangers of landmines.

These examples echo Jacob's warning for outsiders to be wary of "rushing in liberal governance reforms before reconciling the underlying conceptualizations and discourses of security and protection that are contested in existing political relationships" (2014, p. 402). Approaches to landmine contamination may be better undertaken with consideration to the nature of "political contestation" (Jacob 2014, p. 398) on the ground, and the strong level of cultural militarization present in Myanmar, discussed in further detail in the following section.

THE NCA AND LANDMINE USE

On 15 October 2015, the president of Myanmar and representatives of eight EAGs signed the NCA.[7] The negotiations resulted in the inclusion of landmines under the agreement's Chapter Three, on ceasefire-related matters (NCA 2015). The first aspect of the agreement relates to a cessation on laying new mines, and the second outlines the need to undertake de-mining activities.[8]

Despite these positive steps, there is no broad consensus on how to address the issue of landmines in the country (Cathcart 2015). The language in bilateral ceasefire agreements differs from one to the next, and furthermore, the language used in deeds of commitment, while related, is not intended to reflect and nor does it reflect that of bilateral ceasefires. While reaffirming bilateral ceasefires, the relationship of existing bilateral ceasefires to the NCA is yet to be clarified. Nevertheless, it is clear that the NCA is a significant step towards a ban on the use of landmines in Myanmar.

LANDMINES IN MYANMAR'S COMMUNITY SPACES AND INFRASTRUCTURE PROJECTS

After the military takeover of government in 1962, armed conflict in Myanmar moved into borderland areas. The presupposition that "the best way to destroy rebel groups is to destroy the ability of civilians to support them" (Delang cited in Callahan 2003, p. 208), drove the "four cuts" strategy the army adopted: cutting food, funds, intelligence, and recruits from the enemy (Smith 1991, pp. 258–62). During this time, landmines began to appear on village paths, at water source points, in rice storage, and houses, contributing to displacement and chronic emergency conditions for populations living in these areas.[9] Casualties due to landmines increased. In a study on rights indicators and health outcomes, Mullan et al. (2007) show that displaced communities were five times more likely to have an accident with landmines than if they had not been uprooted by conflict.

After the second military takeover in 1988, landmine use became a feature of security arrangements around infrastructure assets like hydropower dams, radio stations, and electricity transmission towers, as well as economic assets, like gold, tin, and jade mines (Lentz 2013). These 'restricted sites' denote areas of military significance as well as land being used for business purposes that is not to be accessed by the community.[10]

The evolving nature of landmine use in Myanmar is largely the result of an emerging militarized culture that brought knowledge and use of landmines and improvised explosive devices to local communities, either through their targeting or their defence.[11] These factors have constructed an environment of chronic insecurity that has predisposed communities to enact a series of community protection strategies, including multiple patron-client relations and the use of landmines to actively confront and establish control within an environment of chronic insecurity.

CHRONIC INSECURITY AND THE FORMATION OF POLITICAL COMPLEXES IN MYANMAR

Duffield (2008, p. 9) defines chronic emergency in Myanmar as "the exposure of a population to risk and uncertainty by the exercise of arbitrary personal power". In Myanmar, the exercise of arbitrary power is complicated by its multiple sources and characteristics. While populations are in general terms divided between those under the administrative areas of the state or EAGs, in reality conditions are far more complicated, with local militia, border guard forces, business groups, various administrative agencies, faith-based organizations, and INGOs and local CSOs all part of an "emerging political complex" (Duffield 2014).

South (2012) and Jolliffe (2014) describe the influence of patron-client ties on communities in the southeast of Myanmar, along the Thai border. A core theme in their work is that patron-client relationships do not necessarily translate into relationships of protection. Jolliffe (2014, p. 5) says:

> Where there is a lack of universal protection provided by the state or other institutions, civilians become further dependent on [patron-client] relations. Political conflicts and allegiances are therefore typically a function of compatibilities or incompatibilities with regard to expectations about deference or patronage.

However, not all EAGs position themselves locally as protection actors, even though, "groups identifying with ethnic nationalities in

South-Eastern Myanmar seek to position themselves as — and are often perceived to be — protectors" (Schissler 2016, p. 11). Indeed, traditional modes of patron-client relations can be said to include the use of villagers as labourers, porters, fighters, and as a source of revenue (Taylor 2009). Multiple armed groups in this region tax the populations they dominate, and commit human rights violations, force labour and conscript troops, and take or destroy food, crops, and land (Jolliffe 2014; South 2012). The power of local militia extends across networks of politicians, military officers, and businesses. These networks provide militia leaders access to formal and informal economies. As Yue (this volume) and Callahan (2003) show, there are a variety of political accommodations for militia at sub-national levels, including business concessions and other incentives.

The need for multiple relationships to mitigate the violations of one or more actors is crucial for community survival. Hence, patron-client relations may feature multiple overlapping networks between competing armed actors, businesses, or influential persons. Relationships also extend to a range of respected faith-based representatives, and CSOs who may themselves enter into relationships with the parties to conflict and communities as a means of minimizing conflict and maximizing community protection.

RESPONDING TO CHRONIC INSECURITY WITH COMMUNITY PROTECTION STRATEGIES

Jose and Medie characterize community protection as "activities undertaken during armed conflict (international or non-international) to preserve physical integrity in which the primary decision maker is a civilian or group of civilians" (2015, p. 516). It aims to protect the community against immediate, direct threats to physical integrity imposed by belligerents or traditional protection actors.

In the case of Myanmar, South et al. (2010) categorize self-protection into three strategies of containment, avoidance, and confrontation. These strategies encompass activities like establishing hiding sites in preparation for expected displacement, hiding food stores in the forest, monitoring troop movements, and employing advanced warning systems to alert villagers to approaching army patrols, retrieving food and other supplies left behind at villages during flight, cultivating covert agricultural fields, sharing food with friends and family, using local foods and medicine, accessing indigenous organizations providing cross-border aid, providing community education and social services, and assisting family and community members in the daily challenges of life in hiding (KHRG 2008, pp. 5–7).

As South notes, community protection mechanisms in Myanmar are "highly contextual and time-specific, and must be understood and analysed at the national, community, family and individual levels" (2012, p. 21). While it is clear that protection strategies need to be studied as contingent responses to localized threats, the research used for this chapter found that a consistent pattern throughout the surveyed population was that landmines were among the community protection measures used (MRE WG 2014, 2015). In the area of southeast Myanmar where the surveys were conducted, twenty-two per cent of respondents reported that "mines keep their village safe", with women reporting a higher level (twenty-six per cent) than men (twenty per cent). In separate locations of Myanmar two key informants mentioned that around half of the villagers in their areas know how to make homemade mines.[12]

Despite respondents' insistence that landmines are a form of protection, sixty-five per cent of respondents in the southeast reported a landmine accident in their village, and forty-eight per cent of all those interviewed in the southeast reported that landmines are a problem in their daily lives (MRE WG 2014). Therefore, the use of landmines as a community protection strategy is risky, and involves an assessment and balancing of the risks of landmine use with other threats to the community.

RISK ASSESSMENTS

The use of landmines occurs with an assessment of risk. This assessment comprises two parts: first, an assessment of the risks of using explosive devices; and, second, an assessment of the risk of using landmines compared to other risks.

Many communities have developed what Andersson et al. (2003) refer to as a level of "mine smartness" that is learned from interaction with armed actors. In this way it is possible to show how individuals create their own response mechanisms while living in contaminated areas, and that engagement with mines often occurs through a risk assessment process that "makes sense to them" (Andersson et al. 2003, p. 873). In Myanmar such assessments take place in the context of communities that have long been deliberately using this knowledge to handle and deploy ordnance in order to protect their assets. Communities' interaction with explosive devices is not a sign of ignorance, but is evidence of learned local practices grounded in militarized norms formed by social, political, and economic interactions.

For many communities in Myanmar landmine use presents an unenviable choice between exposure to risks from other threats, the need for food security and future livelihood versus the risk of injury. The objective of villagers in conflict areas is to somehow balance the multitude of risks they face on a daily basis in order to survive. As South (2012, p. 21) writes, "Self-protection and survival mechanisms often involve taking tough decisions... between safety and livelihood security. Many self-protection strategies expose vulnerable people to further risks." These further risks include the risk of losing crops, village stores of rice, and orchards, which are weighed against the risk of using landmines as a form of protection.

Obviously, the presence of landmines laid by the community itself brings with it the risk of accidents. When respondents to the KAP surveys were asked to list the kind of activities victims or survivors of explosions were engaged in when they had an accident, sixty-five per cent reported that accidents most commonly result from villagers entering mined areas to collect forest products (MRE WG 2014). Concerns for food security and daily survival override other factors.[13] As Bottomley (2001, p. 12) says, "The risk of not being able to feed a family or to secure land can sometimes only be addressed through undertaking a high risk activity" like navigating mined forests in search of produce.

Despite these risks, research conducted by Schissler (2016, p. 5) reported that communities expressed concern that though ceasefires improved freedom of movement, they had increased the number of business activities in former civil war areas. These activities may or may not have the support of the local communities. Feedback from six stakeholders in five states and regions in the east of Myanmar confirmed that the use of landmines as a means of community protection had not reduced significantly after ceasefires. Communities are retaining the use of landmines as a means to protect their resources from new threats from businesses and developers. Even with a series of bilateral and national ceasefires signed, local protection concerns remain, with one stakeholder stating bluntly that, "If we remove our landmines then our forest would be gone."[14] Another said, "It is too early for de-mining as many businesses are entering these areas."[15] Ceasefires are exposing communities to new and perhaps more serious threats than those they encountered previously. In response, communities continue to resort to protection strategies that include the use of landmines to contain outside encroachment and protect their assets.

INFORMATION SHARING ABOUT LANDMINE USE

Stakeholders and respondents at all levels often spoke of landmines being a "sensitive issue". This sensitivity is partly associated with the fear of negative consequences for sharing information regarding the whereabouts and types of landmines. That is, villagers fear that individuals, families, and communities might be targeted for interrogation or be more exposed to human rights violations if they are identified as having knowledge of, or involvement with, explosive devices. Consequently, people keep quiet about their knowledge, as exemplified in statements during interviews like, "I did not dare to talk about this to anyone because I was worried… I might get… trouble", and, "I have never told about this to anyone. I am able to talk about this only when you came".[16]

Internally displaced populations in Kachin and northern Shan States show an even higher level of sensitivity than others, with just over one quarter of respondents in these locations stating they would not talk about an explosive device they had seen (MRE WG 2015).

Despite this fear of reporting to others, more than two-thirds of men and women stated they knew what landmines were. But when these respondents were asked to list their sources of information, nearly half chose not to respond and a third responded 'don't know' (MRE WG 2014).

Community protection strategies aim to promote survival, and the chances of survival are improved if silence is kept regarding landmines and their locations. Communities thereby retain local knowledge, giving them more power in their relations with belligerent patrons and other outsiders. For instance, one informant spoke of an EAG member being injured from landmines set by local communities. The EAG then came to the village and implored the community that "they did not want to harm them, but to just tell where the landmines were".[17]

Information is shared predominantly through person-to-person contact. Nearly a quarter (twenty-three per cent) of all households reported that information on explosive devices around and near the village was shared between and among villagers, the Myanmar military, EAGs, and other parties using 'business mines' in person (MRE WG 2014). But such information is shared not necessarily to prevent harm, but rather as a warning not to go near areas under the control of whoever is using landmines.

Information is not often shared using signage. According to the MRE WG (2014) data, just over one percent of respondents would set a 'warning sign' if they saw an explosive device. Of forty-five interviews with landmine survivors or their families, thirty-seven stated that the area where the accident occurred was not marked as dangerous.

Norms for landmine use partly depend on myths. For example, numerous informants mentioned that homemade devices made from bamboo only last one rainy season or six months. In fact, it is difficult to know the durability of these devices because testing the reliability of a homemade device after a rainy season is not something to be encouraged. In any event, the combination of myths with norms of landmine use presents a considerable challenge to anyone seeking to implement risk education interventions with populations actively engaging with explosive devices.

FINDING A WAY FORWARD

This concluding section presents two approaches to responding to the use of landmines in Myanmar. It directs action in terms of how international organizations and actors operating outside conflict areas can best engage with communities to have more impact for the safety of populations, retain local agency, and create more opportunity for local voices in nascent political dialogue in these areas. One intervention operates at a community level, while the second focuses on sub-national and joint state administration.

When asked about the best way to inform people about how to keep safe around explosive devices, the majority of respondents (thirty-six per cent) stated that people should organize themselves (MRE WG 2014). As one said, "Fitting in with local contexts is the best, and if people can organize themselves, it's perfect."[18]

A community-based participatory systems model of conflict dynamics is one method that can promote village agency to deal with landmines (Jolliffe 2015). Such an approach can lead to a better understanding of not only how communities are responding to a range of threats, but the various strategies they have adopted in response. From this starting point, the identification of existing, durable, and safe coping mechanisms with communities can occur, while reducing potentially harmful strategies that leave communities exposed to further risks. Jolliffe (2015) points to how community-level engagement can result in the formulation of localized indicators to measure progress towards security.

A second and broader approach is to promote non-militarized responses. But in encountering the complex nature of landmine use, traditional risk education and information-sharing models need to be re-examined to ensure the safety of populations and enable a secure environment absent of mines for development to occur. A model of mine action needs to be designed that seeks not only to warn populations of dangers, but also responds to the chronic insecurity, for communities to live in sustainable safe and secure environments. Mine action needs to be in coalitions to prevent triggers for landmine use, including "unlawful land grabbing incidents", and the promotion of a "safe and peaceful living environment for communities".[19]

Interim arrangements to diminish landmine use are also important. Chapter six of the NCA includes a number of areas for interim arrangements while political dialogue gets underway, including "projects regarding the health, education and socio-economic development of civilians" (NCA 2015, p. 10). Interim arrangements can also bring the opportunity to build legitimacy, participation, and inclusion of local populations in interim governing authorities, which have the potential to engage local populations on key issues and promote a high level of inclusion that can reduce landmine use more effectively than other measures. Such inclusion will be critical to address the chronic insecurity that has given rise to militarized community approaches, and to promote non-militarized responses to local security concerns.

Notes

1 In discussion with author, April 2013.
2 Refer to <http://www.icbl.org>.
3 In December 2012, the MRE KAP survey was identified as a priority of the Mine Risk Education Working Group (MRE WG). The author served as MRE Specialist to this project. The views expressed in this paper are solely those of

the author and not those of the MRE WG, UNICEF or DanChurchAid (DCA).
4   Ceasefires that have included the issue of landmines in their text include the Karenni National Progressive Party 3rd, Union Level (23 October 2013); KNU, 2nd Pre State Level (12 January 2012); KNU 2nd Union Level (4 September 2012); RCSS, State Level (2 December 2011); KIA (10 October 2013).
5   According to Geneva Call, the following non-state armed groups have signed deeds of commitment against the use of landmines: Arakan Rohingya National Organization, CNF/Army, KNU/KNLA, Lahu Democratic Front, National Unity Party of Arakan, Pa'O Peoples Liberation Organization, Palaung State Liberation Front /Ta-an National Liberation Army (PSLF/TNLA), <http://www.genevacall.org/how-we-work/armed-non-state-actors/>. Accessed 1 May 2015.
6   EAG representative, Yangon, in discussion with the author, 2013.
7   The eight signatories are: All Burma Students' Democratic Front (ABSDF), Arakan Liberation Party (ALP), Chin National Front (CNF), Democratic Karen Benevolent Army (DKBA), Karen National Liberation Army-Peace Council (KNLA-PC), Karen National Union (KNU), Pa-O National Liberation Organization (PNLO), Restoration Council of Shan State (RCSS).
8   NCA, Chapter Three, "(a) Cease the following actions in ceasefire areas: troop movements for territorial control, reconnaissance, recruitment, armed attacks, laying of mines, acts of violence, destruction of property, and launching of military offensive... (e) Undertake de-mining activities to clear mines laid by troops from all sides in accordance with the progress of the peace process and coordinate mine action activities in close consultation with the Government of the Republic of the Union of Myanmar."<http://www.eprpinformation.org/files/recent-events/Myanmar-s-peace-process-a-nationwide-ceasefire-remains-elusive--19sept-2015.pdf>. Accessed 27 February 2016.
9   Most commonly reported locations of landmines identified through desk survey and key informant interviews include military installations, along paths, near hydropower dams, roads, electricity transmission lines, bridges, farms, and orchards.
10 MRE WG Team Leaders, in discussion with the author, December 2014.
11 Improvised explosive devices are similar in action to landmines however are made from bottles, tins, bamboo, or pipe and are often referred to locally as 'homemade mines'.
12 Civil society representatives, Kachin, Kayin, and Kayah States, 2014.
13 Civil society representatives, Kayin State, discussion with author, March, 2015.
14 Village leader, in discussion with MRE KAP Team, May 2013.
15 Civil society representative, Yangon, in discussion with the author, 2014.
16 Farmer, in discussion with MRE KAP Team, 2013; casual worker, in discussion with MRE KAP Team, 2013.

17 Village leaders, Bago East, in discussion with the author, 2013.
18 Civil society representative, Mon State, March 2015.
19 Civil society and government representatives, various locations, in discussion with the author, 2015.

References

Andersson, Neil, Aparna Swaminathan, Charlie Whitaker, and Melissa Roche. "Mine Smartness and the Community Voice in Mine Risk Education: Lessons from Afghanistan and Angola". *Third World Quarterly* 24, no. 5 (2003): 883–87.

Bottomley, Ruth. "Crossing the Divide: Landmines, Villagers and Organizations". International Peace Research Institute report, 2001 <http://file.prio.no/Publication_files/Prio/Bottomley%20(2003)%20Crossing%20the%20Divide%20(PRIO%20Report%201-03).pdf>. Accessed 27 February 2016.

Callahan, Mary. *Making Enemies: War and State Building in Burma*. New York: Cornell University Press, 2003.

Cathcart, Gregory. "Myanmar's Minefields: Landmines are the Missing Link in Ceasefire Process". *New Mandala* 12 October 2015 <http://asiapacific.anu.edu.au/newmandala/2015/10/12/myanmars-minefields/>. Accessed 26 January, 2016.

Delang, Claudio O. *Suffering in Silence: The Human Rights Nightmare of the Karen People of Burma*. Karen Human Rights Group. Parkland: Universal, 2000.

Duffield, Mark. "On the Edge of 'No Man's Land': Chronic Emergency in Myanmar". Department of Politics, University of Bristol, Working Paper No. 01-08, 2008 <http://www.bristol.ac.uk/media-library/sites/spais/migrated/documents/duffield0108.pdf>. Accessed 27 February 2016.

———. *Global Governance and the New Wars: the Making of Development and Security*. Kindle edition, 2014.

Geneva Call. "Humanitarian Impact of Landmines in Burma/Myanmar 2011". 2011 <http://www.genevacall.org/wp-content/uploads/dlm_uploads/2013/12/Humanitarian-Impact-of-Landmines-in-Burma-Myanmar.pdf>. Accessed 26 February 2016.

Humanitarian Country Team. "Durable Solutions to Displacement in Kachin and Shan States: Guidance Note on Standards and Principles". August 2014 <http://www.themimu.info/sites/themimu.info/files/documents/Ref_Doc_Durable_Solutions_Kachin_HCT_2014.pdf>. Accessed 27 February 2016.

Jacob, Cecilia. "Practising Civilian Protection: Human Security in Myanmar and Cambodia". *Security Dialogue* 45, no. 4 (2014): 391–408.

Jolliffe, Kim. "Myanmar: Ethnic Conflict and Social Services". The Asia Foundation, June 2004 <https://asiafoundation.org/resources/pdfs/

MMEthnicConflictandSocialServices.pdf>. Accessed 27 February 2016.

———."Ceasefires and Durable Solutions in Myanmar: A Lessons Learned Review". *New Issues in Refugee Research*, Research Paper No. 271, 2014 <http://www.unhcr.org/533927c39.html>. Accessed 27 February 2016.

———. "Letting Communities Take the Lead: Building IDP Rehabilitation Programmes around Community Approaches to Protection". Unpublished, 2015.

Jose, Betcy and Peace Medie. "Understanding Why and How Civilians Resort to Self-Protection in Armed Conflict". *International Studies Review* 17 (2015): 515–35.

Karen Human Rights Group (KHRG). "Village Agency: Rural Rights and Resistance in a Militarised Karen State". 25 November 2008 <http://khrg.org/2008/11/village-agency-rural-rights-and-resistance-militarized-karen-state>. Accessed 27 February 2016.

Lentz, Kirsten. "Assessment of Landmine Victims' and Survivors' Needs in Kachin, Kayah, and Kayin States, Myanmar". Unpublished report, Yangon, 2013.

Local Resource Centre. "Opportunities". 8 December 2013 <http://lrcmyanmar.org/en/opportunities/us-embassy-grants-announcement-%E2%80%93-landmine-stabilization-initiative-small-grants>. Accessed 13 December 2013.

Min Zaw Oo."Understanding Myanmar's Peace Process: Ceasefire Agreements: Catalyzing Reflection". 2014 <http://www.swisspeace.ch/fileadmin/user_upload/Media/Publications/Catalyzing_Reflections_2_2014_online.pdf>. Accessed 27 February 2016.

Moser-Puangsuwan, Yeshua. "Seeds of Destruction". *Burma Debate* 7, no. 4 (2000): 4–10.

Moser-Puangsuwan, Yeshua, and Andrew Selth. "Myanmar's Forgotten Minefields". *Jane's Intelligence Review* 12, no. 10 (2000): 38–42.

MPC. "Mine Action Centre". 2015 <http://www.myanmarpeace.org/programs/myanmar_mine_action_center>. Accessed 24 February 2016.

MRE WG. "Knowledge Attitude and Practice Survey: Impact of Landmines and Other Explosive Remnants of War in South East Myanmar". Unpublished report, Mine Risk Education Working Group, Yangon, 2014.

———."Knowledge Attitude and Practice Survey: Impact of Landmines and Other Explosive Remnants of War in Kachin and Northern Shan". Unpublished report, Mine Risk Education Working Group, Yangon, 2015.

Mullan, Luke, Adam Richards, Catherine Lee, Voravit Suwanvanichkij, Cynthia Maung, Mhan Mahn, Chris Beyrer, and Thomas Lee. "Population-based Survey Methods to Quantify Associations Between Human Rights Violations and Health Outcomes Among Internally Displaced Persons in Eastern Burma". *Journal of Epidemiology Community Health* 61, no. 10 (2007): 908–14.

Myanmar Peace Support Initiative. "Lessons Learned from MPSI's Work Supporting the Peace Process in Myanmar: March 2012 to March 2014". Myanmar Peace Support Initiative, Yangon, March 2014 <http://www.burmalibrary.org/

docs17/MPSI_Lessons_Learned_Paper-March_2014-en-red.pdf>. Accessed 3 September 2015.

Myanmar Times. "De-mining Delayed Until Peace Agreed". *Myanmar Times*, 8 December 2014 <http://www.mmtimes.com/index.php/national-news/12470-de-mining-delayed-until-peace-agreed.html>. Accessed 29 April 2015.

NCA. Nationwide Ceasefire Agreement between the Government of the Republic of the Union of Myanmar and Ethnic Armed Organisations, unofficial English translation, 2015 <http://www.eprpinformation.org/files/recent-events/Myanmar-s-peace-process-a-nationwide-ceasefire-remains-elusive--19sept-2015.pdf>. Accessed 27 February 2016.

NPA."First Landmine Survey Activities in Myanmar's History Taking Place". Norwegian Peoples Aid, 13 October 2013 <http://www.npaid.org/News/News-archive/2013/First-landmine-survey-activities-in-Myanmar-s-history-taking-place>. Accessed 13 December 2013.

Schissler, Matt. "Potential Refugee Return in Eastern Myanmar: Exploring the Relevance of a Study into Local Protection Concerns, Plans, and Aspirations". Yangon: Local to Global, 2016.

Selth, Andrew. "Landmines in Burma: The Military Dimension". *Burma Debate* 7, no. 4 (2000): 10–20.

Smith, Martin. *Burma: Insurgency and the Politics of Ethnicity*, London: Zed, 1991.

South, Ashley. "The Politics of Protection in Burma". *Critical Asian Studies* 44, no. 2 (2012): 175–204.

South, Ashley, Malin Perhult, and Nils Carstensen. "Conflict and Survival: Self-protection in South-east Burma". Asia Programme Paper ASP PP 2010/04, September 2010, <https://www.chathamhouse.org/sites/files/chathamhouse/public/Research/Asia/0910pp_burma.pdf>. Accessed 27 February 2016.

South, Ashley, Simon Harrigan, Simon Corbett, Richard Horsey, Susanne Kempel, Henrik Fröjmark, and Nils Carstensen. "Local to Global Protection in Myanmar (Burma), Sudan, South Sudan and Zimbabwe". Humanitarian Practice Network, Network Paper, February 2012 <http://www.cmi.no/file/1538-Local-to-Global-Protection-in-Myanmar-Burma-Sudan-South-Sudan-and-Zimbabwe.pdf>. Accessed 11 January 2014.

Taylor, Robert. *The State in Myanmar*. Singapore: NUS Press, 2009.

UN CRC. *Consideration of Reports Submitted by States Parties under Article 44 of the Convention*, United Nations Committee on the Rights of the Child, CRC/C/MMR/CO/3-4 (14 March 2012), <http://www2.ohchr.org/english/bodies/crc/docs/co/CRC_C_MMR_CO_3-4.pdf>. Accessed 4 April 2016.

III

Elections and After

7

THE 2015 ELECTIONS AND CONFLICT DYNAMICS IN MYANMAR

Michael Lidauer

The watershed Myanmar 2015 elections are widely regarded as more credible and inclusive than any previous polls in the country, and were largely experienced as peaceful and without disruptions. Despite a mostly quiet election day, the electoral process, however, was not free of conflict. One major cluster of conflicts impacting the electoral process revolved around tensions between ethnic armed groups (EAGs) and the national government's military forces, the Tatmadaw — usually termed 'ethnic conflict' (see Laoutides and Ware, this volume). Another cluster of conflicts concerned the growing anti-Muslim sentiment, with the potential for violent escalation. A third conflict cluster evolved around questions of constitutional justice.[1] This chapter briefly outlines the conceptual framework for elections and conflict, and then proceeds by reviewing the major clusters. The section on elections and the peace process is followed by a discussion of a little understood element of the electoral process, the partial cancellation of elections. The chapter concludes by summarizing some nascent conflict-mitigating measures of the 2015 electoral process and provides an outlook for challenges ahead.

ELECTORAL PROCESS AND RESULTS IN BRIEF

Despite low expectations based on historical experience and criticism in the period prior to 8 November 2015, the Union Election Commission (UEC) enabled a positive election-day experience for most of Myanmar's voters, and left little doubt that the will of the electorate was respected. The voter list, digitized and publicized for public scrutiny — which had been criticized for inconsistencies and omissions in earlier versions — stood its test on election day. More than a year prior to the polls the UEC engaged in unprecedented stakeholder meetings with political parties and CSOs. It introduced new integrity measures such as transparent ballot boxes, numbered seals, and indelible ink to create better safeguards in polling procedures, and supported the dissemination of voter education materials, including in the mass media and by new communication technologies. International and national observers were deployed in large numbers, all across the country and throughout the pre-election and election day period, with limitations only in conflict-affected areas and around military installations. Observers largely agreed in their assessments of an overall positive election day, while also sharing concerns about undemocratic restrictions in the electoral legal framework.[2]

The National League for Democracy (NLD) won an historic victory, similar to its 1990 results. It now dominates the upper and the lower houses of the Pyidaungsu Hluttaw, the legislature at union level, in such a way that it can nominate two vice-presidents and select the president; and can oppose, propose, or pass any law without consent of the opposition — with the exception of changes to the constitution which are regulated under chapter 12. Section 436(a), in particular, requires the consent of military members of parliament who still hold twenty-five per cent of the Pyidaungsu Hluttaw. The NLD was also successful in the race for most region and state legislatures, winning the majority in all regions (two with 100 per cent of the elected seats) and in the three eastern ethnic states (Mon, Kayah, Kayin). The winning party also returned fifty per cent of the total number of seats, that is, including military representatives' seats, for the Chin State Hluttaw, and around forty-nine per cent in Kachin State. The Arakan National Party (ANP) was the most successful party in Rakhine State (see Than Tun, this volume). The large Shan State holds the only legislature where the Union Solidarity and Development Party (USDP) remains the strongest single political party, followed by the Shan

Nationalities League for Democracy (SNLD). Thus, together with the members of parliament appointed from the military, the USDP has the ability to form a working majority in the Shan State Hluttaw.[3]

The challenges for the incoming government are vast. They include continued economic liberalization, democratic reforms, continuation of the peace process, the necessary balance of power with the military, and hardly any experience in governance. Challenges also come from the overwhelming NLD victory itself: how will the victor engage with the less successful in the future? Very few parties that decided against a boycott in 2010, as the NLD and its allies did, won seats five years later. While a diversity of ethnic representation continues to exist in parliament, most members are from the NLD. As the Transnational Institute (TNI 2015, p. 12) notes, "Ethnic-based parties, in contrast, hold few seats which is reminiscent of Myanmar's post-independence democratic period." Ahead lies an unscripted future, including the resolution of major conflicts, which were prominent throughout the electoral process. However, all sides, including the military, have made reconciliatory signals in the early post-election period.

THE NEXUS OF ELECTIONS AND CONFLICT

As a point of departure, this chapter suggests that elections are rarely the root cause of conflict, but have the potential to exacerbate pre-existing levels of conflict. Further, the angle on conflict taken here is wider than a mere focus on electoral violence occurring during the campaign period, on election day, or in its immediate aftermath, which is usually defined by its intentional character (for example, Höglund 2009). The analysis of conflict and its entanglements with the electoral process should not be limited to a focus on escalation of physical violence, but also extend to forms of structural violence and disenfranchisement, although mitigation strategies derived from such an analysis should aim to minimize the risks of physical harm.

Practitioner communities supporting elections internationally increasingly view elections as cyclical (Tuccinardi et al. 2007). This allows their analysis over a longer time frame and takes the preparations and organization of the ballot into account. The longer periods of the electoral cycle are less visible to the public eye and grow in intensity as election day approaches.

The key elements towards the end of the electoral cycle are the review and finalization of the legal framework governing the elections; the production or update of the voter roll until its finalization; the deadline for the registration of political parties; the deadline for the nomination of candidates; the electoral campaign period; the definition of electoral constituencies and the allocation of polling stations; arrangements for electoral security; the training of polling staff; the production and distribution of electoral materials, in particular ballots and relevant forms to administer electoral procedures; the arrangements for results management; and the adjudication of complaints that arise during the entire process. All these elements can trigger conflicts, or assist in their mitigation, at various levels and at particular times, albeit with differing degrees of intensity and impact.

ELECTIONS AND THE PEACE PROCESS

Myanmar and its territorial sovereignty have been consistently challenged by armed actors since the colonial era. Subsequent centralist military regimes offered truces to these actors without achieving lasting peace. When President Thein Sein took office in 2011, he made peace with EAGs a major goal of his term. While some old ceasefires were reconfirmed and new bilateral ceasefires could be agreed, there has also been fierce fighting in recent years, including the use of heavy artillery and air strikes. The bilateral ceasefire with the Kachin Independence Organisation (KIO), which was in place since 1994 and gave Kachin State a period of relative stability, broke in 2011 (see Farrelly 2014).

Since then, armed conflict has been ongoing in parts of Kachin State and northern Shan State, and it continued over the electoral period. For the first time since 2009, on 9 February 2015, fighting broke out between the Tatmadaw and the Myanmar National Democratic Alliance Army at the Chinese border in the northeastern corner of Shan State, in the Kokang SAZ. On 17 February, the president declared a state of emergency and martial law in the area, and transferred executive and judicial powers to the commander-in-chief. This was the first time during Thein Sein's term that martial law had been declared. The state of emergency remained in place until mid-November, about one week after the elections.

Notwithstanding the escalation of conflict at the beginning of the electoral year, and the continuation and outbreak of fighting on various fronts, a (partial) Nationwide Ceasefire Agreement (NCA) was signed less than a month prior to the elections, on 15 October 2015. Eight EAGs signed the NCA, while others were not allowed to participate, and more abstained from signing for this reason.[4] The signing ceremony had been preceded by a first agreement on a draft ceasefire text on 31 March, but negotiations continued for another six months.[5]

During all this time, the peace negotiations were largely disconnected from the electoral process. Although President Thein Sein repeatedly called on all sides to work towards both peaceful elections and an NCA, the processes had no visible institutional links on the side of state agencies. Both the UEC and the Myanmar Peace Center (MPC) — entrusted with the facilitation of ceasefire negotiations on behalf of the Union Peacemaking Working Committee (UPWC) — were careful to stay within the boundaries of their respective mandates (see Su Mon Thazin Aung, this volume). The UEC had some encounters with EAGs, but did not appear to pursue contact as part of a broader policy. Opportunities for convergence of the two processes were not explicitly pursued. For example, it could have been conceivable to tie agreements for ceasefire monitoring mechanisms to arrangements for electoral security, but this did not occur, partly because the NCA was agreed much later than initially expected — and too late to have a substantive impact on the electoral process.

This is not to say that the electoral and peace processes were unrelated. In an interview conducted in February 2014, chief negotiator Minister U Aung Min had already expressed concerns that the window of opportunity to reach a conclusive agreement would be closing ahead of national elections. Indeed, for much of 2015, elections were perceived to disrupt the longer-term peace negotiations, which were in principle open ended. Unlike in other countries where a brokered peace deal set the timing for elections, in Myanmar the electoral time frame was constitutionally mandated. At the same time, the raised stakes of the peace process created risks in the security environment ahead of the polls. Outbursts of violence occurred before or between crucial negotiation meetings, in particular in Kachin State and northern Shan State. Perceptions that violence preceded key meetings possibly as a deliberate strategy may have deepened the trust deficit in the talks.

It can be tempting to paint the potential electoral interests of ethnic armed actors and their relationships with political parties in black and white, but any attempt to do so would oversimplify matters. Based on their historical experience with the 2010 elections (and for Kachin State, also the 2012 by-elections), most stakeholders had no trust in the election administration. The upcoming elections were also not a priority for most armed groups and their constituents. Their attention was on fighting, advancing the ongoing peace negotiations toward the NCA, maintaining the bilateral ceasefires, and profiting from them through increased access to local markets and services. For many EAGs, their continued non-acceptance of the 2008 Constitution also contradicted an intensified interest in elections, even if an earlier change of their legal status would have allowed increased engagement. Some alleged that EAGs denied political parties access to their territories, however, many said they would not disrupt the electoral process even prior to the NCA. It is in this context that elections were partially cancelled.

The partial cancellation of elections

The 2015 elections did not take place in all parts of the country. Elections were cancelled (postponed) in seven townships and partially in some townships in 416 additional wards or village tracts[6] in conflict-affected areas, as announced by the UEC in two rounds, on 12 and 27 October 2015.[7] The number of excluded voters did probably not exceed half a million (see TNI 2015, p. 5), or roughly 1.5 per cent of the population registered to vote. The October notifications were largely expected by observers and followed a similar pattern of announcements ahead of the 2010 elections. Nevertheless, the cancellations are one of the least understood and least transparent elements of the Myanmar elections.

The authority to cancel and postpone elections lies with the UEC, and ultimately with its chairman; however, the decision-making process is informed from below. Administrative personnel with electoral duties at ward and village tract level inform township and district subcommissions. The state/region subcommissions then provide the recommendation to postpone elections, if needed, to their superiors in Naypyitaw. While the internal administration of this process appears to involve several levels, the decision-making for cancellations is little understood outside the involved apparatus. There were some negotiations around whether to hold elections under the condition of volatile ceasefires — for example in Kayin State's Kyainseikgyi township or in northern Shan State's Mongmit township —

however, if these negotiations occurred at all, they usually took place at the local level, between village administrators and members of armed groups, while higher-level subcommissions, and even the central UEC, could be entirely unaware of them.

The elections' postponement is based on UEC law section 10f and section 50 of the electoral laws.[8] The language of these laws, as in many areas of the electoral legal framework, is ambiguous, and vulnerable to different interpretations. Sections 10f and 50 establish that the UEC has the authority to postpone elections in constituencies where a natural disaster prevents them, or where the security situation makes voter list updates and polling impossible. While the 'security situation' is not further clarified, the laws state that elections can be partially cancelled within a constituency, and that results from such constituencies are valid if fifty-one per cent of all enrolled constituents participate in the elections. Excluding eligible voters in conflict areas and only needing fifty-one per cent of registered voters to hold an election increases malapportionment, with the potential of creating easy-to-win seats. The natural disasters during the 2015 rainy season did not result in election postponement. All cancellations in 2015 were for security reasons.

UEC public communications did little to clarify the reason for cancellations beyond a simple reference to security. The ambiguity of this language, the lack of public communications and transparent decision-making, or of a publicized participatory approach that would involve various stakeholders led to speculation about the potentially arbitrary or politically motivated nature of these decisions. Such assumptions are grounded in past electoral experiences. Partial cancellations are related to concerns about the potential misuse of advance votes (often of military voters) and about candidates using the influence of local militia to coerce voters. Allegations like this occurred in ceasefire areas where, from the perspective of the voters affected by the cancellations (for example, in Kyainseikgyi), there were no obvious security threats (see HURFOM 2015).

Relative to 2010, and as a result of new or renewed bilateral ceasefires, the southeast witnessed significant improvements to its 2015 electoral space. Most Kayah State townships were affected by cancellations in 2010, but none were in 2015. In Mon State, the nine village tracts without elections in 2010 were reduced to one. In Kayin State, the electoral space increased by approximately a third over this period.[9] Shan State is the only place where cancellations also led to vacant seats in the legislature, and the number would have remained consistent with 2010 had a second round of cancellations not occurred on 27 October. In Kachin State, the number of partial cancellations increased from 2010, however, this did not directly lead to increased disenfranchisement, as will be explained below.

The cancellations must be understood in their respective geographical and political contexts, but with few exceptions they have one element in common — the absence of the state. In most situations where elections were cancelled, a voter list had never been established. Creating the voter list requires data from local offices, namely the Department of Immigration and Population at township level, and offices of the General Administration Department (GAD) at ward and village tract level.[10] In addition, the GAD fulfils electoral functions on the lower levels of the administration. Thus, if there is no GAD at the local level, there is no voter list and no office to organize elections in that area.

Therefore, the partial election cancellations seem to equate to the absence of the state's administrative capacity in most cases. This is particularly evident in the areas under the control of the KIO in Kachin State; in those parts of Hpapun township under control of Karen National Liberation Army (KNLA) Brigade 5 in Kayin State; in territories controlled by the United Wa State Army (UWSA) in the Wa Self-Administered Division (SAD), and by the National Democratic Alliance Army (NDAA) in Mongla township in Shan State, formerly termed Special Regions 2 and 4. Only a few of the cancellations declared on 12 October concerned areas assessed as having the potential for actual violence on election day, or that saw physical disruptions to earlier phases of the electoral cycle, such as the voter list display. These exceptional cases included the conflict-ridden township of Mansi in southern Kachin State, and Kawkareik township in Kayin State, where tensions between the state security apparatus and several EAGs caused insecurity along the Asia Highway during the voter list update period.

The cancellations have different administrative consequences, depending on the size of the administrative units concerned. Vacant seats occur only where elections are cancelled for an entire constituency; this was the case for seven townships in Shan State, resulting in seven vacant seats in the Pyithu Hluttaw and fourteen vacant seats in the Shan State Hluttaw (the Amyotha Hluttaw is not affected). Contra to this, the cancellation of elections in specific wards and village tracts smaller than a constituency do not translate into vacant seats in the legislature, leading to the disenfranchisement of voters as the election goes ahead regardless of their involvement, as well as candidates coming to power in seats without universal suffrage of their constituents.[11]

There was a lengthy preparation for the first announcement of cancellations on 12 October. It occurred somewhat later than expected as the UEC was busy with candidate scrutiny and its contestation (see below) in September. The second announcement, less than two weeks before election day, seemed to occur as an ad hoc response to real security concerns. On 27 October, elections were cancelled for the two townships of Monshu and Kyethi, as well as for eight additional village tracts in neighbouring Tangyan township in Shan State.[12] These cancellations followed the responsible district subcommission's demand to partially cancel elections after fighting had broken out between the Tatmadaw and the Shan State Army-North (SSA-N). The subcommission later argued that they could not "send the ballots" and had genuine concerns about the safety of electoral personnel and materials if elections went ahead.[13] Political spectators disputed the legitimacy of this decision. Representatives of other EAGs understood the escalation of fighting in this area as a consequence of the SSA-N's non-participation in the NCA signing ceremony on 15 October, and the Tatmadaw's attacks — similar to those in Mohnyin township, Kachin State, with "unusual intensity" (TNI 2015, p. 4) — as a punishment for their absence.[14] The SNLD accused the UEC of political motivation, seeing the cancelled constituencies as potentially safe wins for its party. Meanwhile the SNLD's direct political opponent, the SNDP, encouraged and welcomed the UEC's decision to safeguard campaigners' safety and voters' rights, which, from its perspective, were under threat.[15]

While the UEC might have had good reason to cancel elections in most cases, due to past experience few stakeholders trusted the genuineness of their motivations prior to the 2015 elections. The UEC's decisions were also interpreted as synonymous with decisions of the Tatmadaw and other state institutions, while in reality they might not have been related. The collective positive experience of the 2015 elections, and the generally well-trusted results, may lead to increased confidence in this particular government institution in the future. More clarity about UEC law section 10f and election laws section 50 would help to avoid the potential for politically motivated contrasting interpretations of partial election cancellations. Currently, these suspensions are a more complex phenomenon related to different reasoning, motivations, and opinions than a simple 'security' explanation might suggest.

Electoral versus census space

From the perspective of the state's access to its peripheries, it is interesting to compare the 2015 partial election cancellations with the 2014 census. There are apparent overlaps in areas where neither the census nor the elections were possible, where enumerators experienced hindrances, or where data for the census were provided by the local administration of armed actors rather than by government enumerators.[16]

The census reports share some information about accessibility and collaboration between the state and ethnic armed actors in ceasefire areas. Apart from Rakhine State, where the government's refusal to allow the term Rohingya as self-ascription led to a situation where the census was not fully conducted in ten out of seventeen townships (see below), the population count also faced accessibility restrictions in Kachin State and Kayin State. In Kachin State, the KIO did not allow enumerators to count people in villages under their control, leaving twenty-five village tracts (ninety-seven villages) out of the census. In parts of Hpapun township of Kayin State, the KNLA denied access to enumerators and provided their own data about the total number of households and population by gender. As a consequence, the populations in these areas were estimated and included in the overall census results, but not in the analysis and presentation of detailed information (MoIP 2015, pp. 8–10).

The Kachin and Hpapun situations during the census parallel the non-accessibility experiences with the establishment of the voter list in these areas. However, the census seems to have been possible in other locations where the voter list was not established, in particular in the Wa SAD townships under UWSA control, and in Mongla, which is under NDAA control. One explanation is that the leaders of these armed groups might have had an interest in knowing how many people reside in their realm, for purposes of recruitment or taxation, but had no interest in their populations' participation in general elections.

ANTI-MUSLIM SENTIMENT AND DISENFRANCHISEMENT

Anti-Muslim sentiment in Myanmar is not a novelty of the political transition, but results from the country's historical ethno-linguistic complexity. Expressions of Buddhist nationalism earned integral status in Burmese politics during the anti-colonial struggle. Religious legitimation of political power was relevant for all regimes following independence — parliamentary, socialist, and military. This continues to be so both for state and opposition leaders of the Burmese mainstream (Schober 2006, p. 91). Those who are perceived as foreigners — including Indians, Chinese, and Muslims — were often targeted in times of political crisis. Extremist expression and violence linked to Buddhist-inspired nationalism was already part of monks' riots in the 1920s and 1930s. There are also reports of occasional anti-Muslim violence over the period of the Ne Win and SLORC/SPDC governments. Egreteau (2011) argues that contemporary 'Islamophobia' has developed as a broader 'Indophobia' — Indians were perceived as agents of the colonial regime — and was reduced to its anti-Muslim direction over the last period of the military regime.

New freedom of expression, coupled with the use of new technologies, led to an increase in religiously framed political hate speech, both offline and online (see Schissler 2016), prior to the electoral contest. The major protagonists were religiously conservative and extremist monks such as Ashin Wirathu, who was convicted for political instigation in 2003, but was released along with other political prisoners in 2012. Since 2012, the increase in anti-Muslim sentiment became visible in public space with the emergence of the 969 movement and its Buy Buddhist campaign. The political policy agenda of the Organization for the Protection of Race and Religion, known by its abbreviation MaBaTha, founded in early 2014, started to target the legislature more directly with the propagation of four laws relating to interreligious marriage, religious conversion, monogamy, and population control (Walton and Hayward 2014, pp. 12–16). Acknowledging that these movements are "a reflexive defense against what is perceived by some to be the threat of a globally spreading Islam, as well as the motivation to preserve and promote Buddhist practice and behavior in Myanmar during a time of significant change", Walton and Hayward (2014, p. x) argue that they are inherently political in nature.

Ahead of the elections, the political process appeared increasingly held hostage to Buddhist-nationalist discourses. Neither incumbents nor the opposition could afford to publicly display any empathy towards Muslim minority causes during the campaign, or risk losing votes.

Deadlock in Rakhine State

Internationally, anti-Muslim sentiment, inter-communal violence, and Muslim disenfranchisement in Myanmar are mostly associated with Rakhine State and the disputed legal status of its Muslim population. These developments are part of the national discourse on Islam, and are sometimes directly influenced by extremist Buddhist leaders. The dire humanitarian situation of most Muslims in northern Rakhine State led INGOs and NGOs to provide support, although this was at times hindered by the military government. The aid was mainly directed towards returning refugees, but was perceived to leave out the majority of the Rakhine population, which in Myanmar is also marginalized and poor. This situation hardened the Rakhines' deep dislike of their Muslim neighbours.

The 1982 Citizenship Law (which establishes complex rules governing citizenship by descent), its 1983 Procedures, and a citizenship inspection process in 1989 worsened the already difficult conditions for Muslim people in Rakhine State to acquire or maintain citizenship status — and, in fact, made many who had citizenship stateless. While this has been the case for nearly two decades, the politics of identity and identity labels increased over recent years and notably worsened in the 2015 pre-election context. Prior to 2012, Muslims lived as integrated minorities in Sittwe and across many townships of northern/central Rakhine State — although settlements were often separated in rural areas where the impoverished Muslim population is cut off from the outside world.

Following the rape of a Rakhine Buddhist woman by Muslim men and retaliation for this act with a revenge killing of Muslim travellers in May/June 2012, violence erupted in and around the state capital of Sittwe and subsequently led to the displacement of 145,000 people (ICG 2014). The great majority of the displaced live in Sittwe and neighbouring townships. While many are stateless Muslims, Rakhine and Kaman — who are officially Myanmar ethnic nationals — are also included. For most of these people, return to their place of origin is not expected anytime soon.[17] As a result of the 2012 violence and displacement, the March/April 2014 census exercise could not be fully carried out from Sittwe northwards, thus affecting ten out of Rakhine State's seventeen townships.

The census results proclaimed an estimated total population of over three million inhabitants, making Rakhine State the second-most populated ethnic state after Shan State. Of the total, nearly 2.1 million were enumerated, however an estimated 1,090,000 were not (MoIP 2015, p. 9).[18] It is believed these were largely Rohingya, or 'Bengalis', without citizenship. The government had previously committed to allow self-identification as Rohingya as a response to the question on ethnicity in the census questionnaire. Following pressure from Buddhist nationalist groups, this possibility was revoked just prior to the start of the count. This last-minute decision led to a variation in the enumeration practice across the townships concerned, and households where people decided to self-identify as Rohingya were not taken into account. The disputes around this led to new outbreaks of violence in Sittwe.

The term Rohingya — also used by international advocacy groups to speak of Muslims in Rakhine State — has gained more weight in recent years. Before the violence of 2012, it was mainly significant for Muslims in the northern parts of the state, but less so for those who were more integrated in Sittwe and in central townships. While for some Muslims in Rakhine State this term is still not the label of choice, its use has become more important for many and helps to forge more of a political identity (see ICG 2014, p. 23). For the ethnic Rakhine as much as for the union government, the term Rohingya is unacceptable, and the very existence of a Rohingya group in Myanmar is denied. Instead, most people in Myanmar use the term 'Bengali' which clearly carries connotations of Muslims as foreigners whose citizenship status should be rightfully denied, or at least verified.[19]

The lack of a compromise term such as 'Rakhine Muslim' rendered the 2014 census and pilot citizenship verification impossible to execute fully, or at least very difficult to implement. From mid-2014, the government implemented a voluntary pilot citizenship verification process in Myebon township. The ethnic Rakhine thought this would end allegedly illicit Muslim claims to citizenship. However, more applicants obtained at least 'naturalized' if not full citizenship than were expected.[20] The process was stopped (or at least did not proceed to other townships) over this controversy and resumed in the beginning of 2015, but with few applications. In informal conversations, Ministry of Immigration and

Population employees have said this would be the Rohingyas'"last chance to register", and that "the conditions after this will be very different, especially with a new government in place", without specifying the reason for this perception.[21] In this situation, franchise was linked to citizenship, constituting a departure from past practices.

In 2010, the holders of temporary registration cards (TRCs) — so-called 'white cards' — were encouraged to take part in the elections. The outgoing SPDC regime distributed more white cards to increase the turnout for the USDP. However, the political rights of the formally stateless population were again infringed in late 2014 with an amendment of the political party registration law, which deprived white-card holders of the right to found or be members of political parties. As a consequence, the UEC required all parties to change their membership lists.

The next controversy arose at the beginning of 2015, with a Pyidaungsu Hluttaw draft national referendum bill, stimulating a new debate around temporary identity certificate enfranchisement. Ashin Wirathu said in a press statement, "I warn [parliament] not to betray the over 50 million national people by giving priority to the over one million illegal people. If you allow them to vote in the coming election, I will lead the people to fight against them all."[22] Other press statements called for public protests in Rakhine State and Yangon. The president turned the situation around by declaring the expiry of white cards altogether by 31 March 2015. The two-month period for collection started on 1 April, and facilitated by village leaders the cards were handed in without much resistance. As a consequence, white-card holders were not included in the voter list updates, which started about the same time these decisions were taken. The electoral laws were later amended accordingly; it was estimated that half a million voters were disenfranchised by these changes in the legal framework (TNI 2015, p. 5).

A year ahead of the ballot, fears were high that Rakhine State was steering towards another significant outbreak of violence and potential humanitarian disaster. From a perspective of electoral security, the large-scale disenfranchisement of formerly eligible voters decreased the risk for violence to escalate, but the environment remained charged. The electoral contest turned into a battle between the ANP, the USDP, and the NLD. The ANP emerged as the most successful party, albeit with lower results than anticipated and more seats lost to the NLD than expected.[23] Following the expiry of white cards, Muslim voters hardly participated in the electoral process in Rakhine State, with the exception of Kaman voters in Thandwe, some dozen remaining Muslim voters in Maungdaw, Sittwe, and in a small number of IDP camps where electoral arrangements were made for a few voters who legally qualified as citizens. Kaman voters who were caught up in the violence of 2012 and had been displaced (for example, from Kyauk Phyu to Pauktaw or Sittwe), and had lost their ID documents, lost their right to vote. In Myebon, as a consequence of the 2014 pilot citizenship verification, around a thousand people who had accepted being called 'Bengali' and who were rewarded with citizenship regained their voting rights. However, deprived of the freedom to move, they cast their ballots secluded from other voters inside their settlement, and expressed fears about possible retaliation if their vote would stand out as different from the overall township results.[24]

Loss of union-level representation

Soon after the Rakhine State crisis in 2012, waves of violence also occurred in other parts of Myanmar, starting in Meikhtila in March 2013. Most incidents followed a similar pattern, with a small dispute between Buddhists and Muslims escalating quickly, resulting in the loss of life and the destruction of mosques and other property. The involvement of "dark forces", a "hidden power", or a "third hand" was attributed to these events, implying the instrumentation of violence against Muslims for political purposes (see ICG 2013).

Given MaBaTha's growing voice and its apparent popularity ahead of the ballot, increasingly open statements by Wirathu and others against the NLD and its leader, and some political parties' use of Buddhist-nationalist campaign rhetoric, many analysts saw the risk of another wave of anti-Muslim violence increasing with the electoral competition. With few execptions religiously motivated violence did not occur during the campaign period, and nationalist parties were surprisingly unsuccessful at union level. However, it would be short-sighted to believe that anti-Muslim sentiment, advocacy and the potential for religiously inspired violence have disappeared with the relative calm of election day, and the NLD victory (see Walton 2015).

Disenfranchisement also occurred with the candidate nomination deadline in August 2015. As a result of increased anti-Muslim sentiment, and in a break from the past, neither the USDP nor the NLD fielded a single Muslim candidate in the electoral race. Furthermore, the candidate nomination process revealed intensified scrutiny to verify candidate eligibility based on the 2010 electoral laws, in particular in relation to candidates' citizenship. As of 2 September 2015, eighty-eight candidates had been rejected by the UEC, with the majority coming from Rakhine State (twenty-eight) and Yangon Region (twenty-four). Following massive criticism of these decisions, including from the international community, several candidate rejections were later revoked. However, in Rakhine State, based on the combined effects of restrictions to political parties, voter disenfranchisement, and increased candidate scrutiny, Muslims have lost — with the exception of a few remaining voters who might have voted for the NLD — any electoral representation. This is quite dramatic, and adds to the series of future governance challenges and to the inheritance of a worsening human rights situation in Rakhine State with an unresolved citizenship problem. How the NLD will deal with the problems and interests of citizen and non-state Muslims who do not have any representative of their own in the legislatures remains to be seen.

IN SEARCH OF SOLUTIONS

Demands for reform by the former Burmese opposition and ethnic actors coincide with constitutional reform debates that have been part of the political transition process since it started. After the 2012 by-elections, expectations were high that significant changes of the 2008 Constitution could happen prior to 2015. The most prominent elements that many outside the hitherto governing elite want to see changed are the participation of military appointees in the legislature, the qualification criteria for presidential candidates which by design make Aung San Suu Kyi ineligible for this post, and the further establishment of a federal system, as well as the conditions for changing the constitution which is de facto not possible without military consent (see Lidauer 2014). Ethnic parties' demands for constitutional changes also include the possibility of electing chief ministers of states and regions directly, rather than have them appointed by the president from among elected or appointed state or region members of parliament, as is currently the case.

Despite the introduction of the draft bill for a national referendum to change the Constitution — which triggered the legal formalisation of TRC holder disenfranchisement — a referendum did not take place prior to the 2015 elections. Attempts to bring about constitutional changes included a parliamentary commission 2013/2014, an NLD signature campaign in 2014, some high-level talks between leaders since 2014, and a vote for selected constitutional amendments in parliament in 2015, which did not change any of the constitutional conditions disputed by the majority of the opposition at that time. The obstacles to changing the Constitution will likely see much debate over the tenure of the NLD government. It remains to be seen to what extent these debates will also take place outside the legislature, to which the NLD brings electoral legitimacy.

The partial NCA, which has now become President Thein Sein's legacy, established the idea of a structured political dialogue. Quite remarkably, given the major electoral process taking place at the same time, the government and EAG signatories followed a rigid three-month time frame to establish the structures foreseen in the NCA, including the Joint Monitoring Committee (JMC), and the Union Political Dialogue Joint Committee (UPDJC). The UPDJC led to the first Union Peace Conference held in Naypyitaw between 12 and 17 January 2016. Aung San Suu Kyi had not attended the NCA signing ceremony, and no NLD representative signed the document. Despite its initial scepticism about the outcomes of the USDP- and Tatmadaw-led peace process (and about the MPC as the vehicle to facilitate the negotiations), the NLD joined the UPDJC drafting committee after the elections, and Suu Kyi spoke at the opening of the Union Peace Conference alongside the president, the commander-in-chief, and senior EAG leaders. If and how the NLD will use the nascent peace and political dialogue structures — which could include constitutional reform — is not yet apparent.[25] Of course, the electoral process could not bring about constitutional change by itself, and how the core disputed elements will be resolved, if at all, remains to be seen.

CONCLUSION

Despite considerable fears, the 2015 elections were not marred by electoral violence. These fears were fed by the long-term armed conflict between the Tatmadaw and EAGs and escalation of fighting with unusual ferocity during the electoral period; the recent history of inter-communal violence in Rakhine State and beyond, with anti-Muslim rhetoric becoming a dominating feature during the election period; and in view of the major stakes at this watershed election for old and new power brokers. Further research into why the ballot remained peaceful should be encouraged; for now, it appears that the political will for peaceful elections was strong enough, and the costs of escalating political violence deemed too high to bear. International support, incentives, and diplomatic pressure for credible and peaceful elections also contributed to a peaceful transfer of power.

The lessons learned during this electoral process should be transferred from the old to the new UEC leadership. A new cycle of capacity building in the UEC should have a dedicated focus on conflict sensitivity and reaching conflict-affected communities, such as the internally displaced. Conflict-affected communities and their representatives (whether members of political parties or EAGs) should become targeted beneficiaries of civic and voter education in the future, in particular in ceasefire areas and areas where elections were cancelled. Whatever parliamentary or extra-parliamentary discussion and decision-making forums will develop, they should include and address outstanding electoral reforms. The existing majoritarian electoral system deserves a review in a participatory manner, although it is unlikely the NLD would embrace major change to the current system, which helped it to convert the popular vote to a disproportionately high number of seats (see Lemargie et al 2014). If the existing system remains, however, to enable a more equal suffrage, as a minimum the new administration would be advised to review the constituency boundaries to avoid another election with severe malapportionment. As the existing boundaries derive from the 2008 Constitution and new delimitation would require constitutional change, this topic has to be addressed in a transparent and consultative manner.

The UEC proved open to enhancing the electoral process towards international standards. Some of these measures were developed following international advice, such as new integrity measures for the polls, increased interaction with political parties and CSOs, and intensified voter education. Other elements of the process came from within the institution. New measures to mitigate the risks of electoral violence included the introduction of a political party Code of Conduct, signed by almost all registered parties; the introduction of UEC-led mediation committees, which helped diffuse tensions between parties in some cases; the introduction of police-led electoral security management committees, largely consisting of administrators and security forces, to operationalize electoral security around election day; and some improvements concerning the use, costs, and transparency of the electoral dispute resolution process. All these measures deserve further development to make them more participatory, transparent, and functional. In any case, future electoral stakeholders have a better foundation to work from now than prior to the 2015 elections.

Notes

1 This chapter cannot deal with all nuances of conflict which occurred during the electoral period. For example, it omits conflicts within the (formerly) governing, military-proxy elite, or a detailed discussion of the electoral conditions for internally displaced persons in conflict-affected areas.
2 See the reports of international election observation missions, that is, ANFREL (2015), EU EOM (2015), and TCC EOM (2015).
3 The UEC publicized official election results via its results centre in Naypyitaw in the period between 9 and 20 November 2015, and later on its websites via the following links (last accessed 5 February 2015): http://uecmyanmar.org/index.php/2014-02-11-08-31-43/884-1-12-2015-pyithuhluttaw, http://uecmyanmar.org/index.php/2014-02-11-08-31-43/885-1-12-2015-amyotharhluttaw, http://uecmyanmar.org/index.php/2014-02-11-08-31-43/886-1-12-2015-sanddhluttaw, http://uecmyanmar.org/index.php/2014-02-11-08-31-43/887-1-12-2015-nationality. Compare the IFES-MIMU results maps for further details: <http://www.themimu.info/election>. Accessed 5 February 2015.
4 The following eight armed groups participated in the NCA: All Burma Students' Democratic Front (ABSDF), Arakan Liberation Party (ALP), Chin National Front (CNF), Democratic Karen Benevolent Army (DKBA), Karen National Liberation Army-Peace Council (KNLA-PC), Karen National Union (KNU), Pa-O National Liberation Organization (PNLO), Restoration Council of Shan State (RCSS). Together with the leaders of these groups, the NCA was signed by the president, the vice presidents, the commander-in-chief, the deputy commander-in chief, the speakers of the Pyidaungsu Hluttaw and other members of parliament on behalf of the government. Representatives of the UN, the EU, China, India, Thailand, and Japan were invited to sign as international witnesses.
5 The author has written elsewhere in more detail about this period (Lidauer 2015).
6 For an overview of Myanmar's administrative structure see <http://www.themimu.info/sites/themimu.info/files/documents/Myanmar_Administrative_Structure_Aug_2015.pdf>. Accessed 5 February 2015.
7 UEC Notifications No 61-65/2015 (October 12) and No 67/2015 (October 27).
8 Together with the Union Election Commission Law and the Political Party

Registration Law, the election laws extend to the Amyotha Hluttaw, Pyithu Hluttaw, and State and Region Hluttaw laws. All these laws have been in force since 2010, and some have been amended since (see Lidauer and Saphy 2014).

9   Elections were also cancelled in forty-one village tracts in Kyaukkyi and Shwegyin townships in eastern Bago Region. Note that the UEC annnouncements of cancellations in 2010 did not include eastern Bago, but it is almost certain that there were no elections as this area had been under KNU control for decades. The 2010 notifications only cover areas where elections were officially cancelled, while the number of areas where elections did not take place in practice might have been significantly higher.

10 See the UEC FAQ on Voter List Update, February 2015. This and other electoral reference documents can be found on <http://www.merin-online.org/english-resources/>. Accessed 6 February 2015.

11 In several situations in Kachin State and in northern Shan State, the cancellations concern areas that have been vacated during years of conflict, meaning that villages were either destroyed or left at some point during the last two to three decades. The names of these places are nevertheless still part of official records and get included in constituency demarcation, and therefore elections were declared for these locations in the first place. In these cases, the cancellations can be interpreted as rectifying an administrative error while still relating to the security narrative commonly used to explain the phenomenon.

12 The second announcement included the partial cancellations of elections in Hopang township in the Wa SAD which appeared to have been forgotten in the first notification.

13 Interview with the Loilen subcommission on 7 November 2015.

14 Interview with an RCSS Liaison Officer on 12 January 2016.

15 Radio Free Asia on 27 October 2015, <http://www.rfa.org/english/news/myanmar/election-10272015172919.html> Accessed 5 February 2016.

16 The census data is inherently different from the voter list as it relates to anonymous household-based information from people who were present at particular locations during the enumeration. The voter list consists of data of individuals based on their registration status. Census enumeration was conducted in a proactive manner, while the voter list was at first established passively, on the basis of household lists and GAD logbooks, before voters were encouraged to actively check their inclusion on the list. This is not to say that census data were of no use for electoral preparations, but to underline that the census did not generate the voter list. Census data can be used to interpret patterns in the voter list with degrees of approximation, and can be used to interpret particular elements of the process, for example, literacy in relation to voter education or the availability of ID documents among voters, while acknowledging that gaps remain.

17 People who were displaced within their home communities in rural areas started to resettle in February 2015.
18 For want of more detailed information, the data contained in the 2013 Rakhine State Commission Report are still regarded as the most accurate, although changes might have occurred due to refugee departures, notably during the 2015 boat crisis.
19 In a joint press conference with US Secretary of State John Kerry on 22 May 2016, Daw Aung San Suu Kyi said that neither of the "emotive terms" Rohingya and Bengali should be used (Mizzima, 22 May 2016), which constitutes a change in governmental practice.
20 The above-mentioned 1982 Citizenship Law established three categories of citizenship: full, naturalized, and associate.
21 Conversation with the author on 25 March 2015.
22 Press release on 3 February 2015, translation by IFES.
23 It was expected that the NLD could be successful in southern Rakhine State; the wins in the island constituency of Munaung, where ANP leader Dr Aye Maung stood unsuccessfully, were not expected.
24 Interview with IDP camp leaders in Myebon on 29 October 2015.
25 Since the inauguration of the new government, the MPC has been renamed the National Reconciliation and Peace Centre and a new peace conference has been announced.

References

Asian Network for Free Elections (ANFREL). "Interim Report on the 2015 Myanmar General and Local Elections", 10 November 2015 <http://anfrel.org/wp-content/uploads/2015/11/ANFREL-Interim-Report-on-the-2015-Myanmar-General-Elections.pdf>. Acccessed 6 February 2015.

Egreteau, Renaud. "Burmese Indians in Contemporary Burma: Heritage, Influence, and Perceptions since 1988". *Asian Ethnicity* 12, no. 1 (2011), 33–54.

European Union Election Observation Mission (EU EOM). "Preliminary Statement", 10 November 2015 <http://www.eueom.eu/files/dmfile/101115-ps-myanmar_en.pdf>. Accessed 6 February 2015.

Farrelly, Nicholas. "War, Law, Politics: Reflections on Violence and the Kachin". In *Law, Society and Transition in Myanmar*, edited by Melissa Crouch and Tim Lindsey. Oxford: Hart Publishing, 2014.

Höglund, Kristine. "Electoral Violence in Conflict-Ridden Societies: Concepts, Causes, and Consequences". *Terrorism and Political Violence* 21, no. 3 (2009): 412–27.

Human Rights Foundation of Monland (HURFOM). "Burma 2015: Ballot Denied.

Disenfranchised Voters in Kyar Inn Seik Gyi Township, Karen State", November 2015 <http://rehmonnya.org/reports/Ballot-Denied-Full-Report-Eng.pdf>. Accessed 6 February 2015.

International Crisis Group (ICG). "The Dark Side of Transition: Violence Against Muslims in Myanmar". *Asia Report* 251, 2013 <http://www.crisisgroup.org/~/media/Files/asia/south-east-asia/burma-myanmar/251-the-dark-side-of-transition-violence-against-muslims-in-myanmar.pdf>. Accessed 6 February 2015.

———. "Myanmar: The Politics of Rakhine State". *Asia Report* 261, 2014 <http://www.crisisgroup.org/en/regions/asia/south-east-asia/myanmar/261-myanmar-the-politics-of-rakhine-state.aspx>. Accessed 6 February 2015.

———. "The Myanmar Elections: Results and Implications". *Asia Briefing* 147, 2015 <http://www.crisisgroup.org/en/regions/asia/south-east-asia/myanmar/b147-the-myanmar-elections-results-and-implications.aspx>. Accessed 6 February 2015.

Lemargie, Kyle, Andrew Reynolds, Peter Erben, and David Ennis. "Electoral System Choice in Myanmar's Democratization Debate". In *Debating Democratization in Myanmar*, edited by Nick Cheesman, Nicholas Farrelly and Trevor Wilson. Singapore: ISEAS, 2014.

Lidauer, Michael. "Towards a New State in Myanmar". In *Burma/Myanmar: Where Now?* edited by Mikael Gravers and Flemming Ytzen. Copenhagen: NIAS Press, 2014.

———. "Background Briefing on Electoral Risks: Elections in Areas Affected by Armed Conflict". IFES internal report, 12 October 2015, pp. 13–22.

Lidauer, Michael and Gilles Saphy. "Elections and the Reform Agenda". In *Law, Society and Transition in Myanmar,* edited by Melissa Crouch and Tim Lindsey. Oxford: Hart Publishing, 2014.

Ministry of Immigration and Population (MoIP), Department of Population. "The 2014 Myanmar Population and Housing Census. The Union Report". Census Report Volume 2, 2015 <http://unstats.un.org/unsd/demographic/sources/census/2010_phc/Myanmar/MMR-2015-05.pdf>. Accessed 6 February 2015.

Mizzima. "Aung San Suu Kyi Calls for Patience Over 'Rohingya' Controversy". Mizzima 22 May 2016. <http://mizzima.com/news-domestic/aung-san-suu-kyi-calls-patience-over-'rohingya'-controversy>. Accessed 23 May 2016.

Schissler, Matthew. "New Technologies, Established Practices: Developing Narratives of Muslim Threat in Myanmar." In *Islam and the State in Myanmar: Muslim-Buddhist Relations and the Politics of Belonging*, edited by Melissa Crouch. Oxford: Oxford University Press, 2016.

Schober, Juliane. "Buddhism in Burma. Engagement with Modernity". In *Buddhism in World Cultures. Comparative Perspectives*, edited by S.C. Berkwitz, Santa Barbara, CA: ABC-CLIO, 2006.

The Carter Center Election Observation Mission (TCC EOM). "Preliminary Statement". 10 November 2015 <http://www.cartercenter.org/resources/pdfs/news/peace_publications/election_reports/Myanmar-Preliminary-Statement-111015.pdf>. Accessed 6 February 2015.

Transnational Institute (TNI). "The 2015 General Elections in Myanmar: What Now for Ethnic Politics?" *Myanmar Policy Briefing* 17, December 2015 <https://www.tni.org/files/publication-downloads/bpb17_web_def.pdf>. Accessed 6 February 2015.

Tuccinardi, Domenico, Paul Guerin and others. *Focus on Effective Electoral Assistance*. 2007 <http://aceproject.org/ace-en/focus/focus-on-effective-electoral-assistance>. Accessed 6 February 2015.

Walton, Matthew J. and Susan Hayward. "Contesting Buddhist Narratives. Democratisation, Nationalism, and Communal Violence in Myanmar". *Policy Studies* 71. Honolulu: East-West Center, 2014.

Walton, Matthew J. "The Post-election Future of Buddhist Nationalism in Myanmar". *East Asia Forum*, 19 November 2015 <http://www.eastasiaforum.org/2015/11/19/the-post-election-future-of-buddhist-nationalism-in-myanmar/>. Accessed 6 February 2015.

8

INSTITUTIONS IN MYANMAR'S 2015 ELECTION

The Election Commission, International Agencies, and the Military

Chaw Chaw Sein

Myanmar successfully held an historic general election on 8 November 2015 under President U Thein Sein's government. Local people as well as the international community welcomed the election outcome, where the National League for Democracy (NLD) won by a landslide, with 77.1 per cent of seats nationwide. The ruling Union Solidarity and Development Party (USDP) won only 117 seats out of 1,150, or 10.2 per cent of the total.

In the pre-election period, some people assumed the election would not be free and fair. Even though by-elections had been held successfully on 1 April 2012 and had brought members of the NLD to parliament, they pointed to general mistrust of the Union Election Commission (UEC), as well as to the removal of the Speaker of the Legislature Thura U Shwe Mann as a member of the USDP Executive Committee by a so-called internal party coup. Furthermore, Myanmar was hit hard by heavy rain and flooding between July and August 2015, which led to speculation that the election might not be held, or might be conducted improperly. Nevertheless, when it was conducted, it attracted praise from home and abroad.

The success of the 2015 election was in part due to the respective roles played by certain key institutions. This paper will concentrate on the roles of the UEC, international agencies, and the military, or Tatmadaw.[1] Today, electoral commissions are integral to conducting democratic elections, and in Myanmar too, the role of the newly created UEC was essential to the success of the 2015 election. In countries like Myanmar without a strong tradition of regular elections, international agencies are an important enabling factor in conducting a successful election. In the case of Myanmar, 2015 was the first time the government opened the door to international observer missions and capacity-building organizations, which contributed in important ways to the election outcome. Lastly, the election could not be held successfully without the complaisance of the Tatmadaw, which has a record of having played an obstructionist or spoiling role. Although questions remain about the role of the military in the post-election power transition and in the work of the forthcoming legislature, it was true to its word in allowing the 2015 election to proceed smoothly, and in remaining committed to the process for the transfer of power to a new government despite the NLD's overwhelming victory.

THE UNION ELECTION COMMISSION

A crucial ingredient for a credible election is an independent electoral commission. Although Myanmar's current UEC is new, the country has prior experience with similar institutions. After independence in 1948, general elections in 1951 and 1956 were held under the management of a single election commissioner. In 1960, the first commission with three members was formed, all of them civilians. Each of these elections resulted in transfer of government to the successful party.[2] For the 1990 election a five-member commission was formed, four from a civilian background and one a retired brigadier general (SLORC 1991, p. 401).

The 1990 election, which was held under a military government, was fair in a broad sense. The NLD won a landslide victory with an estimated eighty-two per cent of the vote, but the military declined to transfer power for want of a constitution at that time. After years of rule, the Tatmadaw government adopted a seven-step road map for Myanmar's democratic transformation. As part of the process, a new election commission was established in April 2009 under the terms of the 2008 Constitution of Myanmar. It was formed with eighteen members chaired by U Thein Soe, who came from a military background.[3]

The first general election the new commission took responsibility for under the new constitution was held in 2010 (see Horsey 2012; Skidmore and Wilson 2012). It prepared for the electoral process in just eight months, during which time all necessary preparations, such as delimitation of constituencies, enacting of rules and regulations, formation of sub-commissions, preparation for polling booth stations, calling for candidates, and many other things, had to be done. Training for the sub-commissioners as well as the members of polling booths was conducted urgently. Voter education could not reach out to all people, especially in remote areas. Unfortunately, the lack of census data as well as mismanagement and lack of funding hampered the quality of the electoral process.

The conduct and results of the election, which the NLD boycotted, were criticized by locals and the international community. The major criticism of the election commission was that the USDP, which was formed under the leadership of retired military officers, won a landslide victory with the aid of advance votes. Other criticisms and questions concerned the commission's lack of experience and capacity, the process for appointment of ballot officers, restrictions on party campaigns, flaws in the list of registered voters, and ambiguity between practical and legal circumstances. The commission was in a dilemma concerning its power and function, as legally it was supposed to be neutral but in fact it was obligated to comply with government instructions and enable the USDP victory.

When the new administration had been set up by President U Thein Sein, the election commission was classed as a union-level organization with the nomination of the president and approval of the Hluttaw, or parliament, in accordance with the 2008 Constitution. The UEC was criticized again because it was chaired by U Tin Aye, a former senior military officer who was appointed by presidential nomination. Almost all members came from the former election commission, although they were mostly civilians.[4]

The year 2015 was the last in the term of President U Thein Sein's government. So elections had to be carried out to form a new government and convene a new parliament. Holding a successful election in 2015 was the top priority of the UEC, and for U Thein Sein's government as well. the president stressed his commitment to conducting free and fair elections in his monthly radio talk, stating that "my government under its executive authority and within the bounds of its executive power, will ensure that the elections are free and fair" (Thein Sein 2015).

Although the president promised to hold a free and fair election, people still mistrusted the government and did not think that the UEC could do its work credibly, given its record in 2010. Moreover, 2015 was a critical year for Myanmar for many other reasons. The country had to sign a nationwide ceasefire agreement (see Su Mon Thazin Aung, this volume), rehabilitate flood victims, solve the problems of labour and student strikes and land grabbing issues, among other things (see Pedersen 2014). Many were worried the election would be marred by violence in some areas, due to rising nationalism and religious extremism. Under these complex circumstances, the UEC had to tackle a range of issues and challenges in the pre-election period.

The UEC would not easily convince political parties or civil society organizations (CSOs) to trust it. To address the trust deficit, the UEC launched an information centre in Yangon and a new website on 27 May 2015 where eligible voters could check their names against voting lists compiled by the commission.[5] Meeting with the Myanmar Press Council and CSOs to discuss a draft Code of Conduct for observers and political parties, it sought to demonstrate its willingness to conduct a free and fair election. The draft code was discussed with the over sixty local CSOs and international organizations in December 2014. About two-thirds of the original code was changed in line with CSOs' requests.

The poor capacity of the UEC and its staff was one of the biggest challenges. Chairman U Tin Aye frankly admitted in interviews on Skynet News during October 2015 that the UEC could not manage at the two lowest tiers of administration, the township and ward or village levels, due to a shortage of staff (Skynet 2015). Although it had been recruiting through the Union Civil Services Training, these new staff would become available only after mid-2016. He explained that mistakes happened because of poor management, and expressed concerns about the difficulties of capacity building and the material limitations of the UEC. Therefore, he encouraged international and local donors to supply basic needs for the UEC staff.

One reason for the lack of staff and capacity was indeed under-funding, in part caused by a sense that the election would cost too much at a time when the government had limited resources for other urgent matters. On 17 March 2015, the UEC proposed a 5700.811 million kyat (US$5.4 million) budget to parliament for the cost of the 2015 election, to erect polling stations, produce ballots, hold receptions for volunteers at voting booths, and so on. One parliamentarian raised a question about the UEC's budget proposal, which was equivalent to the cost of building 126 Rural Health Centers (RHCs). Building RHCs was one of the Millenium Development Goals (MDGs) to be accomplished in 2015. The point was that holding a national election would cost a lot to the national budget that could be used elsewhere. The Hluttaw decided to record that motion.

In the lead-up to the election the UEC was criticized both by political parties and CSOs over the issuing of registered voters lists; the drafting of a Code of Conduct for the media, election observers, and CSOs; cancelling of the election in some constituencies (see Lidauer, this volume); and the way international election observers were allocated to different regions.

One of the issues that caught attention was advance votes, which had caused public concern in the 2010 general elections. In 2015 similar questions were raised about what would happen with the advance votes, but whereas the problem in 2010 was one of fraud, in 2015 it turned out for the most part to be one of capacity. When advance voting began in some Myanmar embassies abroad, especially in Singapore where hundreds of thousands of Myanmar citizens work, information was posted on social media about inconsistent voting procedures and ballots. It was a huge task for Myanmar embassies to arrange convenient advance voting due to their lack of prior experience and limited staff. Voters were confused and there were problems associated with the short time frame and lack of cooperation among government officials, the UEC, and staff at embassies.

The UEC's efforts to police the activities of campaigning political parties also attracted attention. With locals and the international community watching, the UEC needed to take a firm stand and act as an independent body, not as a partisan of one party or another. It issued warnings to parties about various activities. For example, it called on the United Nationalities Alliance to avoid supporting student protests over a new National Education Law in early 2015 (Hein Ko Soe 2015). It also warned the Mon National Party, which published a joint statement with the New Mon State Party, a group still in armed struggle against the central government (Lawi Weng

2015). It raised concerns over unofficial election campaigns and party promises, especially from the ruling party. For example, the minister for industry distributed gifts in fifteen villages in Min Kin township to get people to vote for the USDP (Ye Mon and Wa Lone 2015).

The largest number of complaints arose over the voter lists. Although the UEC disseminated preliminary voter lists across the country and invited people to correct mistakes for fourteen days starting on 7 September 2015, few people checked the lists, and errors were only made known later. In the end, the UEC released preliminary voter lists four times, but a correct listing could not be compiled as political parties criticized the process and did not cooperate in getting people to check their details.

Voting rights for people who lived in slum areas also became a significant unresolved issue. Legally, people living as squatters and in slums are not eligible to register as residents of a constituency, since they have no definite address and no official household registration in a town or ward. This made it impossible for the UEC to register these people. Furthermore, the commission also had to be aware that a big movement of people into slums around Yangon area could significantly affect election outcomes. This happened in 2010, particularly in South Okkalapa constituency, where a large number of fishermen from Ayeyarwady Region deliberately moved into the constituency and voted as migrant workers in Yangon Region. Nevertheless, the UEC did agree to relax its rules for migrant workers to vote in their current constituencies, even though formally they should not have been able to do so (Eleven Myanmar 2015). However, political parties continuously emphasized the voting rights of those in slums; they pointed out that citizens' right to vote was at odds with the law.

Despite all the speculation, accusations, and rumours just before the election, the real essence of holding an election through public participation could be observed on election day, 8 November 2015. Long queues waited outside ballot stations at dawn. The enthuastic and disciplined participation of the public showed how Myanmar could hold free, fair, and transparent general elections for the first time in decades. As the vote counting went on, nearly all election observers, both local and international, clearly stated that the election was overall fairly free and transparent. This successful achievement was the result of the politically active Myanmar community, and the relentless efforts of the UEC, political parties, and a handful of CSOs as well as international groups that came to Myanmar before and during the process to communicate their skills and offer their experience.

INTERNATIONAL AGENCIES

International agencies were active in providing electoral assistance to the UEC, political parties, and a variety of CSOs in anticipation of the 2015 election. The primary agency providing financial and technical assistance was USAID. It coordinated activities with the United Kingdom's Department for International Development and Australia's Department of Foreign Affairs and Trade. They provided funding for the International Foundation for Electoral Systems (IFES), the National Democratic Institute (NDI), and the International Republican Institute's (IRI) operations in the country. Furthermore, European Union support included grants to civil society groups, media training, police training, and technical assistance to the UEC in drafting the Code of Conduct for election observers (Myanma Alin 2015).

Ahead of the election, the NDI provided technical assistance to Myanmar's parliament through the creation of a Parliamentary Resource Center in Naypyitaw, and training to strengthen parliamentary processes and the reform agenda. NDI also worked with CSOs to facilitate peer-to peer training and best practices. NDI trained some 5,000 citizens as election observers to monitor electoral processes before and during election day (NDI 2015).

IRI focuses on strengthening political parties. It provided training workshops to all parties — from the NLD and USDP to small ethnic parties — to teach them how to conduct campaigns, organize internal party structures, and develop party platforms. It also supported civil society groups engaged in voter and civic education campaigns.

In addition, with funding from Norway, the International Institute for Democracy and Electoral Assistance (IDEA), together with the Danish Institute for Parties and Democracy, and Democracy Reporting International operated in Myanmar on a new 2015 electoral trust-building initiative. IDEA also provided technical assistance to the UEC via workshops on how to use IDEA's Electoral Risk Management tool, to identify potential trouble areas before the election.

In 1990 and 2010, foreign observers were not allowed to monitor and scrutinize general elections. In the 2012 by-election, only observers from Southeast Asian countries were invited. Thus, 2015 marked the first time in Myanmar's election history that international observers other than those from nearby countries were invited. In total, the UEC issued accreditation cards to 470 diplomats from thirty-two international embassies, 465 staff from six international election observation bodies, 183 staff from nine international organizations assisting in electoral processes, and 9,406 staff of local observation organizations.[6]

Among them, the Carter Center and European Union organized sizeable missions. The Asian Network for Free Elections (ANFREL), a regional network of CSOs focused on election monitoring, was also actively involved. The organization had been working in Myanmar furtively since 1999, and it partners with local CSOs and media organizations to develop talent and support their efforts to deepen civic engagement.

Although international observers and election support agencies generally came to Myanmar with goodwill, they met with mixed responses among local actors. From the perspective of political parties, the critical question was how development partners would distribute their assistance to parties. Some questioned whether international assistance should be accepted at all. For instance, U Sai Leik, spokesperson for the Shan Nationalities League for Democracy, said his party had received no support and was unsure who was benefiting from the international programme. He said, "We have never accepted any assistance from international donors yet" (Ei Ei Toe Lwin and Dinmore 2015). The Rakhine National Party expressed its view that parties should not accept direct international assistance according to the 2008 Constitution. CSOs argued that foreign assistance had little impact at the grassroots level where it was needed, and it could only reach parties or civil society groups with close ties to the UEC.

The general consensus among observers themselves was that the election was fair. For instance, during its press conference, the European Union's election observation mission stressed that the elections was well-run and peaceful (Lambsdorff 2015). The 150 or so European Union observers had reached more than 500 polling stations across the country and reported very positively on the voting process, with ninety-five per cent rating the process as 'good' or 'very good'. However, their assessment was that the process of in-constituency and out-of-constituency advance voting was less well managed and transparent.

In some other settings scholars have pointed to how election observers' reports reveal as much about their own biases as about what has actually taken place in an election (see Kelly 2010). As this was the first time Myanmar allowed international observers in large numbers, it is not possible to make a comparison with earlier experiences and it is also hard to identify the biases, strengths, and weaknesses of foreign election observers' missions. Also, given the NLD won with such a convincing margin, questions of bias were less relevant than if had it won with only a slim majority.

THE TATMADAW

In order to understand the role of the Tatmadaw in Myanmar electoral politics, one must look back to history. As civil war has lasted for many decades, military involvement in politics is strong. As long as the state is weak and unable to manage political instability, military involvement in politics cannot be easily changed, even with good electoral outcomes. On two previous occasions free and fair elections were held under military rule: in 1960, and again in 1990. Yet, these elections were followed by long periods of military rule, and most people have negative views about the military's role in politics since the failed democracy uprising of 1988.

Today it cannot be denied that Myanmar's path to democratization in recent years was made possible by military officers. But even since the transition to democracy began, some civilian posts have been taken by military officers. So in the eyes of Myanmar people, the military continues to be treated with distrust and hostility. Events like the silver jubilee anniversary commemoration of the 1990 election at the Judson Center, and efforts by elected members of parliament from 1990 to launch legal proceedings against some members of the military junta for breaking electoral laws cause uneasiness for the military (Lun Min Maung 2015). Criticism and hatred of the military expressed on Facebook and other social media do little to bring civilians and the military closer together. Yet, without trust between civilians and the military, it will be difficult for the present number of seats in parliament reserved for the military to be reduced from twenty-five per cent.

For its part, the military has been trying to improve its professionalism in order to rid itself of old habits. The National Defence College, which trains colonels and high-ranking officials, has been upgrading its curricula since 2008, after the constitution was promulgated. Courses on civil-military relations, democracy, and human rights are now a part of the curriculum. Visiting military delegations from abroad, such as the United States, embolden the military to open up and re-engage with the West.

Some colonels are being sent to the United States for further professional training. Also, in 2015, Commander-in-Chief Senior General Min Aung Hlaing held regional seminars on defence and frequently took military friendship tours to Japan, Indonesia, Thailand, Malaysia, India, Israel, Russia, and China, to improve professionalism with the support of partners inside and outside the region.[7]

Throughout 2015, the military insisted it would be on guard to ensure that the election would be fair. Commander-in-Chief Senior General Min Aung Hlaing said that "any armed pressure or threats to voters couldn't be allowed in the General Elections" (Global New Light of Myanmar 2015), although he did not elaborate. At the time of the election, he took a leaf out of the president's book by being more open and engaging in dealing with the public and media on the military's role, especially in addressing questions about the transfer of power to the newly elected parties. After casting his vote, the commander responded to questions raised by the media. He said that there was no reason not to accept the election results. In a November 23 interview with the *Washington Post* posted to the senior general's Facebook page, he showed positive signs that power would be transferred peacefully. At a meeting with political parties in Yangon on 15 November 2015, the president, himself a former army general, also stressed that the current government would work for a smooth transition in line with existing laws, regulations, and procedures, and would do so calmly, peacefully, and smoothly so as not to cause concerns about the power transfer.

The questions are not surprising, given that in 1990 the election was held freely but it did not result in a power transfer. The reason given by the military to refuse to transfer power at that time was lack of a constitution. People still mistrust the government and Tatmadaw when it comes to the transfer of power, meetings with the NLD leader Daw Aung San Suu Kyi notwithstanding. The events of 1990 caused massive trauma for the political development of Myanmar, and fears of a U-turn or military coup will take time and many more confidence-building measures to dissipate.

CONCLUSION

The 2015 general election fulfilled the high hopes of people of Myanmar to vote freely and fairly, avoiding pre- and post-election instability. It was successful due to the cooperative efforts of the UEC, government, military, CSOs, media, and international observers. The UEC as an integral institution proved up to the task, despite skepticism about its role. International agencies, as important supporters of democratic development, also made major contributions. Overall, the UEC has proven to be a welcome development, as many reforms have taken place that put it in a much more favourable light at the end of 2015 than only a few years before. The willingness of the UEC to work with international and local observer missions is a significant feature of its changed circumstances.

The military went along with the 2015 election and did not obstruct or play a spoiling role, despite ample opportunities should it have wished to do so. It stayed neutral, as it did in the 2012 by-election. Reducing the Tatmadaw's involvement in politics remains a matter to be dealt with through consideration of history, and building of trust. Significant challenges lie ahead and it is by no means certain that Myanmar's political transition will go smoothly, but the 2015 election marks an historic achievement on the path to a democratic Myanmar, one for which all institutions involved deserve credit, as well as the politically active and discerning Myanmar public.

Appendix

Election commission members, 1960 election

1. Thadoe Thudama U Tin
2. Thadoe Mahar Thayey Sithu U Chan Tun Aung
3. Wanna Kyaw Htin U Ohn Pe

Election commission members, 1990 election

1. U Ba Htay
2. U Saw Kyar Doe
3. U San Maung
4. Saya Chae
5. U Kyaw Nyunt
6. U Aye Maung

Election commission members, 2010 election

1. U Thein Soe
2. U In Zaw Naw
3. U Khin Maung Nu
4. U Saw Ba Hlaing
5. Dr Ba Maung
6. U Nyunt Tin
7. U Maung Thar Hla
8. Dr Sai Kham Hlaing
9. U Aung Myint
10. U Myint Naing
11. Dr Tin Aung Aye
12. Dr Daw Myint Kyi
13. Daw Khin Hla Myint
14. U Thar Oo
15. Dr Maung Htoo
16. U Thar Htoo
17. U Win Kyi

Election commission members, 2015 election

1. U Tin Aye
2. U Tin Htun
3. Dr. Daw Myint Kyi
4. U Win Kyi
5. U Win Ko
6. U Myint Naing
7. U Aung Myint
8. U Nyunt Tin
9. N Zaw Naung
10. Saw Ba Hlaing
11. Sai Khum Win
12. Ha Ki
13. Dr. Maung Maung Kyi
14. Sai Nun Taung
15. Sai Htun Thein
16. Dr. Sai San Win

Notes

1 In addition to sources cited, the contents of this chapter are drawn from two roundtable sessions on the election results held at the Department of International Relations, University of Yangon, on 9 and 13 November 2015. The first roundtable was a closed session of faculty members, while the second brought faculty together with colleagues from the Myanmar Research Centre, Australian National University.
2 For general discussion of the history of elections and their management in Myanmar, see history section of the UEC website, http://uecmyanmar.org.
3 Biographies of election commission members are available on the UEC website.
4 A list of election commissioners is provided in the appendix.
5 The website address is http://checkvoterlist.uecmyanmar.org/. Aside from the website, the UEC also made mobile apps available for people working from telephones and tablets.
6 See the section of the UEC website on international cooperation for details.
7 Trip details available on Senior General Min Aung Hlaing's Facebook page.

References

Ei Ei Toe Lwin and Guy Dinmore. "Political Parties Wary of Foreign Election Aid". *Myanmar Times*, 5 March 2015 <http://www.mmtimes.com/index.php/national-news/13340-political-parties-wary-of-foreign-election-aid.html>. Accessed 8 May 2015.

Eleven Myanmar. "Domestic Migrant Workers Can Vote in Current Constituencies". *Eleven Myanmar*, 30 September 2015 <http://www.elevenmyanmar.com/politics/domestic-migrant-workers-can-vote-in-current-constituencies.html>. Accessed 2 October 2015.

Global New Light of Myanmar. "Speech Delivered by Commander-in-Chief of Defence Services, Senior General Thayaysithu Min Aung Hlaing at the Parade of the 70th Armed Forces Day Held on 27th March, 2015". *Global New Light of Myanmar*, 28 March 2015 <http://globalnewlightofmyanmar.com>. Accessed 8 May 2015.

Hein Ko Soe. "Election Commission Tells UNA to Stay Out of Student Protest". *Mizzima*, 24 February 2014 <http://www.mizzima.com/news-domestic/election-commission-tells-una-stay-out-student-protests/>. Accessed 8 May 2015.

Horsey, Richard. "Myanmar's Political Landscape Following the 2010 Elections: Starting with a Glass Nine-tenths Empty?" In *Myanmar's Transition: Openings, Obstacles and Opportunities*, edited by Nick Cheesman, Monique Skidmore, and Trevor Wilson. Singapore: Institute of Southeast Asian Studies, 2012.

Kelly, Judith. "Election Observers and their Biases". *Journal of Democracy* 21, no. 3 (2010): 158–72.

Lambsdorff, Alexander. "Myanmar Elections Better Than Expected, Say EU Observers-video". *The Guardian*, 10 November 2015. <http://www.theguardian.com/world/video/2015/nov/10/myanmar-elections-better-than-expected-say-eu-observers-video>. Accessed 11 November 2015.

Lawi Weng. "Elections Commission to Question Mon Party Over Joint Statement with Rebels". *The Irrawaddy*, 6 April 2015. <http://www.irrawaddy.org>. Accessed 8 May 2015.

Lun Min Maung. "NLD Shuns 1990 Election Ceremony". *Myanmar Times*, 28 May 2015 <http://www.mmtimes.com/index/php/national-news/14720-nld-shuns-1990-election-ceremony.html>. Accessed 23 January 2016.

Myanma Alin. "Code of Conduct Issued for Domestic and International Elections Observers". *Myanma Alin*, 20 March 2015, p. 3. In Burmese.

National Democratic Institute (NDI). "Burmese Vote in First Open National Election in 25 Years". National Democratic Institute, 9 November 2015. <http://www.ndi.org/burma_elections_Nov_2015_story>. Accessed 9 November 2015.

Pedersen, Morten. "Myanmar's Democratic Opening: The Process and Prospect of Reform". In *Debating Democratisation in Myanmar*, edited by Nick Cheesman, Nicholas Farrelly, and Trevor Wilson. Singapore: Institute of Southeast Asian Studies, 2014.

Skidmore, Monique and Trevor Wilson. "Interpreting the Transition in Myanmar". In *Myanmar's Transition: Openings, Obstacles and Opportunities*, edited by Nick Cheesman, Monique Skidmore, and Trevor Wilson. Singapore: Institute of Southeast Asian Studies, 2012.

Skynet. "Interview with Union Election Commission Chairman U Tin Aye", Skynet Hluttaw Channel, 7 October 2015. In Burmese.

State Law and Order Restoration Council (SLORC). *Chronicle of the State Law and Order Restoration Council 1988–1991*. Yangon: Publishing Committee of State Law and Order Restoration Council, 1991. In Burmese.

Thein Sein. President U Thein Sein's Radio Address. 3 November, 2015 <http://www.president-office.gov.mm/?q=media-room/>. In Burmese.

Ye Mon and Wa Lone. "Minister Faces Vote-buying Allegations in Kayah State". *Myanmar Times*, 3 September 2015 <http://www.mmtimes.com/index.php/national-news/16289-minister-faces-vote-buying-allegations-in-kayah-state-html>. Accessed 5 September 2015.

9

ETHNICITY AND BUDDHIST NATIONALISM IN THE 2015 RAKHINE STATE ELECTION RESULTS

Than Tun

Myanmar's 2015 election was distinguished by the overwhelming victory of the National League for Democracy (NLD), not only at the national level, but also in most of the states — the home of minority ethnic nationalities that were considered to be politically dominated by ethnic parties. The exceptions to this 'Red Wave' were Shan and Rakhine States where the NLD did not win the majority of seats. In Rakhine State, the Arakan (Rakhine) National Party (ANP) won most seats, making it the largest ethnic party in the national parliament and in a State Hluttaw. The ANP's win in Rakhine State has implications at the national level, not just for electoral reasons but, more importantly, for the political significance of ethnic politics and Buddhist nationalism in Myanmar.

The electoral victory of the ANP has been explained in terms of ethnicity that centred on the ANP's abilities to draw support from the Rakhine ethnic community and Buddhist nationalism in relation to the communal antagonism against the Muslim community prevailing across

Rakhine State. In contrast to political parties from other ethnic groups who were unable to form a united political front in the 2015 election, the ANP was reported as the united front gaining an exceptional level of support from the Rakhine constituency. The popular support among the Buddhist Rakhine for their leaders' strong stance against the Muslim communities and the prevalence of public perception that the NLD was pro-Muslim were also identified as key reasons for the Rakhine State electoral exceptionalism.

However, the ANP victory was not as comprehensive as it might first appear to have been. It lost all townships of Thandwe District to the NLD, and gained most of its seats with small margins, with a large majority of votes only in Sittwe District.[1] The exclusion of most Muslim voters in the northern district of Maungdaw resulted in shared electoral victories between the ANP and the Tatmadaw-established Union Solidarity and Development Party (USDP). The differences in voting patterns and election results showed support was not uniform across the state. A detailed analysis of the electoral results at the constituency level can show the reasons for these differences, and give insights into the influence that ethnicity and Buddhist nationalism have among the Rakhine. Moreover, the Rakhine State situation can be juxtaposed with other parts of Myanmar and the NLD wins, shedding light on the reason for the overall rather insignificant effect of Buddhist nationalism on the 2015 elections.

As this chapter aims to put the Rakhine State electoral results in the national context of the NLD's landslide victory, in the next section I outline how the election outcome was predicted and then explained by most analysts, especially in relation to ethnicity and Buddhist nationalism. In the subsequent section I discuss the ideological origins of the ANP to show that it is the manifestation of a long history of Rakhine ethno-nationalism despite being less than two years old. Then, I present detailed information on voting patterns in Rakhine State to show that the ANP support is strongest in northern townships, and gradually weakens towards the south. The final section discusses the ANP as a credible alternative to the NLD in Rakhine State, while the USDP was not a credible alternative in the whole of Myanmar. The electoral results in Rakhine State showed the relative influence of Buddhist nationalism in Myanmar, and the electoral victory of the NLD should not under-emphasize this influence in understanding Myanmar's politics and society.

EXCEPTIONALISM OF RAKHINE STATE ELECTION RESULTS

Most analysts of politics in Myanmar, including myself, were not expecting the NLD to get an absolute majority in the national parliament, even though it would win the largest number of seats, or that it would dominate in most State Hluttaws. This prediction was based on two assumptions: political allegiances would go to ethnic parties in the states, and the influence of the Buddhist nationalists who were campaigning against the NLD would be significant. Post-election readings of the NLD's stunning victory risked under-recognizing the continued relevance of these phenomena to Myanmar's political and social conditions.

The first assumption was that most ethnic parties would receive somewhat stronger support in the states (see ICG 2015b; Kyaw San Wai and Kumada 2015; Medail 2015; Nguyen 2015). It was predicted that ethnic parties, with a substantial number of ethnic seats, would become key players at least in state assemblies, if not at the national level. Ethnic groups would vote as a block, overcoming the organizational and financial challenges faced by the ethnic political leaderships (Berliner 2015).

The second assumption was based on the perceived popularity of MaBaTha (Committee for Protection of Race and Religion), which campaigned against the NLD in the election. The rise of Buddhist nationalism, initially as the 969 movement and later as MaBaTha, was linked to the anti-Muslim riots between 2012 and 2014. Starting with the Rakhine riots in June 2012 in Rakhine State, sixteen violent incidents against Muslim communities occurred across the country by June 2014 (Min Zin 2015). Capitalizing on these events and the associated communal sentiments, the Buddhist nationalist movement achieved popularity in Myanmar.

MaBaTha viewed the NLD and its party leader Daw Aung San Suu Kyi as pro-Muslim for their stance on the rule of law and communal tolerance. Moreover, there were reports of weakening support for the NLD throughout the country, especially in 2014. For example, the NLD's signature campaign for amendment of the Constitution received five million signatures from the whole country, which some considered a relatively small proportion of the population (Htoo Thant 2014). Citing large MaBaTha public events and the local rumours, some said that the NLD had lost the sizeable support it enjoyed before 2011. Looking at the popular MaBaTha events, it was assumed that the popularity of Daw Aung San Suu Kyi and the NLD had decreased with the rise of anti-Muslim sentiment in Myanmar.

Despite the attempts from the NLD and Aung San Suu Kyi to discard the 'pro-Muslim' image, such as by expelling party members with temporary residency cards, or 'white card' holders (Yen Snaing 2015) and not selecting a single Muslim candidate (Hindstrom 2015), the Buddhist nationalists endorsed President U Thein Sein and the USDP (Hnin Yadana Zaw and Soldkowski 2015). It was expected that the NLD would win most seats in the election, but was unlikely to gain more than a two-thirds majority needed to form the parliamentary majority outright and the government, taking into account the quarter of seats held by the military.

In the end, the NLD got an absolute majority in both houses of parliament and also in eleven of the fourteen regional assemblies (TNI 2015). It won more than fifty per cent of the seats in five states, and it became the largest party in Kachin State. Many of the ethnic political parties failed to win any seats, either in the national or the regional assemblies of the ethnic majority states. The ethnic parties at the national level did worse than in the controversial 2010 election, going down from fifteen to nine per cent of seats (ICG 2015a, p. 4).

The failure of ethnic parties to get votes, with the notable exception of the Rakhine and Shan States, is explained as being due to a proliferation of parties, lack of resources, weak local politics, failure to translate ethnic identity to votes, the charisma of Aung San Suu Kyi, possible perceptions of these ethnic parties as having close ties with the military, and the effective reach of the national parties at the local level (Burke 2015). The potency of MaBaTha and the importance of Buddhist nationalism in the election were questioned too.

Yet the insights on ethnicity and religion that were underlying the wrong predictions were based on established scholarship on Myanmar. Therefore, the NLD's electoral victory either demands rethinking or rejection of these two assumptions on the roles of ethnicity and religion in Myanmar's politics. This requires us to reconsider the link between an individual's ethnicity, aspects of one's social identity in everyday life, ethnic nationalism, and political mobilization based on the community's ethnic identification. We need to re-apprise the link between the political importance and the cultural ubiquity of Buddhism in Myanmar. But to do that, we need to take into account those elements and conditions in Rakhine State that made it an exception in 2015.

THE ARAKAN NATIONAL PARTY AND RAKHINE ETHNO-NATIONALISM

Rakhine State had exceptional circumstances, which influenced the election results in the state. The largest communal violence in Myanmar occurred in the state between 2012 and 2013 (ICG 2013; Kipgen 2013; Walton and Hayward 2014). While the communal antagonism continued through ongoing segregation and continuous political mobilizations on communal issues, such as the inclusion or exclusion of 'Rohingya' as an ethnic identity in the census process, attacks against INGO offices in Sittwe and rejection of the voting rights of white-card holders (Min Zin 2015) inflamed the situation.

The white-card voting right cancellation was significant because most people from Muslim communities in Rakhine State were not able to vote in 2015, although they had participated in the 2010 election (Lun Min Mang 2015; Samet 2015). This changed the composition of voters in many townships, especially in Maungdaw District. Before the 2010 election, the military junta issued 750,000 Temporary National Identity Cards or 'white cards' in Rakhine State for the people who are controversially referred to as 'Bengalis' or 'Rohingya'. The USDP received a considerable proportion of votes from the Muslim community with a large number of white card voters, and it won seats with Muslim representatives in Maungdaw and Buthidaung townships in 2010 (O'Toole 2014). The cancellation of white card voters' rights massively reduced the size of these constituencies and removed the Muslim population from the vote. In 2010, 211,328 people in Maungdaw township lodged valid votes, and in Buthidaung there were 129,909 people.[2] The eligible voter numbers would still have been higher than these figures. For the 2015 election, Myanmar's Union Election Commission (UEC) reported eligible voters in Maungdaw were just 24,008, and in Buthidaung, 36,069. Moreover, the Commission also disqualified Muslim candidates, citing citizenship issues over their parents' identities and backgrounds (Ei Ei Toe Lwin 2015). This resulted in only Buddhist candidates standing in these townships. As a direct consequence, the overwhelming majority of the residents in Maungdaw and some people in Sittwe District were unable to vote in the 2015 election (Long 2015b). Furthermore, it made less electoral competition for the ANP candidates in these constituencies.

These circumstances contributed quite significantly to the Buddhist nationalist agenda in Rakhine State against the NLD, while favouring those identified with the communal sentiments. The religiously based antagonism was particularly significant because Rakhine ethnicity is articulated in terms of Buddhism (de Mersan 2015, p. 46; Leider 2008). Both ethno-nationalism and Buddhist nationalism that dominated pre-election discussions seemed to have converged to give the ANP electoral dominance in Rakhine State. The relevance of Rakhine ethno-nationalism is that the ANP portrayed itself as the vanguard of the Rakhine ethnic movement. The influence of Buddhist nationalism in Rakhine State also meant that those candidates who identified with anti-Muslim sentiments would have done well in the township where communal conflicts were more severe and religious antagonism was intense. The ANP's background and the detailed voting patterns at the township or constituency level show the strength and characteristics of Rakhine ethno-nationalism and Buddhist nationalism in Rakhine State during the 2015 election.

The ANP, through its leaders and formation process, has come to be not just a political party representing people of Rakhine ethnicity, but also the party working for the aspirations of ethno-nationalism, especially Arakanese (the former name of Rakhine State) sovereignty. The ANP itself is relatively young. It was only officially established in April 2014. However it has a long history, since it was formed through the merger of two existing Rakhine political parties, namely the Arakan League for Democracy (ALD), formed in 1989, and the Rakhine Nationalities Development Party (RNDP), formed in 2009. The merger discussions started early in 2012 (Ei Ei Toe Lwin 2012), however the actual dissolution of each party and establishment of a single leadership mechanism only occurred in February 2014, with official registration in March 2014.

The ALD was the most prominent Arakanese political party in the 1990 election, winning the third largest number of seats (eleven) at the national level, one more than the junta-backed National Unity Party. The most significant ALD politician during its 1990 electoral campaign was the late U Oo Tha Tun,[3] the champion of Arakanese sovereignty and ancient Arakanese history. After 1990, the ALD was driven underground and was limited to a few public activities around the involvement of its new leader, U Aye Thar Aung, in national politics as General Secretary of the Committee Representing the People's Parliament (CRPP), in close collaboration with the NLD. The ALD also joined the NLD-led 2010 election boycott, but re-registered in 2012.

In 2009 the RNDP was set up to seize the electoral opportunities emerging from the initial small opening in the 2010 elections within the authoritarian context of military rule but in a period of high civil society mobilization (de Mersan 2015). RNDP members had political and socio-cultural activist backgrounds in the Rakhine ethno-nationalist movement, and many older leaders were former members of the ALD from the 1990s. The RNDP fielded a total of 44 candidates in the 2010 elections, and it won 35 seats consisting of 7 Amyotha Hluttaw, 9 Pyithu Hluttaw, and 19 State and Region Hluttaw seats (Burma News International 2011). It became a prominent political player at the national level, partly because of the explosive communal violence in Rakhine State and the prominent role of its chairman, Dr Aye Maung, in key national political events, such as the top-level six-party talks in April 2015 (Htoo Thant and Pyae Thet Phyo 2015). Despite its marginal political position in the state government, the RNDP in Rakhine State led many major political successes on the religious-nationalist agenda, such as the white-card holder vote cancellation, promulgation of the religion and race protection laws, and the rejection of the Organization of Islamic Cooperation and campaign against international aid agencies for their alleged bias towards the Muslim community.

The ALD and RNDP were two parties with significant political capital themselves, but their merger was especially important for ethno-nationalists. Achieving unity of various Rakhine political forces was a key ethno-nationalist desire, which had been expressed more strongly among the armed organizations based in the border area. Although the armed movements dated back to Myanmar independence from Britain, there had been little or no armed activity in Rakhine State since the late 1970s. The lack of potency of the ethno-nationalist armed activities was attributed partly to the divisive nature of Rakhine political groups. Despite their low profile, there have been many attempts to unite these smaller groups. In 1997, four Rakhine armed groups formed as the National United Party of Arakan, only to disintegrate again within two or three years. The Arakan National Council was formed in 2004, which also disbanded within a few years. As a result of the divisive nature of Rakhine politics, the unity of key political entities had become an important aspiration among the ethno-nationalists. The merger of the ALD and RNDP addressed this aspiration of Rakhine ethno-nationalism.

The unity of the ANP faced internal and external challenges just before the 2015 election campaign. Internal conflicts are said to have occurred along the original party lines. The disagreements centred around the candidate selections between the former RNDP members who dominated the party leadership and the former ALD members with longer histories of anti-junta activism (Mratt Kyaw Thu 2015). At the same time, a new political party based on Rakhine ethnicity, the Arakan Patriotic Party, was created with former members of the ALD (Narinjara News 2015).[4] The Rakhine State National Force Party also emerged as a political party based on Rakhine ethnicity, but it was mostly active in southern townships. Despite these external challenges, the ANP managed to remain a single front with an undivided public face during the election campaign, and it was able to resolve internal disagreements at the time of the election (Long 2015a). This unity that the ANP projected strengthened its claim to represent the long-running Rakhine ethno-nationalist agenda.

The Rakhine ethno-nationalist ultimate aspiration is sovereignty over its ethnic nationality and territory, the Arakan or Rakhine State. It is articulated through narratives of past glories of Buddhist kingdoms and the desire to recover the loss of sovereignty after the conquest of Mrauk-U by the Burmese in 1784 (Leider 2008). The narratives of Arakan as the land of the Mahamuni Buddha Image, which was moved to Mandalay by the Burmese conquerors, dominate Rakhine ethno-nationalist discourse (Leider 2009). The descriptions of rich Arakanese kingdoms juxtaposed with the current status of Rakhine State as the second-poorest region in Myanmar creates an inspiration to return the control of abundant natural resources from the Burman-dominated government to local people. The Rakhine nationalists envisage a Rakhine government with independent control over the state's natural resources and directing them for its development. However, Rakhine political parties, whether they are based inside Myanmar or at the border areas, do not explicitly express 'independence' as their main agenda publicly, but the ethno-nationalist ideas of separatist self-determination remain an important aspect of their aspirations (Ware 2015).

The ANP raised the political agenda of winning all the seats and controlling the State Hluttaw, which would result in an ANP chief minister and state government (Eleven Myanmar 2015). With these political tools, the ANP argued, the state development agenda would be in the hands of the Rakhine people and it would take back their rightful share of benefits from the extraction of its natural resources. This message centred on the ethno-nationalist idea of self-determination, though expressed in the context of the State Hluttaw. Moreover, the argument for the control of the state development agenda resonated strongly with the Rakhine people's desire to see benefits from natural resources and receive local opportunities. This focus was on control of the state development agenda as an alternative policy approach, while its communal approach was as a strong contender for Buddhist nationalist credentials over and above other parties.

The main ANP electoral strategy was to translate Rakhine ethnicity to ethno-nationalist sentiment, and thereby get support for ethno-nationalist development and security policies. As the ANP was identified strongly with an anti-Muslim sentiment, it also received Buddhist-nationalist support. As they went to vote, the people in Rakhine State faced three main electoral choices: inspiration for national change from the NLD; stability and status quo from the USDP, especially in the context of communal segregation; and an advancing ethno-nationalist agenda from the ANP.

DETAILED RESULTS OF THE 2015 ELECTION IN RAKHINE STATE

At the Rakhine State level, the electoral results showed victory for the ANP in terms of seats and popular votes. Compared to the electoral performance of other ethnic parties in their home states, the ANP achieved significantly more in Rakhine State, winning forty-five out of the available sixty-four seats for both houses of national parliament and the State Assembly. The ANP won twelve out of seventeen Pyithu Hluttaw (lower house) seats from Rakhine State, while the NLD gained four, and the USDP one. The ANP also won ten out of twelve seats for the Amyotha Hluttaw (upper house), while the NLD and USDP received only one each. For the State Hluttaw, the ANP won twenty-three out of thirty-four township-based seats. The NLD gained eight seats, and the USDP five. The ANP received seventy per cent of all elected seats from Rakhine State. Full state-wide results for the Pyithu Hluttaw, Amyotha Hluttaw, and State Hluttaw are shown at the end of the chapter.

At the national level, the ANP's electoral representations amounted to only 4.45 per cent in the Amyotha Hluttaw and only 2.7 per cent in the Pyithu Hluttaw. While the ANP received twenty-three seats, or sixty-five per cent, of the elected seats at the state level, this was one seat short of gaining the majority of the Rakhine State Hluttaw, which consists of thirty-five elected and twelve military-appointed members. This means the ANP will be the largest party with forty-nine per cent representation in the State Hluttaw, but it does not have the control of the assembly in its own right. It would have to work together with either the NLD, which controls around nineteen per cent of the state legislature, or the military, with nine members, and the USDP and military coalition of thirty-two per cent with fifteen members.

The ANP won the popular vote in Rakhine State, receiving fifty-one per cent of the valid votes across the state for the combined three houses. The ANP also gained fifty-three per cent of the state's popular vote for the national seats. However it did not win the popular vote for the State Hluttaw, with only forty-nine per cent of all the valid votes (SEDI 2015). At the constituency level, the NLD won in Thandwe District, the southern-most part of the state, while the ANP won most seats and got the largest proportion of votes in Kyaukphyu District, had landslide wins in every seat in Sittwe District, and had a joint victory with the USDP in Maungdaw District.

In Thandwe, the NLD received the strongest support and won all the seats. In three townships in Thandwe and nearby Munaung township, all seats for both national and state levels went to the NLD. In the southern-most Gwa township, the NLD gained more than sixty per cent of the valid votes, which is on par with seats in other parts of the country. However, Gwa was the only Rakhine township where the NLD received the majority vote. In Thandwe, Toungup, and Munaung townships, the NLD got the highest vote, but not the majority. In Munaung Constituency (1) for the State Hluttaw, the NLD defeated the ANP's president, Dr Aye Maung. Despite his high profile, Aye Maung did not win more than twenty-eight per cent of the votes in Munaung. From a historical perspective, the NLD also won with significant majorities in these townships in the 1990 election. These southern townships were also the only places in Rakhine State that Daw Aung San Suu Kyi visited during the 2015 election campaign amid the controversies around her response (or non-response) to the communal conflicts in the state.

In other townships in Kyaukpyu District, namely Kyaukpyu, Ramree, and Ann, the ANP received the highest proportion of votes but not the majority. The ANP won all seats for the national and state assemblies in these two townships, except the State Ann Constituency (1). This seat was won by USDP, for the former chief minister, General Maung Maung Ohn. In the 1990 election, the NLD won all the seats for Kyaukpyu District.

The ANP received a majority of votes in all seats in Sittwe District, except in Myebon Constituency (1) and Ponnagyun Constituency (2) for the State Hluttaw. The Sittwe Constituency (2) was also an exception, since the ANP did not field a candidate but two independents who claimed to have a close association with it received the most votes. In Rathaedaung, Mrauk-U, Pauktaw, Minbya, and Kyauktaw townships, the ANP achieved resounding victories with its share of votes being more than sixty per cent.

In northern Maungdaw district, with the vast majority of residents excluded from voting, the ANP and USDP shared votes and seats. While township-wide seats for Pyithu Hluttaw went to the ANP, the USDP gained one seat for Amyotha Hlutaw from Maungdaw, and two out of four State Hluttaw seats.

In constituencies in these northern townships, the USDP did better than the NLD in terms of votes. These constituencies were among the few where the NLD only gained a small proportion of votes, less than ten per cent. Out of 168 Amyotha Hluttaw seats, the NLD received less than ten per cent in only eight constituencies, and seven of those were in northern Rakhine State[5]. Out of 323 Pyithu Hluttaw seats, the NLD got less than ten per cent of votes in only ten seats. Eight were in Rakhine State. Out of 630 State or Region Hluttaws, the NLD did not gain more than ten per cent of the votes in 34 seats; 16 were from the northern townships in Rakhine State. The electoral results showed that constituencies in northern parts of Rakhine State rejected the NLD.

Buddhist nationalism and anti-Muslim sentiment played a key role in the way people of Buthidaung and Maungdaw voted. The minority Buddhist communities in these townships, which in 2015 were the voting majority, supported either the USDP or ANP. For example, in Buthidaung constituency for the Pyithu Hluttaw, the ANP gained 46 per cent, while the USDP got 40 per cent. The Buddhist communities in Buthidaung and Maungdaw consisted of not just Rakhine people, but also a large number of NaTaLa model villages occupied by military veterans and ethnic minority groups. Detailed voter backgrounds are not available, but it is likely that most of their votes went to the USDP, probably with support from a small proportion of the Muslim community still entitled to vote, delivering it three seats from this district.

In Sittwe District, the exclusion of white-card holders and Rakhine ethnic nationalism created landslide wins for the ANP, gaining an average of sixty-seven per cent of votes. Ethnic nationalism has always been strong in this district of ancient Arakanese monuments and the historic capital of the Arakanese kingdom. The Mahamuni Pagoda, which was considered central in Rakhine ethnic history, was located in Kyauktaw township. The Rakhine people experience Rakhine ethnic nationalism, centred on the historical glory of independent Arakan, in this district in a physically real sense. With this strength of ethnic nationalism, Rakhine ethnic parties have always done well in these townships. The scale of the ANP landslide win here was based firmly on ethnic appeals and communal antagonism, with Muslim people excluded from voting.

Kyaukpyu District also demonstrated the role Buddhist nationalism played in the 2015 elections in Rakhine State. Being at the epicentre of the 2012 communal conflict, the Buddhist Rakhine constituency would not view the NLD favourably. At the same time, people from Kyaukpyu District were given policy alternatives between the ANP, which promised a new conception of governance and development policy, and the USDP, which had not achieved any substantial improvements in these people's lives over the previous five years. Centred on the Shwe Gas project and Kyaukpyu Special Economic Zone activities, the ANP's ethno-nationalist argument of direct benefits for the local people from these mega-projects resonated strongly.

However, ethnic nationalism and Buddhist nationalism failed to get traction in Thandwe District and Munaung township. Historically, Rakhine ethnic nationalism has not been significant in these townships. In the 2010 election, the RNDP did not field any candidates in these constituencies, and in 1990, the NLD won all of these seats. As both Thandwe and Toungup were sites of communal conflict, Buddhist nationalist concerns would have been significant in these constituencies. However, the Buddhist-nationalist agenda against the NLD did not have as strong an impact as in the seats of Meiktila township in Mandalay Region, which went against the NLD and to the USDP (Maung Zaw 2015). In Thandwe District, the NLD's call for political change won out over the Buddhist nationalist calls against Daw Aung San Suu Kyi and the ANP's ethno-nationalist claim on Rakhine ethnicity.

In these townships, three-cornered contests between the ANP, USDP, and NLD occurred as all of them gained more than twenty but less than forty-four per cent, except in Gwa township. While a majority of the people in these townships would be identified as Rakhine, their ethnicity had not automatically translated to ethnic-nationalist aspirations and votes for the ANP. Although there are possibilities that local and personal issues disadvantaged the ANP, such as its choice of candidates or disorganized election campaigns in these townships, these cannot fully account for the fact that in all four southern townships it gained less than thirty per cent of the valid votes.[6] Contrasting the results here to the ANP's share of more than sixty-seven per cent of votes in Sittwe District, a fault line based on ethno-nationalism clearly exists between the northern and southern townships of the state. Despite shared ethnicity, the voting patterns in these townships show that the political sentiments of the Rakhine ethnic group are, in fact, deeply divided.

ANP AS THE BUDDHIST–NATIONALIST ALTERNATIVE

The NLD election victory nationwide surprised MaBaTha leaders, who had openly called for lay supporters not to vote for the NLD (Vogt and Khin Su Wai 2015). Since Myanmar monks are not allowed to vote (or participate formally in politics), MaBaTha office holders did not participate in the election. They could only persuade the lay people to vote for those who would champion their Buddhist-nationalist aspirations.

The central premise of MaBaTha's Buddhist nationalism is that Buddhism in Myanmar is under threat from a Muslim takeover, and the Buddhist community and the government must defend the religion and nation (Walton and Hayward 2014). While this position rests on the fear of Islam, MaBaTha arguments are articulated in terms of cosmological imageries embedded in Buddhist morality, juxtaposed with simplistic readings of global and regional terrorist events (Gravers 2015). However, the articulation of Buddhist morality is not only limited to the communal arguments championed by MaBaTha. Most Myanmar Buddhists would also view other socio-political issues through the lens of personal morality. Gravers points out that in fact "violence, corruption, drugs, gambling, prostitution, and socio-economic decline are seen as problems that can only be repaired by new moral subjects (and leaders) who are able to uproot their moral defilements" (2013, p. 48). From the perspective of Burmese Buddhists, the notion of Buddhist morality is not just about the defence of the religion from other religions, but also about how socio-economic reforms should be conducted.

The ruling party, the USDP, had failed in presenting itself as credible on socio-economic reforms by the standards of Buddhist morality. It had pitched for re-election citing its reform credentials (Barron and Swan Ye

Htut 2015). The USDP government did initiate a large number of reforms, ranging from the peace process, expansion of media freedom to reforms in economic and administrative policies (Pedersen 2015; Tin Maung Maung Than 2014). While there were initial positive reactions to these reforms, none of the main problems relevant to people's everyday lives abated. More importantly, the USDP government was unable to address the corruption, cronyism, and associated conspicuous wealth of its former and current members. Impunity of illicit businesses thriving in Myanmar with the alleged blessing of the retired or existing military and government officials sustained the public distrust of the previous military government and the military-backed USDP administration. This failure led the general public to view the USDP as morally bankrupt. Despite some positive views on the presidency of U Thein Sein, the USDP as a whole did not seem to Myanmar's general public to have any moral authority to take the country forward, remove injustices, and resolve socio-economic problems. Therefore, when the Buddhist-nationalist leaders urged Myanmar's Buddhist majority to back the USDP in the interest of morality, their call contradicted the popular understanding of the USDP as lacking such moral authority. The USDP, even under the relatively popular Thein Sein, was not a viable alternative to the NLD. The NLD's overall victory indicated "most voters' desire for overall political change [being] ranked higher than their concerns about religious issues" (Walton 2015).

In Rakhine State, the ANP offered an alternative to the NLD along ethno-nationalist and religious lines, and in a context that did not exist in most other parts of Myanmar. Rakhine ethno-nationalism provided the ANP with an alternative electoral platform based on Rakhine ethnicity and their communal concerns. However, if we consider the ANP case simply as an exception to the national trend, we run the risk of under-emphasizing the roles that ethnicity and religion continue to play in Myanmar politics more generally, and miss the complexity of ethnicity in the seemingly homogeneous Rakhine community. Over-emphasis on ethnicity and Buddhist nationalism before the election resulted in expectations of their influence that were not well founded, but the post-election wisdom on Myanmar should not simply discount them. Both religion and ethnicity remain salient to Myanmar politics, not only in Rakhine State but in other parts of the country as well.

The electoral strength of the ANP and USDP in Rakhine's southern townships could be an indication of the communal concerns that MaBaTha promoted as being relevant in Myanmar. However, it also indicates that the MaBaTha-backed USDP was not a genuine alternative to the NLD, especially when the whole of Myanmar is aching for change. The NLD victory, despite MaBaTha's rejection, does mean the influences of Buddhist nationalism have dissipated somewhat in Myanmar. Nevertheless, communally focused anti-Muslim sentiment remains important among Buddhists (Walton 2015). The influence of Buddhist nationalism on Myanmar's social and economic life will still need to be factored into any comprehensive analysis of the country's politics for the foreseeable future.

Ethnic nationalism takes many shapes in Myanmar's politics, but most observers have focused primarily on the role of armed organizations (Maung-Thawnghmung 2011). While people who identify as non-Burman ethnic nationalities may not have voted for their ethnic parties, ethnicity remains an important identity aspect and pertinent in other forms, such as cultural, development, or rights organizations.[7] Despite the current weakness of many ethnic parties in the formal assemblies, their aspirations remain relevant to the ethnic minorities (Dolan 2015).

Ultimately the ANP will have very limited opportunities to influence political change and policy institutions in Myanmar. Also, it still faces internal political divisions. In addition to the divide based on support for ethno-nationalism among the Rakhine community, the ANP needs to overcome potential schisms based on personal, positional, and ideological differences. A specific concern is that if the ANP is marginalized in the Rakhine State development agenda despite its strong electoral showing, it could lead to the ANP focusing further on the communal aspects of Rakhine ethno-nationalism, thereby exacerbating existing communal antagonism.

Table 9.1. Percentage votes for main parties for Pyithu Hluttaw in Rakhine State

Constituency		ANP	NLD	USDP	Others
Maungdaw District					
	Maungdaw	51.7	4.7	43.6	N/A
	Buthidaung	45.5	2.7	39.7	12.2
Sittwe District					
	Kyawtaw	68.0	6.9	20.6	4.4
	Rathaedaung	79.5	3.3	14.9	2.4
	Ponnagyun	59.1	14.4	18.7	7.8
	Mrauk-U	75.6	3.8	10.9	9.7
	Pauktaw	73.6	2.7	15.3	8.4
	Sittwe	67.0	3.3	25.6	4.1
	Minbya	62.1	5.8	22.2	9.9
	Myebon	50.8	11.8	27.4	10.1
Kyaukphyu District					
	Kyaukpyu	45.4	13.3	23.5	17.9
	Ramree	44.6	15.4	33.4	6.7
	Ann	29.3	25.9	30.4	14.4
	Munaung	21.8	43.7	28.1	6.4
Thandwe District					
	Thandwae	28.0	37.0	26.1	8.9
	Tungup	26.7	41.6	23.7	8.0
	Gwa	10.7	62.7	21.3	5.2

Ethnicity and Buddhist nationalism in the 2015 Rakhine State election

Table 9.2. Percentage votes for main parties for Amyotha Hluttaw in Rakhine State

Constituency and towns*	ANP	USDP	NLD	Others
Rakhine 7 Maungdaw1	38.8	51.2	5.9	4.1
Rakhine 8 Maungdaw2	58.5	35.4	6.1	N/A
Rakhine 9 Buthidaung	44.7	38.9	6.2	10.2
Rakhine 3 Kyauktaw	67.0	15.6	10.0	7.3
Rakhine 6 Rathedaung, Ponnagyun	60.4	24.1	9.3	6.2
Rakhine 2 Mrauk-U	70.0	13.7	3.6	12.7
Rakhine 5 Pauktaw, Myebon	69.0	17.2	N/A	13.8
Rakhine 1 Sittwe	68.2	21.5	3.1	7.2
Rakhine 4 Minbya	71.2	12.0	3.3	13.5
Rakhine 10 Kyaukphyu, Munaung	38.1	24.7	25.9	11.4
Rakhine 11 Ramree, Ann	43.8	32.4	23.8	N/A
Rakhine 12 Thandwe District	23.5	23.6	44.5	8.4

* Information on townships covered by Amyotha Hluttaw Constituency sourced from *Myanmar Times* <http://www.mmtimes.com/images/mte/2015/di180/amyotha-2015-complete-large.jpg>.

Table 9.3. Percentage votes for main parties for the State Hluttaw in Rakhine State

Constituency	ANP	NLD	USDP	Others
Maungdaw 1	38.7	4.6	51.1	5.6
Maungdaw 2	61.5	N/A	38.5	N/A
Buthidaung 1	22.3	4.6	49.0	24.1
Buthidaung 2	77.9	3.3	18.9	N/A
Kyauktaw 1	63.9	7.0	13.6	15.6
Kyauktaw 2	65.9	4.1	19.0	11.0
Rathaedaung 1	74.6	2.4	17.6	5.4
Rathaedaung 2	62.1	2.3	22.2	13.5
Ponnagyun 1	63.6	8.5	15.9	12.0
Ponnagyun 2	44.1	13.4	14.3	28.1
Mrauk-U 1	75.9	4.7	14.1	5.3
Mrauk-U 2	73.9	5.3	13.1	7.7
Pauktaw 1	66.3	1.9	12.6	19.1
Pauktaw 2	69.3	1.5	10.8	18.4
Sittway 1	66.0	2.3	23.1	8.6
Sittway 2	39.7	3.2	27.5	29.5
Minbya 1	68.7	N/A	19.6	11.7
Minbya 2	51.0	6.5	36.1	6.4
Myebon 1	49.2	N/A	22.9	27.9
Myebon 2	50.6	14.0	27.3	8.1
Kyaukpyu 1	43.1	17.3	17.9	21.7
Kyaukphyu 2	41.5	12.1	29.2	17.1
Ramree 1	47.8	17.0	29.4	5.8
Ramree 2	45.0	16.9	32.4	5.7
Ann 1	12.8	34.0	38.5	14.6
Ann 2	47.3	16.1	24.7	11.9
Munaung 1	29.3	36.1	27.2	7.5
Munaung 2	23.5	40.4	33.4	2.7
Thandwae 1	28.7	34.1	22.3	14.9
Thandwae 2	21.1	36.1	28.6	14.2
Tungup 1	28.4	37.7	21.5	12.4
Tungup 2	23.4	43.9	26.0	6.7
Gwa 1	12.8	62.8	20.9	3.5
Gwa 2	9.3	63.0	20.5	7.1

Notes

1. Rakhine State has four districts consisting of seventeen townships: the southernmost Thandwe District has three, namely Gwa, Thandwe, and Taungup; Kyaukpyu District towards the north has four, Munaung, Ramree, Kyaukpyu, and Ann; Sittwe District has eight, Sittwe, Ponnagyun, Mrauk-U, Kyauktaw, Minbya, Myebon, Pauktaw, and Rathedaung, and the northernmost Maungdaw District at the Bangladesh border has Maungdaw and Buthidaung.
2. Source: MyanmarElections.org 2010 Myanmar elections: Elections Database http://myanmarelections.org/2010_old/
3. U Oo Tha Tun died in August 1990 in Sittwe Prison.
4. The Rakhine State National Force Party was deemed an ally of USDP and its leader had a background with the National Unity Party, the 1990s junta-backed political party. However, individuals involved in the Arakan Patriotic Party generally had opposition backgrounds and were Arakanese activists. Its leader, U Maung Maung Saw, was a painter with a national profile (Zon Pann Pwint 2013). U Maung Maung Saw was involved in the All Arakan Students and Youth Congress in the early 2000s and other activism against the junta in later years.
5. The NLD did not field a candidate for Constituency 5 covering Pauktaw and Myebon townships.
6. The ANP got 29.6 per cent for the State Hluttaw, 29.5 per cent for Pyithu Hluttaw but only 23.6 per cent in the Constituency 12 covering the whole Thandwe District, but did better with around 40 per cent in Kyaukpyu District (SEDI 2015).
7. For discussion, see Welsh and Huang, this volume.

References

Barron, Laignee and Swan Ye Htut. "USDP: We Brought Democracy to Myanmar". *Myanmar Times*, 29 September 2015. <http://www.mmtimes.com/index.php/national-news/16726-usdp-we-brought-democracy-to-myanmar.html>. Accessed 17 January 2016.

Berliner, Tom. "Myanmar Election: Five Things You Should Know". Overseas Development Institute, 5 November 2015. < http://www.odi.org/comment/10045-myanmar-election-2015-democracy-aung-san-suu-kyi-rohingya>. Accessed 17 January 2016.

Burke, Adam. "Why Didn't Ethnic Parties Do Better in Myanmar's Elections?" *New Mandala Inquirer#2*, 2015, < http://asiapacific.anu.edu.au/newmandala>. Accessed 19 January 2016.

Burma News International. "Hobson's Choice: Burma's 2010 Elections". *Burma News*

International, 2011. <http://www.burmalibrary.org/docs11/HobsonsChoice-Burmas-2010-Elections-BNI-red.pdf>. Accessed 17 January 2016.

de Mersan, Alexandra. 2015. "The 2010 Election and the Making of a Parliamentary Representative". In *Metamorphosis: Studies in Social and Political Change in Myanmar*, edited by Renaud Egreteau and François Robinne. Singapore: NUS Press, 2015, pp. 43–68.

Dolan, Richard. "Keeping Afloat After the 'Red Wave'". *New Mandala: Myanmar Votes 2015*, 27 November 2015. <http://asiapacific.anu.edu.au/newmandala/2015/11/27/keeping-afloat-after-the-red-wave/>. Accessed 21 January 2016.

Ei Ei Toe Lwin. "Rakhine Parties Discuss Possible Merger". *Myanmar Times*, 20 September 2012. <http://www.mmtimes.com/index.php/national-news/1647-rakhine-parties-discuss-possible-merger.html>. Accessed 17 January 2016.

———. "Election Commission Rejects Muslim Candidates En Masse". *Myanmar Times*, 1 September 2015. <http://www.mmtimes.com/index.php/national-news/16240-election-commission-rejects-muslim-candidates-en-masse.html>. Accessed 28 January 2016.

Eleven Myanmar. "ANP Boss Plays Ethnic Card". *Eleven Myanmar*, 1 November 2015. <http://www.elevenmyanmar.com/politics/anp-boss-plays-ethnic-card>. Accessed 6 January 2016.

Gravers, Mikael. "Spiritual Politics, Political Religion and Religious Freedom in Burma". *Review of Faith & International Affairs* 11, no. 2 (2013): 46–54.

———. "Anti-Muslim Buddhist Nationalism in Burma and Sri Lanka: Religious Violence and Globalized Imaginaries of Endangered Identities". *Contemporary Buddhism* 16, no. 1 (2015): 1–27.

Hindstrom, Hanna. "NLD Blocked Muslim Candidates to Appease Ma Ba Tha". *Irrawaddy*, 31 August 2015. <http://www.irrawaddy.com/election/news/nld-blocked-muslim-candidates-to-appease-ma-ba-tha-party-member>. Accessed 16 January 2016.

Hnin Yadana Zaw and Antoni Soldkowski. "Myanmar Radical Monk Endorses Ruling Party in Election, Raps Opposition". *Reuters*, 4 October 2015. <http://www.reuters.com/article/us-myanmar-politics-idUSKCN0RY08I20151004>. Accessed 16 January 2016.

Htoo Thant. "NLD Leader Hails Constitution Petition's Five Million Signatures". *Myanmar Times*, 9 August 2014. <http://www.mmtimes.com/index.php/national-news/11278-nld-leader-hails-petition-result-as-unprecedented-in-myanmar.html>. Accessed 15 January 2016.

Htoo Thant and Pyae Thet Phyo. "Six-way Talks Set for April 10 After Speaker Meets Parties". *Myanmar Times*, 7 April 2015. <http://www.mmtimes.com/index.php/national-news/13969-six-way-talks-set-for-april-10-after-speaker-meets-parties.html>. Accessed 15 January 2016.

International Crisis Group (ICG). *The Dark Side of Transition: Violence Against Muslims in Myanmar*. Brussels: ICG, 2013.
———. *The Myanmar Elections: Results and Implications*. Brussels: ICG, 2015a.
———. *Myanmar's Electoral Landscape*. Brussels: ICG, 2015b.
Kipgen, Nehginpao. "Conflict in Rakhine State in Myanmar: Rohingya Muslims' Conundrum". *Journal of Muslim Minority Affairs* 33, no. 2 (2013): 298–310.
Kyaw San Wai and Naoko Kumada. "Ethnicity and Myanmar's Elections". In *RSIS Commentary*. Singapore: S Rajaratnam School of International Studies, 2015.
Leider, Jacques. "Forging Buddhist Credentials as a Tool of Legitimacy and Ethnic Identity: A Study of Arakan's Subjection in Nineteenth-Century Burma". *Journal of the Economic and Social History of the Orient* 51 (2008): 409-59.
———. "Relics, Statues, and Predictions: Interpreting an Apocryphal Sermon of Lord Buddha in Arakan". *Asian Ethnology* 68, no. 2 (2009): 333–64.
Long, Kayleigh. "In Sittwe, An Independent Candidate in Name Only Tells of a Split Within His Party". *Myanmar Times*, 3 November 2015, (2015a). <http://www.mmtimes.com/index.php/national-news/17332-in-sittwe-an-independent-candidate-in-name-only-tells-of-a-split-within-his-party.html>. Accessed 3 January 2016.
———. "Northern Rakhine Facing Major Political Shake-up". *Myanmar Times*, 15 September 2015, (2015b). <http://www.mmtimes.com/index.php/national-news/16481-northern-rakhine-facing-major-political-shake-up.html>. Accessed 5 January 2016.
Lun Min Mang. "Former White-card Holders Cut from Rakhine Voter Lists". *Myanmar Times*, 24 June, 2015. <http://www.mmtimes.com/index.php/national-news/15191-former-white-card-holders-cut-from-rakhine-voter-lists.html>. Accessed 19 January 2016.
Maung Zaw. "Communal Violence Haunts Meiktila Vote". *Myanmar Times* 12 November 2015. <http://www.mmtimes.com/index.php/national-news/17584-communal-violence-haunts-meiktila-vote.html>. Accessed 16 January 2016.
Maung-Thawnghmung, Ardeth. *Beyond Armed Resistance: Ethnonational Politics in Burma*. Washington: East-West Center, 2011.
Medail, Cecile. "Ethnic Conflict and the Vote". *New Mandala: Myanmar Votes 2015*, 7 November 2015. < http://asiapacific.anu.edu.au/newmandala/2015/11/07/ethnic-conflict-and-the-vote/>. Accessed 21 January 2016.
Min Zin. "Anti-Muslim Violence in Burma: Why Now?" *Social Research* 82, no. 2 (2015): 375–97.
Mratt Kyaw Thu. "Rakhine National Party in 'Chaos'". *Myanmar Times*, 26 June 2015. <http://www.mmtimes.com/index.php/national-news/15221-rakhine-national-party-in-chaos.html>. Accessed 4 January 2016.
Narinjara News. "New Political Party Formed in Arakan State". *Narinjara News*

13 March 2015 <http://www.bnionline.net/news/arakan-state/item/425-new-political-party-formed-in-arakan-state.html>. Accessed 4 January 2016.

Nguyen, Phuong. "Myanmar's Electoral Landscape Vibrant, But Fraught with Uncertainties". *PacNet*. Hawaii: Center for Strategic and International Studies, 2015.

O'Toole, Bill. "How the USDP Went from Courting to Spurning Rakhine State's Muslims". *Myanmar Times*, 3 November 2014. <http://www.mmtimes.com/index.php/national-news/12150-how-the-usdp-went-from-courting-to-spurning-rakhine-state-s-muslims.html>. Accessed 28 January 2016.

Pedersen, Morten B. "Myanmar in 2014: Tacking Against the Wind". *Southeast Asian Affairs* 2015, no.1 (2015): 223–45.

Samet, Oren. "The Explosive Politics of Voting Rights in Myanmar". *The Diplomat*, 4 March 2015. <http://thediplomat.com/2015/03/the-explosive-politics-of-voting-rights-in-myanmar/>. Accessed 1 January 2016.

Social and Economic Development Initiative (SEDI). "2015 Elections in Rakhine State: A Statistical Analysis". *SEDI Occasional Paper*. Sittwe: SEDI, 2015.

Tin Maung Maung Than. "Myanmar in 2013: At the Halfway Mark". *Asian Survey* 54, no. 1 (2014): 22–29.

Transnational Institute (TNI). "The 2015 General Election in Myanmar: What Now for Ethnic Politics?" Myanmar Policy Briefing No 17. Amsterdam: TNI, 2015.

Vogt, R.J. and Khin Su Wai. "U Wirathu 'Surprised' by Strong NLD Victory". *Myanmar Times*, 12 November 2015. <http://www.mmtimes.com/index.php/national-news/17586-u-wirathu-surprised-by-strong-nld-victory.html>. Accessed 16 January 2016.

Walton, Matthew J. "The Post-election Future of Buddhist Nationalism in Myanmar". *East Asia Forum*, 19 November 2015. <http://www.eastasiaforum.org/2015/11/19/the-post-election-future-of-buddhist-nationalism-in-myanmar/>. Accessed 19 January 2016.

Walton, Matthew J. and Susan Hayward. *Contesting Buddhist Narratives: Democratization, Nationalism, and Communal Violence in Myanmar*. Vol. 71, East-West Center Policy Studies. Honolulu: East-West Center, 2014.

Ware, Anthony. "Secessionist Aspects to the Buddhist-Muslim sectarian Conflict in Rakhine State, Myanmar". In *Territorial Separatism in Global Politics*, edited by Damien Kingsbury and Costas Laoutides. Milton Park: Routledge, 2015.

Yen Snaing. "NLD Expels 20,000 White Card Holders From Party". *Irrawaddy*, 17 March 2015. <http://www.irrawaddy.com/election/news/nld-expels-20000-white-card-holders-from-party>. Accessed 16 January 2016.

Zon Pann Pwint. "Portraits of the Peacemakers of Myanmar". *Myanmar Times*, 4 August 2013. <http://www.mmtimes.com/index.php/lifestyle/7687-portraits-of-the-peacemakers-of-myanmar.html>. Accessed 5 January 2016.

10

THE HLUTTAW AND CONFLICTS IN MYANMAR

Chit Win

In the five years from when its transition from a military regime began in 2011, Myanmar faced a number of conflicts old and new that had profound influence on the breadth and depth of the transition. The Myitsone dam crisis and subsequent suspension of the project in 2011 changed the way the international community saw the transition (Skidmore and Wilson 2012, p. 7). On the other hand, communal violence in Rakhine State and in several parts of Myanmar in 2012 was portrayed as a setback at a time when reforms were bringing high hopes to the future of Myanmar (Wilson 2014, p. 13). Subsequently, the Letpadaung copper mine dispute and clashes with the police and protesters in 2013; land-grabbing disputes between government agencies, the military, and the local people in 2013; clashes between the Constitutional Tribunal of the Union (CTU) and the legislature on the status of the legislative commissions in 2012; and the student movement on educational bill amendments that turned violent in 2015 were obvious examples of conflicts that have had serious impacts on the course of reforms.

Myanmar's legislature, the Hluttaw, was involved in accommodating these transitional conflicts and its effectiveness and assertiveness were not always the same.[1] For instance, its involvement in the ethnic conflict and the peace negotiations was more ceremonial than crucial (Ei Ei Toe Lwin 2013). Next, the Hluttaw was mostly silent on the communal violence in Rakhine State (Ei Ei Toe Lwin 2014a). While it was less responsive to violent clashes like the Letpadaung copper mine conflict, the legislature was quick to flex its muscles against the CTU when the latter ruled against the legislature (Nardi 2012). Moreover, while the government showed signs of compromise with the students on the amendments to the national education bill, the Hluttaw was firm in its process, and rejected the deadline set by the student movement to amend the law (Htoo Thant and Mratt Kyaw Thu 2015). In land-grabbing disputes, the legislature was proactive and had substantial achievements (Thiri Min Tun 2012).

Each of the conflicts was different in nature and therefore required a different legislative response. Some were long-standing conflicts such as the peace process, while some were new, as in the case of communal violence. Some were fast moving as in the case of Letpadaung copper mine conflict, while some encountered many bureaucratic hurdles as in the case of land-grabbing conflicts. Therefore, the legislature's response and its influence were understandably different in each case.

Contributing to a broader literature with empirical evidence from Myanmar, this chapter attempts to understand the role of the legislature in conflict resolution by looking at the Hluttaw's response to major issues and conflicts during its first term (2011–16). In order to better capture its characteristics, it looks at three different types of conflict mentioned above that can be regarded as important challenges in Myanmar's nascent transition. They are: (i) resource-based disputes; (ii) borderland conflicts and peace negotiations; and (iii) communal violence.

In each case study, I look at the assertiveness and effectiveness of the legislature and the type of legislative tools applied. In particular, I am interested in the use of conventional legislative tools such as consultation and dialogue among lawmakers and with stakeholders, and during legislative debates. The main goal of my chapter is neither to discuss legislative politics (including factional politics and clientelism) nor to compare specific legislative responses to these conflicts, but rather to extract empirical data from them in order to better understand the Hluttaw's institutional characteristics.

LEGISLATURES INSTITUTIONALIZE CONFLICTS

Legislatures are breeding grounds for conflicts, but institutionalize them so that they do not become violent (Olson 1994, p.7). Lawmakers from different parties and factions have different interests and policies towards national issues, and conflicts are part and parcel of the process in reaching a solution. Legislatures serve as shock absorbers to conflicts so they do not create unrest, instability, or violence. They are rule-based forums to transform differences into solutions accepted by all the stakeholders through accountable and transparent decision-making. Legislators representing various societies through their constituencies can reflect their views on equal footing inside the legislature. Because their performance is usually judged at the next election, they tend to be more responsive to the public than the executive, and are more sensitive to public sentiment, real or perceived. As people's representatives, legislature brings legitimacy (Norton 1990), and so do their conflict resolution efforts. However, the role of the legislature in conflict resolution is often overlooked because the executive and law-enforcement agencies are the ones dealing directly with conflicts. To make matters worse, legislatures in countries undergoing transition are usually developing countries that lack institutional capability to respond to conflict (Yace de Mel 2013, p.22).

There are several ways legislatures can directly or indirectly accommodate domestic political, economic, and social conflicts using legislative tools (Stapenhurst, O'Brien, and Johnston 2008, pp. 5–9). First of all, legislatures provide avenues for dialogue and consultation, which require interaction among legislators and respective stakeholders. Next, through their oversight function, legislatures can make government more accountable, thus reducing conflicts arising from executive incompetence. Legislatures can proactively prevent conflict by promulgating laws. On the other hand, legislatures can also exacerbate or create new conflicts.

Empirical evidence suggests the parliamentary role in conflict is mixed. There are examples of parliaments playing a pivotal role in managing conflicts. During peace talks in Sri Lanka in 1997, the ruling People's Alliance Party reached an agreement with the opposition United National Party to adopt a bipartisan approach and seek consensus to speak with one voice. During tension between Rwanda and Uganda in 2002, both sides were able to ease the tension through bilateral parliamentary visits, which helped to convey that the people of both countries did not want war. In

Australia, the parliament contributed to the reconciliation process with Aboriginal people by setting up the Council for Aboriginal Reconciliation in 2000 (O'Brien 2008, pp. 36–37). In Aceh, Indonesia, the regional parliament passed the Aceh Truth and Reconciliation bylaw, an historic step toward reconciliation in the province (Amnesty International 2014). On the other hand, parliaments have on occasion been responsible for escalating the intensity of conflict, such as in Rwanda in 1994, the Lebanese civil war during the 1970s and 1980s, Algerian unrest in 1990s, and the Ukrainian crisis in 2013, among others. In each of these cases, the conflicts arose from electoral resentment and the institutional arrangement of parliament, which gave an advantage to the majority, leaving minorities vulnerable.

MYANMAR'S LEGISLATURE

The establishment of the legislatures at the union and local levels in 2011 symbolized Myanmar's transition from a military to quasi-civilian rule. Myanmar was without a legislature for over two decades. Since then it has become an avenue for the people to address their issues and concerns through conventional legislative functions of representation, lawmaking, and oversight which people had not experienced for a generation. Asserting its autonomy with a non-partisan approach to oversight of the executive and with the inclusion since 2012 of the opposition figure Daw Aung San Suu Kyi as a legislator, the Hluttaw has become a symbol of Myanmar's transformation (Kean 2014, p. 65).

On the other hand, the Hluttaw faced a major institutional challenge while performing its functions. Institutionally, the legislature had serious constraints set by the 2008 Constitution. Firstly, the legislature had no check and balance mechanism on the military and it had little say on executive appointments.[2] The legislative oversight mechanism of the executive relied mainly on motions and questions raised during the plenary sessions. Secondly, the legislature had capacity constraints. Its members were new and so were the support staff, who received little or no training. Committees were still at their infancy and lacking technical competence. These issues were compounded by lack of facilities and services, such as offices and research services usually provided in established legislatures.

Christina Fink (2015, p. 327) has reflected on the work of Myanmar's legislature as supplementing the reform process despite its institutional constraints. She sketched the executive dominance in policymaking while the military took care of security affairs, including the borderland conflict. However, she argued that lawmakers used legislative tools at their disposal to fulfil their mandate and she attributed this better than expected accomplishment to the role of the speakers, political space for minority parties within tolerable boundaries inside the legislature, and the effective engagement by community-based organizations for giving input. Renaud Egreteau (2014, p. 60) accepted the positive role played by the Hluttaw with a cautious warning that lack of capacity, institutional constraints, and signs of emerging clientelist and patrimonial politics may undermine the "euphoric optimism" of the legislature in the long run.

THE HLUTTAW'S RESPONSE TO CONFLICTS

Resource-based disputes

During the transition one of the most contentious resource-based disputes affecting all the country was conflict that arose from land grabbing by the military, government agencies, and business companies. According to the government, from September 2013 to September 2014, there were 7,615 cases of land-grabbing disputes at its peak, covering over 122,300 hectares of land: comparable to the size of Hong Kong (President's Office 2014a). During the military regime, land grabbing was mostly carried out by the military to extend its bases and the government for various development projects. But because of increased business opportunities, coupled with a surge in foreign direct investment, the private sector led by business cronies became increasingly involved in land grabbing through formal and informal means (Woods 2014). At the same time, thanks to significant freedom of expression garnered during the transition, people started to express their grievances on their land being grabbed with less fear.

The land-grabbing issue was initially introduced into the legislature on 26 September 2011 by the Public Complaints and Petition Committee of the Amyotha Hluttaw after receiving an alarming number of complaints of land grabbing by private entities. The committee chair U Aung Nyein from the ruling USDP said in his speech, "Mishandling of local authorities, not abiding by the laws and lacking co-ordination has resulted in the loss of confidence in the government by the public. Therefore, it is about time that the government consider solving the land grabbing issues between farmers and private entrepreneurs" (Amyotha Hluttaw 2011). His speech truly reflected what had been happening on the ground as business firms' thirst for land increased.

The government was defensive on the issue, but promised to tackle it. The legislature decided to get involved strongly and formed an investigation commission on land grabbing when one of the Union Solidarity and Development Party (USDP) leaders took the initiative. U Tin Htut, chairman of the Farmers, Workers and Youth Affairs Committee of the Pyithu Hluttaw, raised a motion after receiving petitions from farmers (Pyidaungsu Hluttaw 2012). The legislature was non-partisan and it received a lot of attention with forty-six legislators debating the issue. A number of lawmakers took a proactive approach, liaising for their constituencies, while other lawmakers were passive and relied entirely on the commission.[3] The commission report was submitted to the president in seven parts from September 2013 to September 2014 (President's Office 2014b).

On 16 September 2013, soon after the submission of the first report on 20 August 2013, the president formed a Central Committee on Land Administration led by the Vice President Nyan Tun to solve land-grabbing issues. Public media was heavily involved in amplifying grievances. The issue received national attention on 4 February 2014 when police forcibly removed more than 1,000 families of Thamee Kalay village from Hlegu township in Yangon region because they resided on land owned by the military (DVB 2014). With mounting land-grabbing conflict, the Hluttaw investigation commission on land grabbing tabled a motion on 20 February 2014. Afterwards, the Speaker Thura U Shwe Mann urged the president to intervene and set a deadline to solve the crisis before the harvest season ended in September 2014 (Pyidaungsu Hluttaw 2014). The president responded immediately by requesting the legislators to cooperate with the Central Committee on Land Administration in order to solve the crisis effectively, and to be aware of the real situation rather than constantly pressuring the executive. Subsequently, on 30 April 2014, the president gave an interim report to the Hluttaw, claiming the government was doing its best to solve the land-grabbing crisis (President's Office 2014b), followed by opening of land administration offices across the country. On 19 December 2014, the government announced the status of almost

8,000 cases of land-grabbing complaints. A quarter of them (about 40,000 hectares or one-third of the land grabbed) was to be returned to the original owners, with another quarter mostly between private entities to be settled through judicial process (President's Office 2014a). In addition, the military decided to return to the farmers another 122,000 hectares of land that was grabbed but unused.

In a nutshell, the Hluttaw was non-partisan and persistent on the issue and it was led in this matter by a senior USDP figure. However, there were no consultations between lawmakers and the military representatives that make up twenty-five per cent of seats in the legislature, whose institution was responsible for massive land grabbing. Rather than effectively engaging affected constituencies, the representative function of the concerned lawmakers was limited to questions and motions in the debate. The support of the speaker was important in follow-up and putting pressure on the executive.

Borderland conflicts and peace negotiations

One of the symbols of Myanmar's transition has been the attempt at national reconciliation, in addition to political and economic liberalization. During his inaugural address on 31 March 2011, President U Thein Sein offered an olive branch to ethnic armed groups (EAGs). Afterwards, there were rounds of peace talks: eleven union-level and three state-level ceasefire agreements were signed with fourteen EAGs. In the meantime, a draft nationwide ceasefire agreement was negotiated between the Myanmar government represented by the Union Peacemaking Central Committee (UPCC) and its Working Committee (UPWC), and EAGs represented by the Nationwide Ceasefire Co-ordination Team (NCCT). After seven rounds of negotiation, both sides agreed to a single draft text for a nationwide ceasefire agreement. The next step was to initiate political dialogue. However, there were a number of major and minor setbacks, most notably in Kachin State in 2013 and in Kokang Self Administered Zone in 2015.

The legislature was keen to get involved in the peace process and was persistent in working for the peace process since its inception. But after an initial push, the role of the legislature diminished as the peace process mechanism began to function (see Su Mon Thazin Aung, this volume). There were altogether eight motions and nine questions raised to the Hluttaw, pushing the government to work harder on it. The Speaker Thura U Shwe

Mann called for the National Security and Defence Council, the highest executive body overseeing security affairs of the state, to coordinate on the peace process with the executive (Pyithu Hluttaw 2013). In its 2014–15 budget proposal, the executive was praised for allocating US$7 million for the peace process (Yen Snaing 2014). But it was the Hluttaw that had sought funding for the peace process a year earlier, squeezing it from unimportant projects (Pyidaungsu Hluttaw 2013).[4] There were extensive informal consultations between ethnic lawmakers and the military representatives, as both were involved directly or indirectly in the borderland conflict.[5]

While it was highly non-partisan and received most support from the speakers and lawmakers, the first motion on peace was rejected, for two reasons: (i) the Hluttaw overwhelmingly controlled by the USDP did not want to undermine its president who announced his peace initiative a few days later;[6] and (ii) the Hluttaw was reluctant to accept motions from non-USDP parties in the early days. Amid renewed conflict in Kachin State in 2013, the Hluttaw also adopted four motions on ending conflict in Kachin State but to no avail. In the meantime, the government formed the UPCC and UPWC on 19 May 2012. Prominent ethnic legislators from the ruling and ethnic parties were included as members (President's Office 2012).[7] On the other hand, Union Minister U Aung Min facilitated by the Myanmar Peace Centre (MPC) did most of the nitty-gritty work (see Su Mon Thazin Aung, this volume). Participation of ethnic legislators in the UPWC was largely ceremonial. The Hluttaw has its own peace committee but its involvement in the peace process was again notional rather than substantial.[8] As U Hkyet Hting Nan from the Amyotha Hluttaw explained:

> In the beginning, ethnic armed group representatives did not trust us and saw us as collaborators of the ruling party and its government. Though these perceptions are diminishing, we still have limitations in participating in the peace process. The government not the Hluttaw is leading the talks. But the Hluttaw is ultimately responsible for legitimizing the whole peace process. Therefore, I am happy to be part of it.[9]

While his presence legitimized the process, he seemed frustrated with his inability to influence the dialogue substantively, because there was no major role for a legislator to play. Most of the negotiations were dealt with directly by the military and the executive.

Ethnic legislators — except for a few prominent ones who had come from ethnic armed groups — were not confident in participating in the peace process. EAG members had direct or indirect connections with the legislators, especially from ethnic parties. Through them, they learned how the Hluttaw works, as explained by the Kayin legislator Mahn Aung Tin Myint:

> I am not in the peace committee and I don't know why. But I was able to explain our parliamentary experiences to my old colleagues [EAG members] when they visited Naypyitaw during the national census launching ceremony. The relationship between us [ethnic legislators] and ethic armed group members is tricky. We know each other very well but we have to play safe because we can breach the Unlawful Associations Act.[10]

The Hluttaw tried to use all available options to accommodate half-century long borderland conflicts and to get involved in the peace process. Conventional tools such as consultations among stakeholders, executive oversight, promulgation of laws, and budget scrutiny were used. Lawmakers were able to show themselves as role models, engaging in a rule-based forum where conflicts are institutionalized. Questions and motions were again used extensively to express the concerns of the legislature. But, as mentioned above, the role of the legislature was more of a legitimizing and supporting role than a mediating one.

Communal violence

While Myanmar was praised for its peaceful transition, it was disrupted by the communal violence in Rakhine State and subsequent violence across Myanmar from 2012 to 2014, which was regarded as a significant shift, if not setback in Myanmar's transition (ICG 2013). Sparked by a rape and murders in June 2012, it quickly escalated into a widespread communal conflict between Rakhine and Muslims (Bengali/Rohingya).[11] According to the Rakhine State government estimates, 192 people died and 6,614 homes were destroyed in eleven of the state's eighteen townships in 2012 alone (Rakhine Inquiry Commission 2012, p. 31). The violence was followed by numerous outbreaks of communal clashes in various parts of Myanmar, most notably in Meiktila where forty-four people were killed and 1,818 homes destroyed (Pyidaungsu Hluttaw 2013).

Unlike in the peace process, the role of the Hluttaw in tackling communal conflict was quite modest. The Hluttaw did not denounce these conflicts nor urge the government to take prompt actions. There were no formal consultations between Rakhine and Muslim legislators, nor with the public. Apart from validating the presidential decrees on the States of Emergency in Rakhine State and Meiktila, the Hluttaw's involvement was minimal, for three reasons: (i) the Hluttaw was slow to respond to the fast-moving nature of communal conflict compared to the executive, and its options were limited to consultations, oversight of the government, and law-making; (ii) it was an extremely sensitive issue and legislators did not want to be branded either as ultra-nationalists or Muslim sympathizers; and (iii) while it has tried its best to accommodate ethnic conflicts, the legislature was unprepared for this type of communal conflict based on religious lines. Only three Muslims sat in the Hluttaw. There are ad hoc committees for ethnic groups affairs, but not on religious minorities such as Christians and Muslims, which make up about eleven per cent of the total population (CSO 2012).

Though its involvement was weak, the Hluttaw was effective in preventing itself from becoming a source of conflict. After the Rakhine conflict, the legislature dealt with nine non-binding questions and five binding motions on communal violence.[12] Seven of these questions came from Rakhine Nationalities Development Party legislators and they were based on Rakhine resentment of Muslims. At the same time, none of the Muslim legislators raised any questions or motions in the legislature. Moreover, in the Rakhine State Hluttaw, four Muslims from Buthidaung and Maungdaw took long leave and quietly disappeared.[13] Next, the Hluttaw considered five motions on communal violence. Three were rejected citing their sensitivity and their potential to trigger more violence. One of the USDP motions was opposed by its own members.[14] Two were noted as requiring no action from the executive. According to an interview with an anonymous legislator, some of the motions were too sensitive and were rejected outright by the speakers. The legislature was careful not to escalate tension. A military legislator reflected on the atmosphere inside the legislature:

> The Hluttaw seemed quiet on communal conflict in Rakhine State. But it wasn't. Though we may have been silent in plenary sessions, there were a lot of informal discussions among us. Muslim legislators felt that everyone was against them. At the same time, Rakhine legislators felt that their questions and motions were rejected intentionally by the speakers. In reality, the speakers were conducting debates carefully so as not to become a source of conflict. And no one wanted to touch these issues publicly.[15]

In February 2014, the president requested the legislature to draft the controversial bills on religious conversion, interfaith marriage, population control, and polygamy, popularly known as the *myo-saunt-upade* (laws on protection of race and religion). Instead of drafting these bills, the legislature returned the ball back to the executive by suggesting that these bills be drafted by the respective government agencies and they submit them to the legislature. This was a smart move by the Speaker Thura Shwe Mann, because it prevented ultra-nationalist lawmakers and groups from influencing the drafting process.

The Hluttaw could have been involved proactively on the communal conflicts. There were avenues for dialogue between Rakhine and Muslim legislators, but they were never realized at a formal level. The legislators could have played a mediator role in the crisis, but instead they were even accused of escalating the crisis.[16] It was weak and ineffective in responding to conflict due to its sensitivity and constraints. At the very least, it was able to prevent itself from negatively influencing the conflicts by rejecting radical motions and toning down sensitive bills.

ANALYSING THE RESPONSE

These three case studies together reflect the characteristics of the Hluttaw in responding to various conflicts, and reveal its institutional strengths and weaknesses. As mentioned in the introduction, these conflicts differed from each other. Yet there were a number of approaches repeatedly taken by the legislature such as the non-partisan approach, the use of questions and motions, and the influence of the speakers. Whether in a transitional or established legislature and regardless of institutional constraints, lawmakers can play a crucial role in their societies and strengthen peace-building through consultation and mediation (Miall, Ramsbotham, and Woodhouse 2003, p. 216). And yet, Myanmar's legislature was not able to use its consultation mechanism effectively. There was no formal interaction between lawmakers and very little with concerned stakeholders.

Non-partisan legislature

One reason the Hluttaw spoke with one voice in responding to these three conflicts was the non-partisan nature of the legislature. In all three cases, the legislative motions received non-partisan support. On communal violence, the USDP party members rejected their party's own motion. In the first term of the Hluttaw, voting patterns were not based on party lines. This is because the USDP overwhelmingly controlled the Hluttaw, there was no eminent threat and in order to show the robustness and legitimacy of the Hluttaw, a non-partisan approach was encouraged. Unless it would fundamentally affect party interest, legislators were free to vote based on their own positions.[17] In some cases, legislative committee members from different parties even voted in a bloc.[18] The non-partisan nature of the legislature was relevant when dealing with the executive. However, the military supported the government's position on most issues, even when USDP lawmakers, whose own party was in power, voted against it.

Figure 10.1. represents the non-partisan nature of the legislature, taking motions as a proxy. Because of its numerical superiority, the USDP tabled more motions than non-USDP members. Despite its overwhelming control of the legislature, around one-third of motions rejected were from USDP.

Figure 10.1 Non-partisan legislature, 2011–14

The non-partisan nature of the Hluttaw can be taken as an institutional legacy of earlier parliaments. With bitter memories of the factional power struggle during the post-independence period of the 1950s and early 1960s, the new Myanmar legislature was careful not to be portrayed as divided, at least in the public eye. Furthermore, in order to legitimise the legislature, ethnic and minor parties including the opposition National League for Democracy (NLD) were represented inclusively in the legislative committees in accordance with their number of seats, even though it was not mandatory by law.¹⁹ Non-partisanship was achieved because: (i) the speakers had absolute power to command the direction of the legislature; (ii) the USDP had an overwhelming majority; and (iii) ethnic and minor parties allowed themselves to be co-opted by the USDP willingly and chose cooperation rather than confrontation, so they were able to build a certain degree of trust that they were all working for a common goal.²⁰

On the other hand, the non-partisan approach had its limits. It made some of the lawmakers lose interest and disengage themselves from their duties. Dissenting party voices were marginalized because of this approach and therefore it was harder for internal factional consultation, especially during communal conflicts where exchange of information was crucial among legislators.

But the legislature was not always non-partisan. When it came to party interest, it was undoubtedly divided. During the debate on the electoral system and the constitutional review, since the NLD and ethnic parties could not challenge the USDP in terms of numbers, some legislators boycotted the debate by taking leave, and some resigned from the electoral system review commission as a sign of protest (Ei Ei Toe Lwin 2014b).

Questions and motions as primary legislative tools

Another common characteristic exhibited from these three conflicts was the extensive use of questions and motions as legislative tools. Consultations within the legislature were not practised, other than in informal discussion during coffee breaks and in the corridors. A public hearing mechanism was activated only in 2015, during the student movement over a new national educational law, and on protection of race and religion bills. This was partly because the Hluttaw was new to this idea and there were no coordinating mechanisms among legislators other than administrative procedures within the legislature.

Moreover, when dealing with the ethnic armed leaders, legislators were hesitant to engage actively because they were perceived to be inferior to other actors and as newcomers to politics, while the former had decades of experience in their roles, and held guns. "No man is above the law but the gun is," a Kayin legislator from the Amyotha Hluttaw told me during my fieldwork in 2014. Furthermore, at the constituency level, legislators received no respect from local authorities, as they had no direct power, though this trend has been diminishing.²¹ Therefore, the main weapon of choice for the legislators was questions and motions, which they could table to the legislature subject to approval of the speaker. Figure 10.2 represents the frequency of the use of questions and motions from 2011 to 2014.

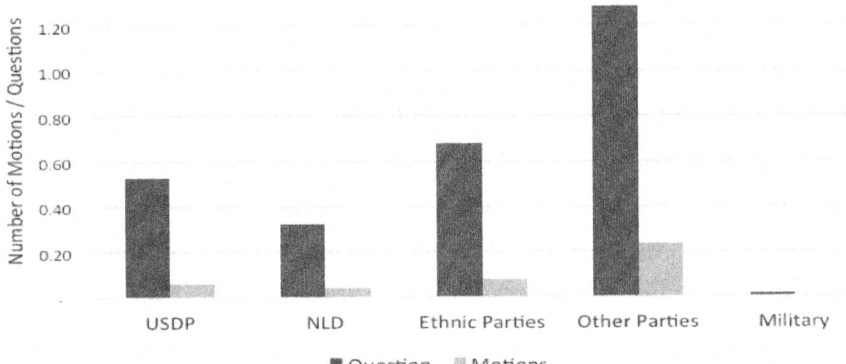

Figure 10.2. Questions and motions, 2011–14 (per session, per legislator)

Legislators usually started their attempts by raising questions, and tabled them as motions when they felt more confident. Questions were usually addressed to the executive for explanation and confirmation but they are not binding. A motion is a lot more difficult and takes more time to prepare than a question. It must pass a number of steps: approval from the speaker, approval from the legislature to be debated as a motion, and a vote passed as a motion. In addition, motions are regarded as legislative oversight of the executive and the latter is required to implement them, though there is no constitutional measure to force compliance. Because of over-reliance on questions and motions and because of the indirect nature of legislative tools (that is, through the executive), the legislature had little influence dealing with the conflict, as in the case of the peace process and communal violence. Moreover, on fast-moving issues like communal violence and the Letpadaung conflict, there is no way the legislature can react to the changing situation in real time. But because it can exert constitutional pressure on the executive, it has a strong oversight influence as seen in land-grabbing issues.

Other than these tools, public complaints and petitions proved to be the main sources of collecting information from the public. When speaking with the Public Complaints and Petition Committee of the Amyotha Hluttaw during my fieldwork in March 2014, I was told that the committee received five to ten complaints/petitions per week on average. Most came from Yangon and Mandalay and were mainly about unfair judicial verdicts in civil and criminal cases, and power abuse by local authorities.[22] The committee had no executive power to deal with them and it had to forward the complaints to the respective government agencies. However, the committee was effective in following up on these issues and could pressure the executive to respond to them.

Everything depends on the speakers

The speakers' absolute power is important in understanding the Hluttaw characteristics in responding to conflict. In established democracies, little importance is given to the role of the speaker.[23] The emphasis is on the leader of the ruling/majority party or the opposition/minority partly. But in Myanmar, the speaker has additional powers: (i) he can call for and adjourn plenary sessions at his own discretion; (ii) every motion and question needs his prior approval; (iii) his decision is final and cannot be protested; and (iv) he has control over the voting method.[24] Not only does he bring order, he also directs and controls the pace of the legislature. Thus, Myanmar's speakers are not just conductors, but also commanders.

The role of the speakers was prominent during communal violence, when they were able to control the legislature from making provocative speeches or even debating the issue. It was also the speakers who influenced the executive to expedite the bureaucratic process in tackling land-grabbing issues, and who were instrumental in confronting the executive by impeaching the CTU (Nardi 2012). While their powers were absolute, they were instrumental in resolving conflicts. For instance, through their shepherding, the nature of the debate on communal violence changed from making emotional speeches to finding solutions. During the Rakhine conflict the discussion had focused on either the Rakhine–Muslim dynamic or the necessity of ensuring rule of law and security in conflict-affected areas, but during the Meiktila violence, the debate was more on the lack of co-ordination between the parliament and the government and finding ways to improve the rule of law.

Institutional characteristics

The responsiveness and the effectiveness of a legislature to conflict reveals its institutional characteristics and its power. While the conventional functions of legislatures (representation, lawmaking, and oversight) are the same, each legislature is unique in a number of ways based on its historical legacy and political culture. As for Myanmar, it is institutionally different in two ways: (i) the presence of the military representatives and their veto power to any constitutional amendments; and, (ii) the inheritance from the past two post-independence legislatures.

The main difference between the current and previous parliaments of Myanmar (post-independence parliament of 1948–62 and one-party socialist era of 1974–88) is the presence of unelected military representation and the military veto to the constitutional amendment process. With memories of highly partisan and fierce power struggles between political factions in the post-independence parliamentary era that became a pretext for coups in Myanmar, everyone was careful not to offend each other personally or politically and non-partisan co-operation was encouraged from the beginning.[25] Therefore, I argue that the institutional design of Myanmar's legislature seeks to avoid chaos and disorder in the legislature, as witnessed during the post-independence parliament, by giving absolute power to the speakers and addressing frequent coup d'états by giving the role of constitutional defender to the military inside the legislature.

In addition, the current legislature has links with its two predecessors. When the constitution was discussed by the National Convention in the 1990s and 2000s, the government sought no technical cooperation from outside, nor was any offered. Learning from history was most effective. Interviews with State Constitution Drafting Commission staff suggest adherence to precedent was observed in codifying the 2008 Constitution.[26] Apart from adapting legislative procedures from the post-independence parliament, the new constitution also inherited arrangements from the socialist era.[27] Because the legislature at that time practised a single party system and there was no opposition party, questions and motions were directed to the government. Following this tradition, in the new Hluttaw, questions are directed to the government rather than the ruling party. In this way, the legislature itself became the opposition to the government. Therefore, the Hluttaw from 2011 to 2015 preferred dealing with the executive rather than consulting within the legislature.

CONCLUSION

The role of Myanmar's legislature in responding to conflicts was similar to its counterparts elsewhere in some aspects, but different in several ways. While legislatures are usually equipped with similar legislative tools of representation, executive oversight and lawmaking mechanisms, their institutional characteristics greatly shape the way they use these instruments. In Myanmar's case, lawmakers were reluctant to use their representative functions because these were new to them and institutionally not so favourable. But the Hluttaw's advantage came from its non-partisan approach, speaking with one voice and controlling itself so as not to be involved in exacerbating conflicts.

The Hluttaw has been hailed as a symbol of Myanmar's transition for its autonomy, inclusiveness, and its oversight of the executive. Haunted by the horrible memories of factionalism in the post-independence parliamentary system, the Hluttaw has tried to take a non-partisan approach as much as possible. This approach, combined with the socialist parliamentary style of the legislature questioning the executive, led the whole house to become an opposition to the executive. This made the house strong when encountering the executive, as in the case of the CTU and oversight of the executive.

All these characteristics of the legislature can be attributed to power entrusted to the reform-minded leaders of the legislature: the two speakers. The important role of the speakers affirmed the old tradition of Myanmar society where agency is more important than the institution. Because they had extraordinary power to significantly influence the legislature, they were able to operate skilfully. These institutional practices would no doubt be passed on to the next Hluttaw after the 2015 election. The new political arrangement would be a lot different than the first Hluttaw, as the NLD becomes the ruling party. Whether the new Hluttaw will try to inherit or reject institutional practices from its predecessor, such as the non-partisan nature of the Hluttaw, remains to be seen. Nonetheless, Myanmar's first legislature should be credited for its attempt to mediate conflicts regardless of its institutional constraints and transitional challenges.

Notes

1. Unless otherwise mentioned, the "legislature" in this chapter refers to the union level: Pyithu Hluttaw (People's Assembly), Amyotha Hluttaw (Nationalities Assembly) and joint sitting of these two assemblies known as Pyidaungsu Hluttaw (Union Assembly).
2. For more details on institutional constraints of Myanmar's legislature, see Williams (2014).
3. Interview with U Aung Zin, National Democratic Front legislator from Pyithu Hluttaw on 31 January 2014.
4. On 26 February 2013, at the Fourteenth Day of the Pyidaungsu Hluttaw Sixth Plenary Session, USDP lawmaker U Hla Swe proposed to revise the budget by giving an example of peace investment in Sri Lanka.
5. Interview with a Wa legislator from Pyithu Hluttaw on 26 March 2014.
6. Interview with a legislator from Pyithu Hluttaw on 17 February 2014.
7. There are eighteen ethnic legislators from Amyotha and Pyithu Hluttaw representing equally. Among them, eight were from USDP and the rest from ethnic parties.
8. The Pyithu Hluttaw has a fifteen-member National Races Affairs, Uplifting of Rural Livelihood and Internal Peace Implementation Committee and the Amyotha Hluttaw has a ten-member National Races Affairs, De-escalating Conflicts and Peace Process Committee.
9. Interview with U Hkyet Hting Nan, Kachin legislator from Amyotha Hluttaw, on 5 June 2015.
10. Interview with Mahn Aung Tin Myint, Kayin legislator from Amyotha Hluttaw on 28 February 2014. On the Unlawful Associations Act see Su Mon Thazin Aung, this volume.
11. Because of the politicized nature of the use of "Bengali" and "Rohingya", the author chooses to use the general term "Muslims".
12. Observations made from fourth to ninth plenary sessions of the Hluttaw, July 2012- March 2014.
13. Interview an RNDP legislator from Rakhine State Hluttaw on 13 March 2014.
14. On 13 August 2012, a Rakhine USDP legislator called for a motion to urge the government to prevent violence, illegal immigrants and to draft a strategy in the aftermath of communal violence in Rakhine State. A legislator from his own party challenged his motion. Later, he didn't receive enough support and his motion was rejected.
15. Interview with a military legislator from Amyotha Hluttaw on 11 February 2014.
16. During communal conflict in Thandwe, in Rakhine State, police arrested the local RNDP chairman.

17 Interview with an NLD legislator from Amyotha Hluttaw on 27 February 2014.
18 On 19 March 2014, when the Hluttaw debated a new electricity scheme, members of the Pyithu Hluttaw Committee on Investment and Industrial Development voted together as a bloc against a rate hike.
19 At the second plenary session of the Amyotha Hluttaw on 1 March 2011, the Speaker U Khin Aung Myint justified the allocation to the membership of legislative committees based on the party ratio, on geography and on the qualifications of the individual legislators.
20 Interview with a Kayin legislator from Pyithu Hluttaw on 1 February 2014.
21 Interview with an RNDP legislator from Rakhine State Hluttaw on 13 March 2014.
22 Based on my discussion with U Sein Tin Win, Speaker of Yangon Region Hluttaw on 4 July 2015, this was also true in state and region legislatures. For instance, the number of complaint letters received by the Yangon Region Hluttaw increased from eighty three in 2011 to almost six hundred in 2013 and 2014.
23 However, there are six possible ways where a speaker can influence the legislature through (i) administrative staff, (ii) allocation of resources and facilities such as staff, office space and equipment, (iii) assembly's schedule, (iv) interpreting procedural rules, (v) plenary session, and (vi) as an active party member (Bach 1999).
24 The Hluttaw rules allow the speaker to choose (i) electronic secret ballot; (ii) paper secret ballot; and (iii) voting by standing up. In addition, voice voting is widely used. Unlike other legislative institutions, Myanmar uses secret ballots. Voice voting is commonly used by the speaker for procedural matters. It is also used when the speaker wants to get it quickly endorsed without any opposition from the floor. Voting by standing up can also be intimidating especially if the speaker is in favour of the other positions to the member's preference. It is usually applied when there is an objection to the voice voting. And unless legislators really oppose a particular decision of the plenary, they would rarely stand up.
25 Interview with U Khin Aung Myint, Speaker of Amyotha Hluttaw on 6 July 2015.
26 See ICG (2009).
27 The constitutional amendment procedure, seating arrangement within the legislature, and fifteen-member legislative committees (each from seven states and regions plus a leader) are all taken from the 1974 Constitution.

References

Amnesty International. "Indonesia: Aceh Parliament Passes Truth Commission Bylaw". Amnesty International, 2014.

Amyotha Hluttaw. "Report of the Twenty Fifth Day of the Second Plenary Session of the First Amyotha Hluttaw (26 September 2011)". Naypyitaw, 2011.

Bach, Stanley. "The Office of the Speaker in Comparative Perspective". *Journal of Legislative Studies* 5, no. 3–4 (1999): 209–54.

Central Statistical Organization (CSO). "Statistical Yearbook 2011". Naypyitaw: Central Statistical Organization, 2012.

Democratic Voice of Burma (DVB). "Settlers Forcibly Evicted in Hlegu Township". *Democratic Voice of Burma*, 10 February 2014. <http://www.dvb.no/dvb-video/settlers-forced-out-of-homes-in-hlegu-myanmar-burma/37042>. Accessed 11 November 2015.

Egreteau, Renaud. "Emerging Patterns of Parliamentary Politics". In *Myanmar: The Dynamics of an Evolving Polity*, edited by David I. Steinberg. London: Lynne Rienner Publishers, 2014.

Ei Ei Toe Lwin. "Government Meets MPs to Talk Peace". *Myanmar Times*, 29 July 2013. <http://www.mmtimes.com/index.php/national-news/7627-government-meets-mps-to-talk-peace.html>. Accessed 11 November 2015.

———. "Hluttaw Stays Silent on Ethnic Conflicts". *Myanmar Times*, 18 August 2014a. <http://www.mmtimes.com/index.php/national-news/mandalay-upper-myanmar/11310-hluttaw-stays-silent-on-conflicts.html>. Accessed 11 November 2015.

———. "Speaker Seeks Middle Ground on Proportional Representation". *Myanmar Times*, 4 August 2014b. <http://www.mmtimes.com/index.php/in-depth/11267-speaker-seeks-middle-ground-on-proportional-representation.html>. Accessed 11 November 2015.

Fink, Christina. "Myanmar's Proactive National Legislature". *Social Research* 82, no. 2 (2015): 327–54.

Htoo Thant, and Mratt Kyaw Thu. "Lower House Rejects Students' Demand to Form Unions Freely". *Myanmar Times*, 8 April 2015. <http://www.mmtimes.com/index.php/national-news/13979-lower-house-rejects-students-demand-to-form-unions-freely.html>. Accessed 11 November 2015.

International Crisis Group (ICG). "Myanmar: Towards the Elections". *Asia Report*, Yangon / Brussels: International Crisis Group, 2009.

———. "The Dark Side of Transition: Violence against Muslims in Myanmar". *Asia Report*, Yangon / Brussels: International Crisis Group, 2013.

Kean, Thomas. "Myanmar's Parliament: From Scorn to Significance". In *Debating Democratization in Myanmar*, edited by Nick Cheesman, Nicholas Farrelly and Trevor Wilson. Singapore: Institute of Southeast Asian Studies, 2014.

Miall, Hugh, Oliver Ramsbotham, and Tom Woodhouse. *Contemporary Conflict Resolution: The Prevention, Management, and Transformation of Deadly Conflicts.* Cambridge: Polity, 2003.

Nardi, Dominic J. "After Impeachment, a Balancing Act". *Myanmar Times,* 1 October 2012. <http://www.mmtimes.com/index.php/national-news/2013-after-impeachment-a-balancing-act.html>. Accessed 11 November 2015.

Norton, Philip. "Legislatures". In *Legislatures,* edited by Philip Norton. Oxford: Oxford University Press, 1990.

O'Brien, Mitchell. "Making Parliament More Representative". In *Parliaments as Peacebuilders in Conflict-Affected Countries,* edited by Mitchell O'Brien, Rick Stapenhurst and Johnston Niall. Washington D.C.: World Bank, 2008.

Olson, David M. *Democratic Legislative Institutions: A Comparative View.* Armonk and New York: M. E. Sharpe, 1994.

President's Office. "Formation of Union Peacemaking Central Committee and Working Committee". Naypyitaw: President's Office, 18 May 2012.

———. "Stats Report on the Solving the People's Grievances on the Grabbing of Farm Lands and Other Lands". Naypyitaw: President's Office, 30 April 2014a.

———. "Press Release". Naypyitaw: President's Office, 19 December 2014b.

Pyidaungsu Hluttaw. "Report of the First Day of the Fourth Plenary Session of the First Pyidaungsu Hluttaw (4 July 2012)". Naypyitaw, 2012.

———. "Report of the Special Session of the First Pyidaungsu Hluttaw (20 May 2013)". Naypyitaw, 2013.

———. "Report of the 19th Day of the Ninth Plenary Session of the First Pyidaungsu Hluttaw (3 March 2013)". Naypyitaw, 2014.

Pyithu Hluttaw. "Report of the Fifth Day of the Seventh Plenary Session of the First Pyithu Hluttaw (2 July 2013)". Naypyitaw, 2013.

Rakhine Inquiry Commission. "Final Report of Inquiry Commission on Sectarian Violence in Rakhine State". Naypyitaw: Inquiry Commission on Sectarian Violence in Rakhine State, 2012.

Skidmore, Monique, and Trevor Wilson. "Interpreting the Transition in Myanmar". In *Myanmar's Transition: Openings, Obstacles and Opportunities,* edited by Nick Cheesman, Monique Skidmore and Trevor Wilson. Singapore: Institute of Southeast Asian Studies, 2012.

Stapenhurst, Rick, Mitchell O'Brien, and Niall Johnston. "Introduction: Parliaments as Peacebuilders". In *Parliaments as Peacebuilders in Conflict-Affected Countries,* edited by Mitchell O'Brien, Rick Stapenhurst and Johnston Niall. Washington D.C.: The World Bank, 2008.

Thiri Min Tun. "Reps Ignore Ministry on Land-Grab Committee". *Myanmar Times,* 30 July 2012. <http://www.mmtimes.com/index.php/national-news/243-reps-ignore-ministry-on-land-grab-committee.html>. Accessed 11 November 2015.

Williams, David C. "What's So Bad About Burma's 2008 Constitution? A Guide for the Perplexed". In *Law, Society and Transition in Myanmar*, edited by Melissa Crouch and Tim Lindsey. Oxford and Portland, Oregon: Hart Publishing, 2014.

Wilson, Trevor. "Debating Democratization in Myanmar". In *Debating Democratization in Myanmar*, edited by Nick Cheesman, Nicholas Farrelly and Trevor Wilson. Singapore: Institute of Southeast Asian Studies, 2014.

Woods, Kevin. "A Political Anatomy of Land Grabs". *Myanmar Times*, 3 March 2014. <http://www.mmtimes.com/index.php/national-news/9740-a-political-anatomy-of-land-grabs.html>. Accessed 11 November 2015.

Yace de Mel, Laurette Andree. "Summary Record Presented by Mrs. Laurette Andree Yace De Mel, Conference Rapporteur". In *The Role of Parliament in Conflict Prevention and Management in West Africa*. Abidjan: National Assembly of Cote d'Ivoire and Inter-Parliamentary Union, 2013.

Yen Snaing. "Burma Govt Requests $7m for Peace Process". *The Irrawaddy*, 16 January 2014. <http://www.irrawaddy.org/burma/burma-govt-requests-7m-peace-process.html>. Accessed 11 November 2015.

11

LEGISLATING REFORM?
Law and Conflict in Myanmar

Melissa Crouch

What is the relationship between law and conflict? In particular, what role does law-making play in avoiding, managing, or exacerbating conflict? This chapter considers these issues in the context of Myanmar. Legal reform often occurs at moments of political conflict, crisis, and change, and this is also the case in Myanmar. Law reform may be undertaken for a range of reasons — to update, amend, or replace existing laws, to introduce a new policy, or to set a strategic direction in a particular area of reform.

Underneath these efforts at law reform in transitional contexts such as Myanmar there are often two implicit assumptions at play. First, it is sometimes assumed that law has not played an important role in Myanmar in the past. Second, it is assumed that in the post-2011 political transition era, law can and will make a more important contribution to the reform process. At the core of these assumptions is the idea that law helps, rather than hinders, conflict. I suggest that the relationship between law and conflict is more complex, and this is illustrated in the case of Myanmar.

Conflict in Myanmar is often referred to in the context of disputes over land, armed conflict between ethnic groups and the military, or violence directed against Muslims, as other chapters in this volume demonstrate (see in particular Chit Win, this volume). In this chapter, however, I examine conflict from a different angle by exploring the dual capacity of law as a tool to manage conflict, but also as an instrument that can be used to exacerbate conflict.

One way that law has been analysed in relation to conflict is in terms of the connection between law and violence. In his classic opening line, "Legal interpretation takes place in a field of pain and death", Robert Cover (1995) focuses on the way violence is primarily evident in law through the process of interpretation. While the idea of interpretation is conceived in various ways due to the textual nature of law, this is often considered in terms of legal interpretation by the courts. The scholarship that has developed around Cover's work on law and violence includes focus on judicial interpretation and the role of judges, as well as its connection to criminal trials, practices of punishment, and torture (Cover 1995; Sarat and Kearns 1993; Sarat 2001).

Building on Cover's work, Sarat and Kearns (1993) identify several ways that violence justifies the existence of law, despite the fact that modern law denies that its origins lie in violence. This includes the way violence offers the reason for the establishment of a legal system; violence justifies the existence of law; and violence acts as one means through which the law is enforced. While Sarat and Kearns' edited volume covers a range of topics, many contributions focus on criminal law, penal sanctions, and the role of the courts. This focus on courts and the role of a judge presumes that disputes can and will be heard in court.

But what about in legal systems where cases never have a chance to get to court in the first instance? This may be particularly true in authoritarian or transitional regimes, where there are few opportunities for individuals to challenge government decisions, or where, in fact, the system is designed so that individuals will not be able to review government decisions. When we look at the internal structure and lines of authority set out in legislation in Myanmar, it is clear that few matters between individuals and the state are ever able to go to court. The courts are primarily concerned with matters of criminal law, family law, and civil law, while most legislation passed in the reform period explicitly anticipates that disputes will not be able to go to court.

This chapter therefore looks to lawmaking by parliament, and the dual capacity of law to both manage and engender conflict. There has been broad recognition that the Union Parliament, a new body in the legal landscape of Myanmar, has found its voice and begun to assert its power in the past few years (ICG 2013; Kean 2014). In fact, we could go as far as to say that parliament has been the most aggressive institution in the period from 2011–2015, resisting any perceived or real attempts by the president or the courts to limit its power. Scholarship has drawn attention to the personalities and political parties in the Union Parliament, particularly the military representatives (Egreteau 2015a, 2015b; Kean 2013; Republic of the Union of Myanmar 2013). There has also been a focus on the process of lawmaking in parliament, that is, the increase in lawmaking activities, the vigour of debate, and attention to the role of members of parliament in the legislative process, including which members or political parties proposed, supported, or rejected which bills (ICG 2013; see also Chit Win, this volume). This has highlighted the way military officers have not always voted in line with the majority Union Solidarity and Development Party (USDP), nor in a uniform bloc. However, there has been less focus on the substance and form of laws passed by parliament in light of past lawmaking practices, nor acknowledgement of the role of parliament in relation to conflict.

In 2010, its final year in power, the military junta known as the State Peace and Development Council passed a range of legislative reforms in preparation for the new political regime. Since 2011, there has been an increase in legislative reform in areas as diverse as foreign investment; farmland; labour rights; media reforms; civil society organizations, and the Central Bank. The first new Union Parliament sat in fourteen sessions from 2011 to 2015 and debated a wide range of policy reforms. Law reform that in many other countries would have taken years has seemingly appeared overnight. Yet many of these reforms are not necessarily new, and follow a pattern set by the previous military government, which did undertake legislative reform after 1988 and the democracy uprising. In fact, the military regime was meticulous in recording and publishing its legislative activities. Since 1988, all legislation in Myanmar has been published in annual edited volumes, in both English and Burmese (see Union of Myanmar 1999–2013).[1] All laws are published in the government-run Government Gazette as well as in some local newspapers, and more recently online on various government websites. There is, therefore, greater accessibility to the law in Myanmar than in the past (presuming internet access, which remains unreliable).

In this chapter I focus on the relationship between conflict and the Union Parliament's legislative output from 2010 to 2015. First, I question the extent to which the law reform agenda differs from past patterns of law-making, particularly in terms of the way law relates to conflict. I identify and explore three main issues on the legislative reform agenda: structural governance reforms; economic and business reforms; and social reforms. I suggest many of these reforms have been informed by past debates and efforts at law reform. While each of these three areas of change have generated new tensions and conflict between key institutions and actors, in many ways there is continuity in terms of law's relation to conflict. I then consider these legal reforms in terms of their textual content and structure. I explore the ways these laws have been used to manage and avoid conflict, primarily by keeping disputes away from the courts. At the same time, some laws in this period of political uncertainty have, intentionally or unintentionally, exacerbated conflict. I conclude with reflections on the direction of the law reform agenda, suggesting the need for greater awareness of the dual capacity of law to both prevent and foster conflict in Myanmar.

STRUCTURAL GOVERNANCE REFORMS: CONFLICT BETWEEN INSTITUTIONS

The first major area of reform has been structural governance reforms that implemented the new constitutional and legal system. These structural reforms put in place the implementing laws required under the Constitution, yet most did not add significantly to the text of the Constitution itself. In establishing the three arms of government, and the role of the military in governance, the law has sought to manage conflict between key governance institutions, both old institutions (such as the military), revamped institutions, and new institutions. It has done this primarily by giving the president and the executive significant power and control, particularly over the courts. It has also generated new layers of institutional conflict, particularly between the president and the parliament, and towards the Constitutional Tribunal. I illustrate these new areas of conflict concerning the institutional legal framework through the constitutional amendment proposals of 2015.

Given that Myanmar has not had a bicameral parliament since 1962, the introduction of a bicameral Union Parliament is a significant feature of the initial structural reforms. The first laws passed in anticipation of the functioning of parliament related to the powers, roles, and responsibilities of the Pyithu Hluttaw, the Amyotha Hluttaw, and the Pyidaungsu Hluttaw.[2] The Union Parliament has authority to pass legislation within the eleven areas allocated to it under the constitution, which are broad in scope. The list of legislative matters includes: defence and security; foreign affairs; finance and planning; economy; agriculture; energy, electricity, forestry and mining; industry; transport, communication, and construction; social sector (education, health); management; and the judiciary. The Union Parliament has residual legislative power, while a narrow range of powers are elaborated for the states and regions. The lawmaking process is heavily centralized, and legislative power has been the subject of constitutional amendment, rather than judicial interpretation. The amendments approved in July 2015 set out further details of the legislative and taxation powers of the states and regions,[3] which suggest that courts are less likely to play a role in the interpretation of the scope of these powers.

In addition, the state and region governments have been established with their own unicameral parliaments and a limited measure of independence from the union government.[4] While the most controversial aspect has been that the president appoints the chief ministers of the states and regions, an unsuccessful attempt was made in 2015 to amend the constitution so that chief ministers could be appointed by a majority of elected representatives. The desire for greater devolution of power to the states and regions and independence of the Hluttaws from the central government are likely to lead to further reform in the future.

At both the central and regional levels of governance, changes to the rules on elections have been another area of reform. Prior to 2010, Myanmar had not held elections for ten years, and so the Union Election Commission was reconstituted to oversee the electoral process.[5] In addition, legislation has been passed on the electoral process in relation to each of these houses and levels of government,[6] as well as for the registration of political parties more generally.[7] One of the key issues that arose was the possibility of proportional representation. The debate on whether to replace the first past the post system with proportional representation, covered in more detail by Lidauer (this volume) generated conflict between the

USDP and the National League for Democracy (NLD), because the proposal was perceived by the NLD as an attempt to undermine its potential for success at the 2015 elections. The amendments to the electoral laws in late 2014 that, among other matters, operated to exclude temporary identity card holders from voting (contrary to past political practise), was one of the darker sides of reform. This change effectively meant that those who hold temporary identity cards (many of whom are Muslim) were unable to vote or run for elections in 2015.

There have been structural reforms in relation to the executive that vests power in the new offices of the president, vice-presidents and ministers. The president's power is wide, and President Thein Sein's (March 2011– March 2016) initiatives have at times been resisted by the parliament. For example, Thein Sein established the Myanmar National Human Rights Commission ('the Commission') by executive order, but when it came time to approve the budget, the parliament refused until the commission was established by law.[8] In addition, Thein Sein has not hesitated to use his power to refer draft bills back to the Union Parliament with suggestions for reform, although under the constitution the Union Parliament has the final say on legislation, with law coming into force fourteen days from assent regardless of the president's opinion.

The legal framework on the administration extends to the newly established self-administered zones, which were born out of the ceasefire deals of the 1990s. These zones are part of the state's strategy to be seen to grant symbolic recognition to select ethnic groups (Crouch 2015b).[9] As Ricky Yue (this volume) notes in relation to the Pa-O Self-Administered Zone, these areas largely exist and function beyond the realm of national law. The reform agenda has also led to laws on local governance, including the administration of Naypyitaw Council, Yangon and Mandalay City Development Council, and the Ward and Village Administration, which is one of the most important administrative units of government at the local level (Chit Saw, Kyi Pyar and Arnold 2014).[10] Overall, power remains concentrated in the central government, although there are persistent calls for greater decentralization of power.

Given the change in legal institutions and authorities, an early law provided that some new institutions replaced existing ones and where legislation mentions these old institutions, it should be taken as referring to the new institution. For example, this 'rebadging' exercise included the replacement of all references in law to the chairperson of the State Peace and Development Council (SPDC) with the president; the replacement of the chairperson of the state/division SPDC with the chief minister of the state or region; and the replacement of the District Peace and Development Council with the General Administration Department.[11] Similar laws were introduced during the socialist and then later military regime which gave new names to existing structures and organizations. In this way, many 'new' structures in the post-2011 period are simply positions or institutions that have been rebranded, and remain steeped in the governance habits of the old regime.

The new laws passed since 2010 continue to subordinate the courts to executive and parliamentary control. The courts are the branch of government least affected by the transition process so far. The constitution and subsequent law on the judiciary does attend to details previously absent from regulation, such as the process for the selection, appointment, tenure, and removal of judges (Myint Zan 2012). Some features particular to the judiciary in Myanmar include executive control over judicial appointments, the unusual nature of the court's power to submit bills to parliament but also remain accountable to it, and the insistence that judges are free from party politics, yet they are allowed to run for elections while still in their role as a judge.[12] While several laws have been passed or amended in relation to court procedure and practices, such as the new contempt of court law (Cheesman 2015, p. 243), and the law on writ procedures of the Supreme Court (Crouch 2014),[13] these have not enhanced the independence of the courts. In fact, the introduction of the revised Contempt of Court Law is perhaps telling of the extent that it is still used as a form of punishment today. This law acts as a significant deterrent for lawyers and applicants to bring cases to court, and for the media to cover court proceedings. In one instance in 2015, the Ministry of Information brought a case for contempt against seventeen senior figures of the *Daily Eleven* news group (Kyaw Phone Kyaw 2015), which is in addition to a defamation case related to the coverage of the court trial of five other members of the same media outlet who were accused of defamation for alleging the ministry had misused government funds. The *over*-use of the Contempt of Court Law to target political opponents remains a real way that the courts do violence to the process of justice.

The main structural change in terms of the judiciary has been the introduction of the Constitutional Tribunal (Myint Zan 2012; Nardi 2010), which has added a new source of tension due to its ability to review legislation and executive decisions on matters of constitutionality.[14] The resignation of the first bench in 2012 was a result of tensions between the president, the parliament and the Constitutional Tribunal in relation to the powers of parliamentary committees. This led to amendment to the law in 2013 which reduced the finality of decisions of the tribunal, although this appears to have been restored by further amendments in 2014.[15] The Constitutional Tribunal has insisted it derives its authority primarily from the constitution, and that therefore all of its decisions are final and binding on the government. The distrust displayed by the parliament towards the Constitutional Tribunal has provoked intermittent discussions about abolishing the tribunal and potentially giving jurisdiction for constitutional review to the Supreme Court, yet this will not be able to occur unless the constitution is formally amended. The proposed constitutional amendments in 2015 instead included measures that would have reduced the independence of the Supreme Court by reducing the term of judges to five years, and limiting the authority of decisions of the Constitutional Tribunal. This proposal was unsuccessful.

The reforms introduced in terms of structural governance have created new institutions — including parliament, state governments, and the Constitutional Tribunal among others — and reformed existing institutions, leading to new forms of institutional and political conflict. The laws, and proposals for constitutional amendment, have sought to manage conflict by centralizing power in the president and confining the role of the courts.

ECONOMIC AND BUSINESS REFORMS: CONFLICT BETWEEN COMMERCIAL STAKEHOLDERS

Aside from this first wave of structural reforms, the second theme that many new laws address is economic reforms geared towards more foreign investment and the market economy,[16] including in the banking sector, establishment of special economic zones, and potential reform of the Company Law. These laws manage conflict between commercial stakeholders, the public and private sectors, foreigners and locals, and military businesses. However, these economic reforms have also generated conflict between local stakeholders, and between local stakeholders and foreign investors, in particular by raising fears that such reforms may be too generous to foreign investors. One reason for these laws was to open up the economy, although 1988 officially marked the transition from a socialist economy to a market economy (Turnell 2014a). A key feature of these reforms is that most simply build on law reforms that were introduced post-1988 after the collapse of the socialist regime, extending these reforms a little further. These reforms have reduced the opportunity for individuals to challenge government decisions concerning the application and regulation of licences and permits for various industries in court.

As part of the reform process, some old laws on the economy have been repealed, and this has lifted many restrictions previously used by the military regime to contain and control conflict. For example, the repeal of the 1947 Foreign Exchange Regulation Act and the subsequent decision to float the Kyat in April 2012 was a significant and necessary step forward.[17] This did away with the former discrepancy between the official exchange rate of 6 Kyat to US$1, and the unofficial exchange rate of around 1000 to 1 (see Turnell 2013, 2014a, 2014b). This has attempted to resolve the tension inherent in a system where the unofficial exchange rate was the norm and the official exchange rate benefitted those in power.

One of the first and most significant laws passed in terms of economic reforms was the Foreign Investment Law, passed in 2012 after much debate, followed by a separate law relating to investment by Myanmar citizens.[18] These two laws were combined in 2015, after a more sustained process of public consultation. The Foreign Investment Law seeks to balance the need for certainty and protection of investors' interests with the need to ensure that investment is in the best interests of the country and community. Several issues raise potential for conflict — including tax concessions, land use, and local benefits.

Investors are rewarded with a five-year income-tax break, as well as relief concerning import and export tax. While such tax concessions may be detrimental to local concerns, the law does set a strict standard in terms of labour requirements for skilled positions: twenty-five per cent local employees after five years; fifty per cent after the next five years; and at least seventy-five per cent after the following five years. While this demonstrates acute concern to ensure local Myanmar workers will be appointed to skilled positions, this may be difficult to achieve in practice given the high level of expertise required in some industries.

Another source of tension between government, business, and local communities is that the law grants land use for up to fifty years, with two possible extensions of ten years each. Given that a large number of complaints have been raised about land confiscated by the government past and present, and many of these complaints remain unresolved, the decision to grant such land use concessions for an extended period of time may come under question in some areas. Separate laws have been passed on land use, farmland, and environmental protection (Food Security Working Group 2012),[19] although in reality these reforms have done little to prompt major changes in the regulation of agriculture in Myanmar.

In addition to foreign investment, a new Central Bank law has been introduced.[20] This law granted formal independence for the Central Bank from the Ministry of Finance, reformed the position of the governor of the Central Bank and its board, and restricted the printing of money. The reality, however, is that independence remains something of an illusion. The future operation of banks, including foreign banks, remains limited by the existing Financial Institutions of Myanmar Law. There are multiple tensions in such new areas of regulation — tensions between local and foreign banks; tensions between existing owners of local banks and more recently established local banks; and the general distrust the public has for banks, given their past record in Myanmar.

A further major area of economic reform has been legislation passed to regulate the establishment of Special Economic Zones, marked out for Dawei, Thilawa, Kyauk Pyu, and Kokang areas.[21] The concept itself is not new in Myanmar (Lubeigt 2008; Turnell 2014, p. 194). While the original legislation was modelled on Vietnam and China, further detail was added to the expanded 2014 law, although most of these are minor changes. For example, some legislative changes grant further concessions to developers, such as the period for income tax exemption being extended from the original five years to eight years. The duration for the lease of land has changed slightly, although the overall maximum length of seventy-five years has not changed. The labour requirements have changed to impose a more stringent labour standard for developers by reducing the time frame for employing local skilled workers to twenty-five per cent citizens in the first two years of operation, fifty per cent in the following two years, and seventy-five per cent in the subsequent two years. Finally, while the amendments in 2014 now include the process for dispute resolution, it simply notes that if disputes cannot be resolved between the parties, they must either be resolved in accordance with the contract, or in accordance with existing laws. The law does not establish a new mechanism for resolving disputes or an avenue for independent review.

A large number of other areas in the business and economic sector have been affected by law reform. Mining is one area of change and of competing interests. Although efforts were made to privatize mines in the 1990s and open up to foreign firms, these measures were stunted as Western economic sanctions were imposed. The Mining Law passed in 2015 offers new opportunities for foreign investment and extends the duration of large-scale mining licences, but most certainly will generate issues due to conflicting interests of the government, businesses, and local communities. There are also new laws for specific industries that have broken the monopoly that military companies had on particular sectors, such as the telecommunications sector, with Ooredoo and Telenor now competing with the existing MPT.[22]

Another emerging area of tension is the creation of the Myanmar Stock Exchange. The Stock Exchange was officially launched in December 2015. The Securities Exchange Law lays the foundation for the establishment of the Stock Exchange, and creates the Securities Exchange Supervision Commission (Tun Zaw Mra 2014).[23] The Stock Exchange, however, is majority-owned by Myanma Economic Bank, which remains on the United States sanctions list. While most Western sanctions have been lifted, there are many questions over how remaining sanctions will impact the functioning of new developments such as the Stock Exchange.

Overall, these economic and business reforms build on and extend the legislative foundations set after 1988, yet can now be implemented in an environment where most sanctions have been lifted. While these laws attempt to develop the economy by managing local and foreign interests, they will inevitably remain a source of tension and conflict, particularly in relation to land.

SOCIAL REFORMS: CONFLICT BETWEEN THE STATE AND CIVIL SOCIETY

The third area addressed is social reforms that have had an impact on the role of civil society, and the position of individuals in relation to the state, including labour law, media, religion, education, and the right to peaceful assembly. It is in this area that law reform to some extent represents a break with the past, although much depends on the implementation of these laws in the years to come. While still playing a role in managing conflict, these laws have also given rise to new forms of conflict between the state and civil society.

Central to these reforms have been the rights to organize and freedom of speech, although these rights are not unqualified. Important reforms in the area of labour organizations and dispute settlement have allowed for greater protection of the workers' rights. According to the law, workers are now permitted to form unions and undertake collective bargaining (Kyaw Soe Lwin 2014).[24] A new law on freedom to demonstrate and protest was enacted, although it still required applications to the police for permission to protest, and provides the grounds on which a request could be denied, or criminal prosecutions made.[25] Like many reforms in this area, there are significant problems with implementation, as many applications for a permit to protest never receive a response from authorities, or are denied. Protestors who go ahead with their protests without a permit have been arrested and jailed. This situation prompted parliament to amend the law, which now simply requires consent to be given to all applications for a permit to protest (whereas before a request could be denied). In addition, the term of the maximum sentence that may be imposed for breach of the law has been reduced from two years to one, from one year to six months, and from six months to three months. Yet these amendments are minimal and concerns remain over the implementation of the law to silence criticism of the military, and contain political opposition and student activism. In fact, the violence legitimated by this law — in terms of arrests and imprisonment — demonstrates the way law can be used to effectively sanction and legalise harassment.

The removal of former restrictions on the media has significantly transformed the information space, and this sector is now regulated by a new media law.[26] The media, however, remains subject to certain limitations, for example, as mentioned above, the risk of being charged with contempt of court when reporting court cases perceived to be critical of the government. The new Association Registration Law has opened up greater freedom for civil society organizations. Registration is now voluntary, and no criminal sanctions are attached to non-registration.[27] This is a shift from earlier attitudes heavily circumscribing civil society organizations.

A number of laws on the legislative agenda significantly affect civil society and the freedoms and rights of individuals. One particularly heated debate has been over the National Education Law,[28] which was finally passed in 2014 and amended in 2015. Myanmar has a history of student activism, beginning in the 1920s with student union opposition to a proposed law on Rangoon University (as it was then known). Since the coup in 1962, the education system, including universities, has come under strict government control. During the recent debate over the new National Education Law, a large range of concerns was expressed, not the least of which was that there had been insufficient consultation in the drafting process. This has been further exacerbated by the limits of the new labour laws, which do not allow student unions to be registered under the new laws.

An area where law reform has arisen directly from violence is in relation to the anti-Muslim sentiment and conflict since 2012. One response was a proposal by a group of nationalist monks to introduce four bills that allegedly seek to 'protect' race and religion, that is, to protect Burmans and Buddhists to the exclusion of non-Burmans and non-Buddhists. These four laws were adopted in revised form by parliament and include the Monogamy Law; the Population Control Law; the Buddhist Women's Special Marriage Law; and the Religious Conversion Law.[29] Yet some aspects of these bills have antecedents in existing laws, linked to previous debates and long-held prejudices against Muslims. For example, the Buddhist Women's Special Marriage Law revises an existing law passed in 1954 (though confusingly it does not seem to replace it, see Crouch 2016). What these laws may potentially do is further entrench discrimination and the marginalization of certain groups, particularly Muslims. Combined, these laws are an overt example of the way law engenders and exacerbates conflict, although much will depend on whether the administration enforces them, or whether certain social groups such as monks pressure enforcement agencies to act in certain circumstances.

TEXTUAL PATTERNS IN LAW REFORM

Across these three areas — structural, economic and social – several patterns have emerged in the drafting of law and the way laws have been designed to avoid and manage conflict, while also at times exacerbating conflict between different institutions or between individuals and the state. I will focus on four aspects: the formation of committees close to the executive to avoid conflict; the wide discretion given to government ministers to manage conflict; the exclusion of courts from reviewing executive decisions to keep complaints against government bodies out of court; and the increased level of participation in lawmaking, which has created new tensions. In doing so, these aspects of law reform point to the ongoing close relationship between law and violence, and the way law has been used to silence potential conflict.

First, these laws evince a common pattern of providing for the formation of a committee to oversee certain administrative processes, such as the consideration of an application for an investment permit or licence to use land. These committees usually consist of members of parliament, ministers, and government officials, and therefore have no independence from government. They are given extremely broad discretion under these laws to manage conflict. On the one hand, allowing scope for discretion is a legitimate means to ensure flexibility in decision-making and is well recognized in the common law. On the other hand, excessive discretion must not be granted to allow any kind of decision to be made. In part, this means that because most of the laws have been drafted in such broad terms, the laws have little effect until they are fleshed out in more detail by government regulations, and even then implementation depends on the capacity of ministerial departments.

Another clear pattern in the form of legislative drafting is the tendency to include finality clauses in legislation. Finality clauses (also known as ouster clauses) typically provide that a committee, which has powers of review over a certain application process, has the authority to make final decisions that cannot be reviewed by a court. Many decisions are said to be final and conclusive, including the decisions of the Myanmar Investment Commission;[30] the Region/State Farmland Management Body regarding the use of farmland;[31] the Union Election Commission regarding electoral disputes;[32] a decision of the Minister of Health in relation to licences as a dentist;[33] the Rural Development and Poverty Reduction Working Committee and its decisions on microfinance, among other examples.[34] Such provisions are an attempt to remove the jurisdiction of the court to hear these cases. In this way, it can be said that legislative reform has not empowered the courts, but rather has limited the potential role of the courts because few executive decisions are able to be challenged. Taking this one step further, it can be seen as part of the deliberate ideological project for executive control that is central to the very idea of law and legal institutions in Myanmar. This project has deep historical roots, as has been highlighted in the work of Cheesman (2012a, 2012b) on the restructuring of law and courts from the 1960s.

Both the establishment of commissions and inclusion of finality clauses in law represent a noticeable continuity in lawmaking patterns. Further, all previous regimes in Myanmar went through a similar pattern of affirming that all existing laws remained in force unless otherwise repealed, while also dismantling the existing institutional structures and creating new ones by law. The quasi-civilian government led by Thein Sein has therefore trod a very familiar path in terms of the law-reform process.

Finally, in relation to the process by which laws are made, there have been higher levels of participation and transparency in lawmaking than in the past. This has facilitated a strategy of both managing conflict, in terms of taking into account different perspectives and at times revising draft laws on the recommendations of various civil society groups. The process of consultation, combined with more media freedom, has allowed dissenting voices to be heard. Sustained engagement and consultation with international and local actors was limited prior to 2011. Since then, there has been increased engagement with local actors, the private sector, stakeholders, and civil society; and more engagement with international actors and experts offering comparative examples of legal reform. There are many examples of this, such as the reform of the Media Law, or the introduction of the Foreign Investment Law (Kean 2013, p. 57). Yet for every example of community consultation, there have been many laws that have not included a public consultation process, or issues have been raised over the scale and scope of consultation held.

Although not new, there has been an increase in the level of foreign involvement in the consultation and legal drafting process — from international non-government organizations (INGOs), to consultants, and law firms. For example, under the previous regime, the military made claims that the Child Law No 9/1993 was to fulfil its obligations under the United Nations Convention on the Rights of the Child (although the law is not compatible with this convention).[35] Further, the Anti-trafficking in Persons Law No 5/2005 was said to be drafted with the assistance of international actors and with reference to international standards. This law allows for engagement between international organizations and the Central Body for Suppression of Trafficking in Persons under the Ministry of Home Affairs. Foreign involvement in drafting has become more frequent since 2011, and this has raised local concerns, suspicions and rumours over the agenda of foreign actors. For example, several international organizations were involved in the consultation and drafting of the Small and Medium Enterprise Law (Set Aung 2014, p. 7). There was international help drafting the Central Bank Law (Turnell 2014b, p. 190), and the current process of revising the Company Law is supported by the Asian Development Bank. Some laws have been passed as part of conditionality agreements set by international organizations, such as the Social Security Law.[36] While engagement with foreign expertise creates more opportunities to consider best practice, it has also led to local concerns and rumours of unwarranted foreign influence in the drafting process, resulting in new forms of conflict and tension.

THE FUTURE OF LAW REFORM IN MYANMAR: BEYOND CONFLICT?

Sarat and Kearns observed, "The existence of law stands as a monument to the hope that words can contain and control violence" (1993, p. 2). This is one way to view the legislative reform process in Myanmar — the text of legislation acting as a symbolic source of hope that the future will contain less conflict and violence. Yet legal reform is an inherently uncertain process, particularly in times of political transition. As I have suggested in this chapter, this uncertainty lies in the dual capacity of law to both manage and engender conflict.

The legislative agenda over the past few years in Myanmar is one indication of deep uncertainty in society and is an attempt to counter insecurity about the future. The priorities of the law reform agenda are telling of these tensions. This chapter has demonstrated how law reform is more a reflection of past patterns in lawmaking both in terms of law's relation to conflict and the textual features that determine this. It therefore maintains continuity in how law is used to manage and avoid conflict, particularly by preventing access to the courts. There is also the future potential for new laws to exacerbate conflict between individuals, or between individuals and the state. This adds to the sense of instability and insecurity about the future.

In terms of legislative reform beyond 2015, there are a large number of bills in progress that the new parliament, dominated by the NLD, may address from 2016. Yet given the dramatic shift from the USDP to the

NLD-led government, this may lead to a change in legislative priorities, and potentially to new textual patterns in the making of law. While I have only focused on laws passed by the Union Parliament, as region and state parliaments pass more laws these will also need to be studied.

The real or perceived threat of violence and conflict, as Cover noted, will continue to justify the existence of law. This is also the case in Myanmar, whether it is institutional conflict between branches of government, conflict between different interest groups on economic reforms, or conflict between the state and society on social reforms. The area of law reform likely to undergo significant change in the immediate future is economic and business reform. There are a number of bills being debated or drafted, including amendments to update and revise the Company Act 1914 (Tun 2014); as well as laws passed recently that will need to be implemented, such as the Competition Law and the Arbitration Law. These laws will have an impact on opportunities for foreign investment, as well as how foreign investment is managed in terms of benefits to local communities. Law can be seen as setting the framework within which expectations are managed and potential conflict between different interest groups controlled.

How then should we understand the recent spate of law reform activities since 2011 in Myanmar, and where it is headed? I suggest that the value of analysing law through its relation to violence and conflict is that it promotes awareness of the need for greater caution in law reform and responsiveness to new tensions caused by legal change. This is not to suggest all conflict is negative, but the potential for law to legitimate violence is real. Such awareness would temper the unrealistic expectations that the solution to Myanmar's issues is simply to legislate reform.

Notes

1 Up to 2013, the volumes of Myanmar Laws published by the Office of the Attorney General include 22 volumes in Burmese, and 20 volumes in English.
2 Law Relating to Pyithu Hluttaw No 12/2010; Law Relating to the Pyidaungsu Hluttaw No 11/2010; Law Relating to the Amyotha Hluttaw No 13/2010; there have been several amendments to these laws since then.
3 Law Amending the Union of Myanmar Constitution No 45/2015.
4 Law Relating to the State/Region Government Law No 16/2010.
5 Union Election Commission Law No 1/2010.
6 Region and State Hluttaw Election Law No 5/2010, Law Amending the Region

Hluttaw or State Hluttaw Election Law No 10/2011; Pyithu Hluttaw Election Law No 3/2010, Law Amending the Pyithu Hluttaw Election Law No 8/2011; Amyotha Hluttaw Election Law No 4/2010, Law Amending the Amyotha Hluttaw Election Law No 9/2011.

7 Political Parties Registration Law No 2/2010, and Law Amending the Political Party Registration Law No 11/2011.
8 Myanmar National Human Rights Commission Law No 21/2014.
9 Self-Administered Zone Law No 17/2010.
10 Naypyitaw Council Law No 8/2010; Ward and Village Administration Law No 1/2012, and Ward and Village Administration Amending Act No 7/2012.
11 Law Relating to Adaptation of Expressions No 11/2011.
12 Union Judiciary Law No 20/2010, amended by Judiciary Law 30/2013; and Law on amendment to Judiciary Law No 25/2014.
13 Contempt of Court Law No 17/2013.
14 Constitutional Tribunal of the Union Law No 21/2010.
15 Law Amending the Constitutional Tribunal of the Union Law No 4/2013 and No 46/2014.
16 The Constitution 2008 identifies that Myanmar is based on a market economy (s 35).
17 Foreign Exchange Rate Management Law No 12/2012.
18 Foreign Investment Law No 21/2012; Myanmar Citizens Investment Law No 18/2013.
19 Environmental Conservation Law No 9/2012; Administration of Vacant, Fallow and Virgin Lands Law No 10/2012; Farmland Act No 11/2012.
20 Central Bank of Myanmar Law No 16/2013.
21 Myanmar Special Economic Zones Law No 1/2014 (which replaced Myanmar Special Economic Zone Law No 8/2011 and Dawei Special Economic Zone Law No 17/2011); Kokang Economic Zone, Myanmar Investment Commission Notification 59/2014.
22 Telecommunications Law No 31/2013.
23 Securities Exchange Law No 20/2013.
24 Labour Organisation Law No 7/2011; Labour Disputes Settlement Law No 5/2012.
25 Law Relating to the Right of Peaceful Assembly and Peaceful Procession No 15/2011, amended by Law No 26/2014.
26 Media Law No 12/2014.
27 Registration of Organisations Law No 31/2014.
28 National Education Law No 41/2014.
29 The Population Control Law No 28/2015, the Conversion Law No 48/2015, the Buddhist Women's Special Marriage Law No 50/2015 and the Monogamy Law No 54/2015.

30 The Foreign Investment Law No 21/2012, s 49.
31 Farmland Law No 11/2012, s 25.
32 Union Election Commission Law No 1/2010, s 9.
33 Myanmar Dental Council Law No 15/2011, s 31(6).
34 Microfinance Business Law No 3/2011.
35 I am indebted to Nick Cheesman for pointing out these examples.
36 Social Security Law No 15/2012.

References

Cheesman, Nick. "How an Authoritarian Regime in Burma Used Special Courts to Defeat Judicial Independence". *Law and Society Review* 45, no. 4 (2012a): 801–830.

———. "Myanmar's Courts and the Sounds Money Makes". In *Myanmar's Transition: Openings, Obstacles and Opportunities*, edited by Monique Skidmore and Trevor Wilson. Singapore: Institute of Southeast Asian Studies, 2012b.

———. *Opposing the Rule of Law: How Myanmar's Courts Make Law and Order*. Cambridge: Cambridge University Press, 2015.

Chit Saw, Kyi Pyar and Matthew Arnold, *Administering the State: An Overview of the General Administration Department*. Yangon, Asia Foundation and MDRI, 2014.

Cover, Robert. "Violence and the Law". In *Narrative, Violence and the Law: The Essays of Robert Cover*, edited by Martha Minow, Michael Ryan and Austin Sarat. Ann Arbor: University of Michigan Press, 1995.

Crouch, Melissa. "The Common Law and the Constitutional Writs in Myanmar". In *Law, Society and Transition in Myanmar*, edited by in Melissa Crouch and Tim Lindsey. Oxford: Hart Publishing, 2014.

———. "Ethnic Rights and Constitutional Change: The Constitutional Recognition of Ethnic Nationalities in Myanmar". In *Central-local Relations in Asian Constitutional Systems*, edited by in Andrew Harding and Mark Sidel. Oxford: Hart Publishing, 2015.

———. "Promiscuity, Polygyny and the Power of Revenge: The Past and Future of Burmese Buddhist Law in Myanmar". *Asian Journal of Law and Society*, 3, no. 1 (2016): 85–104.

Egreteau, Renaud *Military Delegates in Myanmar's Legislature: What Do They Do? What Will They Continue To Do?* Institute of Southeast Asian Studies policy paper. Singapore: Institute of Southeast Asian Studies, 2015a.

———. "Who are the Military Delegates in Myanmar's 2010–2015 Union Legislature?" *Sojourn* 18, no. 2 (2015b): 338–370.

Food Security Working Group, *Legal Review of Recently Enacted Farmland Law and Vacant, Fallow and Virgin Lands Management Law: Improving the Legal and Policy Frameworks Relating to Land Management in Myanmar*. Forest Trends Association,

November 2012.

Human Rights Resource Centre (HRRC) *Keeping the Faith: A Study of Freedom of Thought Conscience and Religion in ASEAN: Myanmar*. Jakarta: University of Indonesia, 2015, pp. 321–60.

International Crisis Group (ICG). *Not a Rubber Stamp: Myanmar's Legislature in a Time of Transition*. 2013, <http://www.icg.org>. Accessed 10 January 2016.

———. *Myanmar's Electoral Landscape*. April 2015, <http://www.icg.org>. Accessed 10 January 2016.

Kean, Thomas. "Myanmar's Parliament: From Scorn to Significance". In *Debating Democratization in Myanmar*, edited by Nick Cheesman, Nicholas Farrelly and Trevor Wilson. Singapore, Institute of Southeast Asian Studies, 2013.

Kyaw Phone Kyaw. "Government Suit Against 'Eleven' Editors Prompts Criticism". *The Myanmar Times*, 22 June 2015, http://www.mmtimes.com/index.php/national-news/15127-government-suit-against-eleven-editors-prompts-criticism.html. Accessed 10 January 2016.

Kyaw Soe Lwin. "Legal Perspectives on Industrial Disputes in Myanmar". In *Law, Society and Transition in Myanmar*, edited by Melissa Crouch and Tim Lindsey. Oxford: Hart Publishing, 2014.

Lubeigt, Guy. "Industrial Zones in Burma and Burmese Labour in Thailand". In *Myanmar: The State, Community and the Environment*, edited by Monique Skidmore and Trevor Wilson. Canberra: ANU, 2008.

Mieno, Fumiharu. "Determinants of Debt, Bank Loans, and Trade Credit of Private Firms in the Transition Period: The Case of Myanmar". In *Recovering Financial Systems: China and Asian Transition Economies*, edited by Mariko Watanabe. United Kingdom, Palgrave Macmillan, 2006.

Myint Zan. "The New Supreme Court and Constitutional Tribunal: Marginal Improvements for Judicial Independence or More of the Same?". In *Myanmar's Transition: Openings, Obstacles and Opportunities*, edited by Monique Skidmore and Trevor Wilson. Singapore: Institute of Southeast Asian Studies, 2012.

Nardi, Dominic. "Discipline-Flourishing Constitutional Review: A Legal and Political Analysis of Myanmar's New Constitutional Tribunal". *Australian Journal of Asian Law* 12, no. 1 (2010): 1-34.

Republic of the Union of Myanmar, *The Parliaments of Myanmar 2013*. Yangon: MCM Publishing, 2014.

Sarat, Austin and Thomas R. Kearns. "Introduction". In *Law's Violence*, edited by Austin Sarat and Thomas R. Kearns. Ann Arbor: University of Michigan Press, 1993.

Sarat, Austin, ed., *Law, Violence and the Possibility of Justice*. Princeton: Princeton University Press, 2001.

Set Aung, Winston. "Myanmar Reforms Gathering Momentum". In *Debating Democratization in Myanmar*, edited by Nick Cheesman, Nicholas Farrelly and

Trevor Wilson. Singapore: Institute of Southeast Asian Studies, 2014.
Tun, Melinda. "A Principled Approach to Company Law Reform in Myanmar". In *Law, Society and Transition in Myanmar*, edited by Melissa Crouch and Tim Lindsey. Oxford: Hart Publishing, 2014.
Tun Zaw Mra. "The Securities Exchange Law and Prospectus Regulation: Early Sketches of Equity Capital Market Law and Regulation in Myanmar". In *Law, Society and Transition in Myanmar*, edited by Melissa Crouch and Tim Lindsey. Oxford: Hart Publishing, 2014.
Turnell, Sean. "Banking and Financial Regulation and Reform in Myanmar". *Journal of Southeast Asian Economies* 31, no. 2 (2013): 225–40.
―――. "Legislative Foundations of Myanmar's Economic Reforms". In *Law, Society and Transition in Myanmar*, edited by Melissa Crouch and Tim Lindsey. Oxford: Hart Publishing, 2014a.
―――. "The Glass Has Water: A Stocktake of Myanmar's Economic Reforms". In *Debating Democratization in Myanmar*, edited by Nick Cheesman, Nicholas Farrelly and Trevor Wilson. Singapore: Institute of Southeast Asian Studies, 2014b.
Union of Myanmar, *Myanmar Laws*. Yangon: The Office of the Attorney General, 1999–2013. (22 volumes from 1988 to 2013 in Burmese, 20 volumes in English.)
Williams, David. "What's so Bad about Burma's Constitution?" In *Law, Society and Transition in Myanmar*, edited by Melissa Crouch and Tim Lindsey. Oxford: Hart Publishing, 2014.

IV
Us and Them

12

MAKING SENSE OF REACTIONS TO COMMUNAL VIOLENCE IN MYANMAR

Tamas Wells

In June 2012 the rape and murder of a Buddhist girl in Western Rakhine State sparked reprisals against Muslim communities. The resulting cycles of communal violence in the following months left hundreds dead, and thousands displaced. The tensions in Rakhine State continued through 2012, and by early 2013 the violence began to spread to other areas of the country. In Meiktila, in the country's central dry zone, a dispute in a jewellery store saw an escalation of violence and the burning of significant parts of the Muslim quarter, including mosques and schools. Through the rest of 2013 tensions remained high, and there continued to be isolated incidents of violence, especially in Rakhine State.

In October 2013, Mishal Husain interviewed Daw Aung San Suu Kyi on the BBC's *Today* programme. When asked about growing communal conflict between Buddhists and Muslims in Myanmar, Suu Kyi responded, "This is what the world needs to understand: that the fear is not just on the side of the Muslims, but on the side of the Buddhists as well. Yes, Muslims have been targeted, but also Buddhists have been subjected to violence" (BBC 2013). And when finally asked pointedly whether she condemned the anti-Muslim violence, she replied that, "I condemn any movement that is based on hatred and extremism" (BBC 2013).

Over the next few days, Suu Kyi was heavily criticized by the Western media for supposedly defending Buddhist extremism. *Daily Telegraph* reporter David Blair said that the interview had "sent a shiver down my spine" and that her attitudes toward Muslims were "deeply disturbing" (Blair 2013). Others described the interview as a "fall from grace" from the democracy icon (4News). One commentator even suggested that Suu Kyi should now be "shunned by the international community" (4News). While this condemnation was focused specifically on Aung San Suu Kyi, it was representative of a shift that was also taking place in the attitudes of the international aid community toward the democracy movement.

Previously, like Suu Kyi, democracy activists and opposition leaders had been considered allies of Western aid organizations' interests in the country. Yet this perception shifted dramatically with the contrasting reactions to reports of violence against Muslims. A Western donor representative interviewed for this research summed it up by saying that the international aid community "has never felt further from the Burmese democracy movement" (Interview 27, 2013 English).[1] The lack of sympathy for Muslim communities and the failure of some activists to condemn violence was seen as "extremely disappointing" (Interview 3, 2013 English). And a number of international aid workers said they were shocked to hear the way some local activists — many of whom they had known for some time — responded.

This chapter asks the question, *why have there been such contrasting reactions to the communal violence?* Many Western aid agencies and aid workers have been long-term supporters and allies of the Burmese democracy movement.[2] Why then has there been such a diversity of reactions between actors who supposedly have the same goal of "democracy"?

In this chapter I use a narrative approach to argue that different reactions to these incidents of communal violence are embedded within varied accounts of the country's democratization. Based on field research in 2013 and 2014, I argue that the starkly contrasting reactions are not a surprising anomaly amidst a wider consensus about what democratization means. Rather, they are windows onto broader differences in the way challenges and democratic visions for the country are constructed. "Democracy" in

Myanmar does not have a single meaning but rather, it is — to use Gallie's (1956) phrase — an "essentially contested concept". Acknowledging this essentially contested nature of democracy can help make sense of why, especially in aid programmes, there have been such contrasting reactions to the issue of Buddhist–Muslim tension.

Furthermore, I argue that analysis of narratives can illuminate reasons why dialogue about communal violence is so challenging. For some aid workers, universal human rights function as an inviolable foundation that guides discussion about democracy or communal violence. Meanwhile, for many Burmese activists and opposition leaders, notions of unity and protection of the majority are assumed to be necessary foundations for debate. Given the way narratives construct different absolute or inviolable components of democracy, dialogue may not always be progressive and generative of consensus.

This chapter is divided into three sections. I first describe a narrative approach as a way of highlighting the essentially contested nature of the concept of "democracy", shedding light on why there has been such diversity of reactions to communal violence. Next I describe the contrasting ways democratization is commonly narrated within the international donor community, and also among activists in the Burmese democracy movement. Crucially, I highlight that, while Western donor representatives often emphasize *liberal* institution-based democracy and the underlying values of rights and minority protection, in the opposition movement democracy is often described in more personal and *moral* terms with contests over values of unity and majority protection. Finally, I conclude that acknowledgement of these wider narratives can be a step toward increasing the intelligibility of contrasting reactions to Buddhist–Muslim tension in Myanmar.

A NARRATIVE APPROACH

In the last few decades, the idea of narrative has emerged as a popular "portmanteau" (Andrews, Squire and Tamboukou 2008, p. 2) stretching across a range of fields. In this chapter, narrative is taken to mean an account of events related to a political issue that serves to collectively construct a problem and a desired solution (Boswell 2013; Roe 1989). A narrative approach can be valuable in showing how problems and solutions can be constructed in different ways. Responses to political issues, such as communal violence, can flow from wider collective stories about the country's transition. In this sense they can reveal different forms of "common sense" about "democracy" — not only emphasizing that there are multiple ways of understanding "democracy" (or its equivalents in other languages), but also that each of these narratives may be "valid on its own terms" (van Eeten 2007, p. 254). My approach to this study was thus situated in an emerging stream of scholarship (Frechette 2007; Schaffer 2014; Walton 2013) exploring meanings of "democracy" around the world using interpretive (rather than survey-based) methodologies.

By highlighting the different ways of constructing political problems and solutions, a narrative approach is valuable in exploring what Gallie (1956) describes as "essentially contested concepts". These are concepts that "inevitably involve endless disputes about their proper uses on the part of their users" (Gallie 1956, p. 169). Or as Patent suggests, they are "concepts which by nature invite disagreement over their meaning" (2010, p. 205). For example, in describing democracy one may appeal to concepts of "freedom" or "rights", yet these are also impossible to conclusively define. As different local and international actors react to the rise of communal violence, they attach different meanings to the words "democracy" and "democratization".[3]

For Gallie (1956), the utility of "essential contestability" is that it can facilitate mutual understanding about polarizing ideas. By examining the different facets of essentially contested concepts, it might be possible to recognize that one's opponents in a contest may also have internally valid perspectives. In this sense, Gallie assumed that the contestation over meaning would lead to "mutual recognition" (1956, p. 172) between rival actors and "progressive competition" (1956, p. 189). There would be a mutual sharpening of arguments through dialogue. Gaining consensus about the appropriate use of the concept may not be possible but, as Gallie explains, "it may yet be possible to explain or show the rationality of a given individual's continued use … of the concept in question" (1956, p. 189). And importantly, he suggests that not recognizing the essentially contested nature of concepts can lead to the "the chronic human peril of underestimating the value of one's opponents' position" (Gallie 1956, p. 193).

Freeden (1996) builds on Gallie's ideas, suggesting that contestation does not necessarily always lead to mutual recognition and, further, that argumentation is not always "progressive". Even if there is open debate, Freeden suggests "a concept may be impoverished during competition over its interpretation" (1996, p. 60). For example, differences in the meanings given to the word "democracy" can feasibly remain largely invisible in social interactions between activists and donor representatives in aid programmes. Debate over the issue of communal violence may also result in frustration, and little or no refinement of concepts. Thus, while Gallie's idea of essential contestability can help to explain divergence in the ways concepts are employed, along with Freeden (1996), I argue that the nature of contestation is not always "progressive".

It should be noted that the focus on communal violence in this research was, in some ways, accidental. The initial aim was to explore narratives of democratization from within the Burmese democracy movement and to compare these with prominent narratives in the international donor community. My field research, through 2013 and 2014, involved interviews with over fifty activists, opposition leaders, and donor representatives, review of donor program and strategy documents, and participation in a number of donor and political party meetings. Thus there was no initial intent to highlight the growing issue of violence in Myanmar. However, in the course of the research it became clear that, when asked about their perspectives on democratization, many participants sought to draw on the example of reactions to communal violence. Thus, in interviews, clear connections were made between assumptions about the ideal direction of the country's democratization and how the issue of communal violence should be addressed.

Data in the form of interview transcripts, field notes, and strategy and project documents was analysed according to its presentation of the primary obstacles to democratization in Myanmar and the vision of democracy. While there was some diversity in the examples given of problems and visions, responses clustered into broad and contrasting narratives about democratization. The next section outlines the various different ways international aid workers, activists, and opposition leaders narrated democratization and how these narratives linked to different reactions to communal violence.

CONTRASTING NARRATIVES OF DEMOCRATIZATION

Western donor agencies

In considering narratives of democratization and the new rift between the Western aid community and democracy movement, it is crucial the spotlight of investigation does not only fall on one side. Studies by Walton and Hayward (2013) and Kyaw San Wai (2014) have made valuable efforts to outline Burmese Buddhist perspectives and underlying reasoning which informs reactions to communal violence. Yet the arguments put forward by Western actors are less commonly unpacked. Therefore, in this section I begin by outlining a perspective on communal violence in Myanmar — and its grounding in wider assumptions about democratization — which is common among international aid workers. Of course, there is diversity between different Western actors and agencies, so there needs to be some caution about essentialising a uniquely "Western" position. Narratives here are treated as "decentred" — in the sense that there is no single or homogenous way individuals relate the story.[4]

The study revealed that many international aid workers were surprised and dismayed at the reactions of leaders in the opposition movement to news of incidents of violence in Meiktila or Rakhine State. Michael,[5] a European donor representative, described Aung San Suu Kyi's BBC interview as "deeply disappointing" (Interview 37, 2014 English), suggesting she was making a calculated political choice to refrain from condemning the violence. Meanwhile, Claire, an aid agency manager, was concerned about the way the public had responded, not only to violence against Rohingya, but also the wider hostility toward Muslims. She said, "When it was just the Rohingya ... you felt here is this one group that people are just mental about. But then when Meiktila happened ... It was brutal and totally shocking" (Interview 17, 2013 English).

Thus in some ways, the explanations of aid workers reflected international media portrayals of prominent Burmese opposition leaders and activists as "mental", or in the case of Aung San Suu Kyi, insincere. Yet concern was also directed not only toward leaders, but also toward Bamar aid workers within their own, or partner, organisations.[6] Thomas, an international agency director said, "I have no idea how many times my head office is saying 'something is happening in Rakhine [regarding religious violence], what are our local partners doing about this?' I try to say 'well you know many of our partners are part of the problem'" (Interview 27, 2013 English).

For many Western aid workers, the uncovering of these religious tensions in Burmese society since 2012 has been a sobering experience. "I don't know how democracy can progress in a society where people have these kinds of views", was the conclusion of another European donor adviser (Interview 19, 2013 English). Reflecting on the long-term Western advocacy and support to the Burmese democracy movement, Thomas concluded, "Look at what [Western human rights organizations] are saying publicly [about Myanmar's democracy movement]. This country is going to hell. The forces that we have believed in, I don't see how we can work with them any more" (Interview 27, 2013 English).

While there has been widespread concern in international agencies about reactions to anti-Muslim violence, these perspectives are also positioned within a wider liberal narrative of "democratization". Reactions to communal violence are consistent with underlying narratives which construct certain problems and solutions for Myanmar's democratization. One crucial element in framing narratives is the question of how political struggle, contests, and conflict can be contained in society. Proponents of this liberal narrative assume that political contest in society is best contained through formal democratic institutions (Interview 39, 2014 English). Procedures and institutions, such as free and fair elections, a representative parliament, and an independent judiciary, can provide the structure where political contests can be removed from the personalized realm and placed in a formal one. One agency manager (Interview 4, 2013 English) suggested that, as countries democratize, they move from informal and personalized systems to formal and regulated ones.

Yet underlying the formal procedures of government — which may vary from country to country — many Western participants pointed to a set of underlying values. Perceived to be at the core of these is a commitment to the universality of human rights. Michael said that in discussing the issue of communal violence with local organizations, he sought to establish human rights as a common principle from which they may be able to build consensus (Interview 37, 2014 English). Yet he was deeply frustrated in his attempts:

I am quite good at talking to young people about human rights but here I have failed miserably ... Even trying to say things like "My daughter is three and a half and she is sick and I take her to the hospital. If a Rohingya [Muslim minority group] girl gets sick and desperately needs help, don't you think she should get it?" "No" [they say] ... And I tried all these things in my toolbox (Interview 37, 2014 English).

In interactions between Western aid workers and activists and opposition leaders, aid workers often assumed that recognition of universal human rights was an inviolable platform. And when Bamar actors failed to frame dialogue in this category, interaction was often described as no longer being possible. "Nothing works", Michael concluded after failing to establish human rights as a common platform. "I have to admit I really can't discuss this any more. I have to give up. I am really disappointed" (Interview 37, 2014 English).

Along with universal human rights, any vision of democracy is also seen to necessarily embrace acceptance of multiple — especially minority — voices. "In [my country], we say that the measure of a true democracy is not majority rule but how minority voices are heard and incorporated," said another participant (Interview 19, 2013 English). As this quote suggests, the acceptance of multiple voices extends to the respect and protection of minorities. "The more you can respect minorities the better", she continued (Interview 19, 2013 English). Myanmar moving towards clearer protection of the Muslim minority — and other ethnic minority groups such as the Kachin and Karen — was essential for any "genuine" measure of democracy. In this way, for proponents of the *liberal* narrative of democratization in Myanmar, human rights and protection of minorities are values that must be part of the foundation of any future vision of "democracy". Though the structure or procedures of formal democratic institutions may vary, it is essential they are grounded in these liberal values.

I now turn to a set of contrasting interpretations from activists and opposition leaders in the Burmese democracy movement. While respect of human rights and minority protection are perceived by many international aid workers to be necessary components of democracy, among activists, debate commonly focuses on the values of unity and the need for protection of the Bamar majority.

Burmese democracy movement

It is difficult to understand reactions from within the Burmese democracy movement without acknowledging the historical trajectories of democratic thought in Myanmar. In particular, I argue that the values of unity and protection of the Bamar majority have been especially prominent in democratic thought before and since Burma's independence. And that these values inform current descriptions — by activists and opposition leaders — of the problems and solutions related to the country's democratization.

It is firstly important to note that the initial parliamentary period (1948–62) after independence — under Burma's first prime minister, U Nu — was one of great instability. There was a range of civil wars against both Communist uprisings and also disaffected ethnic minority groups. And there were also significant divisions among Bamar political leaders, eventually leading to a split in U Nu's ruling Anti Fascist People's Freedom League (or *hpasapala*) party. With continuing deep ethnic, religious, and ideological divisions, a key question for political leaders was how to maintain unity in the country and protect the future of the Bamar majority from both its internal and external threats.

U Nu, in particular, was intent on a form of "democracy" where benevolent leaders could unite the fragmented country. He praised the martyr U Aung San for his *cetana*, or benevolence (Houtman 1999, p. 62). In his introduction to U Nu's play *The Wages of Sin*, Law Yone (in Blum et al. 2013, p. 65) remarked:

> U Nu came close to quoting the Bible when he gave his concept of democracy: It is not he who says Lord, Lord who will enter the Kingdom of Heaven, but he who doeth the word of my Father. It is not everyone who says Democracy, Democracy that will find it, but he that doeth what democracy enjoins ... democracy had not failed, but those professing it had failed democracy. In particular those who had preached it constantly had failed to practise it.

In other words, U Nu suggested that many people may talk about democracy, yet it was those who fulfilled the obligations of democracy who were most genuine — those who 'doeth what democracy enjoins' (Law Yone 1961, p. 1). The country of Burma could be knitted together for the first time through a democratic political system led by people with moral character and a willingness to put aside narrow vested interests for the benefit of the country.

There is little doubt that this post-independence struggle — over how to bring unity and protection of the Bamar (or more widely the Buddhist) majority — has influenced subsequent democratic thought in the country.[7] The "disciplined democracy" advocated by the State Peace and Development Council — and more recently the Thein Sein government — attempts to maintain the supposedly stabilizing "guardian" role of the military within governance. And in contemporary narratives of democratization from within the opposition movement, and from leaders such as Aung San Suu Kyi, the fear of disunity also features strongly. Thus when considering recent reactions to communal violence in Myanmar, it is important to place these in the context of modern political thought in the country, and particularly the necessary emphasis on unity, and protection of the majority.

The rise of communal violence and Muslim–Buddhist tension is a pressing concern for the Bamar activists and opposition leaders involved in this study. Yet underlying some of the discussion of Muslim–Buddhist tensions is a *moral* — as opposed to *liberal* — narrative of Myanmar's democratization. The *liberal* narrative is premised on formal procedures and institutions — backed by commitment to universal human rights and protection of minorities — as the primary means of containing political conflicts and tensions in society. In contrast, and echoing U Nu's perspectives, the *moral* narrative of democratization portrays internal change as the primary means of containing political contest. It requires the progressive laying aside of one's own individual interests for the good of the whole (Interview 5, 2013 English). Thus on the one hand, among Western donor agencies the word "democracy" is often imbued with liberal values. And it should be noted that the conceptual relation between liberalism and democracy has its own inherent tensions. Yet on the other hand, among Burmese activists, "democracy" is commonly linked to personal *moral* values such as unity and benevolence (or *cetana*).

For example, activist and writer U Wunna stressed that the primary need in the country's democratization is for leaders who are *tageh seit shi de lu* or "people with true motivation" (Interview 1, 2013 Burmese). Meanwhile, opposition political leader U Aung Naing (Interview 5, 2013 Burmese) pointed to the importance of *cetana* in the country's transition to democracy. In this sense, it is insufficient for a leader to have only knowledge or technical skills in governance. They must also demonstrate moral character. And the personal realm is not part of the problem — as is suggested by the *liberal* narrative — but rather the primary realm where change needs to take place.

Many of the country's current problems are seen to stem from a long-standing *ar nar shin* or dictatorial style of leadership (Interview 1, 2013 Burmese). A true-hearted leader (*tage seit shi de lu*) can provide a means to overcome the everyday conflicts that emerge from the political realm. Supporting this leadership requires a commitment among citizens to unity. For proponents of this narrative, Burma was born into instability and unification of the country under a benevolent leader has been the unrealized goal since the country's independence. Ethnic and ideological division soured the early years of civilian government. And while the decades of military leadership may have enforced a degree of national unity, it came via the *ar nar shin* style of leadership by a self-interested few.

Thus, the unification of the country is seen to require an emphasis on the obligations (as opposed to the rights) of individuals. A member of the National League for Democracy (NLD) (Interview 8, 2013 Burmese) explained that in a democratic country, rights need to be "balanced with obligations". If democracy is about rights alone, it will lead to instability in society, as everyone will be guided by self-interest (Interview 8, 2013 Burmese). Rather, as Aung San Suu Kyi suggests in *Freedom from Fear*, "free men" are the ones who "make themselves fit to bear the responsibilities and to uphold the disciplines which will maintain a free society" (1991, p. 183).

This focus on unity also leads to an emphasis on protection of the country's Buddhist majority from sectarian, minority interests — especially those of Muslims. As one local NGO leader described:

> Buddhism is not confrontational. ... But Muslims in Myanmar are systematically threatening the country, infiltrating into the country. If we keep the status quo they will grab the whole society — which is what happened in Indonesia and Malaysia which were originally Buddhist countries. Muslims are very aggressive. ... Buddhism needs a defence system, otherwise we will have to be backed into the ocean. We do not want to attack, but just defend (Interview 46, 2014 Burmese).

The facts articulated in this quote may be disputed, yet what is important is the underlying logic of majority protection, rooted in a commitment to the ideal of unity. While in the *liberal* narrative, human rights is the inviolable framework through which to consider the issue of communal violence, for some in the democracy movement, the inviolable dimension is unity.

Thus these wider narratives of democratization can reveal the contrasting frameworks through which Muslim–Buddhist tensions are understood.

Yet another crucial dimension illuminated through this study was the contests *within* the democracy movement. The *moral* emphasis on unity and benevolence is not universally accepted and, in fact, its core tenets are deeply challenged by an alternate narrative that highlights the need for cultural reform away from norms of hierarchy. For proponents of this *equality* narrative, the emphasis on benevolent leadership and unity is seen to be deeply problematic. Some perceive an inherent tendency toward abuse of power in Bamar culture and religion. These cultural traits emphasize unity and majority protection and yet consistently allow dictatorial leaders to take control. And this problem is not only considered to lie at the national level of politics but throughout society — in local aid organizations, religious organizations, and even in the family. In order to progress toward genuine democratization, proponents of this *equality* narrative suggest the core elements of the *moral* narrative of democratization need to be questioned. When asked in an interview about the main challenge to Myanmar's democratization, U Tun Kyi, an activist organization leader, said:

> It's the culture ... the hierarchy and religious teaching. The social teaching and religious teaching listened with no criticism ... these are key challenges for the practice of the democracy (Interview 9, 2013 English/Burmese).

In the context of communal violence and Muslim–Buddhist tensions, some activists believe there has been an unfortunate reinforcement of the dominant *moral* narrative of democratization. And this has served to distract from the core issue of reforming Myanmar's wider political culture — and especially the role of the military in governance. At its core, the rise in communal violence is seen to represent yet another failure of the military-dominated government. Or even further, some see anti-Muslim sentiments as having been actively fostered by elements in the government in order to divide the opposition. As one activist argued, "the fear is being instilled by the regime ... I think the regime is taking advantage of this fear and are stoking this fear" (Interview 34, 2014 English).

Whatever the case, Bamar activists who are proponents of this narrative suggest that genuine democratization will entail a wholesale cultural reform and a shift toward greater relational equality — and that the dominant Bamar reactions to the issue of communal violence are a sign of the very problems that need to be addressed. Importantly though, this differs from the *liberal* narrative of democratization in that it is sceptical of the role of formal institutions or procedures in resolving the tensions and conflict inherent in politics. Rather, the *equality* narrative offers a deeper critique of Bamar culture, emphasizing the authoritarian tendencies not only in government but also throughout society.

Thus, between Western donor representatives and Bamar activists and opposition leaders, there is a range of contrasting reactions to the issue of communal violence. I have attempted to demonstrate that these reactions are not just isolated perspectives — which can be explained as irrational or disingenuous — but rather sit in contrasting overarching narratives of the country's democratization. These narratives emphasize different sets of core values and different ways of containing, or rising above, the tensions and conflicts of political life.

CONCLUSION: BEYOND FIXED MEANINGS OF "DEMOCRACY"

Communal violence and Muslim–Buddhist tensions have led to polarized reactions, and there are new lines of fracture between the international aid community and the Bamar democracy movement, and also new divisions in the opposition. I have argued that connecting reactions to communal violence to deeper and contrasting narratives of democratization can help explain why there has been such divergence. Thus assumptions about the meaning of "democracy" are critical in making sense of responses to communal violence.

Importantly, if "democracy" is seen to have a single, universal meaning based in "human rights", then the anti-Muslim perspectives expressed by some in the democracy movement can only be explained as crazy or insincere. In contrast, if democracy is considered to be an "essentially contested concept" (Gallie 1956) — where there is no fixed way of determining its meaning — then connections are revealed between reactions to communal violence and contrasting narratives about the country's democratization.

Given the country's fractious modern history, it is no surprise that within the opposition movement the values of unity and protection of the majority are prominent in debates about the meaning of "democracy".

And for some activists and opposition leaders, unity and protection of the majority are an inviolable platform from which any debate about democracy — or communal violence — must take place. Likewise, it is of little surprise that the values of universal human rights and the protection of minorities play a pivotal role in the narratives of democratization drawn on by many Western aid workers.

Yet this research shows that while Gallie's (1956) ideas of essential contestability can be valuable in making sense of different reactions to communal violence, this study did not reveal competition over rival uses of "democracy" as always "progressive". Rather, debate over "democracy" and appropriate responses to communal violence was often portrayed as either absent, or regressive rather than progressive. As absolute and conflicting components of the meaning of "democracy" were put forward — for example, human rights versus unity — there was generally seen to be little mutual refinement of arguments. Rather, many participants suggested they could no longer debate the issue. Questions of how to respond to communal violence may be so difficult to discuss in aid programs because of differing inviolable assumptions about the nature of democracy.

Explaining the reactions of Aung San Suu Kyi or Burmese activists as either disingenuous, or as a sign of being "crazy", fails to appreciate the many different narratives about the country's democratization. Yet recognition of rival meanings of "democracy" may not necessarily lead to reconciliation of positions. And, in fact, attention to the contested nature of "democracy" can reveal that different positions are even more irreconcilable than we may have hoped. Portraying opposing positions as either irrational or insincere at least provides some finality; recognizing them as alternative forms of democratic thinking can be far more perplexing.

Notes

1 This research involved fifty interviews with Western aid workers, activists and opposition political party leaders conducted in Burmese and English languages by the researcher over a ten-month period in 2013 and 2014. The year and language of the interviews is indicated in in-text citations.
2 It should be noted that while this research focused on the democracy movement in Myanmar, it was more specifically targeted to Bamar or Burman activists, or opposition leaders in the movement. The varied perspectives of actors from ethnic minority background were not addressed directly. This could be an important

topic for future research with a wider scope than the present study.
3   In this chapter I refer to narratives related to "democracy" and "democratization". I recognize that these words are often connected to contrasting concepts — one about a vision of political life and the other about a process of change away from an alternate form of political life, and toward "democracy". These two concepts have their own subfields of scholarly investigation. However, I argue that these concepts are also closely connected. Meanings of "democracy" are built around reactions to particular problems that "democracy" is intended to solve. In other words, the vision of "democracy" depends on an understanding of the process of "democratization". Meanwhile, the meaning of "democratization" is contingent on varying constructions of the vision of "democracy". In this sense, both "democracy" and "democratization" are "essentially contested concepts" and the meaning of one is, in certain respects, contingent on the meaning of the other.
4   I use the word "decentred" here to refer to the understanding that narratives do not have a *core* definition. Bevir and Rhodes (2003, p. 2) suggest that one of the dangers of working at the aggregate level is that "we can neglect the beliefs of the individuals lumped together in a tradition". Decentring an aggregate concept like "narrative" serves to show how within a particular coalition of actors there may be more nuanced strands of narrative.
5   Pseudonyms are used to refer to participants in this study.
6   I use the Myanmar word "Bamar" here to refer to the majority Burman ethnic group.
7   Walton (2015) convincingly traces the theme of unity in Myanmar politics further into the colonial and pre-colonial period.

References

4News. "Aung San Suu Kyi: Falling from Grace", 25 October 2013 <http://blogs.channel4.com/world-news-blog/aung-san-suu-kyi-falling-grace/26332>. Accessed 5 February 2015.

Aung San Suu Kyi. *Freedom from Fear and Other Writings*. London: Viking Press, 1991.

Andrews, Molly, Corinne Squire, and Maria Tamboukou, eds. *Doing Narrative Research*. London: Sage, 2008.

BBC. "Suu Kyi Blames Violence on Climate of Fear", 24 October 2013. <http://www.bbc.com/news/world-asia-24651359>. Accessed 2 February 2015.

Bevir, Mark, and Rod Rhodes. *Interpreting British Governance*. London: Routledge, 2003.

Blair, David. "How Can Aung San Suu Kyi—a Nobel Peace Prize Winner—Fail to Condemn Anti Muslim Violence?" *The Telegraph*, 24 October 2013. <http://blogs.telegraph.co.uk/news/davidblair/100242929/how-can-aung-san-suu-

kyi-a-nobel-peace-prize-winner-fail-to-condemn-anti-muslim-violence/>. Accessed 2 February 2015.

Blum, Franziska, Friederike Trotier, and Hans-Bernd Zöllner (eds). *In Their Own Voice: "Democracy" as Perceived in Burma/Myanmar, 1921–2010*. Passau: University of Passau, 2013

Boswell, John. "Why and How Narrative Matters in Deliberative Systems". *Political Studies* 61, (2013): 620–36.

Frechette, Anne. "Democracy and Democratization Among Tibetans in Exile". *Journal of Asian Studies* 66, no. 1 (2007): 97–127.

Freeden, Michael. *Ideologies and Political Theory: A Conceptual Approach*. London: Oxford University Press, 1996.

Gallie, Walter Bryce. "Essentially Contested Concepts". *Proceedings of the Aristotelian Society* 56 (1956): 167–98.

Houtman Gustaaf. *Mental Culture in Burmese Crisis Politics: Aung San Suu Kyi and the National League for Democracy*. Tokyo: ILCAA, 1999.

Kyaw San Wai. "Myanmar's Religious Violence: A Buddhist Siege Mentality at Work". *Rajaratnam School of International Studies*, no. 37/2014, 20 February 2014.

Patent, Jason D. "A Unified Account of Essentially Contested Concepts". *Proceedings of the Annual Meeting of the Berkeley Linguistics Society* 27, no. 1 (2010): 205–13.

Roe, Emery. "Narrative Analysis for the Policy Analyst: A Case Study of the 1980–1982 Medfly Controversy in California". *Journal of Policy Analysis and Management* 8, no. 2 (1989): 251–73.

Schaffer, Frederic Charles. "Thin Descriptions: The Limits of Survey Research on the Meaning of Democracy". *Polity* 46, no. 3 (2014): 303–30.

Tatmadaw. *The Burmese Road to Socialism: Policy Declaration of the Revolutionary Council*. Yangon: Tatmadaw, 1963. Available at <https://archive.org/stream/TheBurmeseRoadToSocialism/BRS_djvu.txt>. Accessed 24 February 2016.

Van Eeten, Michel J.G. "Narrative Policy Analysis". In *Handbook of Public Policy Analysis: Theory, Politics, and Methods*, edited by F. Fischer and G.J. Miller. New York: CRC Press, 2007.

Walton, Matthew J. "Politics in the Moral Universe: Burmese Buddhist Political Thought". Ph.D. Dissertation, University of Washington, 2013.

———. "The Disciplining Discourse of Unity in Burmese Politics". *Journal of Burma Studies* 19, no. 1 (2015): 1–26.

Walton, Matthew J. and Susan Hayward. *Contesting Buddhist Narratives: Democratization, Nationalism, and Communal Violence in Myanmar*. Honolulu: East West Center, 2013.

13

PUBLIC PERCEPTIONS OF A DIVIDED MYANMAR

Findings from the 2015 Myanmar Asian Barometer Survey

Bridget Welsh and Kai-Ping Huang

A dominant image of Myanmar's politics is one of conflict. Whether it is the bloodshed over fighting in the Kokang region and the exodus of Rohingyas from Rakhine State, the struggle between young students against the police in protest, or the contestation among leaders and between democratic forces led by the National League for Democracy (NLD) and the Tatmadaw, the lens that frames Burmese politics is one of division. This was especially the case in the pivotal year of 2015, the year of the contentious November election that witnessed the decisive victory of the NLD.

Rather than examine underlying dynamics of specific issues or explore the causes of a particular conflict in depth, this chapter looks at conflict from the views of ordinary citizens. It uses the data from the Asian Barometer

Survey (ABS) collected from January through March 2015 to shed light on how the public views cleavages in Myanmar society. The aim is twofold: to describe some of the empirical findings of the ABS related to conflict as well as to offer an alternative understanding of conflict drawing from a different data source — ordinary Myanmar citizens.

The chapter examines public views of conflict generally and analyses how different groups in Myanmar society view conflict. Specifically, it concentrates on two different forms of political identity in Myanmar — ethnicity and religion — and examines the implications of responses to the ABS for understanding the causes and trajectories of conflict associated with these identities. Both cleavages are seen as underlying serious divides in Myanmar; ethnic differences have underscored decades of civil war and continued fighting between the Bamar majority and ethnic minorities, especially those concentrated in the states along Myanmar's borders.[1] Religious differences, notably between the Buddhist majority and Muslim minority, have contributed to religious riots, hate speech, and religious intolerance in recent years (Cheesman and Htoo Kyaw Win 2015; Schissler, Walton, and Phyu Phyu Thi 2015). These divisions have been at the heart of conflict and violence in Myanmar.

By looking at public perceptions of conflict around salient political identities, as well as views related to conflict in general and by minorities, this chapter offers some surprising insights. While the ABS confirms the seriousness of division in Myanmar society, the findings suggest there is considerable common ground across communities for peace building and to reduce tensions. Further, by bringing attention to the views of ordinary citizens, this chapter highlights the need to look beyond elite-oriented studies of conflict in understanding both current dynamics and future trajectories.

MYANMAR ASIAN BAROMETER SURVEY: METHODOLOGY AND FIELDWORK

The 2015 Myanmar ABS survey comprised over 200 questions, including the core questions in the Global Barometer and ABS surveys that allow for cross-regional comparisons, as well as specific questions directly related to Myanmar.[2] The main topics explored ranged from perceptions of governance, trust in institutions and social capital to political culture, partisanship and political participation, and views of democracy, globalization, and regional powers. Many of the Myanmar-specific questions are directly related to conflict and are highlighted below. The public findings of the survey were released in August 2015, with a report available in early 2016.[3] As with the practice of all the ABS data, the Myanmar data will also be available publicly for scholars and practitioners after a one-year embargo, from August 2016.

The Myanmar ABS survey adopted random stratified sampling from available population data provided by the Myanmar Ministry of Immigration and Population and the General Administration Department (GAD). A total of thirty-six sampling points or townships were randomly selected, weighted for a representative distribution between rural and urban areas and including all fifteen major administrative states and regions (including the capital). In each township or sampling point, three villages/wards were randomly selected based on a representative urban-rural even weighting. In each village/ward, fifteen respondents were randomly selected through landmark sampling that assured each citizen in the selected community had an equal chance of being chosen. Landmarks were selected after initial fieldwork and were reviewed after the pilot survey. They included the Union Solidarity and Development Party (USDP) office, the village welcome sign, a religious institution, a non-USDP political party office, a village headman's office/home and more, and were assigned randomly to different interviewers to assure all the households in the community had an equal chance of being chosen. Gender and age distribution was randomly assigned at the landmark sampling level. After the release of the Myanmar census data in May 2015, the data was weighted to conform to the released demographic information, urban-rural differences, as well as the age and gender breakdowns. The sampling methodology complied with the rigor followed in similar ABS and Global Barometer surveys. To assure quality fieldwork, a series of quality control measures — from random checks in the field to retesting by another survey team — were conducted. There is a technical report detailing the sampling and methods.[4]

The ABS was implemented by the Yangon School of Political Science (YSPS) and funded by the Taiwan Foundation for Democracy (TFD) and the National Endowment for Democracy (NED) with volunteer contributions by ABS scholars from National Taiwan University and regional ABS survey network teams.[5] The survey was conducted from January through mid-March 2015 in each of the major states/regions in Myanmar. No replacements had to be made to the thirty-six randomly selected sample points, and the team was fortunate to avoid tensions and fighting in some states/regions with early fieldwork implementation. A total of 1,620 people were surveyed in face-to-face interviews. These interviews took an average of an hour-and-fifteen minutes per respondent. YSPS staff were trained and advised by the ABS team from May 2014 through to the end of the survey in March 2015. The national survey was conducted after a successful pilot survey of 720 respondents during September–October 2014 in Bago. The survey was conducted in Burmese, and in the ethnic minority areas with interpreters in local languages.[6] The survey was carried out with the permission of national and state government authorities, and with the knowledge and cooperation of local township officials. While there were a few minor misunderstandings in the fieldwork with local government officials, the relationship with the government was cordial, as officials facilitated the implementation of an independent national survey. The main challenges in the field included logistical access to locations (as a result of poor transportation infrastructure) and difficult physical conditions, especially in more remote areas such as the Chin State.

As public surveys are a relatively new phenomenon in Myanmar,[7] and the historical record with them, as occurred after the 1990 election, is chequered, another challenge involved public confidence and interaction. There were comprehension issues on some of the questions, particularly among less educated and more remote, less exposed respondents. Significant efforts were made to improve comprehension and question wording during the survey, but there were understandable gaps. Some of the more complicated questions solicited more "don't knows". Given general concerns about the political climate and authoritarian history of Myanmar, the response rate for the ABS survey was very high. It reached seventy-five per cent, with interviewers reporting positive cooperation from the majority of respondents. This shows the viability of seeking public views in Myanmar. The results do indicate, however, that fear and reserve were present, especially with regard to sensitive political questions, as there were higher rates of non-answers to sensitive questions. Cross-regional comparisons with other ABS data show that Myanmar citizens were no less inclined to answer sensitive questions than other countries, especially those in Southeast Asia such as Cambodia, Vietnam, and Malaysia. In fact, on some questions, there were more responses than in other countries, suggesting that in spite of a lack of familiarity with surveys and reserve, Myanmar citizens were eager to share their views. The only area in the Myanmar ABS where there was more reserve was in voting intentions.[8]

A word of caution is also necessary about the interpretation of the results. Survey methodology is limited by the wording of questions. Care was taken in the pilot and pre-tests to work toward comprehension and conceptual clarity in the survey wording in Burmese, moving into more colloquial and accessible vocabulary. Nevertheless, analysis of the findings cannot account for the varied meanings of words and potential multiple (mis)understandings of concepts. Below, the findings are presented with limited speculation on alternative and varied meanings, recognizing that alternative methodologies such as focus groups and ethnography provide more in-depth understandings of terms and their meanings.

CONFLICT-AVERSION AND RECOGNITION

We begin with the findings on how the Myanmar public views conflict. One of the interesting findings of the Myanmar ABS involves political culture, as the ABS shows that Myanmar respondents record the most conservative views among the Southeast Asian countries surveyed. This conservatism extends to how they perceive conflict; Myanmar citizens indicate in the ABS that they are highly conflict-averse.

As part of the political culture battery in the ABS, we ask a series of questions about conflict. Respondents are asked to agree or disagree with the following statements: "Even if there is some disagreement with others, one should avoid the conflict"; "In a group, we should avoid open quarrel to preserve the harmony of the group"; "A person should not insist on his own opinion if his co-workers disagree with him". These questions allow us to understand how individuals view conflict at an individual level. The consistent picture emerging is that Myanmar citizens report that conflict should be avoided. A large majority of the people surveyed (ninety-nine per cent) believe that one should avoid conflict, with eighty-eight per cent and ninety-four per cent expressing similar views with regard to the need to preserve harmony and not insisting on one's views. To put these findings in perspective, Figure 13.1 shows where the Myanmar public stands on conflict avoidance compared to other countries in Southeast Asia, revealing that Myanmar citizens profess a desire to avoid conflict at the individual level which exceeds findings in other countries in the region.

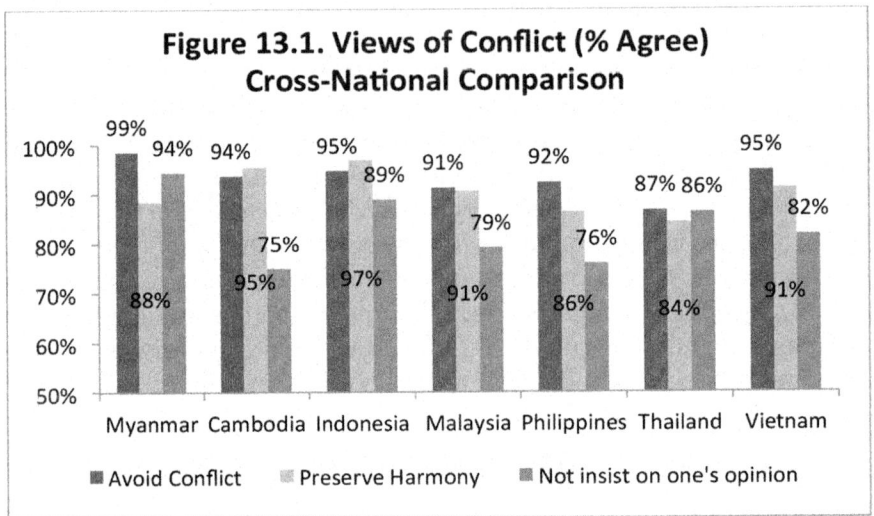

Figure 13.1. Views of Conflict (% Agree) Cross-National Comparison

Part of the reason for this involves recognition of the importance of conflict in society. Seventy-one per cent of Myanmar citizens in the ABS view ethnic conflict as "serious". This recognition extends across divisions, as both ethnic minorities and the Bamar majority hold this view; eighty-three per cent and sixty-seven per cent respectively. Given that most of the ethnic conflicts are concentrated in ethnic minority areas, it is understandable that a larger percentage of the ethnic minority population would see this conflict as serious.

A large percentage of the Myanmar public also sees sharp differences among rich and poor, with citizens split on the government's treatment of communities of different economic backgrounds. Some fifty-one per cent of respondents believe the government treats all groups unfairly. Myanmar citizens are more divided than people in other parts of the region, but what is striking is that a majority of Myanmar citizens see their society as divided along class lines.

ETHNICITY: DIFFERENCE WITH COMMON GROUND

The most prominent division in Myanmar has been ethnicity. Key themes in the literature on ethnic division have involved systemic discrimination on the part of the Bamar majority government towards ethnic minorities, centre-periphery relations with limited decentralization of political power, systematic impoverishment and lack of control of natural resources and land. Scholars vary in their interpretations of the causes of ethnic conflict, but disproportionally the causes are identified as being associated with the actions of Myanmar's military government.

In order to examine variation in how Myanmar citizens look at ethnicity and conflict, we differentiate between the Bamar majority and ethnic minorities. A total of thirty-six different ethnic minorities were surveyed in the ABS, according to their self-identified ethnicity.[9] The breakdown of the different ethnic groups can be found below in Figure 13. 2. The largest share of ethnic minority communities surveyed was Shan, Rakhine, and Kayin. As all of the states were included in the ABS, those included resided in both the periphery as well as the centre.

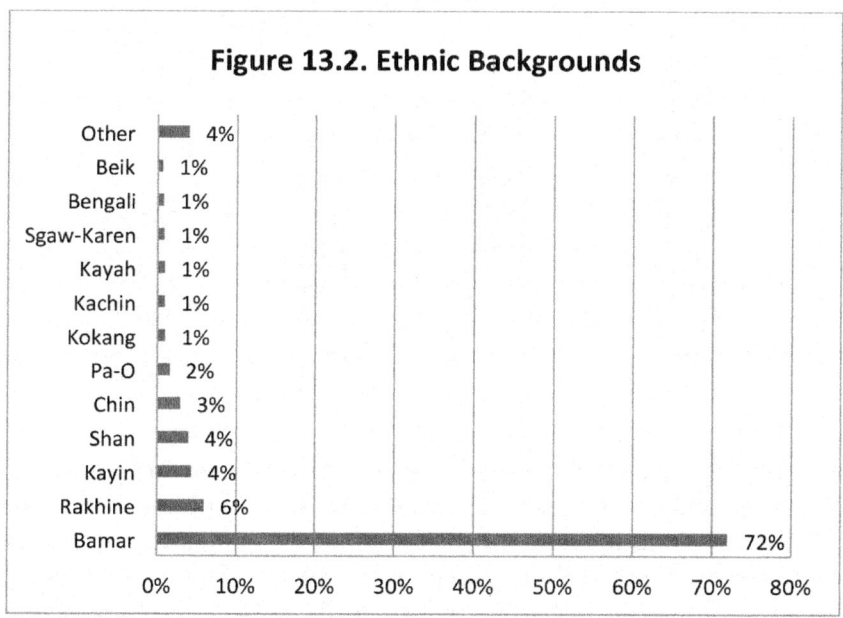

Figure 13.2. Ethnic Backgrounds

The ABS confirms that ethnic minorities perceive discrimination as a matter of concern, believing that there are deep inequalities in how ethnic minorities are treated. Respondents were asked to agree or disagree with the following statement: "All citizens from different ethnic communities in Myanmar are treated equally by the government." As Figure 13.3 shows, only slightly more than a third of ethnic minorities agreed that they received equal treatment from the government, with this number slightly higher in ethnic minority states where ethnic minorities may make up the majority population of the state or an administrative sub-region within it. This view of unequal treatment among ethnic minorities sharply contrasts with that of the Bamar majority, who do not see the issue of inequality along ethnic lines as an issue. Nearly two-thirds of Bamar think there is equal treatment of ethnic minorities. There is a stark difference in how the majority and minorities perceive the government's interventions towards ethnic minorities.

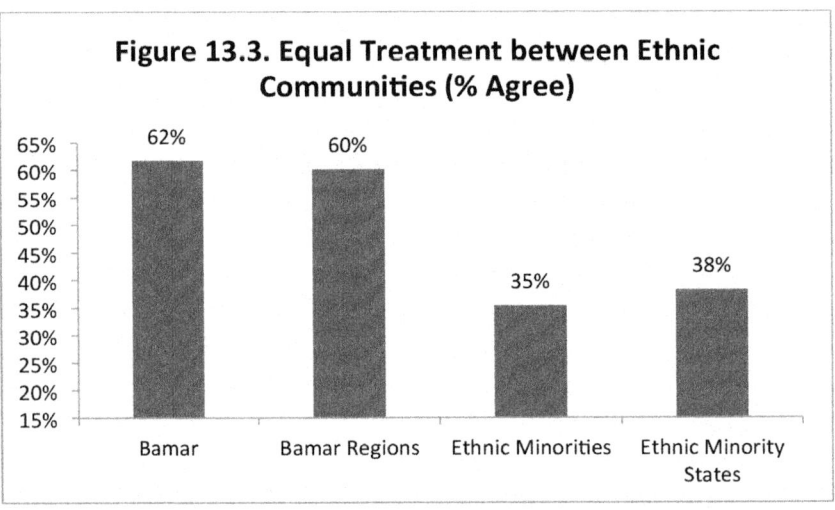

Figure 13.3. Equal Treatment between Ethnic Communities (% Agree)

These concerns about the treatment of the government toward ethnic minorities extend into the evaluation of the current peace process as offering protection for minority rights in the country. Respondents were asked to agree or disagree with the following statement: "The ongoing peace process will protect the rights of ethnic minority groups." While over fifty per cent of respondents view the process positively as a vehicle for rights protection, ethnic minorities are less confident about protection than the Bamar majority, sixty-four per cent compared to seventy-three per cent.

When one moves away from looking at the relationship between ethnic minorities and the government and examines how ethnic minorities perceive differences in society compared to views of the Bamar majority, the differences are not as sharp. Both the Bamar majority and ethnic minorities indicate similar levels of economic difficulties. Slightly over fifty per cent of respondents — Bamar and ethnic minorities alike — say they have difficulty covering basic needs. Poverty is a serious problem in Myanmar and all communities suffer from it.

These shared experiences are echoed when asked about economic vulnerability detailed in Figure 13.4. A majority of nearly all communities acknowledged they would have difficulties making ends meet if they lost their monthly income. Ethnic minorities, especially in ethnic minority states, recorded relatively higher economic vulnerability than citizens in Bamar majority areas. These areas rely heavily on incomes from migrant labour abroad and the diaspora community, which can be irregular sources of income. This finding confirms the view that perceived economic vulnerabilities tend to be slightly higher among ethnic minorities.

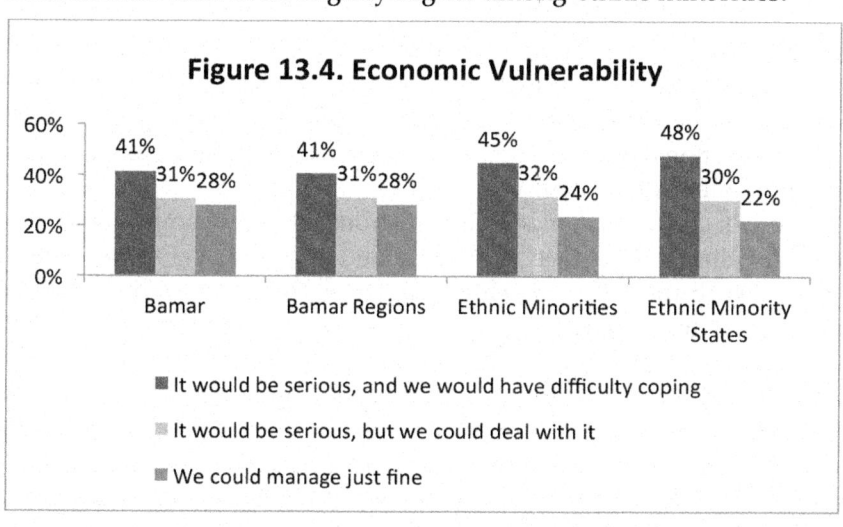

When asked about income distribution, public perceptions differ dramatically. Although a majority of Bamar believe national income distribution is unfair, the perception is more negative among ethnic minorities, as in Figure 13.5 (over page). This reaffirms the more negative perceptions of ethnic minorities regarding discrimination and governance discussed above.

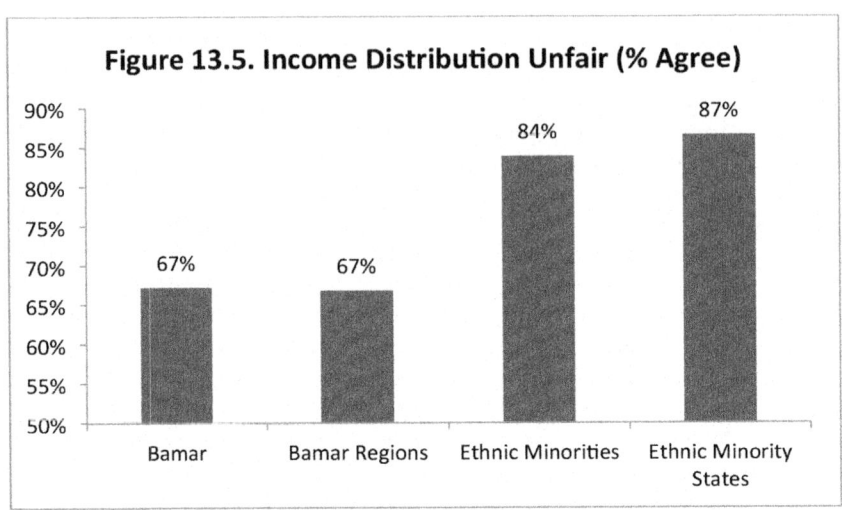

Figure 13.5. Income Distribution Unfair (% Agree)

While the differences among the Bamar majority and ethnic minorities are present, there is considerable common ground on the political solutions to these different views and experiences, notably with regard to decentralization of political power. The ABS asked questions on federalism and autonomy with promising results.

There is consensus among citizens from different communities about strengthening a federal system. Respondents were asked to agree or disagree with the following statement: "We should strengthen a federal system in Myanmar and give more power to state/regional governments." A majority of all the communities concur that a federal system should be strengthened. This support for decentralization exists despite Myanmar not yet having a federal system in place. The percentages are slightly higher among ethnic minorities (seventy-nine per cent compared to seventy per cent), but the shared positive view of decentralizing authority bodes well for measures that can ameliorate ethnic conflict. The numbers increase when Myanmar citizens are asked about the selection of chief ministers who govern states and regions, as over eighty per cent of all communities support decentralizing the choice of leadership of chief ministers to their regional parliaments.

The common ground over decentralization extends to increasing autonomy as well, with over two-thirds supporting increased autonomy, as shown in Figure 13.6. Respondents were asked to agree or disagree with the following statement: "In Myanmar, ethnic minorities should have autonomy in their states/regions." A total of sixty-nine per cent of Bamar support more autonomy for ethnic minorities, with this reaching eighty-three per cent among ethnic minorities. The ABS indicates that while there are clearly different views of the government's engagement of ethnic minorities, there is shared support for measures that have the potential to address ethnic conflict in Myanmar society.

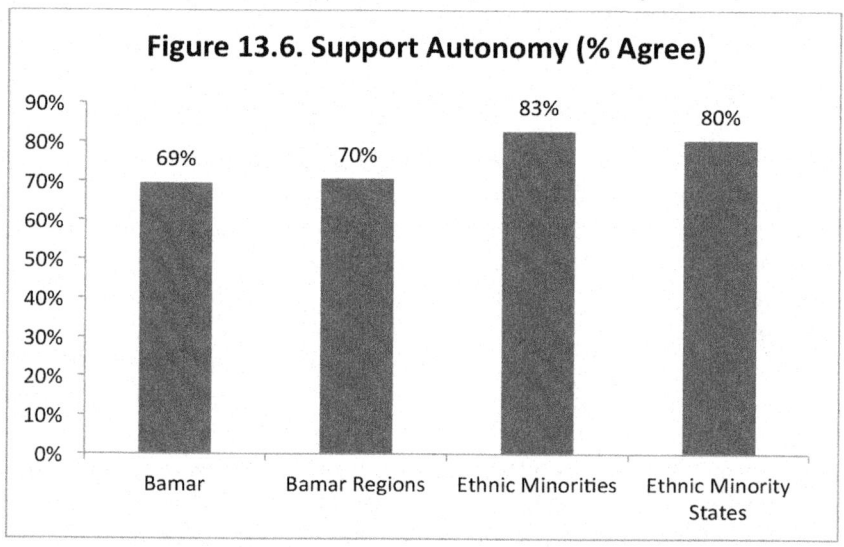

Figure 13.6. Support Autonomy (% Agree)

RELIGION: IMPORTANT BUT NOT ALWAYS DIVISIVE

The picture with regard to religion is less clear-cut. Since the 2012 religious riots against Muslims in a handful of locations in Myanmar, most observers have noted that religious intolerance has increased (for example, Diamond 2014; Mufford 2014). Anti-Muslim sentiment was used to mobilize the electorate in the November 2015 elections (Perera 2015). This effort was largely unsuccessful, but the issues of religious intolerance and division remain prominent and of concern. The ABS foreshadowed the developments in the November polls, indicating that religion is one of the most serious divisions in Myanmar society, but a factor that did not necessarily detract from support for democracy and demands for better governance.

The ABS captured a low number of religious minorities in the survey, only eight per cent, with the large majority of respondents being Buddhist. Despite including religious minorities in all fieldwork teams, the number of Muslims interviewed only reached one per cent. This was one of the areas where the ABS's level of representativeness could have been stronger. We were unlucky in our randomly selected townships, capturing fewer Muslim dominant areas in Rakhine State, for example. We are, however, able to distinguish between Buddhists and non-Buddhists. For further understanding of the impact of religion, we also distinguish between those who self-identify as devout Buddhists compared to those who do not, capturing differences in religiosity as well.

The findings confirm that religion is an important marker of identity, even more prominent than ethnicity. As Figure 13.7 shows, fifty-two per cent of Myanmar citizens are most likely to prioritize religion over ethnicity or national affinity in how they identify themselves. Myanmar citizens were asked to differentiate between religion (bathadaya), race (lumyo), and Myanmar nationality (Myanma amyotha). In fact only fifteen per cent identify with their race first. A third of Myanmar citizens identified with the Myanmar nation. It is noteworthy that a quarter of ethnic minorities prioritized "Myanmar nation" over other markers. Identity is complex, as individuals often change their identity in different circumstances and experience multiple identities, so these results should be interpreted with caution. Nevertheless, the prioritization of religion shows how important it is in Myanmar society, relative to other commonly used markers.

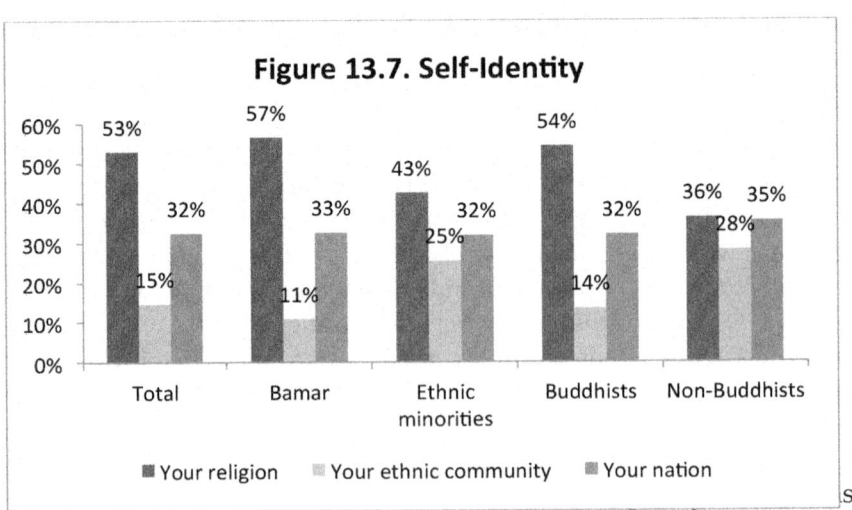

Asia. Nearly three-quarters (seventy-three per cent) profess to practice their faith daily. Of the Buddhists, seventy-four per cent self-identify as devout, with the number of devout being fifty-five per cent for followers of other religions. This level of religious practice confirms long-standing findings of the prominence of religion in Myanmar life (see Smith 1965). The prominence of religion as a marker of identity extends to how Myanmar citizens understand citizenship. Respondents were asked to agree or disagree with the following statement: "Citizenship in Myanmar should be based on religion." A majority of eighty-one per cent agreed that citizenship should be based on religion, with a small minority disagreeing. Disproportionately those that agree that citizenship should be tied to religion are Buddhists. We also found that devout Buddhists were more likely to make this connection, at eighty-nine per cent compared to eighty per cent of non-devout Buddhists. Only forty-eight per cent of non-Buddhists supported citizenship based on religion, which is still a high number given that a minority faith would potentially be at a disadvantage to the majority faith.

Similar high responses for a political role for religion were given to questions involving secular government, with the majority of Myanmar citizens (sixty per cent) believing the government should consult religious authorities when making laws. Respondents were asked to agree or disagree with the following statement: "The government should consult religious authorities when interpreting the laws." A total of fourteen per cent disagreed, with sixteen per cent not answering this question. Of these respondents, devout Buddhists were more inclined to hold non-secular views. These numbers indicate the high prioritization given to religion in political life, especially among those with self-professed higher levels of religiosity.

The ABS did not ask directly about religious conflict. This was deemed too sensitive to be asked by the ABS-YSPS team. There are other questions in the survey that help us understand how religion shapes attitudes toward conflict. We can learn from the ABS questions on political culture. Over ninety per cent of respondents reported conflict-averse positions at the individual level. We also found that religion, notably more devout Buddhism, was associated with reported higher levels of intolerance. Over eighty per cent of devout Buddhists agreed that the society would be chaotic if people had too many different ways of thinking, reflecting less support for pluralism. Generally, stronger religious identity was related to more traditional values. Devout Buddhists have more traditional attitudes compared to other Buddhists and citizens of other religions, as shown in Figure 13.8. To measure traditional values we combine a variety of questions looking at attitudes toward individualism, gender, and social relations. Higher composite scores (with four the highest) indicate higher levels of traditionalism. The findings show a strong relationship between religion and traditionalism. This is not unexpected, as more traditional values have long been seen to include conservative views of religion (see Norris and Inglehart 2009).

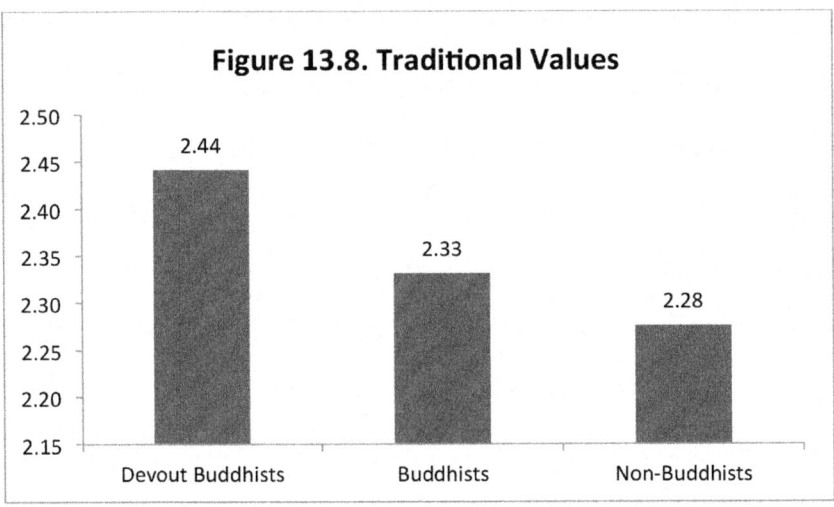

Figure 13.8. Traditional Values

As was the case with ethnicity, religious divisions sharpen when citizens were asked about the treatment of religious communities by the government. Respondents were asked to agree or disagree with the following statement: "All citizens from different religious communities in Myanmar are treated equally by the government." Non-Buddhists expressed concerns, with only forty-four per cent perceiving equal treatment. This compared with nearly two-thirds of Buddhists (sixty-three per cent) and over two-thirds of devout Buddhists (seventy per cent) who agreed with the statement. Religious minorities also had less positive views of religious freedom, with only sixty-one per cent perceiving that religious freedom had improved in the current government, compared to seventy-seven per cent of Buddhists and eighty-two per cent of devout Buddhists. Buddhists perceived considerably more freedom to practice their faith.

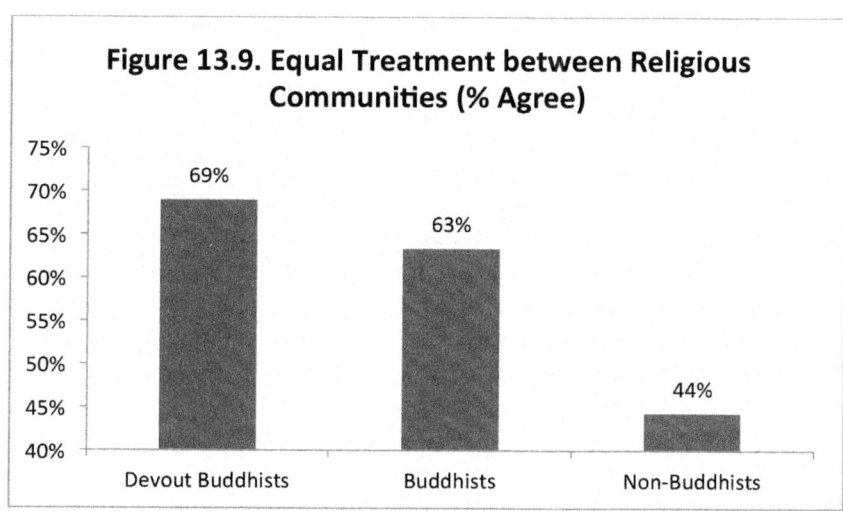

Figure 13.9. Equal Treatment between Religious Communities (% Agree)

Religion is not a significant factor linked to different perceptions of the economy. Religious minorities express similar views about basic needs, poverty, and economic vulnerability as Buddhists: a majority of both groups are poor and vulnerable. While the hate speech towards religious minorities, especially Muslims, often suggests they hold a favorable economic position, the ABS findings do not suggest religious minorities have considerably more economic security than Buddhists. Forty-five per cent of non-Buddhists stated that their income did not cover the needs, compared to fifty-one per cent of Buddhists. In fact, when asked about income distribution, religious minorities reported a more negative view of fairness in income distribution than Buddhists (eighty-five per cent compared to seventy-eight per cent).

Religious minorities in Myanmar have a less positive view of conditions overall when compared to the majority, showing similar trends to those for ethnic minorities. Given that ethnic and religious minority identities often coincide, this is not surprising. At the same time, Buddhists, especially devout Buddhists, expressed stronger views about intolerance and the role of religion in political life, which has the potential to limit the rights of religious minorities and contribute to conflict.

A closer look at the responses of Buddhists reveals that it is not only in the area of the economy that they have common outlooks with non-Buddhists. Buddhists share a commitment to democracy with citizens of other religions, and are as likely to support a more inclusive and democratic alternative for Myanmar. There are no differences reported in the levels of support for democracy across faiths, as seventy-five per cent support democracy over other alternatives. Religious cleavages also do not impact the reported support for different political parties. Even months before the November 2015 election, religion or religiosity did not significantly impact partisan affinity. A majority of all religions, and even devout Buddhists, supported the NLD at statistically the same level, as shown in Figure 13.10. Religion was not a factor that divided Myanmar citizens along party lines. Across faiths a majority of citizens support democracy and wanted a different party at the helm. The voting results in November 2015 confirmed this finding. As with the differences along ethnic lines, religion did not divide Myanmar citizens when it came to potentially bringing about a more inclusive government with support of the NLD.

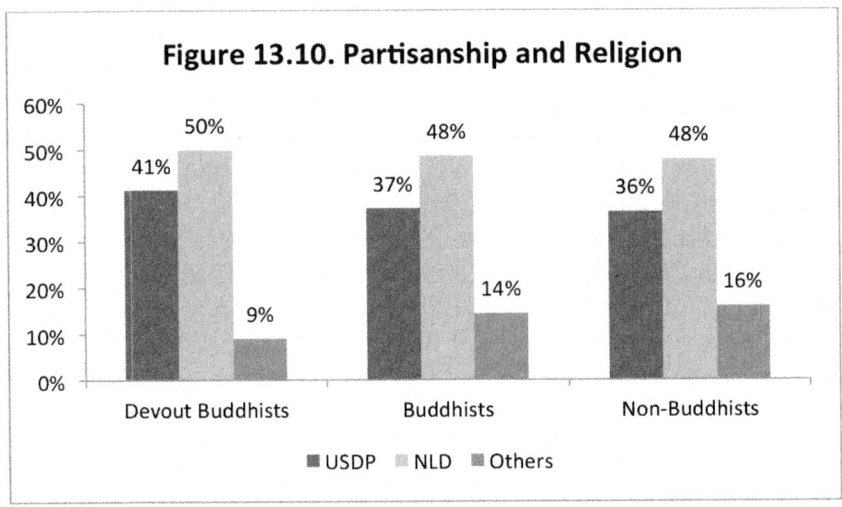

MINORITY CALL FOR CHANGE

Ethnic and religious minorities differed with the Bamar/Buddhist majority in their assessments of the incumbent government at the time of the data collection in 2015. Their reported views are more negative. Only a quarter of non-Buddhists and a third of ethnic minorities reported that the government was responsive to citizens, while this number was over forty per cent for Bamar and Buddhists, as shown in Figure 13.11.

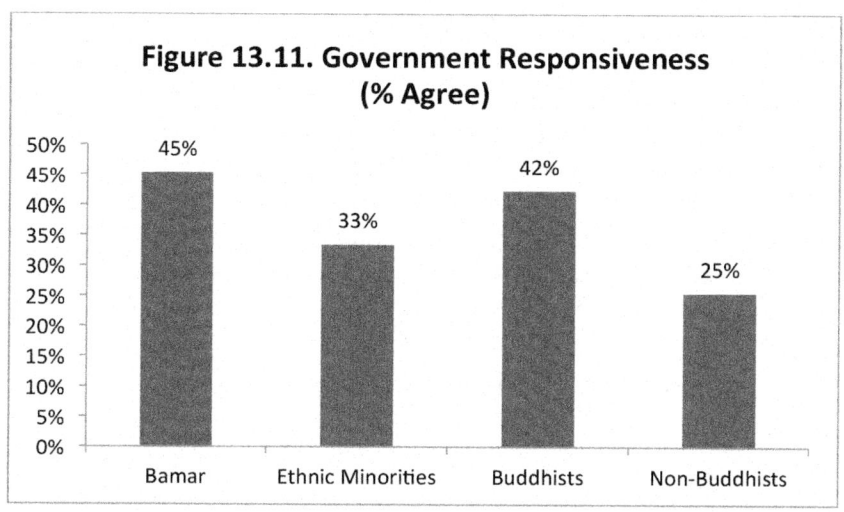

Figure 13.11. Government Responsiveness (% Agree)

The difference between the majority and minorities emerged in response to a question on whether or not the military should be involved in politics. Given the history of the military in conflict, its predominant Bamar/Buddhist composition and association with many of the discriminatory perceptions by minorities, it is not surprising that only a third of minorities reported support for its involvement. Figure 13.12 shows that this is considerably lower than the majority of Bamar/Buddhists, who support the military being involved in politics.

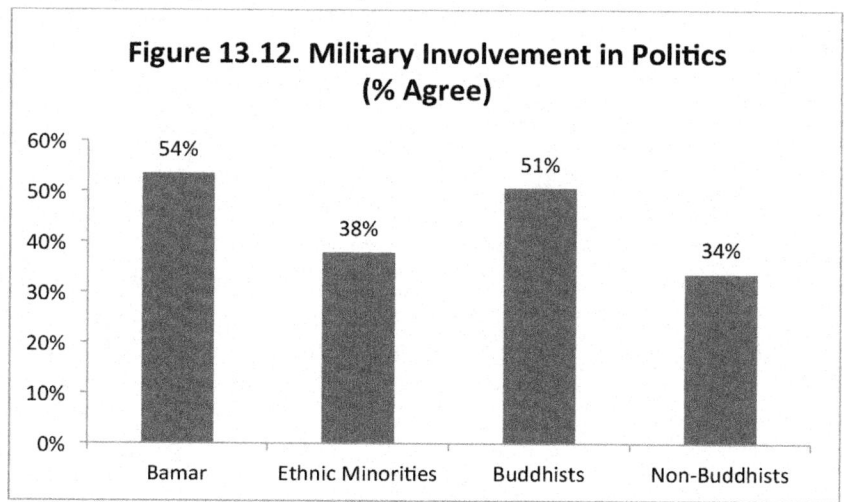

Figure 13.12. Military Involvement in Politics (% Agree)

Minorities also differ from the majority in that they also support broader change in the political system. Respondents were asked the following: "Compared with other systems in the world, would you say our system of government works fine as it is, needs minor change, needs major change, or should be replaced?" While minorities join other Myanmar citizens in calling for change, close to two-thirds of both ethnic and religious minorities believe that the system needs "major" change. Bamar/Buddhists also concur change is needed, but not to the same extent and breadth as minority communities, as shown in Figure 13.13.

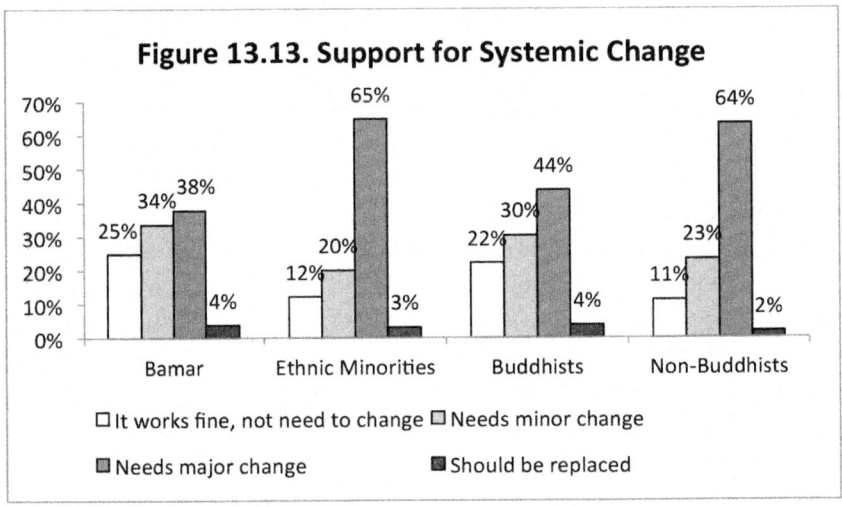

Figure 13.13. Support for Systemic Change

Myanmar citizens want change, but they do not necessarily want the system replaced altogether. Only a small share of all the communities reported selecting to replace the system. The ABS findings suggest that support for change is within the current system, even if there are some citizens who would like this change to be substantive. Myanmar citizens in general are also not inclined to use violence for their political causes. As Figure 13.14 shows, only a small minority, with a slightly higher share of ethnic minorities, is willing to use force. These results suggest that if change can be implemented within the system, this can have important implications for reducing conflict, especially violent conflict, which is only supported by a small share of the population.

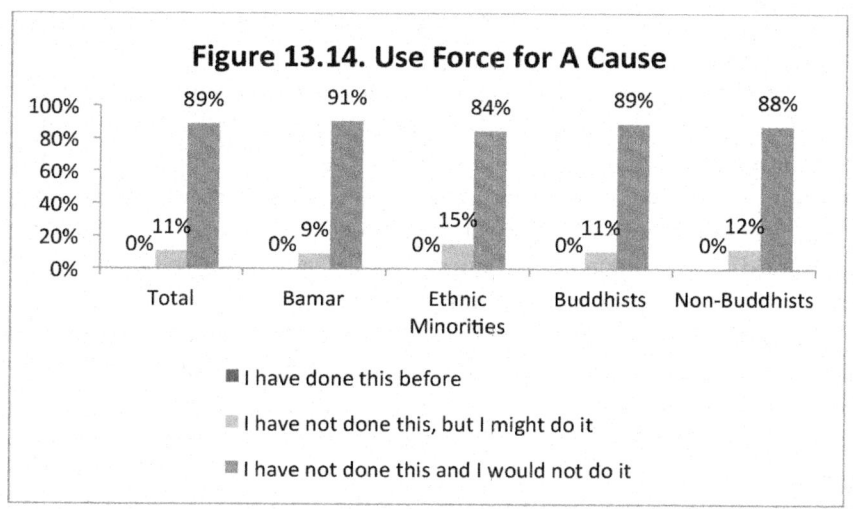

Figure 13.14. Use Force for A Cause

REFLECTIONS AND CONCLUSIONS

Each of these frames of difference — ethnicity, religion, and minorities — point to a similar implication, the need for political change. There is considerable agreement found in the ABS across cleavages on this need for reform, be it for decentralizing authority, strengthening the economy, supporting more inclusive governance and democracy, or systemic change without violence. This similarity bodes well for future trajectories surrounding conflict, as there is broad support reported for measures that have the potential to reduce conflict and public support for reform within the system. The key will be whether the military and elites, including those from the NLD, will be able to build on this public support. Often in analyses of conflict in Myanmar, bringing the public in through measures such as elections is seen to be at odds with reducing conflict. The focus on reducing conflict has rested with the elites in the system, who are seen to use negotiation to resolve differences and reach peace accords. While not dismissing the importance of elite dialogue and discussion as a critical component of reducing conflict in Myanmar, the ABS findings suggest that more confidence should be placed in Myanmar citizens in their understanding and support for measures that reduce conflict. The ABS shows that a majority of Myanmar citizens across cleavages support decentralization, democracy, and political reform, while acknowledging the seriousness of conflict and rejecting violence.

The ABS findings also indicate that reducing conflict will need to address governance issues. This is a theme long emphasized by scholars (for example, Holliday 2008; Kyaw Yin Hlaing 2012). Reported public perceptions of discrimination, inequality, and a lack of government responsiveness by minorities speak to the need to make improvements in how minorities are engaged. An important ingredient for reduced conflict will be a reduced role for the military in politics.

The ABS findings on conflict also suggest the need to rethink the relationship between political culture and conflict. Scholars of political culture have tended to classify Myanmar's political culture as contributing to conflict. Whether in Maung Maung Gyi's (1983) discussion of personalized power, or the tensions in outlooks between the military's nationalism and values and those of society identified by Robert Taylor (1998, 2015) and Mikael Gravers (1999) among others, or the traditional values supporting limited change and the status quo in society emphasized by Mary and Lucien Pye (1985) and Melford Spiro (1982), the focus has been on accounting for the political culture enabling the military to stay in power for so long.

The ABS findings suggest that Myanmar citizens have rather more conflicting values and political attitudes than scholars tend to assume. On the one hand, Myanmar citizens across communities report to be conflict averse at the individual level, while on the other, there are real differences in how they view government and governance. Myanmar citizens are intolerant and deeply religious, yet at the same time they support inclusive parties and democracy. Myanmar citizens are traditional, tied to the past and conservative values, yet they are calling out for change and reform. These contradictions are not uncommon in survey findings, but they do highlight the need to think more carefully about how values and culture in Myanmar society will shape conflict in the future. There is clearly a need to probe further, using different methodologies besides survey research, to understand how the contradictions play out and why.

Limitations notwithstanding, surveys are an important tool to understand public perceptions and the findings of the ABS debunk some of the standard views of conflict in Myanmar. Of all the factors that stand out in the 2015 survey, the one that is perhaps the most important is that there is indeed support in the public for reducing conflict, including the use of force. This goes against the grain of recent work on Myanmar which tends to emphasize tensions and problems rather than shared support for solutions. The hope is that the ABS survey can stimulate further work that will build on its positive findings and help build momentum to reduce divisiveness and conflict in the future.

Notes

1. For good studies on ethnic conflict see for instance Callahan (2007); Fink (2008); Kyaw Yin Hlaing and Ganesan (2007); Smith (1999); South (2008); Walton (2008).
2. For more details regarding the Asian Barometer Survey please see: http://www.asianbarometer.org/. For the Global Barometer see: http://www.globalbarometer.net/.
3. The findings report associated with the fieldwork can be found here: <http://www.asianbarometer.org/survey/wave4-myanmar>.
4. For the technical report: <http://www.asianbarometer.org/survey/wave4-myanmar>.
5. Special thanks to Myat Thu and Myo Aung Htwe of the Yangon School of Political Science, the Myanmar field coordinators Arkar Soe and Nan Nan Thu Kyaw and supervisor and interview teams, as well as colleagues who comprised the Myanmar ABS Team, Huang Min-Hua, Wu Wen-Chin, Alex Chang, Tan Seng Keat, and leadership of the ABS, Yun-han Chu and Yu-Tzung Chang.
6. Along with Burmese, the survey was translated into Shan, Kachin, Mon, Rakhine, Chin, various Kayin dialects, and Mandarin by field interpreters as well as colleagues who comprised the Myanmar ABS Team, Min-Hua Huang, Wen-Chin Wu, Alex Chang, Tan Seng Keat, and leadership of the ABS, Yun-han Chu and Yu-Tzung Chang.
7. Two major surveys were released in 2014, a political poll by the International Republican Institute to be accessed via <http://www.iri.org/resource/iri-survey-burmese-strongly-support-democracy-express-satisfaction-over-country's-current/> and a survey by the Asia Foundation, Myanmar 2014: Civic Knowledge and Values in a Changing Society. <http://asiafoundation.org/publications/pdf/1445>.
8. Over half the respondents did not answer questions involving voting intention, higher than in other ABS surveys. Cross-regional analysis of the responses shows that the level of non-responsiveness was at least twenty per cent higher than other countries. For more details refer to the 2016 Myanmar ABS report.
9. The ethnic groups surveyed include Kachin, Jinghpaw (Kachin), Maru, Lashi, Kayah, Ka-Yun, Kayin, Sgaw Kayin, Shu, Chin, Saline, Mro, Bamar, Dawei, Beik, Mon, Rakhine, Shan, Eng, Kokant, Khamti Shan, Danu, Shan Gyi, Lahu,

Pa-O, Tai-Lem, Maw Shan, Chinese, Indian (Hindu), Bengali, Rohingya, Shan-Pa O, Shan-Chinese, Gawrakhar, Shan-Myanmar, Kayin-Chinese, and Min Dat Chin.

References

Callahan, Mary P. *Political Authority in Burma's Ethnic Minority States: Devolution, Occupation and Coexistence*. Washington DC: East-West Center, 2007.

Cheesman, Nick and Htoo Kyaw Win, eds. *Communal Violence in Myanmar*. Yangon: Myanmar Knowledge Society, 2015.

Diamond, Larry. "The Specter of Mass Killings in Burma". The Atlantic, 31 January 2014 <http://www.theatlantic.com/international/archive/2014/01/the-specter-of-mass-killings-in-burma/283483/>. Accessed 26 December 2015.

Fink, Christina. "Militarization in Burma's Ethnic States: Causes and Consequences". *Contemporary Politics* 14, no. 4 (2008): 447–62.

Gravers, Mikael. *Nationalism as Political Paranoia in Burma: An Essay on the Historical Practice of Power*. London: Curzon Press, 1999.

Holliday, Ian. "Voting and Violence in Myanmar: Nation-Building for a Transition to Democracy". *Asian Survey* 46, no. 6 (2008): 1039–58.

Kyaw Yin Hlaing. "Setting the Rules for Survival: Why the Burmese Military Regime Survives in an Age of Democratization". *Pacific Review* 22, no. 3 (2009): 271–91.

———. "Understanding Recent Political Changes in Myanmar". *Contemporary Southeast Asia* 34, no. 2 (2012): 197–216.

Kyaw Yin Hlaing and N. Ganesan, eds. *Myanmar: State, Society and Ethnicity*. Singapore: ISEAS, 2007.

Maung Maung Gyi. *Burmese Political Values: The Socio-Political Roots of Authoritarianism*. New York: Prager, 1983.

Mufford, Tina. "Identity Under Threat: How Religious Intolerance Threatens Burma's Future". Georgetown Journal of International Affairs, 19 November 2014 <http://journal.georgetown.edu/identity-under-threat-how-religious-intolerance-threatens-burmas-future/>. Accessed 26 December 2015.

Norris, Pippa and Ronald Inglehart. *Sacred and Secular: Religion and Politics Worldwide*. New York: Cambridge University Press, 2009.

Perera, Thusitha. "Ma Ba Tha and the Vote". New Mandala, 2 November 2015 <http://asiapacific.anu.edu.au/newmandala/2015/11/04/ma-ba-tha-and-the-vote/>. Accessed 26 December 2015.

Pye, Mary W. and Lucian W. Pye. *Asian Power and Politics: The Cultural Dimensions of Authority*. London: Belknap Press, 1985.

Schissler, Matthew, Matthew J. Walton and Phyu Phyu Thi. "Threat and Virtuous Defence: Listening to Narratives of Religious Conflict in Six Myanmar Cities". *Myanmar Media and Society Project*, Working Paper 1, no. 1 (2015). <http://

www.sant.ox.ac.uk/sites/default/files/m.mas_working_paper_1.1_-_threat_ and_virtuous_defence_-_july_2015.pdf>. Accessed 26 December 2015.
Smith, Donald E. *Religion and Politics in Burma*. Princeton: Princeton University Press, 1965.
Smith, Martin J. *Burma: Insurgency and the Politics of Ethnicity*. London & New York: Zed Books, 1999.
South, Ashley. *Ethnic Politics in Burma: States of Conflict*. London: Routledge, 2008.
Spiro, Melford E. *Buddhism and Society: A Great Tradition and its Burmese Vicissitudes*. Berkeley: University of California Press, 1982.
Taylor, Robert H. "Political Values and Political Conflict in Burma". In *Burma: Prospects for a Democratic Future*, edited by Robert I. Rotberg. Washington DC: Brookings Institute Press, 1998.
———. "Refighting Old Battles, Compounding Misconceptions: The Politics of Ethnicity in Myanmar Today". In *ISEAS Perspective* #12, 2 March 2015 < http://www.iseas.edu.sg/images/pdf/ISEAS_Perspective_2015_12.pdf>. Accessed 26 December 2015.
Walton, Matthew J. "Ethnicity, Conflict and History in Burma: The Myths of Panglong". *Asian Survey* 48, no. 6 (2008): 889–910.

14

ON ISLAMOPHOBES AND HOLOCAUST DENIERS

Making Sense of Violence, in Myanmar and Elsewhere

Matt Schissler

The theme for the Australian National University (ANU) 2015 Myanmar Update Conference was "Making Sense of Conflict". The weeks leading up to the conference, held in the first week of June, added to the theme's poignancy and urgency; at least 25,000 Muslims were fleeing persecution and poverty by making the dangerous trip from Rakhine State across the Bay of Bengal (UNHCR 2015). My paper at the conference presented findings from research into the ways people in Myanmar talk about this violence and, in particular, how those Buddhists who direct a sense of threat and antagonism towards Muslims explain and justify it. I had spent the preceding six months managing a "listening project", born from my belief that to make sense of conflict we must listen carefully to the way it is discussed in everyday life. This research formed a part of the Myanmar Media and Society (M.MAS) project, a partnership between St Antony's College, Oxford University and the Myanmar ICT for Development Organization (MIDO).[1]

One of the things I raised in my conference presentation was the similarity between discourses about Islam that I was hearing in Myanmar and those I had heard in my home country, the United States. We should note parallels between these discourses, I said, and consider what it may mean that the arguments called upon to justify anti-Muslim sentiments in Myanmar are strikingly similar to those I remember in the US after 9/11. You may notice similarities to discourses in the US or Australia today, I also suggested. The first member of the audience to ask a question refused this parallel. "Why are we spending so much time listening to bigots?" she asked. "Would we give such careful attention to the beliefs of Holocaust deniers?" The question presented a different analogy, in which those expressing anti-Muslim sentiments in Myanmar are equivalent to deniers of the Holocaust. This was its refusal: the question positioned discourses in Myanmar as far from home as possible, more analogous to Holocaust deniers — a fringe group most reviled — than anything commonplace on the streets of Sydney, New York, or London.

I would like to take this question seriously by asking: what are the consequences of such a refusal? Conversely, why might it be important to explore relationships between anti-Muslim discourses currently circulating in Myanmar and those elsewhere? This chapter argues that answering these questions is necessary if we are to make any sense of contemporary communal violence in Myanmar.[2] Noting parallels between anti-Muslim discourses in Myanmar and the West necessitates asking: how shall we explain them? Shall we say they are just a coincidence, or that they reveal a universal truth about Islam? Apparently similar phenomena can arise for different reasons, of course, but both answers seem unsatisfactory; too flippant, too essentialising. Neither would it be satisfactory to say that anti-Muslim discourses in Myanmar are *produced* by those in the West — this would mirror old-fashioned diffusionist anthropology or early historiographies of Southeast Asia, which saw developments within the region as derivative, triggered primarily by external intervention. To say instead that anti-Muslim violence in Myanmar is endogenous would be to locate agency primarily within people in Myanmar. This is an important project, yet such an approach also risks ignoring the parallels I have noted, which would be, in the end, the same as explaining them away as coincidence — or to refuse them altogether.

I do not yet have complete answers to all the questions that animate this chapter; they are part of an ongoing project. But within this space, I want to do three things. First, I will explore persistent features in the construction of narratives of Muslim threat in Myanmar. This opening section will summarize findings from the M.MAS research presented at the ANU Update, as well as draw on observation from everyday life in western Yangon 2013–2015.[3] Second, I will establish that there are both parallels and productive interrelationships between these discourses in Myanmar and those that have come to circulate worldwide since 9/11 and the expansion of the so-called global War on Terror. Establishing this will span two sections of the chapter and will require adding a new set of sources, drawn from analysis of Burmese language posts on social media and observations on their circulation in Myanmar.[4] Finally, the chapter will seek to stake out the importance of recognizing and further examining these parallels and relationships. This chapter is intended for an audience of scholars studying violence in Myanmar, for it suggests a different frame for research. But it is also for people working for peace and against conflict in Myanmar, for it suggests a set of concerns that become more legible when employing such a frame.

PARALLELS: JUSTIFYING A SENSE OF THREAT

As Myanmar was preparing for national elections in November 2015 my own country, the US, was preparing for elections as well. Republican Party candidates expressed fear and antipathy towards Islam. No Muslim should be able to be president, noted the party's frontrunners at the time (Pengelly 2015). Later, one of these leaders proposed an indiscriminate entry ban for all persons of Muslim religion — a policy that at least one poll found sixty-six per cent of Republican Party voters support (Rasmussen Reports 2015). Such sentiment in the US is not universal; other candidates, major media outlets, and sitting politicians have condemned these anti-Muslim statements and policies. But the campaign controversies were not isolated, and they illuminate a common current in American popular discourse that has a long history and has increased in force and prominence since 9/11.

As the US election campaign period began to heat up, I watched candidates and media pundits debate these issues. On Facebook, friends posted links to videos defending and decrying anti-Muslim sentiments. I was reminded of other times when similar exchanges have occurred: "It's not condemning people, it's ideas," a media personality defended his claims about Islam in a televised debate, in which he, other pundits, and a popular film actor exchanged heated views about whether Islam was inherently violent (HBO 2014). The actor had accused the others in the debate of making racist arguments and stereotyping all Muslims; they had relied on sweeping generalizations about Islam, illustrated through references to despicable acts by groups like the Islamic State (Islamic State of Iraq and Syria, ISIS). The video of this debate had been circulating widely in October 2014, almost exactly one year before election campaigning had begun in earnest in either Myanmar or the US, and as I watched it sitting in my apartment in Yangon, the parallels to things I heard in Myanmar were striking. The next morning in the teashop, I sat discussing the news with friends from the neighbourhood in which I lived, two brothers and a third man from their block. One of the brothers looked at me with concern: "Can I ask you about something?" He wanted to talk about ISIS. "They are so horrible", he said. "Why is the US military not making war on them?"

I also think ISIS is horrible, I told him, and I explained that I thought many people in my country were tired of war. I offered my opinions about the effectiveness of US military interventions. This conversation was one of many in an ongoing discussion we had over the years I was living in his neighbourhood. I spent considerable time sitting in teashops and on the corner, talking with him, his brothers, and others in the township about a variety of issues. History, politics, and religion were frequent topics, along with many others more quotidian. In early 2013, I began taking note of debates about Buddhist–Muslim violence, when conversations in the neighbourhood were increasingly turning to what my friends felt to be serious dangers from Islam. Our conversation that morning in October was specific to threats from ISIS; over the years, I had heard this brother and our other friends make a persistent set of arguments about Islam in general, and Muslims in Myanmar, characterized as inherently violent and a threat. These arguments seemed to echo — or were echoed in — the posts I was seeing on social media from back home in the US. These narratives were also making people worry within the Myanmar civil society networks where I was working at the time, prompting notable campaigns calling for peace between religious communities.

In order to better understand the way such ideas about Islam were being justified and whether similar things were being said elsewhere in the country, colleagues and I began the M.MAS Research Project in January 2015.[5] Over the next four months, one colleague and I conducted sixty-eight interviews with seventy-eight people in six cities: Sittwe, Meiktila, Mandalay, Lashio, Pathein, and Mawlamyine.[6] The majority of those we interviewed were Buddhist, but we also interviewed people from the other three major world religious traditions in Myanmar (Muslim, Hindu, Christian). Our interviews were arranged by local youth activists, who helped us select people with an eye to a diversity of gender, educational, and class perspectives. We conducted our interviews in Burmese and arranged translations only when, in a few cases, we spoke with individuals who felt more comfortable speaking in another local language.[7]

We strove to make our interview encounters open-ended and thus initiated only basic questions about people's lives, livelihoods, and their concerns. We did not ask specifically about issues related to religion or conflict. Instead, we approached the research as a "listening project".[8] After initial biographical information was discussed, we asked people to reflect on their primary concerns for their communities and for the country, and then to rank these concerns. In each case we would ask a series of probing questions about the issues they selected as their primary concerns, which ranged from topics including health and education to democracy or civil war. This enabled us to understand the nature of their concerns, with whom they discussed these issues, where they sought related news and information, and how long they had felt this way. While not everyone raised communal conflict as their primary concern, it was rare for the issue not to come up, though the issue was, as might be expected, more salient in areas that had experienced riotous violence than in areas that had not.

It is important to say at the outset that while nearly everyone raised concern about communal conflict, not everyone in Myanmar directs fear and antagonism towards Muslims. Where I lived in western Yangon, for example, friends who expressed such feelings about Islam have friends and co-workers who are Muslim, and have happily participated in campaigns to promote interfaith peace. The brothers mentioned above, for example, have had on their front door — for two years now — a sticker bearing the message "I will not be the cause of racial or religious violence." In the M.MAS listening project, meanwhile, we interviewed people who articulated strong senses of felt contradiction between current tensions and their memories of past coexistence.⁹ To say that people highlighted past coexistence is not to say that there has never been anti-Muslim sentiment in Myanmar, or that Muslims have not been subject to violence at other times. Instead, it means that, for many of the people we spoke to, articulating a sense of prior coexistence entailed doing subsequent interpretive work to reconcile this contradiction:

> Before I joined this association [MaBaTha], I felt that we are all the same human beings in my heart ... There was no discrimination in my mind. Not only I felt this way, all Buddhists have this same feeling. But after the [riots in May 2013] took place, I knew that the situation was not the same any more ... This is the weakness [of Buddhists], we don't know what [Muslims] are doing to our religion, or making our religion shrink. I didn't notice this, but when I studied about it in detail, I found out that it's a dangerous issue. So we have to find ways to protect our religion.¹⁰

Ultimately, our purpose was not to conduct a poll; the point in that M.MAS project research — and this chapter — is to understand how those who express a sense of antagonism towards Islam understand and justify such a sense, not to determine the percentage of the Myanmar population who feel a certain way. By asking people to articulate their concerns, the interview encounter encouraged them to make arguments — and indeed, some of the narrators we listened to approached the encounter as an opportunity to try and persuade us into agreement.

We identified a narrative consistent with our earlier research and with the rhetoric of groups like MaBaTha and 969, which we loosely grouped into two interrelated conceptions of threat. First, Muslims were presented as an existential threat to race and religion. This was the idea that Buddhism or a particular ethnic community in Myanmar was vulnerable, and at real risk of being lost forever. Second, Muslims were depicted as a personal threat, to the narrator or their community of residence. The source of this threat was consistently defined in *religious* terms. Individuals identified the object of their fear using terminology both religious (Islam and Muslim) and racial (*kalar*¹¹ and Bengali). But the arguments we heard rested on a fundamentally religious premise: that Islam is unitary and that it is violent, threatening, and otherwise inferior to Buddhism. This argument about Islam was made as a general, universalized claim. It was also connected to specific religious practices that were highlighted as both objectionable and allegedly intrinsic to Islamic tradition, such as the butchering of cows or mistreatment of women.

A corollary to this was the idea that Islam contains an inherent colonizing imperative and, thus, that Muslims seek to expand and overtake other religions. Some narrators explained this as the meaning of Jihad and Sharia, two words we often heard to be used, though not necessarily well understood. Arguments about the intrinsically dangerous nature of Islam are timeless in their universality, but in some cases narrators situated their arguments temporally, pointing to countries including Afghanistan and Indonesia, which were understood to have once been Buddhist and then lost to Islam. Narrators stated that Buddhism in Myanmar is at similar risk of being "swallowed up". A variety of mechanisms were presented to explain how this could occur, including: use of violence, economic power, and demographic change driven by practices imputed to Muslims — illegal immigration, bearing large numbers of children, incentives for inter-religious marriage, and forced conversion of Buddhist women and subsequent children.

A consideration of the spatial aspects of these arguments further highlights their universality, couched in terms of religion. Claims about Islam were illustrated through three strands of interrelated argument, which can be understood as global, through reference to international events; local or national, through reference to events within Myanmar; and personal, through reference to the experiences of the narrator. The following excerpt from an interview in Lashio, for example, illustrates a synthesis of these three strands of argument:

> The things that happened took place not far from our work place — members of the other religion rape children like your daughter's age, and we read about that in the news and also see it in real life ... Their religion is terrorism. They lured people to convert to their religion by force; they don't have freedom of belief in their religion. If a Burmese Buddhist got married to one of them, every opportunity would be lost. Even a drop of blood from them is very dangerous. The blood of terror. They have been taught this since they were children, so it's very terrifying. We say, don't kill. ... They say, kill — if you kill you will be blessed. ... Now, in the news, we see about their Jihad in other countries, cutting off people's heads. Horrible things, burning people alive. ... I don't want to see our Buddhists suffer like that. That's why I want to show people the horror of their religion. I want everyone to know.[12]

My colleague and I conducted this interview with a woman who works at the central office of the Shan State MaBaTha and so it is not surprising she was a particularly illustrative narrator. She spoke to us earnestly, sometimes seeming to be on the verge of tears, and she told us that she had come to work for MaBaTha because of her desire to protect Buddhism. But her synthesis is not unique: in the course of the M.MAS listening project, as well as my own ethnographic research, I have heard others make varying permutations of these three strands of arguments, drawing on their own experiences, events in Myanmar, and events elsewhere in the world. In the following excerpt from an interview in Mawlamyine, for example, the narrator had just told us that he was afraid to interact with Muslims and we had begun discussing his reasons for such a feeling:

Q: Can you give me some examples?

A: I can give many examples of worldwide incidents. For example, they attacked the World Trade Center in America and you can also see [examples] in Myanmar. They are the sources of these incidents. Nowadays, we are more and more afraid of them and also you can see the situation of ISIS. I don't trust Islam in Myanmar because of this ISIS. For example, Islam [Muslims] from Indonesia are involved in ISIS, so nobody can say that Islam [Muslims] in Myanmar are not involved or participating in the processes of ISIS. That is why we are afraid of them.[13]

In the working paper in which my M.MAS colleagues and I detailed our research findings, we explored all three of these strands of argument, organized in spatial terms, and noted that fears and antagonism towards Muslims in Myanmar were more often justified through reference to international events and events elsewhere in Myanmar than those of personal experience (Schissler, Walton, and Phyu Phyu Thi 2015). Throughout our conversation with the narrator quoted above — a Buddhist man who owns a small business and is an active member of social work activities and opposition political work in his city — he wove together a variety of arguments about events in his area, Myanmar, and the world. But as the above excerpt shows, when given an opportunity to explain his feelings, he opted to emphasize them with reference to events outside Myanmar.

When I have commented on the apparent importance of these references to international events in academic settings, it has sometimes generated outright refusal of the kind that inspired this chapter. In other cases, it has generated questions about the nature of research encounters. Was my presence, as an American, prompting interlocutors in Myanmar to invoke a strand of arguments about international events that they might not otherwise? The question applies to both insights drawn from participant observation and to the M.MAS listening project. There is a grain of truth in this question; I do need to consider carefully whether my presence as a foreigner operates as a confounding variable. Certainly, more times than I can count during conversations in daily life in Yangon, in the M.MAS listening project, and elsewhere in Myanmar, people have made explicit overtures to solidarity with me as an American. For example, "You are an American, you experienced 9/11, so surely you must share my views about Islam", or "You are American? I like America, because it made war on Muslim countries." In other cases, especially with individuals seeking to persuade me, including during some of our M.MAS interviews, there is a clear element of argument selection based on what they assume I would be familiar with or find persuasive as a foreigner. But the point that the remainder of this chapter will make is twofold: that my presence as a potential confounding variable is not sufficient to dismiss the importance of references to a global Islam, and that these references must be considered seriously within any further attempts to make sense of conflict in Myanmar, and for any attempts to support the making of peace.

FROM PARALLELS TO INTERRELATIONSHIPS

By now the parallels between discourses about Islam in Myanmar and those circulating elsewhere, including in the US, should be clear. In both cases, they meet any basic definition of "Islamophobia". This term has been defined in a variety of ways, which Erik Bleich has helpfully synthesised as "indiscriminate negative attitudes or emotions directed at Islam or Muslims" (2011, p. 1585). In this case, what I wish to emphasize is that the narratives in Myanmar and elsewhere treat Islam as homogenous, without distinguishing between diverse religious traditions; that they are applied to both Islam as a religion and to Muslims as followers of Islam; and that they are intensely negative. This is not to advocate that Islamophobia per se is a particularly useful lens for understanding communal conflict in Myanmar — I will return to this point in the conclusion. Instead, employing Bleich's definition highlights the fact that narratives about Islam in Myanmar, the US, and elsewhere meet his definition and, in doing so, have broad shapes and content that are consistent with one another.

The narratives treat Islam similarly, as unitary and Muslims as dangerous, but they also explicitly draw on similar strands of argument. Both are based on an understanding of Islam as a religion that is intrinsically violent, and both use particular examples like ISIS to illustrate this universal claim. There are, of course, key differences: arguments about the vulnerability of Buddhism, and references to instances of Muslims denigrating Buddhism and concerns about demography are common in Myanmar, where they are not in the US. But in both cases, the use of global arguments about Muslims elsewhere is an important part of reinforcing a sense of general threat from Muslims at home. This is a parallel, but in Myanmar it also appears to be a productive interrelationship: the strand of argument about Islam in the world that is used to bolster a larger narrative of Muslim threat in Myanmar explicitly draws on discourses that have grown into global prominence as a part of the "War on Terror". These arguments about Islamic extremism and terrorism are common in the US, as I have discussed, but also exceed individual Western countries and are visible elsewhere, including in Myanmar's regional neighbours such as Sri Lanka, India, and Thailand.

In Myanmar, these arguments not only parallel narratives constructed elsewhere, they explicitly draw on and make use of these discourses as semiotic material. The relationships between these materials — produced elsewhere and used in Myanmar — are most clearly seen on social media. Social media technologies have changed rapidly over the last three years: pre-publication censorship has ended and the percentage of the population with a mobile phone and access to the internet has expanded from seven to forty-five per cent (Myanmar Centre for Responsible Business 2015). In this changing media environment, Facebook has come to be one of the most popular platforms in the country, used by media companies and government officials to publish stories and make official statements — and by people in Myanmar who are actively seeking to collect ideas and pieces of information and use them to construct narratives about the world (Schissler 2016). In online spaces, the circulation of such discourses leaves digital trails that can be compared and traced. People in Myanmar posting on Facebook can evidence news articles, websites, memes, or other content generated by people elsewhere in the world. Such cases illustrate moments when discourses about Islam in the US and other places are not only paralleled in Myanmar, but actively used and adapted.

Such uses became most apparent to me in April 2014, as I observed a contest unfold over the nature of free speech and inter-religious harmony.

In late March an activist group, which came to be known as Pan Zagar (flower speech),[14] gave a press conference speaking out against hate speech, including that of famously anti-Muslim Buddhist leaders such as U Wirathu.[15] The campaign, launched by a respected former political prisoner and backed by key activists in Myanmar civil society, gained quick momentum; over the next month, they helped to inspire — and support — anti-hate speech demonstrations on streets in more than forty-two cities and townships in Myanmar. The campaign also generated a strong presence on social media,[16] in an attempt to shatter what appeared to be a developing anti-Muslim "echo chamber" in Myanmar.[17] As the campaign attracted prominence, however, it also attracted counter-attacks. Among these, an imposter Pan Zagar Facebook page was created at the end of April 2014, mimicking the posts of the original account and initially exhibiting no apparent differences from the original. But after a few days, it also began posting anti-Muslim content centred on the argument that the teachings of Islam constitute hate speech and that the Pan Zagar campaign thus rejected Islam.

The campaign members were unhappy at such a development and felt it was a deliberate attack, designed to discredit their efforts or use their momentum to promote inter-religious conflict.[18] As we discussed this and how to respond, I took careful note of the arguments being wielded against the campaign: the posts purported to quote Islamic teachings at length, though not in good faith, and linked back to an English-language website; the posts were Myanmar language translations of an online article entitled "Is the Quran Hate Propaganda?" (Religion of Peace 2015). The article was originally published on a website maintained by anti-Muslim activists in the US. The site is prominent in a network of websites that En-Chieh Chao (2014, pp. 2–3) has called the post-9/11 "industry of Islamophobia". A user in Myanmar was translating the page to use in an unfolding contest over the nature of free speech and religious coexistence.

The contest over Pan Zagar is an example of the use of anti-Muslim material from the US in Myanmar. It is also an example of the way that analysing anti-Muslim discourses on social media offers a mechanism for considering the influence of my presence as a researcher: posts on social media are a valuable space to examine the construction of narratives about Islam by Myanmar people who are addressing each other and, presumably, not altering their arguments to persuade a foreign researcher. The attacks on Pan Zagar, for example, were clearly addressed to a Myanmar audience —

the posts were translated into Burmese and, at the time, the campaign had yet to attract any notice in the English-language press. We never learned who was behind the imposter Pan Zagar account, though the campaign members had a strong suspicion, so it is not possible to ask the creator or creators of the account why they chose to adapt content generated in the US for Myanmar. But adapt it they did, as useful (semiotic) material in digital form.

The contest over Pan Zagar is not an isolated case. Posts on Facebook that present Islam as a threat make regular and direct use of materials produced by Chao's "industry of Islamophobia" as well as other sources, such as Wikipedia and stories from international news media. In preparation for a training program for youth activists held by M.MAS in July 2015, for example, MIDO members analysed examples of posts on social media that underground monitoring networks had been collecting. Of twenty-seven examples that MIDO members prepared for a collection to be used in the training, seventeen included photos depicting events outside Myanmar.[19] These posts included photos such as of beheadings by ISIS — events of the kind friends in western Yangon brought up for discussion. Other examples included a post in Burmese and purporting to explain Sharia law, along with a link to the English-language Wikipedia page on Sharia. The Burmese-language explanation of Sharia did not match the content on the Wikipedia link; MIDO members explained that they thought the post was cleverly designed to make Burmese-language readers believe that the content had the authority that comes with citation, and that people might be unable to read the source page in English or unlikely to take the time to make a comparison between the two languages. Another example made similar clever use of a Burmese-language explanation along with a link to a story from Radio Australia.

Non-Burmese people outside Myanmar have also sought to offer direct support to people in Myanmar who they perceive to be victimized by Muslims. A series of papers by an American named Rik Heizman (2015), for example, bear incendiary titles such as "History Shows Buddhist Cultures Destroyed By Muslims: Is Arakan Next?" and "False and Manipulative Muslim Media". These papers are posted online for anyone to use — including, in at least one case, a Myanmar government inquiry committee convened to respond to Buddhist–Muslim violence (Republic of the Union of Myanmar 2013, p. 74). Heizman also authored a report for the Arakan Human Rights and Development Organization (2013, p. 11), which local media called "dangerous" (O'Toole 2013) and Elliot Prasse-Freeman described as "factually inaccurate, historically implausible, and poorly written and researched" (2014, pp. 17–18). Heizman is an example of the sometimes strikingly direct relationship between anti-Muslim discourses in Myanmar and elsewhere.

These examples have been of individual websites like The Religion of Peace or individuals like Heizman, but we should not mistake these relationships as individual. They are examples of individuals operating within larger arrangements of power: the positions they take towards Islam are indistinguishable from the political campaigns and debates on mainstream television I discussed above. Chao uses the term "industry of Islamophobia" as a way to group together the Religion of Peace and other similar websites, but the industry is much larger. Indeed, Nathan Lean (2012) has characterized such an industry much more broadly, to encompass not just bloggers, but television, radio, evangelical religious leaders, and politicians. Semiotic materials made use of in Myanmar thus draw not from groups on the fringes and elsewhere but from prominent, integrated, and well-funded networks with broadly analogous (anti-Muslim) ideological goals. Perhaps underscoring this best of all, after 9/11, the then-pariah military regime in Myanmar explicitly sought rapprochement with the US by seeking to align itself with regional counterterrorism efforts (Selth 2004, pp. 116–20).

It should be no surprise, that the spectre of "Islamic terrorism" in Burma has also been taken up by those addressing non-Myanmar audiences. The Religion of Peace website, for example, includes a sidebar displaying a regularly updated tabulation of "Islamic Terror Attacks". The tables used to detail the alleged incidents that aggregate into this number include, among others, attacks in Myanmar.[20] International media outlets such as *The Independent* (UK) and *Newsweek* (Popham 2015; O'Gara 2015) have used speculation about events in Myanmar to reinforce established narratives about global threats from Islamic terrorism. None of these stories appear to be based on any concrete evidence other than that groups including al-Qaeda have used violence against Muslims in Myanmar for the purposes of their own mobilization. They operate as if the potential for Muslim terrorism in Myanmar has already (always) been established.[21] The stories take this presumed potential and apply it to the Southeast Asia region. "Spreading such an idea in Myanmar is a killing licence", a friend, neighbour, and prominent activist told me one evening in July 2015. And while the intended addressees for such stories may not be people in Myanmar, they may be taken up as new and helpful materials in digital form.

Anti-Muslim materials from outside Myanmar also appear to be used as a way to situate fear of Islam within a kind of global community. Posts within the set analysed by MIDO, for example, included a collection of photos from an anti-Muslim demonstration in Australia. Demonstrators in the photo collection carry placards with messages including "Islamic Immigration = Genocide" and "I was beheaded because of Shariah Law".[22] The Burmese-language caption calls on people in Myanmar to similarly demonstrate against Islam. After attacks in Paris during November 2015, meanwhile, at least one French news outlet published a rebuttal to a Myanmar-language story circulating on Facebook captioned "A hundred thousand French people protested on November 22 to kick Muslims out of France." France 24's *The Observers* responded by tracking down the photos used in the Myanmar-language story, discovering that they were repurposed AFP photos from vigils to honour victims of the recent attacks (Team Observers 2015, p. 24).

DEFINING AND EXPANDING THE BOUNDARIES OF THREAT

The preceding section drew on examples from social media for two reasons: first, because digital forms leave trails of circulation that can be easily tracked, making legible times in which anti-Muslim discourse in Myanmar draws on materials produced elsewhere; and second, because social media posts present examples of arguments about Islam in the world that are addressed by and to Myanmar audiences rather than foreigners, resolving concerns about a potential confounding variable. These dynamics are not limited to social media of course. As detailed above, such discussions — reference to international events, news and information circulating between online and offline spaces — were regular occurrences in the everyday life as well as in our M.MAS interviews.

The core point here is that the construction of anti-Muslim narratives circulating *within* Myanmar draws on arguments that are not spatially limited to *inside* Myanmar. Narratives in Myanmar make use of materials emanating from outside the country: in the form of events and authority that can be referenced to strengthen claims applied in Myanmar; and in the form of materials prepared outside the country, often repurposed but sometimes designed explicitly to address Myanmar. To be clear: my argument is not a relative comparison between the importance of arguments situated outside and inside the country. It would be possible, for example, to construct a narrative of Muslim threat that is spatially confined to Myanmar; Muslims could be constructed as threats and illustrated as such by drawing on claims about the content of the religion and examples of alleged misdeeds by only Myanmar Muslims. Certainly, the claim is not that anti-Muslim narratives in Myanmar exist only because they also exist in the US and elsewhere. This would be to both treat events in Myanmar as primarily derivative, and to ignore other times when Muslims in Myanmar have suffered violence.

And yet, we cannot simply dismiss the relationships between narratives in Myanmar and elsewhere, where discourses and references to events inside and outside the country are used as materials to reinforce universal claims about Islamic threat. Strands of argument that are spatially outside Myanmar are what enable the construction of a threat that is perceived to be both inside Myanmar and surrounding it. This narrative presents Islam as a threat that is understood to be global and for which Muslims in Myanmar are the vanguard. In this sense, the interrelationship between narratives about Islam inside and outside Myanmar is a necessary condition for this understanding of threat, though it is not necessarily sufficient. Daw Aung San Suu Kyi has been explicit about the global nature of this perception: "Fear is not just on the side of the Muslims, but on the side of the Buddhists as well," she explained to the BBC in October 2013. "There's a perception that Muslim power, global Muslim power, is very great" (BBC 2013). Non-Burmese observers pilloried her for this interview (Blair 2013),[23] but her placement of domestic fears within a global context was descriptively accurate. The narrative is not that there is anything particularly threatening about Muslims in Myanmar, but instead that Muslims in Myanmar are *no less* threatening than Muslims *anywhere*.

Situating this sense of threat globally helps to explain how an overwhelming demographic majority that controls the state can fear a domestically marginalized minority. But, again, we must not treat the production of narratives about Islam in Myanmar as exclusively derivative: experiences during colonialism, in which large-scale immigration occurred from elsewhere in then-British India, and when Rangoon appeared to be more an Indian city than Burmese, also provide ample material for grounding any sense of demographic vulnerability.[24] Situating this sense of threat globally, however, also enables an indexical relationship in which all Muslims in Myanmar are potentially interchangeable with ISIS and images of ISIS are potentially interchangeable with Myanmar Muslims. This is the relationship by which beholding ISIS is to confirm the violent potential in Islam, and encountering a Muslim in Myanmar is to behold the potential for ISIS-like violence.

The state in Myanmar has repeatedly and explicitly made the argument that some Muslims in Myanmar are also extremists, in the rhetoric of senior officials and through allegations and arrests of purported "terrorists" and Muslim extremist groups (Galache 2015; Murdoch 2015). But in examining the uses of strands of argument from outside Myanmar, we can see the full expanse of this narrative: it says not that there may be *some* Muslims who are *also* extremists but that *all* Muslims always already satisfy the conditions necessary for (potential) extremism. This is an example of an important shift that Veena Das described in her exploration of Hindu–Sikh violence in India: when *"fear of the other* is transformed into the notion that *the other is fearsome"* (1998, p. 125, emphasis in original). In Myanmar, the strands of argument that make reference to global Islam help to construct the boundaries for marking a fearsome Other that is defined along religious lines. During our listening project, narrators described how news of violence by Muslims elsewhere prompted them to direct their gaze towards individual Muslims with uncertainty and concern. In the following excerpt from an interview with a young woman in Mawlamyine, for example, she makes explicit the interchangeable relationship between fears generated by views of ISIS and of Muslims in Myanmar:

> A: According to [what I hear from] other people, I am worried that ISIS will affect us, and in our country we have many Muslims. When I see they [ISIS] cut people's heads off, it will be a problem if this comes to us. Some of my friends tell me, if they see Muslims, they are scared of them even though they might not have [plans of cutting people's heads off] in their mind. It is like seeing the news about that and then having fear when looking at these people [Muslims in Myanmar].
>
> Q: You mention, you are feeling scared, when did you start to feel like that?
>
> A: It happened after seeing that news and the Rakhine problem. Since then the news always pops up about it. I am worried that ISIS's actions will affect the world or will affect our country …

Q: Where do you get this information?

A: On Facebook, my friends show me when they see something there. They warn me to be aware of people's heads being cut off.²⁵

The connection that makes ISIS and people in Myanmar interchangeable operates along a line defined in terms of religion. Outward signs of Islamic piety may entail icons of a religion — but they are also indexed as signs of 'extremism' and the potential for violence; no person can be indexed as Muslim without also being indexed as a threat. The following excerpt from an interview with a youth activist in the Delta illustrates the way religious devotion is taken as a sign for extremism:

> My aunt's husband is Muslim. ... As he is my aunt's husband, we tried to see him as an uncle at first. Later, what happened was, they are very good at mobilizing for their religion. They are very religious people. ... For them, from children to old people, they only trust their god. Then, eventually, they persuaded my aunt to their religion. At first, my aunt worshipped [Buddha] but later, she did not. He would persuade her with different ways until he got it. Now, she and the children who she gave birth to became Muslim. ... I was also a friend with an Islam [Muslim]. ... However, as I observed his behaviour and his beliefs, I noticed that he was very serious in his religious belief. To say it rudely, he was like an extremist. ... At that time, I really wanted to do something to him but I tried to control myself. Later, it was fine. I just let it go and didn't argue with him much.²⁶

In Myanmar, the boundaries of the threat are marked by religion and, so established, with this comes a threat that surrounds a nation, accompanies a religion everywhere, and can draw on source materials from anywhere.

MAKING SENSE OF VIOLENCE IN MYANMAR

What is opened up by considering the potential parallels — and relationships — between anti-Muslim narratives in Myanmar and those narratives developed elsewhere, especially since the expansion of the global "War on Terror" in the years after 9/11? I want to close this chapter by making three arguments:

First, noting these relationships highlights the importance of further research that seeks to understand the way threatening Others are being defined in Myanmar. This is a question about identities: religious, racial, Other. But it is also a question about spatial relationships: internal and external, surrounding and invading. This chapter argues that contemporary objects of violence are being defined in religious terms, as part of a threat being situated globally. Careful comparisons need to be made to other times in Burma when people who were subjected to violence were also Muslim. Such a comparison may underscore the shift described by Renaud Egreteau (2011), from an *Indo*phobia in the colonial era to an *Islamo*phobia later. It may also indicate a limit to "Islamophobia" as a lens for understanding Buddhist–Muslim violence. Contemporary arguments and affects may be about a global Islam, but this may also suggest that they are less about Islam than they are about the place of Myanmar in the world. This, in turn, may suggest an answer to a question raised by Tharaphi Than in her recent comparison of nationalism articulated near the end of British rule and that of contemporary movements. "It is perhaps easier to understand why Ba Cho advocated nationalism to fight against the British imperialism," she wrote, "than why Ma-Ba-Tha perceives the nation is under the threat of what they term as 'those who hold wrong beliefs,' especially during the seemingly peaceful time under one's own Buddhist-Burman government" (Tharaphi Than 2015, p. 16). This chapter does not explain the *motivations* of groups like MaBaTha, but it does highlight the way they are (re)defining a threat at a time when British imperialism is no longer the target.

Second, noting uses of international strands of argument also underscores the way anti-Muslim sentiments are being actively constructed. Reprising Croce and Gramsci, perhaps, history is always contemporary (Kahn 2002, p. 126) — and so is violence. There are many factors helping to lend contemporary anti-Muslim narratives their animating power, which this chapter does not explore. But these narratives are being actively constructed, re-constructed, and contested. This is certainly the case when people seek to reconcile contradictions between their personal friendships and memories that cross or blur religious lines. Conversations in western Yangon, for example, have been at times disturbing or saddening, but at others they have just felt like people seeking to make sense of global events and feelings of vulnerability that are still open and unclear. One way I have heard this accomplished is by friends and neighbours who draw a dividing line between the present and past, marking off remembered times of inter-religious harmony as occurring prior to a recently risen spectre of Islamic terrorism. In this telling, this spectre — presented as a global plot — makes it possible to both have had a lifetime of inter-religious relationships and a new sense of fear that helps repudiate them.

Recognizing uses of anti-Muslim materials from outside Myanmar illustrates that relations of religious antagonism are not necessarily predetermined and ossified in Myanmar. This is not to say that anti-Muslim sentiments have never been articulated in Myanmar — that is manifestly not the case. But just as it is possible to trace long histories of anti-Muslim sentiments in Europe and note novelties in their contemporary mobilization (Mastnak 2010), so too can this be done in Myanmar. Such relations, as Gyanendra Pandey has argued, are never static: they have histories that can be charted (1998, p. xiv). And as this history is made, there are myriad ways outsiders can contribute to violence — as with my friend's articulation of concern over the issuing of a "killing licence". This concern applies to the fearmongering and threat construction of industries of Islamophobia discussed above, but it also applies to more subtle ways that such materials may be injected into an unfolding conflict. A good example of this would be the controversy over Myanmar's first national census in thirty years, which pitted members of civil society and some international non-governmental organizations against the government and backers of the census process, including the United Nations Population Fund (UNFPA) (Htun Htun Min 2014; ICG 2014; Transnational Institute and Burma Centre Netherlands 2014). These groups raised a variety of concerns, including that the decision to include an enumeration of ethnic and religious categories in the census might be used to fuel narratives of demographic vulnerability and encroachment.

Any national census is ambitious, all the more so when conducted for the first time after an extended period, so I do not mean to make any claim here about the particular reasons it was conducted, when, and how it was accomplished. However, considering conversations — debates — regarding the census with its foreign backers in Yangon are nonetheless instructive. My place was not at the centre of these debates but, finding myself unexpectedly in one with a UNFPA employee, I also heard concerns about senses of demographic vulnerability dismissed with an irritated abruptness: "People who are going to hate each other already feel that way and the census won't change anything." The assumption in operation was that Buddhists and Muslims are already at odds and that, more importantly for the discussion in this chapter, proffering new semiotic materials could not alter this. And while, again, we should beware any analysis that treats dynamics in Myanmar as primarily derivative, I hope this chapter has made clear that the boundaries between "people who hate each other" are neither stable nor clearly drawn, that new semiotic materials are actively used, and that in this they are significant.

Finally, considering interrelationships between anti-Muslim narratives in Myanmar and those circulating elsewhere offers an opportunity to situate a critique of these narratives closer to home. Nancy Scheper-Hughes (2002) has asked whether it is ever possible to "make sense" of mass violence. Such an attempt is a quest, she says, that is as old as Job and "as fraught with moral ambiguity for the anthropologist-as-witness as it was for the companions of Job who demanded an explanation compatible with their own views of a just God" (Scheper-Hughes 2002, p. 375). To ask such a question *about* Myanmar, I want to argue, is a quest that requires willingness to question, also, societies and politics *outside* Myanmar. That is, to refuse the parallels and relationships I have raised in this chapter — to cordon off narratives and violence in Myanmar, to treat them as beyond the pale, isolated, more like those of Holocaust deniers than anything else — misses a chance to shine a critical light on global dynamics that continue to be salient fifteen years after 9/11 (Kapferer 1988, p. xii).

Indeed, while some feel the claims of those who would deny the Holocaust should not be given even the legitimacy of a rebuttal, this is not universally the case. In Germany and other countries where there were Nazi collaborators, the years since the Holocaust have given rise to what Michael Geyer (1996, p. 169) has called a "politics of memory" with real stakes: it is not simply a question of whether the Holocaust is "denied"or remembered, but how it is remembered and understood, including the culpability and participation of ordinary people and how the ideologies that undergirded Nazi violence persist today. Attempting to make sense of violence in Myanmar is, meanwhile, an imperative to consider the operation and mobilization of such violence at home. At an event held in Washington DC during September 2015, for example, Myanmar's then foreign minister, Wunna Maung Lwin, compared his government's handling of "illegal immigrants" in Rakhine State to America's own immigration policies. An AP reporter who attended the event described these remarks as triggering "awkward laughter" (Pennington 2015). Such a response is another shameful refusal of what should be no laughing matter — along the Myanmar–Bangladesh border, along the US–Mexico border, and in the parallels and relations between the two. Violence in Myanmar is both related to and illustrative of the violence embedded within narratives that help to justify militarized border regions, indefinite detention and torture, and denial of asylum to refugees. Considering this is a chance to break down distinctions between the way such discourses operate in the place of the self and the Other. Otherwise, to reprise Jean Baudrillard, refusal becomes part of the violence itself.[27]

Notes

1 St Antony's college is home to the Programme in Modern Burmese Studies; MIDO is a leading ICT4D (Information and Communication Technology for Development) organization in Myanmar, founded by a group of activist bloggers, 'techies,' and former political prisoner Nay Phone Latt. The M.MAS project, supported by a grant from the National Endowment for Democracy (NED), organized research and a training programme for youth activists, focused on social science research skills and theoretical approaches to understanding violence.
2 I continue to have reservations about referring to violence in Myanmar as 'communal'. However, in this chapter, I will take the approach of Gyanendra Pandey (1998, p. xiv) and use the term because its vagueness can be helpful: violence in Myanmar has been 'communal' in that it has targeted groups defined as a 'communal' Other, but I am seeking to avoid presumptions about the nature of boundaries drawn between self and Other and instead use empirical material to understand how they are being drawn.
3 For a complete analysis of the findings discussed in this chapter, see Schissler, Walton and Phyu Phyu Thi (2015). Additionally, reflections on observations from this research have been the basis for essays kindly published by the blog *New Mandala*. See <http://asiapacific.anu.edu.au/newmandala/author/matt/>.
4 This analysis also benefits from collaboration with members of M.MAS partner MIDO, whom the author wishes to thank for their insights and support.
5 The author wishes to thank Matthew J. Walton and Phyu Phyu Thi, co-conveners of the project.
6 Because the project was motivated by a desire to understand how people might, explicitly or implicitly, justify violence, research was focused on areas that have experienced violence: Sittwe, Meiktila, Lashio, and Mandalay. However, inspired by the work of Ashutosh Varshney (2003), the project also sought to include perspectives from at least two areas that have not experienced violence: Mawlamyine and Pathein. Mawlamyine was selected because it is the putative location from which the '969' movement was launched. As the capital of Mon State, including it also meant that the project could maintain a research focus that was equally balanced between ethnic states and majority Burman regions. Pathein was selected as the sixth city because the delta is generally excluded

from discussions of religious conflict in Myanmar, yet the research team had heard strong indications that conditions there were tense between religious groups. The delta was also the site of serious conflict during the 1930s (Burma Government 1939a; Brown 2013).

7   M.MAS colleague Phyu Phyu Thi and the author conducted all interviews. Each interview opened with an informed consent process, after which the interview was audio recorded. Selected sections of these audio recordings were then translated and transcribed after all the interviews had been completed and reviewed.

8   In another setting, this research may have been called an oral history. "Listening project" was chosen as the framing because the Phnom Penh based Center for Peace and Conflict Studies (CPCS) has conducted a number of insightful listening projects in Myanmar and the methodology, or at least the name, is familiar for many in Myanmar civil society. CPCS, in turn, has based their approach on methodology developed by Collaborative Development Action/Boston. See, <http://www.centrepeaceconflictstudies.org/> and <http://cdacollaborative.org/>. M.MAS was inspired by the work of these groups but would not arrogate complete fidelity to their approach.

9   For a further discussion of this sense of contradiction, see Schissler, Walton and Phyu Phyu Thi (2015, pp. 15–18).

10 Woman, 38, Buddhist, Myanmar, Lashio, March 2015.

11 The etymology of *'kalar'* is contested and the meaning controversial, but there is no controversy in saying that *'kalar'* signifies 'foreigner', and usually foreigner of South Asian descent. For a comprehensive summary of these debates, see Egreteau (2011, pp. 47–48).

12 Woman, 38, Buddhist, Myanmar, Lashio, March 2015.

13 Man, 36, Buddhist, Chinese/Myanmar, Mawlamyine, March 2015.

14 The campaign took on the name Pan Zagar (flower speech) following initial demonstrations during March 2014 in which activists placed flowers in their mouths to signify their anti-hate speech message, as in 'speak flower speech (not hate speech)'.

15 For reflections on the launch of this campaign and the context in Myanmar at the time, see Schissler (2014).

16 The Pan Zagar Facebook page currently has 75,325 followers. See <http://www.facebook.com/panzagar>. Accessed 1 December 2015.

17 On this echo chamber and the potential for puncturing it, see Schissler (2015).

18 The campaign members were able to use Facebook's complaints procedure to effect the removal of the imposter account, which was in violation of the company's user policies that prohibit identity theft.

19 The posts were selected from a collection maintained by an underground hate-speech monitoring network of youth activists in Myanmar. The group

identifies Facebook posts that they feel may cause conflict or tension within their geographic areas and shares screenshots with their closed network to warn each other and discuss responses. The twenty-seven posts analysed were those most recently shared within the group. Notably, because the group was not using a predefined set of criteria — for example, a standard definition of 'hate speech' — each post shared in the network represents a choice based on the analysis of an individual group member. It is thus particularly telling that, of the posts members identified as cause for concern, a large proportion drew on materials from outside Myanmar.

20 At end of 2015, the number displayed on the website reads 27,359. Data for the years 2012 and 2013 included allegations of attacks by Muslims, including an incident in Meiktila described as "A Buddhist monk is pulled off a motorcycle and burned alive by a Muslim mob." See <http://www.thereligionofpeace.com/attacks-2013.htm>. Accessed 1 December 2015. The site makes no mention of the at least forty-four other people who were killed, including the massacre of twenty-two Muslim children in a school (Physicians for Human Rights 2013).

21 For more in-depth criticisms of such media pieces, see Galache and Pedrosa (2015) and Wade (2015).

22 While the Burmese-language caption describes the demonstration as occurring in France, it is likely that at least some of the photos were taken in Australia. One placard reads, 'Refugees suck Aust dry'.

23 See also Wells, this volume, for a discussion of the way Western diplomats and aid workers responded to this interview.

24 Near the end of colonial rule, immigrants from elsewhere in British India were demographically and economically dominant: fifty-five per cent of total corporate taxes were paid by Indians, compared to just eleven per cent by Burmese. In the 1931 census, meanwhile, Indians made up more than fifty per cent of the Rangoon population (Burma Government 1939b, p. 17).

25 Woman, 34, Christian, Karen, Mawlamyine, March 2015.

26 Man, 20, Buddhist, Myanmar, Pathein February 2015.

27 "Forgetting extermination is part of extermination, because it is also the extermination of memory, of history, of the social, etc. This forgetting is as essential as the event." (Baudrillard 1994, p. 49).

References

Arakan Human Rights and Development Organization. "Conflict and Violence in Arakan (Rakhine) State, Myanmar (Burma): What Is Happening, Why and What To Do". 2013.

Baudrillard, Jean, *Simulacra and Simulation*. Ann Arbor: University of Michigan Press, 1994.

BBC. "Suu Kyi Blames Burma Violence on 'Climate of Fear'", British Broadcasting Corporation, 24 October 2013. <http://www.bbc.co.uk/news/world-asia-24651359>. Accessed 10 May 2014.

Blair, David. "How Can Aung San Suu Kyi — a Nobel Peace Prize Winner — Fail to Condemn Anti-Muslim Violence?" *The Telegraph* (UK), 24 October 2013. <http://blogs.telegraph.co.uk/news/davidblair/100242929/how-can-aung-san-suu-kyi-a-nobel-peace-prize-winner-fail-to-condemn-anti-muslim-violence/>. Accessed 10 May 2014.

Bleich, Erik. "What Is Islamophobia and How Much Is There? Theorizing and Measuring an Emerging Comparative Concept". *American Behavioral Scientist* 55, no.12 (2011): 1581–600.

Brown, Ian, *Burma's Economy in the Twentieth Century*. Cambridge: Cambridge University Press, 2013.

Burma Government. "Final Report of the Riot Inquiry Committee". Rangoon: Government Printing and Stationery, 1939a.

———. "Interim Report of the Riot Inquiry Committee". Rangoon: Government Printing and Stationery, Burma, 1939b.

Chao, En-Chieh. "The-Truth-About-Islam.Com: Ordinary Theories of Racism and Cyber Islamophobia". *Critical Sociology* 41, no.1 (2014): 57–75.

Das, Veena. "Specificities: Official Narratives, Rumour, and the Social Production of Hate". *Social Identities* 4, no. 1 (1998): 109–30.

Egreteau, Renaud. "Burmese Indians in Contemporary Burma: Heritage, Influence, and Perceptions since 1988". *Asian Ethnicity* 12, no. 1 (2011): 33–54.

Galache, Carlos Sardiña. "Prison for Supposed Members of Dubious 'Myanmar Muslim Army'". *DVB Multimedia Group*, 10 December 2015. <http://www.dvb.no/news/prison-for-supposed-members-of-dubious-myanmar-muslim-army/59921>. Accessed 24 December 2015.

Galache, Carlos Sardiña and Veronica Pedrosa. "In Myanmar, Muslims Arrested for Joining Terror Group That Doesn't Exist". *The Intercept*, 25 May 2015. <https://firstlook.org/theintercept/2015/05/25/myanmar-muslims-arrested-joining-terror-group-doesnt-exist/>. Accessed 28 May 2015.

Geyer, Michael. 1996. "The Politics of Memory in Contemporary Germany". In *Radical Evil*, edited by Joan Copjec. New York, London: Verso, 1996.

HBO, *Real Time with Bill Maher: Ben Affleck, Sam Harris and Bill Maher Debate Radical*

Islam, 6 October 2014. <https://www.youtube.com/watch?v=vln9D81eO60>. Accessed 24 December 2015.

Heizman, Rick, 2015. <https://www.scribd.com/user/202722025/Rick-Heizman>. Accessed 1 December 2015.

Htun Htun Min. "Ethnic Organizations Call for Talks with Census Commission". *Myanmar Freedom Daily*, 18 February 2014. <http://www.mmfreedom-daily.com/?p=20109>. Accessed 18 February 2014.

International Crisis Group (ICG). "Myanmar Conflict Alert: A Risky Census — International Crisis Group", 2014. <http://www.crisisgroup.org/en/publication-type/alerts/2014/myanmar-conflict-alert-a-risky-census.aspx>. Accessed 19 February 2014.

Kahn, Beverly L. "Antonio Gramsci's Reformulation of Benedetto Croce's Speculative Idealism". In *Antonio Gramsci: Marxism, Philosophy and Politics*, by James Martin. London; New York: Taylor and Francis, 2002.

Kapferer, Bruce, *Legends of People, Myths of State: Violence, Intolerance, and Political Culture in Sri Lanka and Australia*. New York: Berghahn Books, 2012 [1988].

Lean, Nathan, *The Islamophobia Industry: How the Right Manufactures Fear of Muslims*. New York: Pluto Press, 2012.

Mastnak, Tomaz. "Western Hostility Toward Muslims: A History of the Present". In *IslamophobIa/IslamophIlIa: Beyond the Politics of Enemy and Friend*, edited by Andrew Shryock. Bloomington, IN: Indiana University Press, 2010.

Murdoch, Lindsay. "Politics of Fear: Myanmar's Chilling Facebook Warning Ahead of Election". *The Sydney Morning Herald*, 5 November 2015. <http://www.smh.com.au/world/myanmar-president-thein-seins-chilling-facebook-warning-ahead-of-election-20151104-gkqf7m.html>. Accessed 24 December 2015.

Myanmar Centre for Responsible Business. "Myanmar ICT Sector-Wide Impact Assessment". Sector Wide Social Impact Assessment. Yangon: Myanmar Centre for Responsible Business, 2015. <http://www.myanmar-responsiblebusiness.org/pdf/SWIA/ICT/complete.pdf>. Accessed 3 October 2015.

O'Gara, Eilish. "ISIS Look to Recruit Rohingya Muslims Fleeing Myanmar". *Newsweek*, 2 June 2015. <http://europe.newsweek.com/isis-look-recruit-rohingya-muslims-fleeing-myanmar-328087>. Accessed 24 June 2015.

O'Toole, Bill. "Critics Slam 'Dangerous' Rakhine Report". *The Myanmar Times*, 2 August 2013. <http://www.mmtimes.com/index.php/national-news/7663-critics-slam-dangerous-rakhine-report.html>. Accessed 30 November 2015.

Pandey, Gyanendra, *The Construction of Communalism in Colonial North India*. 2nd ed. New Delhi: Oxford University Press, 1998.

Pengelly, Martin. "Ben Carson Says No Muslim Should Ever Become US President". *The Guardian*, 20 September 2015, sec. US news. <http://www.theguardian.com/us-news/2015/sep/20/ben-carson-no-muslim-us-president-trump-obama>. Accessed 24 December 2015.

Pennington, Matthew. "Myanmar Defends Decision Barring Rohingya from Voting". *AP*, 24 September 2015. <http://bigstory.ap.org/article/9a3fa02d4e4e4b0390d8b92a257dde02/myanmar-defends-decision-barring-rohingya-voting>. Accessed 16 December 2015.

Physicians for Human Rights. "Massacre in Central Burma: Muslim Students Terrorized and Killed in Meiktila". 2013. <http://physiciansforhumanrights.org/library/reports/meiktila-report-may-2013.html>. Accessed 21 March 2014.

Popham, Peter. "Burma's 'Great Terror' Moves a Step Closer as Taliban Urges Rohingya to 'Take up the Sword'". *The Independent* (UK), 14 June 2015. <http://www.independent.co.uk/news/world/asia/burmas-great-terror-moves-a-step-closer-as-taliban-urges-rohingya-to-take-up-the-sword-10319254.html>. Accessed 24 June 2015.

Prasse-Freeman, Elliott. "Fostering an Objectionable Burma Discourse". *Journal of Burma Studies* 18, no. 1 (2014): 97–122.

Rakhine State Inquiry Commission. "Final Report of Inquiry Commission on Sectarian Violence in Rakhine State". Naypyitaw: Government of the Union of Myanmar, 2013.

Rasmussen Reports. "Voters Like Trump's Proposed Muslim Ban", 10 December 2015. <http://www.rasmussenreports.com/public_content/politics/current_events/immigration/december_2015/voters_like_trump_s_proposed_muslim_ban>. Accessed 24 December 2015.

Religion of Peace. "Is the Quran Hate Propaganda?" *The Religion of Peace*, 1 December 2015. <http://www.thereligionofpeace.com/Pages/Quran-Hate.htm>. Accessed 24 December 2015.

Scheper-Hughes, Nancy. 2002. "Coming to Our Senses: Anthropology and Genocide". In *Annihilating Difference: The Anthropology of Genocide*, edited by Alexander Laban Hinton. Berkeley and Los Angeles: University of California Press, 2002.

Schissler, Matt. "May Flowers". *New Mandala*, 17 May 2014. <http://asiapacific.anu.edu.au/newmandala/2014/05/17/may-flowers/>. Accessed 17 May 2014.

———. "American Election Watching in Myanmar: Considering Social Media and Buddhist-Muslim Conflict". In *Communal Violence in Myanmar*, edited by Nick Cheesman and Htoo Kyaw Win. Yangon: Myanmar Knowledge Society, 2015.

———. "New Technologies, Established Practices: Developing Narratives of Muslim Threat in Myanmar". In *Islam and the State in Myanmar: Muslim-Buddhist Relations and the Politics of Belonging*, edited by Melissa Crouch. Oxford University Press, 2016.

Schissler, Matt, Matthew J. Walton and Phyu Phyu Thi. "Threat and Virtuous Defence: Listening to Narratives of Religious Conflict in Six Myanmar Cities". 1:1. M.MAS Working Paper. Oxford: St Antony's College, Oxford University, 2015.

Selth, Andrew. "Burma's Muslims and the War on Terror". *Studies in Conflict and Terrorism* 27, no. 2 (2004): 107–26.
UNHCR. "Some 25,000 Risk Sea Crossings in Bay of Bengal over First Quarter, Almost Double from Year Earlier", 8 May 2015. <http://www.unhcr.org/554c9fae9.html>. Accessed 24 December 2015.
Swe Win. "Protecting Cows — a Buddhist Tradition Revived?" *Myanmar Now*, 17 September 2015. <http://www.myanmar-now.org/news/i/?id=95b1414d-bd48-4531-84e5-1f069be1075f>. Accessed 30 November 2015.
Team Observers. "In Burma, False Claims of French Rally 'to Kick out Muslims'", *France 24, The Observers*, 24 November 2015. <http://observers.france24.com/en/20151124-burma-fake-french-march-muslims-facebook-photo-myanmar>. Accessed 1 December 2015.
Tharaphi Than. "Nationalism, Religion, and Violence: Old and New Wunthanu Movements in Myanmar". *Review of Faith and International Affairs* 13, no. 4 (2015): 12–24.
Transnational Institute and Burma Centre Netherlands. "Ethnicity without Meaning, Data without Context". *Burma Policy Briefing* 13. 2014. <https://www.tni.org/en/briefing/ethnicity-without-meaning-data-without-context>. Accessed 3 December 2015.
Varshney, Ashutosh, *Ethnic Conflict and Civic Life: Hindus and Muslims in India*. 2nd ed. New Haven, CT: Yale University Press, 2003.
Wade, Francis. "The Dangers of Echoing Propaganda On Burma's 'Terrorist Threat'". *Asian Correspondent*, 15 June 2015. <http://asiancorrespondent.com/133551/echoing-propaganda-on-burmas-terrorist-threat/>. Accessed 24 June 2015.

15

BUDDHIST WELFARE AND THE LIMITS OF BIG 'P' POLITICS IN PROVINCIAL MYANMAR

Gerard McCarthy

A few weeks after Myanmar's historic November 2015 national elections, images of opposition leader Daw Aung San Suu Kyi crouching in grass to pick up trash went viral on Facebook. Following high-profile meetings with President Thein Sein, Senior General Min Aung Hlaing and former dictator Than Shwe, Daw Suu made one of her first public appearances since the poll: to collect rubbish in her electorate in Yangon. After fifteen minutes flanked by jostling photographers — who she commanded to "Help pick up the garbage!" — she disappeared back into her car and zoomed away (Fuller 2015).

At the Lady's orders, similar clean ups were occurring across the country, led by local party members and welfare groups. In Taungoo, an hour or so south of Naypyitaw, volunteers from local welfare groups and private schools collected rubbish from the streets surrounding a government housing project next to the railway tracks. Above an entrance to the housing project, a large green signboard erected prior to the November 2015 election declared this a 'USDP [Union Solidarity and Development Party] village'. That morning though, an oversized dump truck backed slowly through the gate, driven by a member of a local welfare group wearing a red T-shirt of Aung San Suu Kyi's National League for Democracy (NLD).

Within the housing project, in a small clearing surrounded by dilapidated wooden houses and filled with decades of accumulated domestic waste, women bathed and washed clothes from a well while chatting about the spectacle surrounding them. As the dump truck reversed into the clearing, NLD candidates fresh from their political clean sweep of the township a few weeks prior helped a squatter move his makeshift bamboo hut out of the path of the incoming vehicle. A few minutes later, a bulldozer driven by an off-duty policeman began to scoop up piles of old rubbish, *lungyis* and even a writhing snake, and dumped everything into the waiting truck.

The businessman who donated the industrial vehicles stood proudly alongside the township development officer, watching as decades of accumulated filth was removed. Both took photos on their phones, loading them to Facebook as local residents looked on, bemused yet pleased. "Is this a political campaign?", I asked the businessman, who was wearing a flashy golf cap to keep the sun off his face. "Oh no, this is charity!", he responded. "Haven't you seen the photos of Daw Suu collecting rubbish in Yangon? This is the same", he insisted.

For most of the 1990s and 2000s, the NLD and its local networks had its social and political action tightly constrained. Meetings were held in secret and public signs of allegiance severely punished. Cooperation with official organs of the Myanmar government was simply inconceivable. After the seismic political shifts of the November 2015 elections, state-society relations are already beginning to evolve in provincial areas. Yet the constellation of welfare groups, businessmen, political party members, and everyday people mobilized that day reveal much about a culture of charitable action in the politics of contemporary Myanmar.

In this chapter I explore the political and ideational role of non-state welfare networks that have developed over decades to fill the welfare gap left by Myanmar's 'thin' authoritarian state. Based on fieldwork conducted throughout 2015 in Taungoo, I argue that ideas and institutions of obligation, reciprocity, and political claim-making — frequently linked to institutions of Buddhist religious institutions — have formulated particular conceptions of 'the political'. Despite the NLD's landslide victory in Myanmar's November 2015 elections, there are shallow expectations of the state in welfare provision. Rather, notions of charity as moral citizenship are widespread and will likely have significant implications for the trajectory of state reform, as well as the mechanisms through which various actors exercise power during the term of the next government.

The chapter has five sections. Sections one and two offer a short history of civil society and the state in Myanmar and in Taungoo, respectively. Section three examines informal mechanisms of reciprocity and party politics in Taungoo. Section four brings the discussion to conceptions of the political, and the emergence of Buddhist nationalist groups in contemporary politics. Section five offers a snapshot of a rural family, particularly the role of religious and welfare groups in their lives and the evolution of their voting intentions throughout 2015. The paper concludes with some observations on what this sociology of Buddhist welfare implies for the development of political culture more broadly in Myanmar during the next phase of transition.

CIVIL SOCIETY: FROM SUPPRESSION TO FLOURISHING

The contemporary role of various non-state institutions in welfare, charity, and reciprocity in provincial Myanmar is tied directly to prior economic, political, and social policies, especially with regard to the regulation of civil society.[1] For much of the Burma Socialist Programme Party (BSPP) period (1974–88), non-state civil society was heavily censored and suppressed. Outside of a handful of authorized class and mass organizations (Taylor 2009, p. 373), all other community or civil society groups not linked to the religious sphere were suppressed or coopted by local military commanders and representatives of the BSPP, leading David Steinberg to comment that "civil society died under the BSPP; perhaps, more accurately, it was murdered" (Steinberg 1999, p. 8). This policy endured until the economic crisis of 1988, which sparked mass uprisings across the country and a coup from within.

The NLD victory in the 1990 election provoked an existential crisis for the new military regime. It embarked on a dual process of state- and nation-building throughout both the centre and periphery of the territory newly named 'Myanmar'. Despite the ongoing surveillance and suppression of overtly 'political' civil society, the continued degradation of the economy in the early to mid-1990s led to worsening livelihoods and welfare throughout the country. With the regime dwindling in revenue and rigidly focused on the consolidation of its new vision of the Myanmar state and nation, few resources were dedicated to filling the gaping hole in 'soft' welfare provision.

The realization of the risks and brutal human costs of these crises prompted the regime to shift its policy towards non-governmental groups. Local military commanders began to negotiate with ostensibly 'non-political' community-based groups for delivery of much-needed social services (Callahan 2001, p. 41). As Myanmar transitioned from state-led socialism to a form of heavily licenced capitalism, petty traders and businessman were encouraged to take an active role in these social welfare groups and lead the provision of local 'public' goods such as roads that the state did not provide directly. In exchange they received public recognition as well as information from local military commanders about the latest project tenders or industry licences.[2] Community groups tending to the social needs of Burmese citizens blossomed as a result of this particular political economy and regime strategy. While overtly 'political' institutions continued to be harassed, one study found an estimated 214,000 community-based organizations (CBOs) operating in every corner of the country (Heidel 2006, p. 60).[3] These groups were forced to accept political domination in exchange for permission to pursue quotidian coping agendas focused on filling the social welfare gap left by the absence of the state and stagnant economy throughout much of the country.[4] While these groups were discursively constrained by the junta, they were permitted to engage in welfare activities and began to play a significant role in helping to mitigate health shocks, deliver basic education, and prevent dire poverty for millions of people.

This vital role was solidified further after the devastation wrought by Cyclone Nargis in 2008 and the inability of the regime to assist in providing immediate or long-term humanitarian assistance to those worst effected. While the regime remained preoccupied with military campaigns and the construction of 'hard infrastructure', religious organizations solidified and frequently significantly expanded their pre-existing role in welfare provision (Smith 2002, p. 26). Based on my ongoing fieldwork in central Myanmar, these welfare networks now form an essential part of the social infrastructure of everyday life in Taungoo and should be considered informal political institutions, the study of which is essential to obtain an understanding of contemporary Burmese political culture.

RELIGIOUS INSTITUTIONS AND THE RISE OF MORAL CITIZENSHIP IN TAUNGOO

The substantive analysis in this chapter is based on largely qualitative, ethnographic fieldwork conducted throughout 2015 in Taungoo, a town positioned on the inner border of areas administered directly and indirectly by the British during the colonial period. Independence bequeathed Taungoo a complex ethnic patchwork comprised of large Bamar Buddhist and Karen Christian communities, as well as sizeable Hindu and Muslim populations. As of 2015, the township has a population of around 160,000, split between twenty-three urban quarters and a series of semi-industrial and farmland areas around five kilometres from the centre of town. Community leaders from all major ethnic and religious groups claim that the township is around sixty per cent ethnically Bamar Buddhist, thirty per cent Karen Christian, and ten per cent 'other' including Shan, Muslim, Hindu and Sikh communities.

Since the liberalizing reforms of 2011, Taungoo has experienced the same blossoming of 'political' civil society as well as substantial growth in government expenditure at local levels. Political party offices have proliferated, with almost every ward and village sporting at least one or two prominent signboards of the NLD or various ethnic or special interest parties, along with USDP offices. However, this culture of formal democratic contestation is evolving amidst an already crowded organizational and ideational sphere defined by moral ideas and institutions of non-state welfare and reciprocity developed since the 1990s, which retain a substantial role in local infrastructures of care and communication.

In Taungoo's Buddhist community, a rich sociology of local welfare and 'traditional' civil society groups has developed at neighbourhood, village, and township levels, often with deep organizational or cosmological links to Buddhism. Many of these groups are the direct beneficiaries of support and legitimacy provided by local monks and abbots (*sayadaws*). For instance, a number of monasteries provide offices and support to lay medical clinics that provide discounted or free treatment both for monks and members of the general public. Local doctors and dozens of non-medical professionals offer their time on a weekly basis at these clinics, engaging in what is perceived as socially productive merit-making, referred to by the Pali-derived term *parahita*.[5] Other monasteries provide ambulances for transportation of critically ill patients from Taungoo General Hospital to better-equipped hospitals in Naypyitaw or Yangon, or provide office space for local neighbourhood funeral associations.

One key example of the synergistic relationship between welfare-oriented social action and religious institutions in central Myanmar is the role played by 'Byama-so', a national funeral association and welfare group founded by monks in Mandalay and now closely tied to the Free Funeral Service run by Myanmar film actor Kyaw Thu. The Taungoo chapter of Byama-so was formed in 2002 with the support of a local monk in response to perceived local profiteering in funeral services. In turn, the patrons for the organization — a broad cross-section of Taungoo's local business elites, civil servants, and even senior Burmese armed forces commanders — provided funds to purchase vans, employ drivers, and construct a new crematorium. Within months of the formation of the entirely Buddhist management committee and the opening of the organization to volunteers in 2002, the cost of basic funeral services was brought down to around US$20 for some small expenses, including fuel and a processing fee, though these expenses are apparently waived entirely for families unable to afford them.[6] As of mid-2015, the organization conducted between forty and sixty funerals each month, with over 600 funerals being assisted by the organization across the township in 2014.

The role of Byama-so as one of the primary township-level arenas of social work in Taungoo was solidified in 2006 when the organization established an offshoot chapter adjacent to Taungoo General Hospital with the support of an elderly local cigar merchant. The social support offered by the organization subsequently expanded beyond its core work in funerals, providing services that supplement the local government-run hospital, including an ambulance service as well as management of a blood bank with over 4000 donors across Taungoo's diverse communities, and sale of discounted oxygen tanks for patients suffering from breathing difficulties. With political liberalization since 2011, Byama-so has retained its centrality in welfare delivery for the town, despite rapid growth in social spending under President Thein Sein's decentralization initiatives. Hundreds of people now engage on a weekly basis in various forms of *parahita* with the organization, including driving funeral cars and ambulances, doing office and paper work, participating in chanting as part of funeral processions, and donating blood for patients at the hospital. One volunteer even helps the widows of former government servants to ensure their spouses' pensions are transferred to them as the entitlement guidelines permit.

Notions of selflessness and merit play an essential role in the discursive framing and logistical operations of Byama-so. The inspiration of Buddhism is evident in the language of merit (*kutho*), loving kindness (*myitta*), compassionate social action (*parahita*), and selfless intention (*sedana*) with which volunteers refer to and reflect on their work, especially at times of difficulty or exhaustion. For instance, blood donors are usually accompanied by a volunteer from these organizations who support and ideationally frame the experience of blood-giving as 'saving lives' and putting into practice the 'value of life' for the 'good of the nation' (see McCarthy forthcoming a). The same language recurs in the Pali blessings recited for donors when they make contributions to various Buddhist organizations, as well as on the stickers that cover the funeral vans and ambulances.

INFORMAL MECHANISMS OF RECIPROCITY

In addition to the role of Buddhist-imbued social institutions, there are also a variety of informal mechanisms of everyday redistribution and reciprocity that are deeply framed by Buddhist social morality. For instance, small giving celebrations are held when a family makes a donation to monks, or when a son becomes a novice monk for a period. Such charitable events, intimately tied to Buddhist economies of gift and merit, play an important role in the cultivation of more formal welfare networks in Buddhist communities. Donations are frequently offered to the hosts of these events by attendees to support many of the aforementioned welfare and social activities organized around monasteries, including ambulance services, health clinics, or Dhamma schools. The donations made at these social events are referred to with the same terminology of merit-making and loving intentions as more formal organizations. These events also solidify social ties across a wide range of spheres, with employers, teachers, neighbours, and monks all invited to attend and follow the procession or share in the meal.

Neighbourhood funeral associations use similar symbolism and language of merit-making to explain the support provided to families of the deceased. The majority of Taungoo's urban wards and rural villages have one of these loosely organized groups. Operating on a per-funeral basis, a number of inner-city groups have over 300 members, each of whom donates around 500 kyat (US$0.39) for every funeral sponsored by their network.[7] Many groups provide a customized receipt for each funeral donation, containing language that emphasizes the merit-making nature of the assistance. Between 70,000 and 150,000 kyat (US$54–116) is subsequently raised from the network to cover the various costs associated with funerals, and related rituals, and social events. These include the costs of gatherings usually held on the day prior to the funeral at the house of the deceased, where the family serves food and offers a small bag of gifts to attendees. The bag frequently contains a small bottle of water, some soap or washing powder, and a plastic fan with the name of the deceased printed on one side, and Pali verses for chanting on the other. The family of the deceased again collects donations at this gathering, with those of a more intimate relationship offering more — typically between 3000 (US$2.33) and 10,000 kyat (US$7.76).

Funerals are thus a major moment of sociality, in which large amounts of money change hands through various mechanisms of risk-pooling and redistribution, some of which is returned in-kind to guests. Attendees I interviewed felt obliged to make contributions both to neighbourhood or village funeral teams out of a combination of intimacy with the family, knowledge of the expense of funerals, a sense of reciprocity that they will receive the same support in the future, and also due to social pressure applied by local authorities. Griffiths (2015) observes that these mechanisms of communal risk-sharing are common across Myanmar and continue to play an essential role in complementing government welfare services, especially for the needy.

Comparative research on new democracies and transitions from authoritarian rule highlight that these types of non-state welfare networks play significant roles in framing discursively and ideologically what is seen to be at stake in the political arena, as well as in influencing how people are drawn into the political process. As Steven Levitsky (2001, 2003) notes, such 'informal institutions' tying social life to political process can be essential to analysis of party organizations, political cleavages, and party systems in many new democracies. Similar studies in Southeast Asia (Nishizaki 2004; 2011) and Africa (Ferguson 2015; MacLean 2010) also emphasize the role of everyday social practices and receipt of welfare assistance in framing individuals' notions of citizenship and rights.

It is no surprise then that political parties seek to engage and mobilize the same practices and networks of charitable welfare that helped many people survive some of the hardest years of Myanmar's authoritarian period. The Taungoo USDP office provides a suite of social welfare assistance including small loans and other services to its members, a legacy of its prior status as a military veterans' assistance organization. In recent years the locus of USDP patronage has expanded somewhat, with the opening of a free medical clinic chaired by a USDP legislator in the 2011–15 parliament treating over 100 people per week. In early 2015 the NLD commenced its own funeral service in Taungoo, with the party now offering one hearse and a people mover for this purpose. It assists with approximately ten funerals per week at the request mostly of party members. While such assistance is a concrete demonstration of the confluence of social and political activism, it is important to note that the NLD funeral service, like the USDP's suite of social services, complements the diversity of welfare groups and reciprocity practices already operating in Taungoo that are discursively and organizationally tied to Buddhism.

POLITICAL ACTIVISM AND UNDERSTANDINGS OF 'THE POLITICAL'

Inherent to the assistance provided by both social and political networks in Taungoo is a deeply moral notion of citizenship which expects very little from the state. Indeed it emphasizes the role of citizens in providing care and assistance to the needy with a 'clean', 'pure', and 'loving' mindset. This language, drawn directly from Buddhist cosmology, frequently replaces appeals to 'rights' which carry connotations in Burmese socio-political discourse not of inviolable entitlement but of an uncertain chance to make claims to authorities (see Prasse-Freeman 2012; 2015a and b).

Even amidst the promise and optimism offered by the November 2015 elections, political candidates and party operatives were realistic about the kinds of changes an NLD government could bring. At a rural 'meet the candidate' event attended by local members of the NLD discussion focused at length on how the party promises to deliver a government that would be more 'cooperative' with local communities. The emphasis was placed on a notion of entitlement in which citizens must not just 'ask' for their rights — as opposed to them being inherently granted — but also take the lead in developmental social action, with support from government.

This focus on 'cooperation' of the state with local social welfare teams highlights the emotional and experiential content of the NLD's oppositional identity. Throughout three party forums that day, candidates as well as local party members shared stories from the military period about disputes they experienced with local authorities who opposed various village social initiatives, as well as the perceived mistreatment of government doctors or teachers being sent to work in remote, rural areas without their consultation and without provision of transportation. These deeply personal stories evoked knowing cheers and claps from the assembled supporters, highlighting the role that these experiences of suppressed or unappreciated social action during the authoritarian period — often as individuals engaged in ostensibly 'apolitical' or *parahita* activities — play in the formation of supporters' deeply emotional oppositional political identity.

The synergistic relationship between small and big 'P' politics in central Myanmar is further demonstrated by the pivotal role religious authorities play in defining what is at stake in the ongoing political transition. This is particularly the case since the outbreak of inter-communal violence in Rakhine State in 2012, and the subsequent proliferation of monks and monasteries aligned with the Buddhist nationalist groups 969 and the Patriotic Association of Myanmar, or MaBaTha. As Brac de la Perriere argues (2015, p. 5), these Buddhist nationalist groups explicitly seek to conjoin three concepts of belonging essential to defining the domain of 'the political' in contemporary Myanmar: the nation (*amyo*), religion as faith professed by individuals (*batha*), and religion as teaching instituted in a 'social space' (*thathana*).

While it has long been common for people to offer their time to support monastic activities, such as preaching events, the relationship between monks and laity increasingly revolves around the various socially oriented projects patronized by monks, including Dhamma Schools, clinics, and ambulance services. Indeed, a notable feature of all MaBaTha-aligned monasteries in Taungoo is the active role that laity play in offering their time and money for activities broadly seen to propagate and put into practice Buddhist virtues of the 'value of life', including volunteering at clinics run out of the monastery, the coordination of flood appeals, or teaching at, cooking for, or managing Dhamma schools (see McCarthy forthcoming a).[8]

This ethic of Buddhist-imbued social work, and the notions of value and Buddhist nationalism that animate it, is frequently contrasted with the practices of Muslims, who, it is claimed, only provide social support to their co-religionists. Muslims are also cited as being inherently violent and sexually or physically abusive towards women. In addition to the popular narrative that Muslims, and Rohingya in particular, are 'bad guests' (see Nyi Nyi Kyaw 2015, p. 56) a direct contrast is made by many informants between what are seen as Buddhist and Muslim notions of good and meritorious social action. References are frequently made to the atrocities of the Islamic State, communal conflict in Rakhine State, and ritual slaughter of cows at Eid Al-Adha. This discourse of meritorious and non-meritorious social action recurs both in offline discussion and increasingly online, especially on the Facebook pages of major Buddhist welfare groups (as discussed in McCarthy forthcoming b). Taungoo's second-largest non-state welfare provider, Twenty-Four Hours, provides a prominent example of the discursive role these groups now play in the context of Myanmar's rapidly changing telecommunications landscape.[9] Throughout 2015, the group Facebook page, run by a prominent volunteer, vocal NLD supporter, and self-professed founding member of MaBaTha in Taungoo, regularly featured images andstories about people who 'value life' and engage in selfless social action of various sorts. Articles or rumours about assaults and violence committed by Muslims in Myanmar and elsewhere were also shared, including horrific images of communal conflict in Rakhine State or atrocities committed by the Islamic State in the Middle East, frequently with comments emphasizing that Muslims 'do not value life' or are inherently violent.

This discourse echoes pre-existing narratives and sentiments about the allegedly rapid growth of Islam and the decline of Buddhism (see Schissler et al. 2015; McCarthy and Menager 2015) that have played a major role in a series of legislative debates in Myanmar's parliament about the regulation of inter-religious conversion and marriage as well as reproductive rights. By August 2015 a package of four laws, which were written and passed at the urging of MaBaTha and its national network of monks and laity, had passed into law. In the process of this campaign, a particular notion of 'the political' was popularized which extends deep into the intimate domestic domains of marriage, religion in the family, and sexual relations and reproduction. Nationally and locally prominent monks urged voters not to lend their support to political candidates who did not vote for the laws. Some also suggested that the NLD's opposition to the laws implies that the party does not care about the 'protection of national religion'.[10]

The role of Buddhist networks, and monks in particular, in defining 'the political' and influencing public opinion was a recurring concern for local political party campaign strategists in the months preceding Myanmar's 2015 elections. In Taungoo, the USDP publicly patronized Buddhism throughout Buddhist lent in August and September by hosting a series of robe-giving and donation celebrations. While such events were certainly public performances of the ongoing patronage the party and regime has provided Buddhism (see Schober 2011), USDP officials also emphasized the importance of maintaining good relations with monks to ensure the party retains its reputation of spiritual merit. Fears about the role of monks in influencing followers to support the USDP were voiced at an NLD strategy meeting prior to the commencement of formal campaigning in September 2015. Concerns were raised that a senior abbot in a village on the fringe of the township, who allegedly influenced villagers to support the USDP during the 2010 elections and 2012 by-elections, might urge his followers not to support the NLD again in 2015. While township party operatives urged local party members to continue their campaign and "take the chance ... for the first time" to engage directly with individual voters, senior village members responded exasperatedly: "The Sayadaw has a lot of influence ... Much more than us!" One candidate subsequently agreed to meet with the abbott and "get him to be a friend" — but also admitted his key objective would be to convince the abbott "not to deny the followers the chance to participate in the election". Such anxieties, and the need for overt strategies to manage religious actors, highlight the sacred position monks and religious institutions play as central nodes of both ritual and social action, creating relationships through which the scope of 'politics' is often (re)defined for everyday people.[11]

'UNDECIDEDS' AND THE CENTRALITY OF BUDDHIST INSTITUTIONS

The 'depoliticizing' legacies of authoritarianism, the effects of recent national-level reforms, and the notions of meritorious social action and moral crisis popularized by Buddhist networks of ritual and welfare have created a context where many citizens are unsure how to define 'politics' and reach decisions about who to support.

A Shan family in a rural village around twenty minutes outside

Taungoo's walled city provides a glimpse into the political notions of Myanmar's 'undecided' voters and the institutions with which their lives are tightly interwoven.[12] The family lives in a compound with two houses, one occupied by the patriarch and matriarch of the family, and the other by one of their sons and his family. The patriarch of the family, now sixty-seven, tills a rice paddy nearby with the help of two oxen that occupy their own corner of the family compound. Meanwhile, their five children — who range in age from their early forties to their twenty-four-year-old daughter — work in local rice, durian, and betel nut plantations, as well as in trade and hospitality.

Financially, the national-level economic reforms of recent years have had a noticeable impact on the family's economic fortunes. The largest family incomes are earned by two children — one who works in a local agricultural trade company, and the other in a restaurant adjacent to one of Taungoo's mid-range hotels, a job she received through the patronage of a prominent local Shan businessman. On a national level, both of these industries — agricultural trade and the services sector — have grown substantially since the commencement of political and economic reforms in 2011. Life is easier than it was five years ago. The family has more income and substantially improved freedom of movement than in the early 2000s. They refer explicitly to national-level reforms when explaining the improvement in their lives, and attribute changes directly to former President Thein Sein; however, they are quick to add that they also admire Aung San Suu Kyi.

Although they acknowledge the impact of national-level reforms on their lives, the family members see themselves and their village as largely self-reliant. When asked about the people or organizations that provide them with assistance, the main social institution they mention is the monastery a few hundred metres down a dusty lane. The family makes substantial donations to support the initiatives of the local monks — including financial and in-kind contributions of both food and their own time as regular volunteers for various monastic projects. They contribute daily to the alms bowls of the local monks, and visit the pagoda nearby for prayer at least twice a week. They estimate that they donate an average of 5000 kyat (US$3.88) to the monastery per month. In a context where the wage for someone employed on a plantation, in a stone quarry, or as a driver is around 50,000 (US$38) kyat a month, this is a substantial proportion of income but is consistent with a pattern across Myanmar, with estimates that at least twenty-five per cent of many people's income is donated to non-state institutions in the absence of any operable income tax.[13] When asked what specific help the government provides them, they struggle to give an example — and eventually point to the electricity grid they were connected to two years before and for which they pay around 4000 kyat (US$3.1) per month.[14]

They do not read newspapers, and get most of their information through discussions with neighbours and, to a lesser extent, television. One family member does have Facebook, courtesy of a recently purchased smartphone, though reception in the village drops out regularly. Local monasteries, the social welfare groups affiliated with them, and the social events framed and lubricated by Buddhist spirituality thus form the major networks through which they encounter information about party politics and the ongoing transition.

With regard to politics, the family repeats many of the same opinions heard in Taungoo's urban core as well as surrounding villages, which recent nationally representative surveys of political attitudes bear out as well.[15] They have a positive evaluation of Aung San Suu Kyi, who they believe has a compassionate mind and, to a slightly less extent, praise former President Thein Sein as a reformer. They are deeply concerned about the status of Buddhism in Myanmar. Seated in front of a vinyl poster erected in their house advertising a meditation event held in the village in 2014, they discussed the issue of immigration to Myanmar, especially what they refer to as the arrival of 'Muslim Bengalis' from Bangladesh.

They are not involved in a political party and, until the political campaign commenced in September 2015, they didn't know if there were any political parties active in their village. Even in the week prior to the November 8 election, they remained undecided about which party they would support, as they were reluctant to express their aspirations or to make a choice that could offend their local headman. After months of vacillation, however, when I visited them in the days following the poll, they proudly showed their indelibly stained pinky fingers and declared they had "voted for change!"

When we discussed what they hoped would change with an NLD government, they were unsure. "Hopefully business gets better now", the father suggested, mentioning that relations with America and Europe may improve. "Maybe the NLD government will cooperate more with the welfare groups", the matriarch said. "We need so many permission letters to do anything. So maybe the NLD can change that system", she explained. Conversation then turned to an upcoming pagoda festival in Taungoo, sponsored by the chairman of CB Bank U Khin Maung Aye. They were planning to attend. "We heard it will be the biggest festival ever held in Taungoo", the patriarch said. "That man [Khin Maung Aye] does a lot of good things for Taungoo", he opined.

CONCLUSION

As Myanmar embarks on a transition from decades of authoritarianism to a form of governance more firmly grounded in 'popular' sovereignty, ideas of 'the political' are emerging that are deeply rooted in moral and religious spheres of social action. For many, the central networks and relationships in their lives are linked to local social and welfare groups intimately tied to religious institutions, ideas, and discourses of merit, compassionate social action, and the value of life. With regime approval and oversight, these groups have increasingly filled the welfare vacuum left by the absence of the state since the mid-1990s. Since the liberalization of 2011, the arenas of social action offered by these networks have helped to popularize a notion of 'politics' that frames propagation and protection of Buddhism as a religion essential to the national psyche and character, and fundamental to notions of 'security'.

In the context of a thin welfare state, thick conceptualizations of moral citizenship and sovereignty are emerging. One of the legacies of Myanmar's authoritarian period is thus the creation of a polity where political claim-making does not necessarily occur via the ballot box. Rather, notions of entitlement and cultures of reciprocity are deeply embedded in social action — frequently of a small 'p' political nature — which seeks to supplement, complement, and increasingly navigate the web of Myanmar's nascent democratic state. In the context of Myanmar's 2015 elections, small 'p' politics of this sort ensured that a formal electoral process was lent a distinctly Buddhist nationalist character. Social welfare groups and networks are working as 'informal' political institutions, essential to the everyday interactions from which political imaginaries and notions of sovereignty and citizenship are being generated.[16] The interaction between formal political actors and these 'informal' political institutions rooted in the legacies of a weak authoritarian state are thus likely to be essential to understanding the long-term development of political organization and political culture in Myanmar's young democracy.

Notes

1. I adopt a broad conception of civil society in this article, including in it any non-profit organization or network not funded by or directly managed by the state. The term does not imply any sense of discursive autonomy or that the activities of civil society groups have a democratic component. Nor does it suggest total autonomy from interference or regulation by the state.
2. Interviews with traders and businessman in Taungoo, 2015 and 2016.
3. Other scholars noting the growth in community-based welfare groups include Helen James (2005), Ashley South (2004), Petrie and South (2014) and Jasmin Lorch (2006, 2007, 2008).
4. Navigating the constraints of regime suppression led organizations to frame their activities and objectives in non-political terms (Heidel 2006, pp. 38–39), a strategy which enabled community groups to both engage and elicit participation from both citizens and state apparatuses.
5. Interviews with volunteers at Taungoo medical centres, April 2015. See Walton (2012, pp. 178–83) for a discussion of *parahita* and Buddhist notions of giving.
6. Interview with local representative of Byama-so in Taungoo, 30 April 2015.
7. Exchange rates are calculated at the average Myanmar Kyat to USD rate for the months of July to October 2015, based on oanda.com historical exchange rates.
8. The commitments of monasteries to MaBaTha are known both by word of mouth as well as by signs hanging at the entrances to their compounds indicating endorsement of the group.
9. With the increasing accessibility of SIM cards (US$1.50) and web-enabled smartphones (US$35), social debate is now increasingly taking digital forms such as SMS and Facebook exchanges for the estimated twenty per cent of the population with access to mobile phones (as of mid-2015).
10. The notion that the NLD is soft on national religion was a feature of the MaBaTha national conference held in Yangon in July 2015, and also recurred in pamphlets distributed both at monasteries and online in Taungoo. In order to skirt electoral regulations about the use of religion issued by the Union Election Commission, the latter did not refer to the NLD explicitly. Instead they referenced "a party focused only on rule of law, education, human rights and livelihoods", an unmistakable reference to the NLD for all of my informants. See Aung Kyaw Min (2015).
11. In fact his village was one of a few in the entire township where USDP won a

larger share of the popular vote at the November 2015 elections than the NLD.
12 According to Asian Barometer research conducted nationwide in early 2015, over fifty per cent of respondents declined to name the party they intended to vote for at the November election. While this reluctance could be due to privacy concerns, the fact that respondents were willing to provide an assessment of President Thein Sein's administration suggests a lack of surety — especially given the research was conducted more than nine months out from the elections. See Welsh and Huang, this volume.
13 Myanmar was recently listed as 'the most generous' country in the world by the World Giving Index. Studies of household budgets and reciprocity in Myanmar are rare, especially on a widespread basis, although the absence of the state and strength of social welfare groups throughout much of the country suggests such findings are likely to be broadly accurate. For a discussion of everyday reciprocity practices, see Griffiths (2015).
14 Further fieldwork revealed that the electricity grid was in fact a community-financed project, not supported by the government, though this family gave credit to the government regardless.
15 See for instance, Asia Foundation (2014), International Republican Institute (2014), Welsh and Huang, this volume.
16 See Geertz (1959), Nishizaki (2011), and MacLean (2010) for overviews of the literature on informal institutions and political processes.

References

Asia Foundation. "Myanmar: Civic Knowledge and Values in a Changing Society". San Francisco/Bangkok: Report for The Asia Foundation, 2014.

Aung Kyaw Min. "Religion Looms Large Over Poll as NLD, Ma Ba Tha Trade Words". *Myanmar Times*, 31 July, 2015.

Brac de la Perriere, Bénédicte. "A Generation of Monks in the Democratic Transition". In *Metamorphosis: Studies in Social and Political Change in Myanmar*, edited by Renaud Egreteau and Francois Robinne. Singapore: National University of Singapore Press, 2015.

Callahan, Mary. "Cracks in the Edifice? Military-Society Relations in Burma Since 1988". In *Strong Regime, Weak State*, by Morten Pedersen, Emily Rudland and R.J. May. Adelaide: Crawford House Publishing, 2001.

Ferguson, James. *Give a Man a Fish: Reflections on the New Politics of Distribution*. Chapel Hill: Duke University Press, 2015.

Fuller, Thomas. "After Victory in Myanmar, Aung San Suu Kyi Quietly Shapes a Transition". *New York Times*, 21 December, 2015.

Geertz, Clifford. "The Javanese Village". In *Local, Ethnic and National Loyalties in*

Village Indonesia, edited by G.W. Skinner. Yale University Cultural Report Series. New Haven: Yale University, 1959.

Griffiths, Michael. "Traditional Social Protection Organizations in Myanmar (*Parahita*): Productive or 'Perverse' Social Capital?" Discussion paper. Yangon: Social Policy & Poverty Research Group, 2015.

Heidel, Brian. *The Growth of Civil Society in Myanmar*. Bangalore: Books for Change, 2006.

International Republican Institute. "Survey of Burma Public Opinion". Yangon: International Republican Institute, 2014.

James, Helen. *Governance and Civil Society in Myanmar: Education, Health and Environment*. London: Routledge Curzon, 2005.

Levitsky, Steven. "An 'Organised Disorganisation': Informal Organisation and the Persistence of Local Party Structures in Argentine Peronism". *Journal of Latin American Studies* 33 (2001): 29–65.

———. *Transforming Labor-Based Parties in Latin America*. Cambridge: Cambridge University Press, 2003.

Lorch, Jasmin. "Civil Society under Authoritarian Rule: The Case of Myanmar". *Südostasien aktuell* 2 (2006): 3–37.

———. "Myanmar's Civil Society — a Patch for the National Education System? The Emergence of Civil Society in Areas of State Weakness". *Südostasien aktuell* 3 (2007): 54–88.

———. "The (Re)-Emergence of Civil Society in Areas of State Weakness: The Case of Education in Burma/Myanmar". In *Dictatorship, Disorder and Decline in Myanmar*, edited by Monique Skidmore and Trevor Wilson. Canberra: ANU E Press, 2008.

MacLean, Lauren. *Informal Institutions and Citizenship in Rural Africa: Risk and Reciprocity in Ghana and Cote D'Ivoire*. Cambridge: Cambridge University Press, 2010.

McCarthy, Gerard. "The Value of Life: Moral Citizenship and Notions of the Nation in Provincial Myanmar". In *Ethnic Politics and Citizenship in Transition Burma/Myanmar* (tentative), edited by Ashley South and Marie Lall. Chiang Mai: Chiang Mai University Press, forthcoming a.

———. "Cyberspaces". In *Routledge Handbook of Contemporary Myanmar*, edited by Nicholas Farrelly, Ian Holliday, and Adam Simpson. London: Routledge, forthcoming b.

McCarthy, Gerard, and Jacqueline Menager. "Viral Rumours and the Quotidian Cultivation of Political Identity in Myanmar's Transition". In *Communal Violence in Myanmar*, edited by Nick Cheesman and Htoo Kyaw Win. Yangon: Myanmar Knowledge Society, 2015.

Nishizaki, Yoshinori. "The Weapon of the Strong: Identity, Community and Domination in Provincial Thailand". Ph.D. dissertation, University of Washington, 2004.

———. *Political Authority and Provincial Identity in Thailand: The Making of Banharn-buri*. Ithaca: Southeast Asia Program Publications Cornell University, 2011.

Nyi Nyi Kyaw. "Alienation, Discrimination, and Securitization: Legal Personhood and Cultural Personhood of Muslims in Myanmar". *Review of Faith & International Affairs* 13, no. 4 (2015): 50–59.

Petrie, Charles and Ashley South. "Development of Civil Society in Myanmar". In *Burma/Myanmar: Where Now?* edited by Mikael Gravers and Flemming Ytzen. Copenhagen: Nordic Institute of Asian Studies Press, 2014.

Prasse-Freeman, Elliot. "Power, Civil Society, and an Inchoate Politics of the Daily in Burma/Myanmar". *Journal of Asian Studies* 71, no. 2 2012: 371–97.

———. "Myanmar Conceptions of Justice and the Rule of Law". In *Myanmar: Dynamics, Change and Continuities*, edited by David Steinberg. Boulder: Lynne Rienner, 2015a.

———. "Resistance without Rights, Regulation without Reassurance: Changing Modes of Governance and the Reconfiguration of Politics in Myanmar". Presentation at Myanmar Governance Network, Yangon. 20 July, 2015b.

Schissler, Matthew; Matthew Walton and Phyu Phyu Thi. "Threat and Virtuous Defence: Listening to Narratives of Religious Conflict in Six Myanmar Cities". Report by Myanmar Media and Society Project. Oxford: University of Oxford, 2015.

Schober, Juliane. *Modern Buddhist Conjunctures in Myanmar. Cultural Narratives, Colonial Legacies and Civil Society*. Honolulu: University of Hawaii Press, 2011.

Smith, Martin. "The Time for Change". Minority Rights Group International 2002. <http://www.minorityrights.org/download.php?id=133>. Accessed 23 June 2014.

South, Ashley. "Political Transition in Myanmar: A New Model for Democratisation". *Contemporary Southeast Asia* 26, no. 2 (2004): 233–55.

Steinberg, David. "A Void in Myanmar: Civil Society in Burma". In *Strengthening Civil Society in Burma: Possibilities and Dilemmas for International NGOs*, edited by Thomas Kramer and Pietje Vervest. Chiang Mai: Silkworm Books, 1999.

Taylor, Robert. *The State in Myanmar*. London: Hurst, 2009.

Walton, Matthew J. "Politics in the Moral Universe: Burmese Buddhist Political Thought". Ph.D. Dissertation. University of Washington 2012.

16

THREAT PERCEPTIONS IN THE MYANMAR–BANGLADESH BORDERLANDS

Helal Mohammed Khan

Many complexities that symbolize Myanmar today stem from its borders, border people, and border regions. From Karen and Shan in the east to Kachin and Wa in the north, to Chin and Rakhine in the west, Myanmar's periphery commotions affect its stability and its peace conditions (ICG 2015). Researchers have studied these phenomena, and their approaches range from queries on Myanmar's borders (for example, Cohen 2013; Morshed 2012; Schendel and de Maaker 2014) to nuanced studies on border people, policies, and regions (notably, Chen 2014; Farrelly 2012; Pate 2010).

The way peripheries have dominated Myanmar's future brings to the fore some old questions: what are the causes of conflicts at these outer regions? How do they relate to border administration, and how do the security echelons operating on either side of the border perceive threats? Do these assessments come from physical, tangible elements of fear? Or do they draw from intangible and often imperceptible fear factors like religion, ethnicity, cultures, and languages of the bordering people?

In this chapter I address some of these queries, using the case of the Rohingya in Rakhine State.[1] Despite a long period of neglect, the story of the Rohingya is increasingly finding an audience in the political arena as well as in academia, and yet the Rohingyas' plight is far from being alleviated. A discussion of the Rohingya offers scope for analyzing not only Myanmar's governance at the fringe areas but also performances by their Bangladesh counterparts, and sheds light on the attendant border management by these respective countries.

Since a number of scholars have delved into ethno-religious issues (Siddiqui 2011), socio-political affairs (Shwe Lu Maung 1989), and non-traditional security matters (Ahmed 2010) relating to the Rohingya, in this chapter I focus on two aspects of traditional security: border management and the conception of threat by the opposing forces of Myanmar and Bangladesh. Drawing examples from past conflicts along the border — and juxtaposing them with findings from the field — I question the way borders are typically managed and the threats constructed. My experiences of past service in this borderland region — with the Bangladesh Army in the early years of the twenty-first century (in areas opposite north-western Rakhine State) and subsequently with the Border Guards during the close of its first decade (in areas west of River Naaf) — help me in this assessment.

The discussion is in three sections. The first introduces the borders and hinterlands between Myanmar and Bangladesh and highlights their geopolitics as well as the bilateral relations between these two countries. Threat perception is introduced in the second section, where I look at the traditional ways of identifying threat by the security units and other authorities at the border. In the third section I offer a few practical recommendations in light of the study and also in light of my personal knowledge of the area and of the people whom I was lucky to have met in the recent past.

INTRODUCING THE MYANMAR–BANGLADESH BORDERLANDS

When we talk about borders or border issues for Myanmar, we often refer to its northern borders, those adjacent to India and China, or the eastern ones with Thailand and Laos, and tend to ignore the lands, rivers, and mountains at the country's far west — those that separate Myanmar from an important neighbour: Bangladesh. This 271-kilometre borderline west of the Arakan Yoma — one of the two mountain ranges that separates the western coastal strip of Myanmar from the central plains — links with River Naaf at the south for 64 kilometres as it extends into the Bay of Bengal. The international boundary runs along the mid-stream of the river, which flows through the townships of Teknaf on the Bangladesh side, and Maungdaw of Myanmar on the other.

The presence of major cities like Cox's Bazar (also Saint Martin's Island, a naval base and a popular tourist spot opposite Myanmar's west coast) for Bangladesh, and Sittwe (previously known as Akyab) hosting the biggest seaport as well as air and naval bases for Myanmar, adds significance to this border region. While urbanization and trade activities around Cox's Bazar and Teknaf have ensured a steady growth for this bordering region in Bangladesh, on the Myanmar side the Rakhine State has largely fallen behind in development.

Post-independence relations between Myanmar and Bangladesh stagnated. Although Myanmar was one of the first few countries to recognize Bangladesh's independence in 1972, only four Bangladeshi heads of government have made state-level visits to Myanmar (the latest in December 2011 when Bangladesh's Prime Minister Sheikh Hasina visited Naypyitaw), with no visits for twenty-three years between 1988 and 2011. Similarly, on the Myanmar side, state-level visits took place in 1974, 1979, 1980, and 2002 — also four in total, and with a similar period of abstention (twenty-two years, between 1980 and 2002). The diplomatic dexterity that saw through successful negotiations in 1978–79 between two generals (Ziaur Rahman for Bangladesh and Ne Win for Burma) to affect a full repatriation of the Rohingya people who flocked to Bangladesh due to military oppression in Arakan somehow lost its impetus along the way (Haque 1993, pp. 129–48).

The countries have not fared better on the trade and business front either. Till 2015, neither country featured in the list of the other's top five export or import destinations (WTO 2015). While Bangladesh has it in her interest to persuade Myanmar to allow cross-border transit to China (Amin 2014), Myanmar, by contrast, has emerged as Bangladesh's major competitor, and has used its geostrategic location to offer transit facilities to India, China, and other Southeast Asian countries. It has consistently opposed Bangladesh's proposal for a southern route of the Asian Highway, citing reasons of national security (Banik 2015).

On the security front, two major Rohingya exoduses (first in 1978–79 and the second in 1992) have dominated border proceedings between these two countries, when the Rohingya people crossed into Bangladesh in large numbers, reportedly due to military oppression in Rakhine State (see Table 1 for details). There were also a few skirmishes in which lives were lost;[2] some involved unilateral violation of borders by the NaSaKa, Myanmar's former border forces.[34] A series of incidents took place in 2008 when Myanmar hired Daewoo to carry out gas exploration in the Bay of Bengal in areas where Bangladesh ordered naval deployments, believing them to be in its own waters. The crisis deepened when Myanmar also initiated troop movements in Rakhine and Chin States opposite the Bangladesh border and which, in turn, triggered war-like deployments of the Bangladesh Army and Border Guards. However, Daewoo withdrew immediately after, without further escalation of tension (Alexander's Gas & Oil Connections 2008; Mizzima 2008).

In recent times relations between the two countries have improved. Apart from diplomatic visits at the top levels, businesspeople have been frequenting both countries relatively easily, thanks to better access due to new air routes offered by several airlines.[5] Although the two countries have not signed a major security pact since the 1980 agreement on border cooperation, a landmark verdict was nonetheless obtained through the International Tribunal on the Law of the Seas in March 2012 concerning delineation of the common maritime boundary in the Bay of Bengal — one that was accepted by both governments (Sen 2014).

THREAT PERCEPTIONS AT THE BORDER

Security — or insecurity for that matter — is subjective, and is usually rooted in the perception of threat (Ahmed 2010, p. 68). This remains true even when the threat is misperceived and proved at a later stage to be without basis. As has been the case with incidents at the Myanmar–Bangladesh border in the past, measures taken on one side — out of a perfect or imperfect understanding of threats — have direct effects on perceptions of the problem on the other side, and affect countermeasures.

The classical or neo-classical realist school may encourage modern nation-states to view their neighbours as the closest possible threat and to develop defence plans accordingly (Lobell 2012, pp. 42–43), but such schemes often end up being counter-productive. Threat perceptions appear to be in play behind certain actions and counteractions at the Myanmar–Bangladesh border as well. It is important that this cognitive play in decision-making is recognized and addressed accordingly (Karakul and Qudrat-Ullah 2008, p. 3).

The domestic view of threat, on the other hand, tends to regard inbound people (that is, immigrants from other countries) as potential sources of problems and conflict (Werz and Conley 2012, pp. 2–3). Thus the borders also find a prominent place in this threat narrative. However, it must be remembered that, in themselves, borders are man-made — 'drawn' rather than 'created' — and hence are subject to debate and prone to violation.

Identifiable threats along the Bangladesh–Myanmar border include social and sociopolitical threats to territory. The two countries share a few threats — un-demarcated land boundaries and cross-border movements by insurgents, for example — where coordination and cooperation is generally easier (evident by the success in maritime boundary delimitation in 2012 or in launching combing operations to support each other along the border). But some threats are more severe for one side than the other — for example, the Rohingya influx, or drug trafficking; issues that arguably affect Bangladesh more than Myanmar. In such cases, appropriate identification of the threat as well as a sympathetic understanding of the mutual value in cooperatively addressing the threat becomes important.

How do the security systems of Myanmar and Bangladesh locate, and deal with, such threats? In addressing this question, the following section will draw from the recent history of conflicts in the region but will restrict itself to bilateral affairs only. Discussion of security related to any third country — for example, the growing Indo–Myanmar military relations and its attendant security impact on Bangladesh — is not included.

Threat perception in Myanmar

In maintaining its western gateway with Bangladesh, Myanmar seems to employ an enhanced level of security and often resorts to unusual levels of action or counteraction, not all of which appear to be well planned. Some observers maintain that the 2008 crisis between Myanmar and Bangladesh might have been an outcome of unintended actions by Myanmar, which were followed by equally unprecedented countermoves (in the form of troop deployment) by Bangladesh.[6]

But such actions may also be attributed to the geographical importance of this resource-rich region. As we know, on the Myanmar side, besides being a source for energy itself, the Rakhine Basin along with several parts of the inland have long been regarded as "an emerging oil and gas province".[7] Myanmar's Energy Ministry announced in March 2015 that four blocks in the Rakhine Basin were allotted for exploration by international firms (Chinese and Indian firms were already participating in the Shwe natural gas project from January 2014). With such a level of investment, the region would have to enjoy increased security attention.

The town of Sittwe, the Rakhine State capital, is also in the region. Sittwe has characteristics that make it an important strategic location in the eyes of any government at Naypyitaw. Firstly, it provides the main communication line (through the Bay of Bengal) to Maungdaw, the township nearest to the Bangladesh border where the largest number of Rohingya live. Secondly, besides its importance as a military base, Sittwe has an airport and a seaport (the latter developed by India under a 2007 agreement);[8] the city is also home to the University of Sittwe, a location for potential anti-government dissent.[9]

Also there is the issue of homegrown threats emanating from Myanmar's long-standing problems with the separatist movements in Rakhine State. Starting from the 1990s, these largely indigenous movements went through an apparent lull in insurgency; however, in recent times there have been reports of fresh attempts to ignite insurgency in the state, especially by the Arakan Army (AA) and the Rohingya Solidarity Organisation (RSO).[10] Part of the AA agenda resonates with the pro-independence sections of the Rakhine, and apparently attracts the Buddhist Rakhine, notably, the Rakhine Nationalities Development Party (Keenan 2015); now Arakan National Party (see Than Tun, this volume). Although religion does not appear to be the key issue in this motivation, the ensuing persecution by the armed forces nonetheless affect the Buddhists and Muslims in the state alike (Karim 2000, p. 1).

The actions by the RSO, on the other hand, may be based not only on their need for self-esteem, but also to salvage their Islamic identity, which helps them stand out — perhaps also to acquire a global appeal — as they strive for equal rights alongside Buddhists. Consequently, their struggles to achieve these rights lead to religious repercussions and, since all too often such interests do not converge, put the two into conflict.

With the large Rohingya population in this border area, however, additional complications also arise. The Myanmar government and the Rakhine administration identify the Rohingya as a threat to their demographic map (Ahmed 2010; Morshed 2012). Alongside the infamous Burma Citizenship Law of 1982, several other discriminatory instruments — the Rakhine Action Plan 2014,[11] for example —also have been used to target the endangered community (Norwegian Burma Committee 2015). On 11 July 2012, the Myanmar president even suggested solving the Rohingya problem by expelling all Rohingyas or by having the United Nations resettle them — a proposal that a United Nations official quickly rejected (Al-Mahmood 2012).

In recent years Myanmar government higher-ups have claimed that the Bangladeshi authorities were pushing in (or allowing illegal migration into Myanmar of) its poor and unemployed from Teknaf, Cox's Bazar, and Chittagong. This is a serious allegation, but no field data were provided by Myanmar sources to substantiate it.[12] Nor was there an instance where Myanmar border authorities intercepted any large number of Bangladeshi migrants outbound to Yangon or any other Myanmar city (excepting the 'boat people', who are destined for longer journeys to third countries). Besides, the socio-economic conditions of Myanmar's bordering towns like Maungdaw or Buthidaung, or that of Rakhine State as a whole, do not bear possibilities for such popular migration from Bangladesh into Myanmar. Similarly, Myanmar's perceived threat from the increasing number of attempts by the Bangladeshis to migrate to Southeast Asia (usually Indonesia or Malaysia) using its land and sea areas also seems to be over-amplified since, after all, they do not seem to threaten its territorial integrity.

Threat perception in Bangladesh

Bangladesh remains one of the few countries in the world facing triangular problems of refugees, non-voluntary migration, and displacement — both environmental and man-made.[13] Its emergence as an independent country also bears testimony to the critical significance of refugee issues and concerns (Ahmed 2010, p. 3). Following this legacy, Bangladesh has over the years maintained a largely humanitarian approach in dealing with the Rohingya, and has exercised restraint in measures and counter-measures involving their exodus along Myanmar borders (Morshed 2012).

Table 16.1 summarises major conflict between Bangladesh and Myanmar over thirty-six years, between 1978 (the year of the first Rohingya exodus) and 2014. It indicates how, during and after the major incidents, the Bangladeshi authorities tried to solve the crises through bilateral meetings, first with their Myanmar counterparts and, only when those measures failed, by resorting to seeking international support. Also, unlike occasional digressions by their Myanmar counterparts, the Bangladeshi forces have not been reported for border violations or any such provocative incidents along the Myanmar borders.

Table 16.1. Major conflicts along the Myanmar–Bangladesh border (1978–2014)

Year	Trigger	Actions	Outcome
1977–79	Operation Nagamin launched in 1977; 200,000 Rohingyas forced across border into Bangladesh in 1978	Bilateral meetings Bangladesh/Myanmar. Appeal to international community for help	Almost all refugees repatriated in six phases (1978–79)
1991	Surprise attack by Myanmar Army on border at Cox's Bazar; another Rohingya exodus begins	3 Bangladesh soldiers killed; arms looted; Bangladesh side shows restraint	Major regional conflict averted
1992	A reported 250,000 Rohingyas enter Bangladesh from Myanmar to escape persecution	Calls for immediate action by international community	Only partial repatriation (inaction since 1996)
2008	Myanmar hires Daewoo to carry out gas exploration in the Bay of Bengal	Believing it to be its own waters, Bangladesh orders naval and military deployments	Tension until Daewoo withdraws, no escalation
2009	Bangladesh puts a case to the International Tribunal for the Law of the Sea in 2009 for maritime boundary demarcation with Myanmar	Myanmar reluctant, but attends tribunal; hearing takes place in September 2011	Tribunal declares verdict in 2012; accepted by both countries
2012	Series of conflicts between Rakhine Buddhists and Rohingya Muslims in northern Rakhine State	By October, Muslims of all ethnicities are targeted in various parts of Myanmar	90,000 Rohingya (Muslim) inhabitants displaced
2014 (Jan)	New wave of violence in Rakhine State	48 or more dead; international community concerned, but no action	No discernible outcome to date
2014 (May)	Myanmar Border Police shoots border patrol inside Bangladesh	One corporal dead; dead body taken inside Myanmar	Dead body returned; temporary tension at border

In a way, such a performance contrasts with the Bangladeshi security forces' actions in other places, for example at the Indian borders where they are occasionally seen to retaliate against provocation by the Border Security Force (BSF) of India.[14] In recent years, however, the Dhaka government has employed excessive controls along the Myanmar border, partly to keep Rohingya infiltration to a minimum (IRIN 2015). But while there are the usual concerns regarding the possibility of mass infiltration, decisions are occasionally made to serve intricate political equations as well. It is alleged that the huge deployment of Bangladeshi troops along the Myanmar borders in 2008 — although reportedly in response to unilateral oil exploration attempts and excessive military movement by Myanmar — may have been partly initiated out of political calculations by the then-caretaker government. Nonetheless a lack of field data and analysis causes speculation about decisions by the paramilitary command or even the political leadership concerning the bordering region from time to time (Sen 2014).

A degree of over-assessment of threat has also prevented humanitarian responses from the Bangladeshi border guards in dealing with refugees. Back in 2008 (during the border crisis with Myanmar) or even in 2012, when the Rohingya were victims of massive oppression in Rakhine State, the Bangladeshi border guards were involved in 'pushing-back' any refuge-seeking Rohingya who happened to reach the west coast — many of whom were hapless women and children. On 11 June 2012 alone, the Border Guards Bangladesh (BGB) sent away eleven boats carrying around 500 Rohingya as they tried to enter Bangladesh through Teknaf via the River Naaf (Barua 2012). Such arbitrary 'push-back' incidents in many cases risked the asylum-seekers' lives and possessions.

Also, the Bangladesh government is increasingly assertive in its own territorial control in the hilly regions and hinterlands along the border. Between February and July 2015, there were a number of military and paramilitary operations inside Bangladesh (in areas west of the Arakan Yoma) to weed out possible miscreants or insurgent hideouts. According to the deputy director general of the BGB, the Bangladeshi government and border forces were not to "allow any separatist forces to establish their bases within Bangladesh" (UNB 2015) (Map 16.1 shows the combing operation areas).

Map 16.1. Security forces' combing operations: Bandarban (Bangladesh) 2015

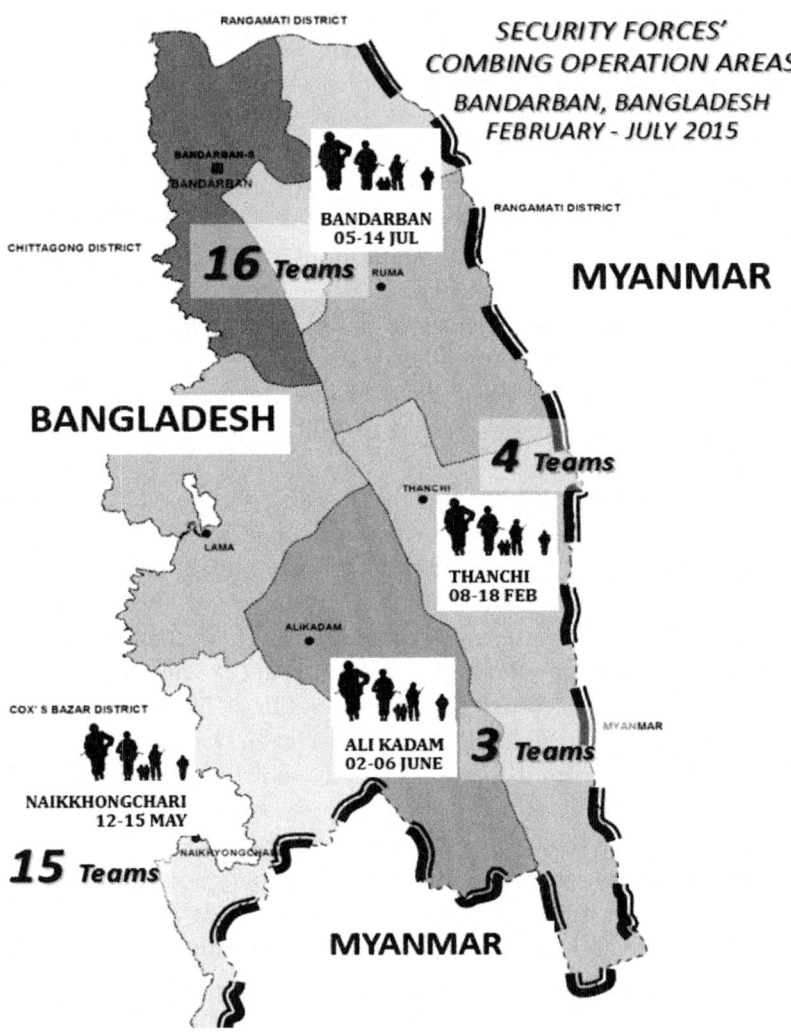

Source: Author's compilation from news sources in Bangladesh

WHAT WE SHOULD DO

In this final section I put forward a few practical recommendations. These are a bare minimum in number, and rather long- and medium-term in scope, but nevertheless important to consider for the security of the Myanmar–Bangladesh border region.

Effective identification of people and control of the border

The population either side of the international border — both in Bangladesh and Myanmar — should be readily identifiable. Procedures for identification should be periodically reviewed. The Rohingya people who have migrated into Bangladesh but are not officially documented (that is, those outside the UNHCR camps in Cox's Bazar) may be registered as Myanmar residents, and not as Bangladeshi citizens. Also, external controls at the border need to be accompanied by appropriate sets of internal controls, something the Bangladeshi authorities seem to lack. Commendably, in the last few years, the local authorities of Cox's Bazar District have introduced stricter verification measures — especially for issuing residents' passports — that could be replicated in other services and sectors.

Freedom of action for local and international agencies

The recent signs of democratic transition in Myanmar call for increased involvement by local and international agencies in strengthening an organized civil society, encouraging constructive dialogue, and overseeing long-term strategies that assist all population groups in Myanmar (HEI 2008). These agencies — especially the UNHCR (which has offices in both Maungdaw and Teknaf) — could be extremely useful in instilling confidence among the Rohingya people so that they do not seek relocation away from their ancestral lands in Rakhine State. This task will require cooperation from the respective authorities in Myanmar. The Bangladesh government should also prevent the local people of Teknaf and Cox's Bazar from pursuing personal gain by providing illegal support for people emigrating from Myanmar. Ultimately, a long-term solution to Myanmar's Rohingya problem lies in a peaceful and stable Rakhine State, and not in hundreds of well-supplied and well-fed UNHCR camps in Teknaf or Maungdaw.

External support and motivation for the Myanmar government to ensure rights for all people living in the borderlands

It is in the best interests of Myanmar that its citizens' rights are protected, including those of the Rohingya. While the Myanmar government needs to take the lead on this issue, other influential governments, INGOs, and the international community as a whole should also continue pursuing and motivating it towards sincere implementation. Countries like Malaysia and Indonesia should consider using the regional forum of Association of Southeast Asian Nations (ASEAN) to put pressure on Myanmar (Malaysia is the current chair, having taken over last year from no other than Myanmar).[15] The Rohingya people should be granted full citizenship and their refugees should be brought back home, and the rights of other ethnic minorities of Myanmar should also be equally protected. Looking at the Rohingya struggles at home and at the amount of outside support they are able to garner, it may be a befitting time for the Myanmar government to assist the community in achieving their democratic rights and rehabilitation, an exercise where they may seek appropriate support from donors and the international community.

Review of the 'Rakhine Action Plan' and scrutiny of ongoing military operations

The Rakhine Action Plan as well as other government decrees and legislation that targets the Rohingya should be rescinded with immediate effect. Proactive and precautionary measures need to be taken to monitor and curb excesses by the Burmese military and security agents along the border, especially against civilians.

Need for more cross-border cooperation beyond the work of government

Bangladesh has a big market and a middle class increasingly engaged in business and trade exchanges that is very much open to cooperating with Myanmar. The planned deep-sea port for Bangladesh at Sonadia is likely to grow into a communications hub which could provide Myanmar and other neighbouring countries with many gains. In the case of Myanmar, its abundance in farmlands, timber, gas, and hydropower could contribute to Bangladesh's needs. Finally, cooperation between Myanmar and Bangladesh should extend towards increasing contact between people through cultural exchanges, sport, education, and other mutually beneficial activities.

CONCLUSION

This chapter has drawn together strands of the debate on issues of border management and threat perceptions by Myanmar and Bangladesh. Imperceptible elements of fear, like the ethno-religious identities of the bordering people, rather than the tangible perception of threats have been the main reasons for confrontations between these two countries for many years. On a brighter side, the people of these countries enjoy ties rooted in their shared histories and cultures. Recovering from a number of diplomatic lows in the 1980s and 1990s, they are now showing signs of improvement in their relations: not only in diplomacy, but also in trade and investment, which could be used by the opposing border forces to increase mutual support and concerted engagement.

Nearly seventy years since independence, the state of Myanmar continues to be a state in formation. It remains one of the most conflict-prone in Asia, but it has much to be optimistic about. Today's Myanmar is identified as a country of many nations, races, ethnicities, and religions; a country that does not belong to any particular group — the majority Bamar or the minority Shan, Kachin, Kayah, Kayin, Rakhine, Rohingya, Mon, Karen, Chinese, or Indian. A democratic framework that genuinely protects the human rights and equality of every citizen of Myanmar without any discrimination is what the people of Myanmar could now aim and strive for. Such inclusiveness would be necessary not only to help re-socialize Myanmar's marginalized people — who, otherwise, may turn to violence and disruption — but would go a long way to see Myanmar's rise as a 'union' in the truest sense, and in so doing help to avert prolonged conflicts with its neighbours.

Notes

1. This study owes its debts to many. First to mention the people connected to the Myanmar Update Conference at the Australian National University. Thanks in particular to the two editors of this volume – Nick Cheesman and Nicholas Farrelly – for bearing the brunt of my loose-knitted drafts. Apart from them I wish to thank Stewart Lone (my mentor, and former member of faculty at the UNSW Canberra), Delwar Hossain (University of Dhaka), and Tareq Mamun (Human Services, Australia) who offered early advice and encouragements. A note of gratitude finally to two anonymous reviewers for their invaluable suggestions of improvements – in some cases which led to total revisions.
2. In one such incident, on 30 May 2014, a Bangladeshi Border Guard was killed by a Myanmar patrol that crossed the border into Bangladesh (Al Jazeera 2014).
3. Dwelling in Myanmar, the Rohingya are sometimes said to be the world's most persecuted minority (Economist 2015). They are an ethnic Muslim group in this majority Buddhist country. Most of the Rohingya reside in the northwestern part of Rakhine State, formerly called Arakan State.
4. The NaSaKa has now been replaced by BSP (Border Security Police), though it is reported that many of the officers and staff have remained the same (Khan 2014).
5. However there has not been any easing of visa restrictions for the business people from either side, who still have to follow certain limitations of movement, especially when entering through the land border or the port at Teknaf.
6. My interview with Major General Shakil Ahmed, the then-Director General Bangladesh Rifles (now BGB) at Gundum, Cox's Bazar; Commanding Officer 42 Rifle Battalion and Detachment Commander DGFI at Teknaf, Cox's Bazar in November 2008.
7. Comment by Phil Loader, Executive Vice President of Global Exploration (ITE Group PLC 2015).
8. India has been developing the port in order to benefit its northeastern provinces (especially the state of Mizoram), which would ensure ocean access via the Kaladan River.
9. Historically, Sittwe has been a breeding ground for political monks in Myanmar: it was the birthplace of U Ottama, the first prominent monk to protest against the colonial British. In 2007 it was the monks of Sittwe who were among the first to participate in anti-government protests.
10. In one of these developments, on 25 August 2015, members of the Arakan Army infiltrated into Bangladesh and opened fire on a BGB patrol near the Bandarban borders that injured a BGB member; the gun battle lasted over six hours. In another incident, on 14 July 2015, BGB rescued two members of the Myanmar army who were abducted by a group of Arakan Army from near

the Bangladesh-Myanmar-India tri-junction area inside the Bandarban region of Bangladesh (UNB 2015).
11 The 'Rakhine Action Plan' is a comprehensive plan that Myanmar government floated in July 2014, and is reportedly in vogue. The Rohingya community believes it is directed against it since it would bar Rohingya subsequently from continuing their legal residency in Rakhine State. Such intentions were evidenced through further illegalization and disenfranchisement attempts by the central government since March 2015, by forcibly confiscating the white cards (the only documentation that a Rohingya usually had to prove their residency) from Rohingya and replacing them with new identification cards. Interestingly, following the announcement of this plan the Myanmar government sent out a three-member team to lobby Western governments and relevant international organisations to accept it as an 'official plan to solve the Rohingya problem' (Norwegian Burma Committee 2015).
12 I base this comment on my attendance at a number of bilateral meetings between Bangladesh and Myanmar border authorities in Cox's Bazar, Teknaf and Maungdaw, between April 2008 to February 2009, and also out of my inspection of documents at the BGB Headquarters in Dhaka later in 2009.
13 Major cases of non-voluntary migration and displacement for Bangladesh affected the tribal people — mostly the Chakma — due to Kaptai Dam project (1978); the tribal and Bengalee people in the 1980s due to insurgency by the 'Shanti Bahini'; and recently, an unidentified number of people who are displaced due to large-scale infrastructure development projects such as the Jamuna Multipurpose Bridge in North Bengal while another large group has been displaced by the natural calamities and other environmental problems at the coastal belt in the south.
14 In one case, in April 2001, the Bangladeshi guards took on a BSF patrol accusing it of deliberately violating the international border with ill intentions, causing huge casualties to the latter. The incident caused a diplomatic spat between the two countries, but did show that the Bangladeshi guards were not indifferent to border violations in general (BBC 2001; Rahman 2013).
15 This view was expressed by Dr. Mahathir Mohammad, former prime minister of Malaysia, at a press conference in Oslo in May 2015.

References

Ahmed, Imtiaz, ed. *The Plight of the Stateless Rohingyas: Responses of the State, Society and the International Community*. Dhaka: University Press Limited, 2010.
Alexander's Gas & Oil Connections. "Myanmar Pulls Out from Bangladesh Waters". Alexander's Gas & Oil Connections, 10 November 2008. <http://www.

gasandoil.com/news/south_east_asia/7bc55418af7ddaa2be5ce45de709b384>. Accessed 21 June 2015.

Al Jazeera. "Tension Along Bangladesh-Myanmar Border". *Al Jazeera* 3 June 2014 <http://www.aljazeera.com/news/asia/2014/06/tension-along-bangladesh-myanmar-border-201463735423134.html>. Accessed 11 April 2015.

Al-Mahmood, Syed Zain. "Persecuted Burmese Tribe Finds No Welcome in Bangladesh". *The Guardian*, 7 August 2012. <http://www.theguardian.com/world/2012/aug/07/bangladesh-persecuted-burmese-tribe-muslim>. Accessed 8 July 2015.

Amin, Zahedul. "Changing Dynamics in Myanmar Impact Bangladesh's Geopolitics". *The Diplomat*, 23 June 2014. <http://thediplomat.com/2014/06/changing-dynamics-in-myanmar-impact-bangladeshs-geopolitics>. Accessed 27 May 2015.

Banik, Ashish. "The way forward in Bangladesh-Myanmar relations". *The Independent*, 22 October 2015. <http://www.theindependentbd.com/printversion/details/20180>. Accessed 28 October 2015.

Barua, Dwaipayan, "Border Guards Push Back 500". *The Daily Star*, 12 June 2012. <http://archive.thedailystar.net/newDesign/print_news.php?nid=237990>. Accessed 23 May 2015.

BBC. "Surprising Outbreak of Hostilities". British Broadcasting Corporation, 19 April 2001. <http://news.bbc.co.uk/1/hi/world/south_asia/1285576.stm>. Accessed 23 May 2015.

Chen, Kai. *Comparative Study of Child Soldiering on Myanmar-China Border*. Singapore: Springer, 2014.

Cohen, David. "China's Myanmar Problem". *The Diplomat*, 17 January 2013. <http://thediplomat.com/2013/01/chinas-myanmar-problem>. Accessed 13 May 2015.

Economist. "The Most Persecuted People on Earth?" *The Economist* 13 June 2015. <http://www.economist.com/news/asia/21654124-myanmars-muslim-minority-have-been-attacked-impunity-stripped-vote-and-driven>. Accessed 15 August 2015.

Farrelly, Nicholas. "Ceasing Ceasefire? Kachin Politics Beyond the Stalemates". In *Myanmar's Transition: Openings, Obstacles, and Opportunities*, edited by Nick Cheesman, Monique Skidmore, and Trevor Wilson. Singapore: Institute of Southeast Asian Studies, 2012.

Haque, Muhammad Shamsul. *Bangladesh in International Politics: The Dilemmas of the Weak States*. Dhaka: The University Press Limited, 1993.

International Crisis Group (ICG). "Myanmar's Electoral Landscape". International Crisis Group, *Asia Report*, Executive Summary, Brussels, 28 April 2015. <http://www.crisisgroup.org/en/regions/asia/south-east-asia/myanmar/266-myanmar-s-electoral-landscape.aspx>. Accessed 21 June 2015.

Institut Québécois des Hautes Études Internationales (HEI). "How the International

Community Can Support UN Efforts in Burma/Myanmar". Report of the Conference held on March 27, 2008 at Château Frontenac in Québec City. Quebec: University of Laval <https://www.csi.hei.ulaval.ca/sites/csi.hei.ulaval.ca/files/Rapports_d_activites/Burma_texte_et_couvert__2_.pdf>. Accessed 27 July 2015.

IRIN (Humanitarian News and Analysis). "Bangladesh-Myanmar Border Tensions Pinch Desperate Rohingya". 19 June 2015. <http://www.irinnews.org/report/100232/bangladesh-myanmar-border-tensions-pinch-desperate-rohingya>. Accessed 29 June 2015.

ITE Group PLC. "New Deal Highlights Potential of Myanmar's Rakhine Basin". *ITE Oil & Gas*, 23 March 2015. <http://www.oilgas-events.com/market-insights/myanmar-sector-news/new-deal-highlights-potential-of-myanmar-s-rakhine-basin/801780830>. Accessed 21 June 2015.

Karakul, Mustafa and Hassan Qudrat-Ullah. "How to Improve Dynamic Decision Making? Practice and Promise". In *Complex Decision Making: Theory and Practice*, edited by in Qudrat-Ullah et al. New York: Springer, 2008.

Karim, Abdul. *The Rohingyas: A Short Account of their History and Culture*. Arakan Historical Society, 2000.

Keenan, Paul. "The Arakan Army's Involvement in Rakhine State". *EBO Background Paper*, 3 July 2015. <https://euroburmaoffice.s3.amazonaws.com/filer_public/49/a3/49a3ea40-fef6-46a7-94a7-5deff91856e5/ebo_background_paper_-_the_arakan_army_involvement_in_rakhine_state.pdf>. Accessed 7 August 2015.

Khan, Sindhi. "Myanmar's Border Police to Resume Nasaka's Oppressive Mechanism Against Rohingya". *Rohingya Vision*, 2 June 2014. <http://www.rvisiontv.com/myanmar-border-police-resume-nasakas-oppressive-mechanism-rohingya>. Accessed 7 July 2015.

Lobell, Steven E. "Threat Assessment, the State, and Foreign Policy: a Neoclassical Realist Model". In *Neoclassical Realism, the State, and Foreign Policy*, edited by Steven E. Lobell. New York: Cambridge University Press, 2012.

Mizzima. "Palpable Tensions Between Burma-Bangladesh on Border". *Mizzima* 14 November 2008. <http://archive-2.mizzima.com/news/regional/1299-palpable-tension-between-burma-bangladesh-on-border.html>. Accessed 21 May 2015.

Morshed, Kaiser. *Bangladesh-Burma Relations*. Stockholm: International Institute for Democracy and Electoral Association (IDEA), 2012. <http://www.idea.int/asia_pacific/burma/upload/chap2.pdf>. Accessed 12 May 2015.

Norwegian Burma Committee [Den norske Burmakomité]. "The Oslo Conference to End Myanmar's Persecution of the Rohingyas", May 2015. <https://www.transcend.org/tms/wp-content/uploads/2015/04/FINAL-VERSION-of-the-Oslo-Conference-announcement.pdf>. Accessed 21 June 2015.

Pate, Tanvi. "Myanmar-Thailand Border Dispute: Prospects for Demarcation". New Delhi: Institute of Peace and Conflict Studies, 2010. <http://www.ipcs.org/article/southeast-asia/myanmar-thailand-border-dispute-prospects-for-demarcation-3186.html>. Accessed 3 July 2015.

Rahman, Major General ALM Fazlur Rahman (former director general of BGB). Interview with *The New Age*. "A Country Should Have Strength to Implement its Political Plans", 20 December 2013. <https://web.archive.org/web/20140222134313/http://newagebd.com/supliment.php?sid=313&id=2142>. Accessed 28 October 2015.

Schendel, Willem Van and Erik de Maaker. "Asian Borderlands: Introducing their Permeability, Strategic Uses and Meanings". *Journal of Borderland Studies* 29 (2014): 3–9.

Sen, Gautam. "Border Tension Between Bangladesh and Myanmar". *IDSA Comment*, 22 August 2014. <http://www.idsa.in/idsacomments/BordertensionbetweenBangladeshMyanmar_gsen_220814>. Accessed 23 May 2015.

Shwe Lu Maung. *Burma: Nationalism and Ideology: An Analysis of Society, Culture and Politics*. Dhaka: University Press Limited, 1989.

Siddiqui, Habib. *Muslim Identity and Demography in the Arakan state of Myanmar*. Pennsylvania, USA, 2011. <https://www.scribd.com/doc/75093911/Muslim-Identity-and-Demography-in-the-Arakan-State-of-Myanmar-By-Habib-Siddiqui-on-10-27-2011>. Accessed 13 April 2015.

United News of Bangladesh (UNB). "BGB Rescues 2 Abducted Myanmar Army Men in Bandarban". *UNB* 15 July 2015. <http://www.unb.com.bd/bgb-myanmar#sthash.8wUGjPfi.dpuf>. Accessed 21 July 2015.

Werz, Michael and Laura Conley. "Climate Change, Migration and Conflict: Addressing complex crisis scenarios in the 21st Century". Center for American Progress, January 2012. <https://www.americanprogress.org/wp-content/uploads/issues/2012/01/pdf/climate_migration.pdf>. Accessed 27 July 2015.

World Trade Organisation (WTO). "Statistics Database Bangladesh and Myanmar". September 2015. <http://stat.wto.org/CountryProfile/WSDBCountryPFView.aspx?Language=E&Country=BD%2cMM>. Accessed 1 October 2015.

V
Conclusion

17

MYANMAR AND THE PROMISE OF THE POLITICAL

Nick Cheesman

For half a century, politics — or rather, the political — were banished from Myanmar. The country's military rulers, having found they lacked political aptitude, instead attempted to generate power "from a society of disconnected singulars" (Wolin 2004, p. 246). In the place of politics, Myanmar got law and order: a mode of association whereby essentially administrative mechanisms coerce people to remain immobilized and quietened (Cheesman 2015a, p. 35).

Well, politics are back. The National League for Democracy, led by Daw Aung San Suu Kyi, has yet again proven itself worthy successor of U Nu's Anti-Fascist People's Freedom League, that unbeatable vote winner of 1950s Burma before the military shut politics down.

But it is not just that with the general election of 2015, on which Michael Lidauer (2016) offers an informative commentary in this publication, we witness the return of politics.[1] The chapters assembled here under the rubric *Conflict in Myanmar* reveal their return from a variety of angles, and in a host of settings.

What does it mean to talk about the return of politics to Myanmar? How are politics differentiated from "the political" promised in this chapter's title? And what is the relationship of each to conflict?

A convenient place to start on these questions may be with the distinction Chantal Mouffe (2005, p. 9) makes between politics and the political, where the former concerns "the set of practices and institutions through which an order is created" for the organisation of human existence, while the latter refers to the "dimension of antagonism" that is constitutive of human relations (see also Wolin 2004, p. 40).[2] For Mouffe, the political does not reside in elections or in a ruling organisation or set of institutions, as Max Weber (1968, pp. 54-55) would have it. Those arrangements are the stuff of politics. The political is more like a condition in which we disagree but also together try to figure out how to decide on stuff that matters without attempting to kill one another. It is a manner of relating to difference, as Dipesh Chakrabarty (2002, p. 140) has written, in which "difference is neither reified nor erased but negotiated".[3] In sum, the political is concerned with rivalry among collectivities recognizing one another as substantive equals who communicate hostility dialogically through fundamentally nonviolent means.

When the political is denied, conflict turns violent. And violence, which is nothing other than a means to some ends, is basically a nonpolitical response to conflict (Arendt 2006, p. 163, again contra Weber, as discussed in Kalyvas 2008, p. 30). This is not to say that violence might not have a possible utility in certain types of political action (Finlay 2009, p. 27), but it has no political meaning of its own (Arendt 1969, p. 51). In general, violence is what occupies the space from which the political has departed. In particular, physical violence subsumes the political in the moment of its performance.[4] Where words fail us, and all that remains is mute bloodshed and brutality, the political dissipates. The *non*political, then, is concerned with enmity between collectivities kept apart and relating to one another as (merely human) enemies who communicate hostility monologically and through fundamentally violent means.

Violent conflict stands apart from and threatens political conflict not only because of its distinctive nonpolitical qualities but also because it has a tendency to reproduce itself. Where conflict is habitually addressed through violence, political habits are eroded and eventually lost. Once that point is reached, as in Myanmar during recent decades, special attention needs to be directed to the political, so as to better articulate and understand what we mean when we say that people are talking and acting politically.

In this concluding chapter of *Conflict in Myanmar,* I read the preceding chapters alongside these three terms — politics, the political, and the nonpolitical. Working through the contributions of my coauthors and with an eye to conflict, my aim is to go some way towards addressing the question of what it means to talk and act politically in Myanmar today, and specifically, how we might differentiate the political from its others. I begin with politics, then the nonpolitical, and lastly, gesture to the promise of the political. I conclude by reflecting upon what threats, in view of the book's contents, the political in Myanmar today encounters.

POLITICS

The lack of political aptitude in Myanmar's military partly explains why it has never been much good at dealing with conflict. It does, of course, excel in violence (see Cheesman 2014a, p. 342). All militaries are violence specialists, and the one in Myanmar has had more opportunities to develop its specialty through armed combat than most.

But if Clausewitz was right that in war politics continues by other means, it is a means that departs from politics, and passes over into some other domain than the political. People may go to war on account of politics, but victory on the battlefield is not ultimately determined politically. Rather, it is determined strategically.

For the longest of times, Myanmar's soldiers favoured strategic solutions to conflict. Violence was their ubiquitous response to antagonism. When meeting intransigent violence, it would be foolhardy to insist on a political response. Consequently, for many people in areas subjected to decades of military violence, political action is implausible. Instead, people in these places respond to their need for security through strategic actions of their own (see Cathcart 2016).

Even where the army did enter negotiations with armed opponents in the 1980s, 1990s and 2000s it treated them not as opportunities for political dialogue, but as a kind of cattle trading. Individual armed groups and commanders who agreed to ceasefires negotiated directly with the military and got moneymaking opportunities, and the army off their back. Most, like the Pa-O National Organisation (see Yue 2016), retained their weapons and a degree of administrative autonomy in the areas where they were active. Although in a few cases the army conceded to ceasefire groups registering political parties, absent of electoral politics and without any commitment to comprehensive strategies for lasting peace, the ceasefires were concerned only with bringing a halt to violence, at least for a time, without addressing the political causes of conflict (see Farrelly 2012, p. 53, 2014, pp. 308-312; Laoutides and Ware 2016; South 2009, pp. 120-121).

Today, things are quite different. Rather than the army negotiating directly with its enemies, from 2012 the government's peace technical team has played an intermediary role. Su Mon Thazin Aung (2016) describes the team as operating at the centre of a "peace policy community" because its functions have not been merely technical. The team has offered support to the presidency on a range of important policies with either direct or indirect consequences for the peace process. Adopting a cautious, piecemeal approach, the team has obtained formally binding commitments from parties where possible, as in the bringing of federalism to the negotiating table; and, informal commitments where necessary to keep things moving, such as by having government officials agree to turn a blind eye to the terms of the Unlawful Associations Act so as to allow armed groups declared as unlawful nevertheless to meet and discuss terms for a nationwide ceasefire.

In other words, the team's role in the peace policy community seems to have been to encourage a kind of embryonic politics. Its efforts do not, in Su Mon Thazin Aung's telling, realize politics anew, but they do at least aspire to do so, insofar as the team was concerned with the establishment of new practices, discourses and institutions than what had hitherto existed. Its activities invite the possibility of the political, inasmuch as it was concerned, up to the end of 2015, at least, with setting terms and conditions that would get collective rivals to the table on more or less equal terms, and have them express their disagreements verbally rather than through use of arms.

Similar ideas and practices animated the inaugural Naypyitaw legislature, from 2011-2016 (Chit Win 2016). The legislature, which even after the election of some NLD members still overwhelmingly comprised of army officers, former army officers and their appointees, attracted interest for being more assertive than many people had expected (as discussed in Kean 2014; Fink 2015). But rather than embrace conflict, the legislature was in its first five years concerned with managing and containing it, adopting methods aimed at obtaining consensus through restrictions on certain debates and control of antagonistic members. Its record was mixed, with strong interventions on disputes over natural resources, inconsistent messages on the peace process, and heavy silence on anti-Muslim violence in 2012 and 2013 (Chit Win 2016; also see Kean 2015).

Whether or not the legislature's non-partisanship successfully contained conflict, forced consensus — which is how I interpret it — is not democratic. Not only is it undemocratic in relation to those persons who were permitted to participate in some form but denied the opportunity to do so in a manner consistent with their aspirations, but also in relation to those persons who were entirely excluded who would otherwise also have become involved.[5] The creating of an appearance of consensus where people would otherwise have acted more antagonistically towards one another, given the opportunity, is what Mouffe wants to warn us against. Suppression of the political does not diminish or eliminate conflict. Instead it channels it into nonpolitical forms.

THE NONPOLITICAL

Melissa Crouch (2016) opens her discussion of the relationship between lawmaking and conflict in Myanmar with a quote from a widely read essay by Robert Cover (1986) on how law is constituted and reproduced through violence — what Walter Benjamin (1978) referred to as lawmaking and law-preserving violence (see also Derrida 1989). To the extent that law is made and remade through the process of interpretation, it depends upon violence for its own existence. And insofar as its response to conflict depends on violence it has certain inherently nonpolitical impulses. Law has the potential to foreclose on the possibility of the political by simple insistence that it be obeyed, on threat of violence for failure to comply.

Where legislative and executive functions are combined, as in Myanmar for the last half-century, the relationship of violence to law is fairly straightforward, insofar as the two are united in a single institution or person. Where some attempt is made to separate the two, even nominally, the relationship of law to violence becomes more problematic.

Crouch explores this uneasy relationship between violence and statute in post-2011 Myanmar. Some of the patterns in the writing of statues she identifies reveal a high degree of continuity with earlier periods, in which lawmaking was essentially an administrative process (see Cheesman 2015a). Other patterns, like new forms of consultation with community groups and international agencies, are evidence of a new kind of nascent politics. As in the case of the politics of policymaking, these practices contain within them glimmers of the political. But cognizant of law's intimate relationship with violence, Crouch warns against unrealistic expectations that the solution to conflict in Myanmar is more legislation. Law as an answer to conflict always brings with it the possibility of diminishing the political through the exercise or threat of violence.

One way that law can act in response to conflict through nonpolitical means is by de-activating the political through the removal of certain issues from the domain in which they can be debated openly and aggressively, or through the removal of people who would otherwise speak and act on those issues from that domain. In modern times, the most effective way law has acted to this end has been to exclude from the political community people who would otherwise belong to it; to refuse them standing or voice through denial or revocation of citizenship (Cheesman 2015a, p. 110), such that a person thereby "ceases to be politically relevant" (Agamben 1998, p. 139). A politically irrelevant person is imperiled not because they are denied legal protections that they might otherwise have had but more specifically because the only possible response to conflict with a person bereft of political qualities can be nonpolitical.

This is why the anti-Muslim and more specifically anti-Rohingya project, aimed at making stateless hundreds of thousands of people in the country's west is so startling and significant.[6] The problem that people who are either self ascribed or are identified as Rohingya — or in the terminology of state, Bengali — encounter is not just that they have had their voting rights cancelled (see Than Tun 2016), although the denial of these rights is symptomatic. Rather, it is that having been denied a place in the political community, the members of this population lack any distinctive political qualities at all. Rendered politically irrelevant, even if the Rohingya can speak, they are not heard (Cheesman 2015b, p. 148).

Ironically, this removal of the Rohingya from the political community "Myanmar" neither liberates their opponents, nor restores to them something of the political that they might have lost or lacked were the Rohingya politically relevant. In fact, it achieves the opposite outcome, since it denies the very possibility of a political solution to conflict, reducing relations between the two communities to physical violence.

Matt Schissler (2016) writes evocatively about how Islamophobes in Myanmar do not feel any more secure or any less fearful for having rendered their enemies politically irrelevant. Rather, they continually articulate fears of existential threats both to themselves personally and to the Buddhist religion, as well as to rather amorphous, loosely attached and weakly conceptualized notions of "race" (see Walton 2013; Nyi Nyi Kyaw 2015). By forcing a collectivity out of the political community that is Myanmar, if not its physical territory, they reduce their relations with that collectivity to violence and its epiphenomena.

This violence might be collective, but it is not political, first, because it wants for an essentially political quality, as already discussed, and secondly, because it emphatically rejects the possibility of political relations with the other. Schissler's interlocutors must characterize Islam as an inherently violent religion. Their project precludes any other characterization. In so doing, it denies the political fundamentally. But it also diminishes the opportunities for political action of its participants, because it robs them of alternatives.

The diminishing of the political through reactions to anti-Muslim violence is evident too in the chapter by Tamas Wells (2016). Bringing the idea of essential contestability (Gallie 1956) to democratization in Myanmar, Wells argues that people interpret this violence differently because they have competing conceptions of democracy. Contrasting what he calls liberal, moral and equality narratives on democracy and democratization, he discusses how each leads its narrators to different explanations for the violence; different conclusions about its implications and different prescriptions for what might be done about it.

Wells emphasizes, and I agree, that argumentation over political ideas need not be progressive. Nevertheless, it does need to be authentic. My concern is that what passes for argumentation in his account may not consist of the dialogue necessary to be authentic, but merely of a number of disconnected monologues. Furthermore, the kind of argumentative exchange necessary for the political is conditional on the bringing together of interlocutors who disagree with one another but who at least recognize the other as someone who is entitled to speak and act politically. Where people who ought to be involved in the argument are denied any political standing, where they are reduced to the "abstract nakedness of being nothing but human" (Arendt 1994, p. 300), these conditions cannot be met.

THE PROMISE OF THE POLITICAL

Where else can we find evidence for the promise of the political in today's Myanmar? The findings of Bridget Welsh and Kai-Ping Huang (2016) perhaps hint at it. Drawing on data from the first-ever Asian Barometer Survey conducted in Myanmar, Welsh and Huang observe that while people there have clearly had enough of violence as a response to conflict, they retain strongly conflicting political values. The survey's respondents appear to reject the nonpolitical responses to conflict of days gone by, while embracing the promise of the political through precisely the type of nonconsensual activity that it entails.[7]

Other writers for *Conflict in Myanmar* go looking for the promise of the political in particular places, and among distinct communities. Gerard McCarthy (2016) goes in search of an emerging "inchoate politics of the daily" (Prasse-Freeman 2012), in the provincial town of Taungoo. Amid rubbish clean ups and funeral services, he identifies a notion of citizenship that has echoes of the moral narrative on democracy about which Wells writes. McCarthy's "political" reveals itself through ostensibly apolitical informal practices of welfare and religious networks. These practices together constitute the means whereby, after decades of nonpolitical behaviour, the political can be excavated and recovered. McCarthy maps political activities across a range of institutions and projects, large and small, and explores the intersections between charity and the reemergence of political parties, as well as advocacy groups. He concludes that the political is expressed in a variety of different forms, which have in common low expectations of the state as a service provider, as well as a deeply religious and specifically Buddhist morality (see also Than Tun 2016).

The problem here, in my view, is that political ideas and practices lead to nonpolitical cul-de-sacs. Absent of Buddhist morality, the non-Buddhist lacks the necessary qualities to act politically. An authentic political relationship with the non-Buddhist becomes impossible. And so rather than being political, this form of morality is potentially corrosive of it. Insofar as the political is reformulated in moral terms of good (us) versus evil (them) the possibility of political engagement is denied.

Two chapters gesture to the political in their discussions of civil war in Kachin State. Costas Laoutides and Anthony Ware (2016) critically reexamine premises that the war is "ethnic" in character. While recognizing that actors and analysts tend to use the language of ethnicity and identity politics in their framing of the conflict, they posit that whereas the discrimination experienced by Kachin might be a proximal cause of conflict, underlying it is more fundamental disagreement about the distribution and form of political power — the kind of disagreement that Welsh and Huang suggest might be indicative of the return of the political to Myanmar more generally.

Jenny Hedström (2016) draws on work in feminist political economy to interpret Kachin women's responses to violence. By recounting how women negotiate and query the gendered roles assigned them, both in their ethno-nationalist struggle and in their households, Hedström urges us to think about how gender inequality is constitutive of conflict.

The engagement of Kachin women with questions of their inequality invites the possibility of a new kind of political activity to come. But it is unlike the embryonic politics through policymaking technical teams and legislative non-partisanship discussed in other chapters. Like Derrida's "democracy to come" (2005, p. 86; see also Mouffe 1993, p. 8), it calls for a militant political critique, with an emancipatory promise both for the women whose narratives it embraces, and for the scholarship of conflict in contemporary Myanmar.

That critique is, of course, rooted in the principle of equality that is essential for the political, insofar as the promise of equality through human organization makes the political possible (Arendt 1994, p. 301).[8] This promise also gives rise to the unavoidable and unending conflict over what equality means and how it is to be realized.

CONCLUSION

Whereas under military government the political was denied to people in Myanmar, today they are again sensing its promise. But, the contents of *Conflict in Myanmar* indicate that the political today also encounters two broadly interrelated threats. Neither of these threats emerges from or is inherently related to the persistence of conflict itself, which is necessary for the political. Rather, each relates to responses to conflict, to attempts to displace or deny conflict and their consequences.

One threat arises from those people who fearful of conflict and, understandably, tired of the violence that it has engendered for so long in Myanmar, aim to establish a kind of politics as technology that can manage conflict without the dangers inherent in the political. Although these efforts are for the most part well intended, in view of the hugely detrimental effects of conflict on the lives of millions in Myanmar, naïve insistence that consensus can be reached by negating the antagonism of the political not only puts the potential for democratic life at risk, but also may increase the likelihood of more violent conflict in the long run. Antagonism is not eliminated, but may instead be suppressed and then re-expressed in basically nonpolitical forms.

These nonpolitical forms, both formal and informal, constitute the other threat that is posed to the political at the current moment in Myanmar. The denial of the political encourages the formation of new groupings that speak the language of politics but attack its institutions; groupings that decline to recognize any kind of political relationship with those towards whom their hostility is directed, that refuse to relate to others' historical and contingent difference by acknowledging and negotiating it, even if the solutions obtained are temporary and for nobody altogether satisfactory.

Like "democracy to come", the promise of the political in some sense must always remain an unfulfilled promise, not because it will be forever deferred but because it is both antagonistic and aporetic — constituted by conflict and uncertainty. But it is the promise of the political that generates and is recognizable in the responses of people in Myanmar to conditions of inequality, and thus that realizes its own possibility. It is the task of scholars of contemporary Myanmar to be attentive both to that possibility, and what it signals for conflict, which is to say, for the political, while being alert to the forces that militate against it.

Notes

1 See also the chapters on the roles in the election of the Union Election Commission, international agencies and the military by Chaw Chaw Sein (2016), and on the Rakhine State election results and ethno-nationalism by Than Tun (2016).
2 Mouffe in dialogue with Carl Schmitt (2007, p. 26), which is why she emphasizes the antagonistic quality of the political. But whereas for Schmitt antagonism is rooted in the distinction between friend and enemy, and the possibility of war, Mouffe argues for a productive antagonism, one that will avoid precisely the danger that Schmitt (2007, pp. 32–33) envisages: the culmination of antagonism in a rudimentary struggle for destruction of the enemy.

3   Chakrabarty talks of this mode of relating to others as ethical rather than political, although he acknowledges that these practices are "never completely autonomous of the larger political field" (2002, p. 144) here designated as politics. Nevertheless, the practices of proximity at the interpersonal level of which he speaks resonate with the conception of the political I argue for in this chapter.
4   Here my discussion is limited to physical violence. For a discussion of violence in Myanmar along both its physical (or personal) and structural dimensions, see Cheesman (2014a).
5   Only three of the 664 members of the first Naypyitaw legislature were Muslims (Chit Win 2016).
6   As Kyaw Min (2015) discussed at the 2015 Myanmar Update conference, podcast available online at: <http://asiapacific.anu.edu.au/news-events/podcasts/address-u-kyaw-min>. See also chapter in this volume by Helal Mohammed Khan (2016).
7   However, just one in a hundred respondents to the ABS survey were Muslim, a disproportionately low number that Welsh and Huang (2016) explain was an unintended consequence of the random survey design.
8   Hence my abiding concern with the rule of law in Myanmar as a preeminently political ideal that rests on the idea of equality, in opposition to law and order, which as a matter of principle rejects equality (Cheesman 2014b, 2015a, p. 262).

References

Agamben, Giorgio. *Homo Sacer: Sovereign Power and Bare Life*. Translated by Daniel Heller-Roazen. Stanford: Stanford University Press, 1998.

Arendt, Hannah. *On Violence*. New York: Harcourt, Brace & World, 1969.

———. *The Origins of Totalitarianism*. 3rd ed. Orlando, FL: Harcourt. 1994 [1951].

———. "What Is Freedom?" In *Between Past and Future: Eight Exercises in Political Thought*. London: Penguin. 2006 [1977].

Benjamin, Walter. "Critique of Violence". In *Reflections: Essays, Aphorisms, Autobiographical Writings*. Translated by Edmund Jephcott. New York: Schocken Books, 1978.

Cathcart, Gregory. "Landmines as a Form of Community Protection in Eastern Myanmar". In Cheesman and Farrelly, eds.

Chakrabarty, Dipesh. "The In-Human and the Ethical in Communal Violence". In *Habitations of Modernity: Essays in the Wake of Subaltern Studies*. Chicago & London: University of Chicago Press, 2002.

Chaw Chaw Sein. "Institutions in Myanmar's 2015 Election: The Election Commission, International Agencies, and the Military". In Cheesman and Farrelly, eds.

Cheesman, Nick. "Democratization, Violence and Myanmar". In *Debating Democratization in Myanmar*, edited by Nick Cheesman, Nicholas Farrelly, and Trevor Wilson. Singapore: Institute of Southeast Asian Studies, 2014a.

———. "What Does the Rule of Law Have to Do with Democratisation (in Myanmar)?" *South East Asia Research* 22, no. 2 (2014b): 213–32.

———. *Opposing the Rule of Law: How Myanmar's Courts Make Law and Order*. Cambridge: Cambridge University Press, 2015a.

———. "The Right to Have Rights". In *Communal Violence in Myanmar*, edited by Nick Cheesman and Htoo Kyaw Win. Yangon: Myanmar Knowledge Society, 2015b.

Cheesman, Nick and Nicholas Farrelly, eds. *Conflict in Myanmar: War, Politics, Religion*. Singapore: Institute of Southeast Asian Studies, 2016.

Chit Win. "The Hluttaw and Conflicts in Myanmar". In Cheesman and Farrelly, eds.

Cover, Robert. "Violence and the Word". *Yale Law Journal* 95, no. 8 (1986): 1601–29.

Crouch, Melissa. "Legislating Reform? Law and Conflict in Myanmar". In Cheesman and Farrelly, eds.

Derrida, Jacques. "Force of Law: The 'Mystical Foundation of Authority'". *Cardozo Law Review* 11, no. 5–6 (1989): 921–1045.

———. *Rogues: Two Essays on Reason*. Translated by Pascale-Anne Brault and Michael Naas. Stanford: Stanford University Press, 2005.

Farrelly, Nicholas. "Ceasing Ceasefire? Kachin Politics Beyond the Stalemates". In *Myanmar's Transition: Openings, Obstacles and Opportunities*, edited by Nick Cheesman, Monique Skidmore, and Trevor Wilson. Singapore: Institute of Southeast Asian Studies, 2012.

———. "War, Law, Politics: Reflections on Violence and the Kachin". In *Law, Society and Transition in Myanmar*, edited by Melissa Crouch and Tim Lindsey. London: Hart, 2014.

Fink, Christina. "Myanmar's Proactive National Legislature". *Social Research* 82, no. 2 (2015): 327–54.

Finlay, Christopher J. "Hannah Arendt's Critique of Violence". *Thesis Eleven* 97, no. 1 (2009): 26–45.

Gallie, W.B. "Essentially Contested Concepts". *Proceedings of the Aristotelian Society* 56 (1956):167–98.

Hedström, Jenny. "A Feminist Political Economy Analysis of Insecurity and Violence in Kachin State". In Cheesman and Farrelly, eds.

Kalyvas, Andreas. *Democracy and the Politics of the Extraordinary: Max Weber, Carl Schmitt, and Hannah Arendt*. New York: Cambridge University Press, 2008.

Kean, Thomas. "Myanmar's Parliament: From Scorn to Significance". In *Debating Democratisation in Myanmar*, edited by Nick Cheesman, Nicholas Farrelly, and Trevor Wilson. Singapore: Institute of Southeast Asian Studies, 2014.

———. "Religious Conflict and Myanmar's Parliament: The Silence in the House".

In *Communal Violence in Myanmar*, edited by Nick Cheesman and Htoo Kyaw Win. Yangon: Myanmar Knowledge Society, 2015.

Khan, Helal Mohammed. "Threat Perceptions in the Myanmar-Bangladesh Borderlands". In Cheesman and Farrelly, eds.

Kyaw Min, U. Who Will Rescue the Rohingya from Their Man-made Tragedy? *Making Sense of Conflict*, Canberra: Myanmar/Burma Update, 6 June 2015.

Laoutides, Costas, and Anthony Ware. "Reexamining the Centrality of Ethnic Identity to the Kachin Conflict". In Cheesman and Farrelly, eds.

Lidauer, Michael. "The 2015 Elections and Conflict Dynamics in Myanmar". In Cheesman and Farrelly, eds.

McCarthy, Gerard. "Buddhist Welfare and the Limits of Big 'P' Politics in Provincial Myanmar". In Cheesman and Farrelly, eds.

Mouffe, Chantal. "Introduction: For an Agonistic Pluralism". In *The Return of the Political*. London & New York: Verso, 1993.

———. *On the Political*. London & New York: Routledge, 2005.

Nyi Nyi Kyaw. "Alienation, Discrimination, and Securitization: Legal Personhood and Cultural Personhood of Muslims in Myanmar". *Review of Faith and International Affairs* 13, no. 4 (2015): 50–59.

Prasse-Freeman, Elliott. "Power, Civil Society, and an Inchoate Politics of the Daily in Burma/Myanmar". *Journal of Asian Studies* 71, no. 2 (2012): 371–97.

Schissler, Matt. "On Islamophobes and Holocaust Deniers: Making Sense of Violence, in Myanmar and Elsewhere". In Cheesman and Farrelly, eds.

Schmitt, Carl. *The Concept of the Political*. Translated by George Schwab. Chicago & London: University of Chicago Press. 2007 [1932].

South, Ashley. *Ethnic Politics in Burma: States of Conflict*. London & New York: Routledge, 2009.

Su Mon Thazin Aung. "The Politics of Policymaking in Transitional Government: A Case Study of the Ethnic Peace Process in Myanmar". In Cheesman and Farrelly, eds.

Than Tun. "Ethnicity and Buddhist Nationalism in the 2015 Rakhine State Election Results". In Cheesman and Farrelly, eds.

Walton, Matthew J. "The 'Wages of Burman-ness': Ethnicity and Burman Privilege in Contemporary Myanmar". *Journal of Contemporary Asia* 43, no. 1 (2013): 1–27.

Weber, Max. *Economy and Society: An Outline of Interpretive Sociology*. Translated by Ephraim Fischoff et al. Edited by Guenther Roth and Claus Wittich. 3 vols. Berkeley, Los Angeles & London: University of California Press, 1968.

Wells, Tamas. "Making Sense of Reactions to Communal Violence in Myanmar". In Cheesman and Farrelly, eds.

Welsh, Bridget, and Kai-Ping Huang. "Public Perceptions of a Divided Myanmar: Findings from the 2015 Myanmar Asian Barometer Survey". In Cheesman and Farrelly, eds.

Wolin, Sheldon S. *Politics and Vision: Continuity and Innovation in Western Political Thought*. Expanded ed. Princeton & Oxford: Princeton University Press, 2004 [1960].

Yue, Ricky. "Pacifying the Frontiers: The Pa-O Self-Administered Zone and the Political Order in the Southern Shan State". In Cheesman and Farrelly, eds.

ABBREVIATIONS AND KEY TERMS

969	Buddhist ethno-nationalist movement
AA	Arakan Army
ABS	Asian Barometer Survey
ABSDF	All Burma Students' Democratic Front
ALD	Arakan League for Democracy
ALP	Arakan Liberation Party
Amyotha Hluttaw	Upper House, Pyidaungsu Hluttaw
ANFREL	Asian Network for Free Elections
ANP	*See* RNP
ANU	Australian National University
Arakan	*See* Rakhine
ASEAN	Association of Southeast Asian Nations
BAD	Border Areas Development
Bamar	*See* Burman
BGB	Border Guards Bangladesh
BGF	Border Guard Force, Myanmar
BSPP	Burma Socialist Programme Party
Burman	Majority ethnic group (or its language); also known as Bamar
CBO	Community-based organisation
CNF	Chin National Front
CPB	Communist Party of Burma

CRPP	Committee Representing the People's Parliament
CSO	Civil society organization
CTU	Constitutional Tribunal of the Union
DCA	DanChurchAid
DEMO	Democracy for Ethnic Minorities Organization
Dhamma	Buddhist conception of natural law
DKBA	Democratic Karen Benevolent Army
EAG	Ethnic armed group
GAD	General Administration Department
Hluttaw	*See* Pyidaungsu Hluttaw
IDEA	Institute for Democracy and Electoral Assistance
IDP	Internally displaced person
IFES	International Foundation for Electoral Systems
INGO	International non-government organisation
IRI	International Republican Institute
ISIS	Islamic State of Iraq and Syria
JMC	Joint Monitoring Committee
Kachin	Ethnic group, language or administrative area in northern Myanmar
Karen	*See* Kayin
Kayin	Ethnic group, language, or administrative area in eastern Myanmar; also known as Karen
KIA	Kachin Independence Army
KIO	Kachin Independence Organization
KNLA	Karen National Liberation Army
KNU	Karen National Union
KRSAN	Kaung Rwai Social Action Network
KWA	Kachin Women's Association
KWAT	Kachin Women's Association, Thailand
KWU	Kachin Women's Union
Kyat	Myanmar currency
Longgyi	Sarong
MaBaTha	[Committee for the Protection of] Race and Religion
MNDAA	Myanmar National Democratic Alliance Army
MPC	Myanmar Peace Center

Naypyitaw	Myanmar national capital; also Naypyidaw or Nay Pyi Taw
NCA	Nationwide Ceasefire Agreement
NCCT	Nationwide Ceasefire Coordination Team
NDAA	National Democratic Alliance Army
NDI	National Democratic Institute
NDSC	National Defence and Security Council
NED	National Endowment for Democracy, USA
NGO	Non-governmental organisation
NLD	National League for Democracy
OIC	Organisation of Islamic Cooperation
PDN	Parami Development Network
PNA	Pa-O National Army
PNLO	Pa-O National Liberation Organization
PNO	Pa-O National Organisation
Pyidaungsu Hluttaw	Union assembly
Pyithu Hluttaw	Lower House, Pyidaungsu Hluttaw
PYO	Pa-Oh Youth Organisation
Rakhine	Ethnic group, language, or administrative area in coastal western Myanmar; also known as Arakan
RCSS	Restoration Council of Shan State
RNDP	Rakhine Nationalities Development Party
RNP	Rakhine National Party (also known as Arakan National Party)
Rohingya	Ethnic group (or language) on coastal border of Bangladesh
RSO	Rohingya Solidarity Organisation
SAD	Self-Administered Division
Sayadaw	Abbot of a Buddhist monastery
SAZ	Self-Administered Zone
Shan	Ethnic group, language, or administrative area in hilly northeast Myanmar
SLORC	State Law and Order Restoration Council
SNDP	Shan Nationalities Democratic Party
SNLD	Shan Nationalities League for Democracy
SNLF	Shanland Nationalities Liberation Front
SPDC	State Peace and Development Council

SSA/-N/-S	Shan State Army/-North/-South
SSNLO	Shan State Nationalities Liberation Organisation
SSNPLO	Shan State Nationalities People's Liberation Organisation
Tatmadaw	Myanmar armed forces
TNLA	Ta'ang National Liberation Army
UEC	Union Election Commission
UNFC	United Nationalities Federal Council
UNFPA	United Nations Population Fund
UNHCR	United Nations High Commissioner for Refugees
UPCC	Union Peacemaking Central Committee
UPDJC	Union Political Dialogue Joint Committee
UPNO	Union Pa-O National Organisation
UPWC	Union Peacemaking Working Committee
USDA	Union Solidarity and Development Association
USDP	Union Solidarity and Development Party
UWSA	United Wa State Army
YSPS	Yangon School of Political Science

INDEX

Notes are indicated by page and note number, for example, "44n6" means note 6 on page 44.

A

Amyotha Hluttaw *see* Hluttaw
Anthias, Floya, 71
anti-Muslim sentiment, 177–82, 233, 254, 255, 358–9
   arguments for, in Myanmar, 288, 289–93, 294
   Buddhist–Muslim violence, 6, 14–15, 16, 149–54, 207–9, 245–6, 250–1, 359
   ISIS and community distrust of Muslims, 288, 292, 294, 296, 300–1, 323
   Islamophobia, 149, 290, 293–4, 302, 359
   Islamophobia industry, 295–6, 297, 303
   media stories on Muslim terrorism threats, 297–8
   non-meritorious social actions ascribed to Muslims, 323
   parallels between discourses in Myanmar and elsewhere, 286, 287–8, 293–300, 302–4
   perceived threat of Islam, 287–94, 359
   see also Buddhist nationalism

Arakan Army, 41, 338
Arakan kingdoms, 184, 188
Arakan League for Democracy, 182–4
Arakan National Council, 183
Arakan National Party (Rakhine National Party), 140, 152, 177–8, 181–5
   as Buddhist-nationalist alternative party, 189–91
   election results (2015), 177–8, 185–9, 193–4
Arakan Patriotic Party, 184, 195n4
armed forces of Myanmar (Tatmadaw), 4
   Bureau of Special Operations, 8–9
   Commander-in-Chief powers, 8
   education, 171–2
   elections and, 164, 171–3
   ethnic composition, 12
   federalism and, 37–8
   "four cuts" strategy, 121, 125
   historic vision of, 56–7
   officers' dual roles, 4
   operations against KIA, 35, 48, 62
   paternalism, 71
   peace talks and, 25–7, 31, 35–8, 40–2, 356

political involvement (citizens' views), 277, 280
Regional Commands, 8
role under Constitution (2008), 4, 8, 35
seats in parliament, 12, 44n7, 171, 214
solutions to conflict, 355–7
warnings to media groups, 41
women in, 86n10
armed groups *see* ethnic armed groups
As'ad, Muhammad Uhaib, 107, 113
Ashin Wirathu, 6, 149, 152, 153
Asia Foundation, 281n7
Asia World, 92
Asian Barometer Survey (2015), Myanmar
conflict-aversion and recognition, 265–6, 279–80, 360
ethnicity, 266–71
governance and political culture, 276–9, 280
methodology, 262–5
religion, 271–6, 280
Asian Development Bank, 236
Asian Network for Free Elections, 170
Aspinall, Edward, 107, 113
Association of Southeast Asian Nations Summits, 5
Aung Min, 79
executive mandate, 30, 33, 44n6
peace plan and, 11, 26, 30–1, 33, 38, 206
Aung Naing, 254
Aung Naing Oo, 26
Aung Nyein, 203
Aung Sa, 95
Aung San, 7, 52–4, 95, 253
Aung San Suu Kyi, 6, 7, 12, 13–14, 85n1, 112
on communal violence, 245–6, 250

on "free men", 255
ineligibility for presidency, 154
NCA and peace dialogue, 155
rubbish collection, 313–14
see also National League for Democracy
Aung Thaung, 30
Australia, 169
Aye Maung, 183
Aye Thar Aung, 182

B

Bamar
Burman paternalism/chauvinism, 56
perceptions of equality/inequality, 266–71
political protection of, 233, 253–4, 255
self-identity, 272
social hierarchical thinking, 56–7
views on governance and political culture, 277–9
see also Buddhist nationalism
Bangladesh
displaced persons from Myanmar, 14–15, 336, 339–40, 341
illegal immigrants in Myanmar, 14, 151, 326, 339
relations with Myanmar, 335–6, 345
see also borderlands, Myanmar–Bangladesh
banks, 230
"Bengali" designation, 151, 153, 159n19, 181 *see also* Rohingya
Bleich, Erik, 293
Border Areas Development, 95, 97
Border Guard Force, 8, 29, 61
borderland conflicts
Bangladesh border, 336, 340
Chinese border, 8–10
CPB role, 56–7

Hluttaw response to, 200, 205–7
Thai border, 10–11
borderlands, Myanmar–Bangladesh
  conflicts, 336, 340
  geopolitics, 334–6, 345
  recommendations for management
    and security, 343–5
  threat perception, 336–7
  threat perception in Bangladesh,
    339–42
  threat perception in Myanmar,
    337–9
borders
  versus frontiers, 93–4
  militarized, 304–5
Buddhism
  perceived threat of Islam to, 290–4,
    323–4
  protection of, 208–9, 233, 253–4,
    323, 327
Buddhist citizens
  religiosity, 273
  self-identity, 272
  Taungoo family case study, 325–7
  traditional values, 274
  views on governance and political
    culture, 276–9
  views on role of religion in society,
    273–6
Buddhist institutions and social
  welfare, 317–21, 327–8
Buddhist morality, 189–90, 360
  contrasted with Muslim practices,
    322–3
  and social welfare, 317–21, 327–8
Buddhist–Muslim violence, 6,
  14–15, 16, 149–54, 207–9, 245–6,
  250–1, 359 *see also* anti-Muslim
  sentiment
Buddhist nationalism, 6, 14, 15, 56,
  149–53, 323–4
  in 2015 election, 178, 179–80
  in 2015 election in Rakhine State,
    181–9
  laws on protection of race and
    religion, 208–9, 233, 323
  principles and Buddhist morality,
    189–91
  see also Bamar; MaBaTha
Bureau of Special Operations No. 1,
  8–9
Burma
  Frontier Areas, 52–3
  independence, 52–4 *see also*
    Panglong Agreement (1947)
  pre-colonial period, 52
  see also Myanmar
Burma Relief Center, 102
Burma Socialist Programme Party
  (BSPP) period, 315
business reforms, 228–31, 236, 237
Buy Buddhist campaign, 149
Byama-so, 318–19
by-elections (2012), 5, 13, 154, 173

C

capacity building, 99, 102, 115n8,
  156, 164, 166 *see also* civil society
  organizations
Carter Center, 170
Cathcart, Gregory S
  chapter by, 17, 121–36
  referenced, 355
ceasefire agreements with EAGs,
  7–11, 25, 29, 30, 47–8, 95–6, 355–6
  Kachin, 7–8, 9, 47–8, 60–1, 62, 142
  Karen, 123
  Kokang, 9–10
  landmine issues and, 123, 125
  nationwide *see* Nationwide
    Ceasefire Agreement
  Shan State, 96–7, 100, 103
  Wa, 10

see also peace talks and agreements (2011–15)
ceasefire capitalism, 60, 92–3, 94, 112–13 *see also* state control
census (2014)
  controversy over, 303
  gaps in, 148
  Rakhine State, 148, 150–1
Central Bank, 230, 236
Central Committee on Land Administration, 204
centre of policy community, defined, 28
cetana, 253–6
Chakrabarty, Dipesh, 354
Chao, En-Chieh, 295, 296, 297
Chaw Chaw Sein
  chapter by, 17, 163–76
  referenced, 365n1
Cheesman, Nick
  chapter by, 18, 353–66
  referenced, 72, 227, 235
Chie Ikeya, 72
Chin people, 95
Chin State elections (2015), 140
China
  relations with Myanmar, 10
  ties with Myanmar ethnic groups, 9–10
  trade with, 8, 9
  trafficking in women to, 81–2
Chit Win
  chapter by, 17, 199–220
  referenced, 222, 223, 356, 357
Christians, 15, 208
Christiansen, Thomas, 36, 38
"chronic emergency", 121–2, 125, 126–8
citizens' views *see* Asian Barometer Survey (2015), Myanmar

citizenship
  citizens' views on, 273
  concept of, 62
  discrimination against Rohingya, 151–2, 181, 339, 344, 358
  notions of, 360
  status and statelessness, 150–4
civil society and the state
  Myanmar, 315–16
  Taungoo, 317–19, 321–4
civil society organizations
  activities causing tension, 106
  community-based organizations, 316
  community protection and, 127
  elections and, 166, 168, 169–71
  funding, 102
  laws concerning, 232
  political socialization agents, 99, 101, 102, 104–5, 113
  see also welfare groups
civilian self-protection *see* community protection
Committee for the Protection of Race and Religion, 15 *see also* MaBaTha
Committee Representing the People's Parliament, 182
communal violence
  Burmese democracy movement reactions to, 245–6, 253–7
  Hluttaw response to, 200, 207–9, 213
  in Meiktila, 15, 207, 208, 245, 250
  Western aid worker reactions to, 246, 250–2
  see also Buddhist–Muslim violence; religious conflict
communist Pa-O *see* Pa-O National Liberation Organization (PNLO)

Communist Party of Burma (CPB), 7, 10, 56–7, 95, 100
community-based organizations, 316 *see also* civil society organizations; welfare groups
community protection
 patron-client ties, 126–7
 strategies, 122, 127–8, 129, 131–2
concepts, "essentially contested", 247, 248, 257
conflict
 among institutions of state, 224–8
 community protection in, 122, 126–9, 131–2
 drivers of, 49–50
 economic reforms and, 228–31
 elections and, 139, 141–2
 gender and, 67–73, 77–8
 Hluttaw response *see* Hluttaw response to conflicts
 parliamentary role in, 201–2
 politics/"the political" and, 353–62
 social reforms and, 231–3
 views on (cross-national comparison), 266
 views on (Myanmar citizens), 265–6, 279–81, 360
 violence and, 354–5
 see also armed forces of Myanmar; ethnic armed groups; female soldiers; Kachin conflict
Constitution (2008)
 armed forces role, 4, 8, 35
 change process, 140
 codification, 214
 "crimes committed during conflict" clauses, 75, 85n5
 legislature and, 202–3
 reform, 62, 154–5, 156, 225
 state ownership of resources, 59
 see also Myanmar government

Constitutional Tribunal, 227–8
contempt of court law, 227
courts, 222, 225, 227–8, 234–5
Cover, Robert, 222, 357
Crouch, Melissa
 chapter by, 17, 221–41
 referenced, 14, 227, 233, 357–8

D

DanChurchAid, 122
Danish Institute for Parties and Democracy, 169
Das, Veena, 93
de-mining *see under* landmine use
"demobilize, disarm, reintegration" (DDR) policy, 26, 31
democracy
 Burmese democracy movement, 253–4
 citizens' views on, 275–6, 280
 concepts of, 246–9, 252, 254, 255, 257–8, 359
 CSO promotion of, 99, 101, 102, 104–5, 115n8
 democratization narratives, 250–7, 359
 pro-democracy camp, southern Shan State, 101
Democracy for Ethnic Minorities Organization (DEMO), 99, 101, 102
Democracy Reporting International, 169
Department for International Development (UK), 169
Department of Foreign Affairs and Trade (Australia), 169
Department of Immigration and Population (Myanmar), 146
Department of Social Welfare (Myanmar), 122, 123

"disciplined democracy", 254
discrimination *see* anti-Muslim sentiment; ethnic minorities; inequality
displaced persons
  in Bangladesh, 14–15, 336, 340, 347n13
  exiles from Myanmar, 4
  internally displaced, 8, 14–15, 150–1, 153
  in Thailand, 4, 11
  see also Rohingya
drug lords *see* frontier strongmen
drug trafficking, 10, 92, 97, 100, 337
Duffield, Mark, 122, 126

E

East Asia Summits, 5
economic reforms, 228–31, 236, 237
economic vulnerability, citizens' views on, 269–70, 275
economy, informal, 78, 81–2, 127
education law, 232–3
Egreteau, Renaud, 149, 203, 302
88 Generation Group, 101, 106
elections (prior to 2010), 164–5, 171, 172
  election commissions, 164–5, 173
  Rakhine political parties, 182–3
elections (2010), 5, 12, 99, 100, 107, 111, 145
  electoral commission, 165, 174
  Muslim participation, 181
  RNDP and, 182
  see also by-elections (2012)
elections (2015), 5–6, 11, 13, 99, 100, 107–8, 111
  armed forces (Tatmadaw) and, 164, 172–3
  Buddhist nationalism in *see* Buddhist nationalism

cancellations, 144–8
challenges, 163–4, 166–8
conduct of, 140–1, 144–8, 165–71, 172–3
conflict and, 139, 141–2
credibility, 139, 140, 147, 155–6, 163–4, 166, 168, 170, 172, 173
disenfranchised groups, 15, 149–54, 168, 178, 181, 226
electoral commission *see* Union Election Commission
funding, 167
international agencies' assistance, 164, 169–71
international observers, 164, 169–71
peace process and, 142–8
Rakhine State *see* Rakhine State elections (2015)
reforms, 156–7
results, 140–1, 163
electoral commissions, 164–5
  members, 173–4
  UEC *see* Union Election Commission
electoral reform, 156–7, 225–6
enrichment *see* wealth (enrichment)
entrepreneurs, 92
equality *see* inequality
"equality" narrative in democratization, 256–7
"essentially contested concepts", 247, 248, 257
ethnic armed groups (EAGs), 3–4, 7–11, 30
  ceasefires *see* ceasefire agreements with EAGs
  co-optation into frontier management, 93–4, 107–14
  community support for, 60, 82–3, 84
  deeds of commitment, 123

patron-client relationships, 126–7
peace talks and, 11, 25–7, 29–31, 34–42
rivalry amongst, 97, 99, 100, 101, 106
in southern Shan State *see* Shan State, southern
unlawful associations, 39–41, 42
see also political violence
ethnic identity
  conflict and, 49–52
  ethnicity as identity marker, 272
  Kachin nationalism and, 52–4, 58–60
  territorial claims and, 59
ethnic minorities, 345
  alliance groups, 35
  Bamar attitudes to, 56
  China's ties with, 9–10
  democratization and, 250, 252
  discrimination against, 54–6, 250
  economic vulnerability, 269–70
  elected representatives, 13, 141, 206–7 *see also* Arakan National Party; ethnic political parties
  perceptions of equality/inequality, 266–71, 274–5, 280
  political issues and, 12
  self-determination *see* self-determination ambitions
  self-identity, 272
  Shan State *see* Pa-O people; Shan people
  summit meetings, 39–41, 42
  views on governance and political culture, 277–9
  see also anti-Muslim sentiment; religious conflict; Rohingya
ethnic nationalism
  Kachin, 52–4, 55, 58–60, 62–3
  women's roles in upholding, 71–2, 76, 80, 82, 83–5

see also Buddhist nationalism
ethnic political parties, 141, 154, 177–80, 182–4, 188, 191 *see also* names *of parties*
Euro-Burma Office, 30
European Union, 169, 170
exiles and migrants from Myanmar, 4
see also displaced persons
extractive industries, 8, 60, 92, 97, 103
see also mining laws; resources

F

Farrelly, Nicholas
  chapter by, 3–21
  referenced, 7, 14, 142
federalism, 26, 29, 31, 36–8, 42, 154
  armed forces (Tatmadaw) attitude to, 37–8
  citizens' views on, 270
  Panglong Agreement (1947) and, 52–4, 55
female soldiers
  contribution of, 80, 84–5
  excluded from combat, 77–8, 86n10
  motivation, 76, 82, 83, 85n7
  in Tatmadaw, 86n10
  see also women
feminist political economy analysis, 68, 69, 70, 73–4, 80, 82, 84 *see also* gendered insecurity and gendered relations
financial institutions, 230
Fink, Christina, 202–3
floods, 5
foreign grants
  to civil society organizations, 102
  in peace process, 34, 44n6
foreign investment laws, 228–31, 237
"four cuts" (Myanmar army strategy), 121, 125
Freeden, Michael, 248–9

freedom of speech, 232
Frontier Areas, Burma, 52–3
frontier strongmen, 92
  devolution of state management to, 93, 94, 101, 102–4, 107–14
frontiers versus borders, 93–4 *see also* borderland conflicts; borders
funeral associations, 318, 319–20 *see also* welfare groups

G

Gallie, Walter Bryce, 247, 248–9
gender analysis in Myanmar studies, 71–3
gender equality/inequality *see* inequality
gendered insecurity and gendered relations
  in the community, 78–80
  in the household, 69, 82–3
  in IDP camps, 80–2
  research studies, 68–9, 71–3
  at the state level, 75–6
  violence and, 69, 73–4, 79–80, 361
  within KIA, 77–8
General Administration Department (Myanmar), 146
general elections *see* elections
Geneva Call, 123
Golden Island Hotel Group, 103
governance reforms, 224–8
governing roles
  female representation in, 70
  leadership style, 253, 254–5
  women excluded from, 70, 72–3, 75, 78–80, 83
  women leaders, 85n1
government of Myanmar *see* Myanmar government
greed as driver of conflict, 49–50

grievance as driver of conflict, 49–50, 51, 55–8
gumsa vs *gumlao*, 57–8

H

Harn Yawnghwe, 30
Harriden, Jessica, 72
Hedström, Jenny
  chapter by, 17, 67–89
  referenced, 9, 361
Heizman, Rik, 296–7
Hkyet Hting Nan, 206
Hla Maung Swe, 33
Hla Pe, 95
Hluttaw
  characteristics, 213–14, 215, 223
  establishment and challenges, 202–3
  lawmaking process, 225, 235–6, 357–8
  speakers' role, 213, 215
  voting methods, 217n24
  see also legislation
Hluttaw response to conflicts
  borderland conflicts and peace negotiations, 200, 205–7
  communal violence, 200, 207–9, 213
  non-partisan approach, 205, 209–11, 215, 356–7
  public complaints and petitions, 212–13
  public consultation, 211, 235
  questions and motions as legislative tools, 207, 211–13
  record, 356–8
  resource-based disputes, 200, 203–5, 213
  speakers' role, 213, 215
Holocaust and the "politics of memory", 304

households
    female-headed households, 68, 76, 82–3
    gendered insecurity and gendered relations, 69, 82–3
Htin Kyaw, 6
Huang, Kai-Ping
    chapter by, 18, 261–83
    referenced, 11, 54, 360, 361
human rights principles, 251–2, 254

I

identity markers, 272 *see also* ethnic identity
ideologies of sociopolitical organization, 56–8, 61–3
Indophobia, 149, 302
inequality
    citizens' views on, 266–71, 274–5, 280
    gender equality indicators, 76
    institutionalized discrimination, 54–6, 69
    of women, 68, 69–70, 73–4, 75–6, 83, 361
    see also gendered insecurity and gendered relations; women
informal economy, 78, 81–2, 127
insecurity *see* gendered insecurity and gendered relations
internally displaced persons, 8, 14–15, 150–1, 153
internally displaced persons' camps
    electoral arrangements, 153
    gendered roles in, 80, 81
    security concerns of women, 81–2
international agencies
    2015 election and, 169–71
    in borderlands, 343
    non-government organisations, 102, 105, 107, 123, 235–6
    reactions to communal violence, 246, 250–2
International Foundation for Electoral Systems, 169
international funding *see* foreign grants
International Institute for Democracy and Electoral Assistance (IDEA), 169
International Republican Institute, 169, 281n7
investment laws, 228–31, 237
Islam
    perceived threat to Buddhism, 290–4, 323–4
    see also anti-Muslim sentiment; Muslims
Islamic State of Iraq and Syria (ISIS), 288, 292, 294, 296, 300–1, 323
Islamophobia, 149, 290, 293–4, 302, 359
    industry of, 295–6, 297, 303
    see also anti-Muslim sentiment

J

Jacob, Cecilia, 124
Joint Monitoring Committee, 155
Jolliffe, Kim, 126, 132
judiciary, 227–8

K

Kachin conflict, 31, 35, 47, 142, 360–1
    Burman paternalism/chauvinism and, 56–7, 60
    ceasefire agreements, 7–8, 9, 47–8, 60–1, 62, 142
    community support for, 60, 82–3, 84
    control of territory and resources, 58–60
    discrimination as cause, 54–6

framed as ethnic conflict, 49–52,
   360–1
framed as resource-driven conflict,
   48, 59–60
fundamental issues, 61–3
historical narratives and, 52–4
Panglong Agreement (1947) and,
   52–4, 55
women's participation in, 69, 70,
   77–8, 79–80, 361
see also Kachin Independence Army
Kachin Independence Army, 31, 35,
   58, 68
   accord (2013), 62
   ceasefire agreement (1994–2011),
      7–8, 9, 47–8, 60–1, 62, 142
   peace agreement (2015) and, 11, 62
   return to conflict, 8–9, 48, 54, 61
   women soldiers *see* female soldiers
   women's supporting roles, 77–8,
      80, 82, 83–5, 361
Kachin Independence Organisation,
   39–40, 54, 58, 68
   ceasefire agreement (1994–2011),
      47–8, 60–1, 62, 142
   census enumeration prevented by,
      148
   community support for, 60, 82–3
   role of, 80
   women's roles in, 77–8
Kachin people
   ethnic identification, 52–4, 55
   impact of war, 8–9, 58, 80–3
   nationalism, 52–4, 55, 58–60, 62–3
   Panglong Agreement (1947), 95
   self-determination denied, 55–6,
      60–3
   sense of collective identity, 58
   significance of territory, 55, 58–60
   social ideals, 56–7
   views in the peace process, 79

Kachin State
   census (2014), 148
   conflict *see* Kachin conflict
   elections (2015), 140, 146
   female-headed households, 68, 76,
      82–3
   gender-based violence, 74, 79, 80–2
   gender differences in society, 68, 76
   people *see* Kachin people
   shadow economy, 78, 81–2
   Special Region 2, 9
Kachin State Peace and Development
   Council, 4
Kachin women *see under* Kachin
   conflict; women
Kachin Women's Association, 68, 78
Kachin Women's Association
   Thailand, 68
Kachin Women's Union, 68
Kaman people, 14–15, 150, 153
Karen National Liberation Army
   (KNLA)
   census enumeration prevented by,
      148
   elections (2015) and, 146
Karen National Union, 30, 34, 39–40,
   62, 123
Karen people, 52, 95, 317 *see also*
   Kayin people
Kaung Rwai Social Action Network
   (KRSAN), 99, 101, 102, 104–5, 106
Kayah people, 10–11
Kayah State elections (2015), 140, 145
Kayin people, 10–11 *see also* Karen
   people
Kayin State
   census (2014), 148
   elections (2015), 140, 146
Kearns, Thomas R, 222, 236
Khan, Helal Mohammed
   chapter by, 18, 333–50

Khin Aung Myint, 4–5, 13, 16
Khin Maung Aye, 327
Khin Maung Latt, 115n14
Khin Yi, 33
Khun Sa, 100
Knowledge, Attitude, and Practices (KAP) surveys on landmine use, 122, 129
Kokang rebel forces (1950s), 85n1
Kokang Region, Shan State, 9–10
  see also Myanmar National Democratic Alliance Army
Korf, Benedikt, 93
Kyauk Sein Nagar (Gems) Limited, 103
Kyaw Sein, 95
Kyaw Yin Hlaing, 33

L

labour organizations, 232
Lake Inle, 91, 103, 115n14
land tenure and use, 12
  Hluttaw response to land grabbing, 200, 203–5, 213
  laws, 229–30
  see also territory, control of
landmine accidents and deaths, 121, 125, 128, 129, 131
landmine use
  behavioural change, 122, 123, 131–2
  for community protection, 122, 128–30, 132
  de-mining, 123–5
  information sharing about, 130–1
  international responses, 122, 123
  minimization of, 131–2
  NCA and, 125
  population surveys, 122
  purposes, 122, 125–6, 128–30
  risk assessment, 122, 128–30
  risk education, 123, 124, 131–2

language education policy, 12
Laoutides, Costas
  chapter by, 17, 47–65
  referenced, 139, 360–1
Lashio, Shan State, 15, 291
law reform, 221, 223–4, 233–7 see also legislation
Law Yone, 253
Le Muer, Pierre-Yves, 93–4
leadership see governing roles
Lean, Nathan, 297
legislation
  contempt of court law, 227
  economic reforms, 228–31, 236, 237
  finality clauses, 234–5
  lawmaking process, 225, 235–6
  laws on protection of race and religion, 208–9, 233, 323
  publication of, 223–4
  social reforms, 231–3, 236
  structural governance reforms, 224–8
  see also law reform
legislatures, 201–2
  of Myanmar see Hluttaw
Lidauer, Michael
  chapter by, 17, 139–61
  referenced, 12, 167, 225, 353
"listening project" on anti-Muslim discourses, 285–6, 289–90
  findings see under anti-Muslim sentiment
Lo Hsing Han, 92

M

MaBaTha, 15, 149, 153, 179, 290, 302, 323 see also Buddhist nationalism
Mahn Aung Tin Myint, 207
Maung Maung Saw, 195n4

McCarthy, Gerard
   chapter by, 18, 313–31
   referenced, 360
media
   armed forces (Tatmadaw) and, 41
   laws concerning, 232
   stories on Muslim terrorism threat, 297–8
   views on peace process, 34, 42
   see also social media
Meiktila, 15, 207, 208, 245, 250
Mi Mi Khaing, 72
migrants and exiles from Myanmar, 4
   see also displaced persons
military forces see armed forces of Myanmar (Tatmadaw)
militia see ethnic armed groups
Min Aung Hlaing, 8, 172
Min Zaw Oo, 33
Mine Risk Education Working Group, 122, 123, 133n3
mines (landmines) see landmine accidents and deaths; landmine use
mining laws, 231 see also extractive industries; resources
Mon National Party, 167–8
Mon people, 10–11
Mon State elections (2015), 140, 145
Mong Tai Army, 100
monks
   donations to, 322, 325–6
   political activism, 6, 149, 152, 153, 323–4
   respect for, 113, 324
   social welfare activities, 322
   see also religious organizations
Mouffe, Chantal, 354, 357
Muslims, 13, 14–15, 208
   disenfranchisement of, 15, 149–54, 178, 181, 226
   ISIS and community distrust of Muslims, 288, 292, 294, 296, 300–1, 323
   NLD pro-Muslim image, 178, 179–80
   population of Rakhine State, 150–3, 343
   social actions contrasted with those of Buddhists, 322–3
   tolerance towards, 14, 179, 289–90, 295
   views/violence against see anti-Muslim sentiment
   see also Rohingya
Myanmar army see armed forces of Myanmar (Tatmadaw)
Myanmar citizens' views see Asian Barometer Survey (2015), Myanmar
Myanmar Egress, 30, 101
Myanmar government, 3–7, 11–14
   citizens' views on governance and political culture, 276–9
   committee processes, 234–5
   ethnic group violence and, 7–11
   executive power, 226
   issues faced, 12
   military support for, 8, 12
   peace-making efforts see peace talks and agreements
   relations with Bangladesh, 335–6, 345
   relations with China, 10
   see also Burma; Constitution (2008); Hluttaw; political system of Myanmar; state control; state/regional-level governments; Thein Sein government
Myanmar legislature see Hluttaw
Myanmar Mine Action Centre, 124

Myanmar National Democratic Alliance Army, 9–10, 31, 36, 41, 142
Myanmar Peace Center (MPC), 11, 27, 101
  goals, 34
  international support for, 32
  membership, 33–4, 41–2
  negotiation and decision-making approach, 28, 36–42, 44n6
  power of, 34
  role, 32–3, 35, 41–2, 124
  stakeholders, 34–6
Myanmar Press Council, 41, 166
Myanmar Stock Exchange, 231
Myanmar studies, gender perspective in, 71–3
Myanmar Update conferences, 16
Myint Swe, 6
Myitkyina, 8–9
myo-saunt-upade (laws on protection of race and religion), 208–9, 233, 323

N

Nang Hern Kham, 85n1
narcotics *see* drug trafficking
narrative approach, 246–9
National Defence and Security Council, 35, 38, 44n5, 44n8
National Defence College, 171
National Democratic Alliance Army (NDAA), 146, 148
National Democratic Institute (NDI), 169
National Endowment for Democracy (NED), 102, 263
National League for Democracy (NLD)
  1990s and 2000s, 314

by-elections (2012), 5, 13
charitable welfare initiatives, 321
elections (1990), 164–5
elections (2010), 5, 12, 165
elections (2015), 5–6, 11, 13, 108, 112, 140, 163
elections (2015) in Rakhine State, 179–80, 185–94
  in government, 6–7, 11–14, 18, 141
  NCA and peace dialogue, 155
  pro-Muslim image, 178, 179–80
  in southern Shan State, 101
National United Party of Arakan, 183
National Unity Party, 182, 195n4
nationalism, 272
  inherently gendered, 71–3
  see also Buddhist nationalism; ethnic nationalism
nationalist Pa-O *see* Pa-O National Organization (PNLO)
Nationwide Ceasefire Agreement, 11, 31, 205
  consequent dialogues, 155, 205–7
  landmine use and, 125, 132
  participants, 26, 39–40, 62, 114, 143, 157n4
  see also peace talks and agreements (2011–15)
Nationwide Ceasefire Coordination Team, 11, 35, 39–41
Nay Win Tun, 92, 103, 104, 107
Ne Win, 7, 44n4
negotiation and decision-making
  in general, 28, 32, 38–9
  MPC approach, 28, 36–41
Neuhold, Christine, 36, 38
969 movement, 149, 290
Norway, 169
Nu, U, 253

O

Oo Tha Tun, 182
Open Society Foundation, 102
opium interests *see* drug trafficking
Organization for the Protection of Race and Religion (MaBaTha), 15, 149, 153, 179, 290, 302, 323 *see also* Buddhist nationalism
the Other, fear of, 300–1, 305n2

P

Pa-O National Army, 92, 110, 116n27
  see also Nay Win Tun
Pa-O National Liberation Organization (PNLO), 98–9, 101
  ceasefire agreement (1994), 103–4
  ceasefire agreement (2015), 114
  rivalry with other groups, 100, 106
  UPNO and, 114
Pa-O National Organization (PNO), 95, 98–9, 101
  areas of control, 96
  attitude to KRSAN, 105
  business operations, 103
  ceasefire agreement (1991), 96, 103
  control of village leaders, 108–11, 113
  election performance, 107–8, 111–13, 116n22
  in frontier pacification, 103–4
  rivalry with other groups, 97, 99, 100, 106
  tangible benefits for Pa-O community, 113–14
Pa-O people, 95
  political groups, 98–9, 101 *see also* Pa-O National Liberation Organization (PNLO); Pa-O National Organization (PNO)
  relationship with Shan, 95, 97
  see also Shan State, southern

Pa-O Self-Administered Zone, 93, 116n22
  political order, 103–5, 111–14
  village tract system, 108–11
Pa-Oh Youth Organization (PYO), 99, 101, 102
Pan Zagar activist group, 295–6
Pandey, Gyanendra, 303, 305n2
Panglong Agreement (1947), 7, 52–4, 55, 95
parahita, 317–19
Parami Development Network (PDN), 99, 101, 113
parliaments, 201–2
  of Myanmar. *see* Hluttaw
Patent, Jason D, 248
patron-client relationships, 126–7
patronage *see* ceasefire capitalism; foreign grants
peace related to gender equality, 76
peace talks and agreements (2011–15)
  election process and, 142–4
  Hluttaw response to, 200, 205–7
  Nationwide Ceasefire Agreement *see* Nationwide Ceasefire Agreement
  negotiation and decision-making approaches, 28, 36–42, 44n6
  process, 11, 25–7, 29–31, 356
  women omitted from talks, 77, 79
  see also ceasefire agreements with EAGs; Myanmar Peace Center
people trafficking, 74, 81–2, 83
  anti-trafficking law, 235
piecemeal approach in negotiation, 28, 38–9
  employed by MPC, 28, 36–41, 42
policy community, 28, 32, 42 *see also* Myanmar Peace Center
political economy
  conducive to state control *see* ceasefire capitalism

CSOs and, 102, 105
political exiles *see* exiles and migrants from Myanmar
political groups in southern Shan State
   international civil society organizations, 102, 105
   Pa-O community, 97–9, 101
   political order, 103–7, 111–14
   Shan community, 97, 99–101
political socialization agents, 99, 102, 104–5
political system of Myanmar
   citizens' views on governance and political culture, 276–81
   ethnic group representation, 12–13
   groups not well-represented, 13
   partisanship and religion (survey results), 276
   see also elections
political violence
   defined, 69
   use of force for a cause (survey results), 278–9
   women's participation/support, 69, 70, 72, 76, 77–8, 80, 83–5
   see also Kachin conflict
"politics of memory", 304
politics/"the political", 353–62
   distinction between "politics" and "the political", 354–5
   influence of Buddhist networks, 323–4
   the nonpolitical, 357–9, 362
   notions of, 321–4, 327–8
   undecided voters, 325–7
Poole, Deborah, 93
poverty and violence, 68, 73–4, 81–2, 83, 84
power, exercise of
   arbitrary, 121, 126

soft power, 112, 113–14
see also sociopolitical organization; state control
presidential powers, 226
Program for the Progress of the Border Areas and National Races Development, 95, 97
protest rights, 232
Pyidaungsu Hluttaw *see* Hluttaw
Pyithu Hluttaw *see* Hluttaw

R

Raeymaekers, Timothy, 93
Rakhine Action Plan, 339, 344
Rakhine National Party, 170
Rakhine National Party (Arakan National Party), 140, 152, 177–8, 181–5
   as Buddhist-nationalist alternative party, 189–91
   election results (2015), 177–8, 185–9, 193–4
Rakhine Nationalities Development Party (RNDP), 182–4, 338
Rakhine State, 4
   census (2014), 148, 150–1
   districts, 195n1
   Muslim population, 150–3, 343
   political parties, 181–5 *see also* Rakhine National Party
   religious conflict, 6, 14–15, 338
   separatist movements, 338
Rakhine State elections (2015)
   ANP and Rakhine ethno-nationalism, 181–5
   ANP as alternative to NLD, 189–91
   disenfranchisement, 152–4, 181
   results, 177–80, 185–9
   voting patterns, 193–4
Rakhine State National Force Party, 184, 195n4

rape *see* sexual violence
religion
   citizens' views on, 271–6, 280
Religion of Peace website, 295, 297
religious conflict, 6, 14–15, 149, 150–3, 245–6, 250–1, 262, 271 *see also* communal violence
religious minorities, 15, 208–9 *see also* ethnic minorities; Muslims
religious organizations
   political and social activism, 321–3
   social welfare services, 317–21, 327, 360
   see also Buddhist nationalism; monks
religious tolerance, 14, 179, 289–90, 295
resource-based disputes, 48, 51, 55, 58–60
   Hluttaw response to, 200, 203–5, 213
resources
   control of, 59, 97
   insurgent financing from, 59
   royalty distribution, 12
   see also extractive industries
Restoration Council of Shan State (RCSS), 101, 106
   ceasefire agreement (2011), 92, 100
   relationship with SNLD, 111–12
   see also Shan State Army — South
rights of individuals, 232–3
rights to organize and protest, 232
Rohingya, 14, 334
   designations (Rohingya/Bengali), 14, 151, 153, 159n19, 181
   discrimination against, 250, 339, 340, 341, 358
   exoduses to Bangladesh, 14–15, 336, 340, 341
   franchise and citizenship, 151–2, 181, 339, 344, 358

   self-identification, 148, 151
   solutions for plight of, 343–5
Rohingya Solidarity Organisation (RSO), 338
Ruby Dragon group of companies, 92, 103

S

Saha, Jonathan, 72
Sai Leik, 170
Sai Mauk Kham, 31
Salai Ngun Cung Lian, 33
Sao Yawd Serk, 100
Sarat, Austin, 222, 236
Scheper-Hughes, Nancy, 303
Schissler, Matt
   chapter by, 14, 18, 285–311
   referenced, 127, 129, 149, 361
Schmitt, Carl, 365n2
self-administered zones, 226 *see also* Pa-O Self-Administered Zone
self-determination ambitions, 154
   Arakanese political parties, 184–5
   citizens' views on, 270–1
   Kachin, 55–6, 60–3
   Pa-O, 101, 113
   Shan, 111, 112
self-protection (communities) *see* community protection
17(1) issue (unlawful association), 39–41, 42
sexual violence, 71–4, 79–82
   absence of legal protection, 75
   in IDP camps, 81–2
   inequality and, 75
   in Kachin State, 74
shadow economies, 78, 81–2, 127
Shan National United Front, 100 *see also* Shan State Army
Shan Nationalities Democratic Party (SNDP), 100, 101, 147

election performance, 111, 113
Shan Nationalities League for Democracy (SNLD), 100, 101, 147, 170
 election performance, 111, 141
 relationship with RCSS/SSA-S, 111–12
Shan people, 10–11
 ethnic armed groups, 99–100 *see also* Shan State Army
 relationship with Pa-O, 95, 97
 Taungoo family case study, 325–7
Shan State, 4
 ceasefire capitalism, 92–3, 94, 101, 112–13
 communities *see* Pa-O people; Shan people
 consequences of war, 8–9
 elections (2015), 140–1, 145–7
 Kokang Region conflict, 9–10
 religious conflict, 15
 Special Region 1, 10
 Special Region 3, 96
 Special Region 6, 96, 99
 Wa armed groups, 7, 10
 see also Pa-O Self-Administered Zone
Shan State, southern
 elections (2015), 111–12
 ethnic struggle, 95–7
 political actors, 97–102, 111–12
 political order, 103–7, 111–14
 rivalry among ethnic armed groups, 97, 99, 100, 101, 106
Shan State Army
 areas of control, 96, 97
 ceasefire agreement (1989), 96, 100
 rivalry with other groups, 97, 100
 see also Restoration Council of Shan State
Shan State Army — North, 147

Shan State Army — South (SSA-S)
 ceasefire agreement (2011), 92, 100
 establishment, 97, 100
 relationship with SNLD, 111–12
 rivalry with other groups, 100, 101, 106
Shan State Independence Army, 100
 see also Shan State Army
Shan State Nationalities Liberation Organization (SSNLO), 98 *see also* Pa-O National Liberation Organization (PNLO)
Shan State Nationalities People's Liberation Organization (SSNPLO), 98
 areas of control, 96
 ceasefire agreement (1994), 96
 rivalry with other groups, 97, 99
Shan State Restoration Council, 100
 see also Restoration Council of Shan State
Shanland Nationalities Liberation Front (SNLF), 98 *see also* Pa-O National Organization (PNO)
Shwe Mann, 5, 13, 44n6, 164, 204, 205–6, 209
smuggling, 100 *see also* drug trafficking; people trafficking
social media dissemination of anti-Muslim sentiment, 294–8, 323
social reforms, 231–3, 236
social services, 315–16
socio-economic inequality *see* inequality; poverty
sociopolitical organization
 control over territory, 59–60
 Kachin/Burman ideological differences, 56–8, 61–3
Soe Thein, 30, 33
soft power, 112, 113–14
Soros, George, 102

South, Ashley, 127, 128, 129
Southeast Asian Games, 5
Special Economic Zones, 230
state control
   borders versus frontiers, 93–4
   ceasefire capitalism and, 60, 92–3, 94, 112–13
   divide-and-rule strategy, 97, 99, 103–4, 106
   through co-optation of local armed groups, 93–4, 101, 102–14
   see also Myanmar government
state control, opposition to see ethnic armed groups; Kachin conflict; self-determination ambitions
State Counsellor, 12
State Law and Order Restoration Council, 95, 100, 103, 114n7
State Peace and Development Council, 4, 13, 223, 254
state/regional-level governments
   devolution of powers to (issue), 12, 225
   peace talks and, 29
Steinberg, David, 315
Stock Exchange, 231
Su Mon Thazin Aung
   chapter by, 17, 25–46
   referenced, 11, 356
Supreme Court, 227, 228
surveys of Myanmar citizens, 264, 281n7
   ABS see Asian Barometer Survey (2015), Myanmar
   "listening project" on anti-Muslim discourses see anti-Muslim sentiment

T

Ta'ang National Liberation Army, 31, 41

Taiwan Foundation for Democracy, 263
Tatmadaw see armed forces of Myanmar (Tatmadaw)
Taungoo
   family life, 325–7
   political and social activism, 321–4
   population characteristics, 317
   religious institutions, 317–19
   welfare groups and services, 317–21
territory, control of, 58–60 see also land tenure and use
Tha Kalei, 99
Thailand
   border region conflicts, 10
   displaced persons from Myanmar, 4, 11
Than Tun
   chapter by, 177–98, 365n1
   referenced, 358, 360, 365n1
Tharaphi Than, 302
Thein Sein, 4
Thein Sein government, 4–5, 12, 14
   "disciplined democracy", 254
   elections see elections (2015)
   ethnic policy, 29
   executive power, 226
   law reform process, 235
   martial law, 142
   MPC influence, 32–3, 35
   peace-making process, 11, 25–6, 29–31, 41–2, 142, 205, 206
   see also Myanmar Peace Center
Thein Soe, 165
Thein Zaw, 30, 31
Tiger Head see Shan Nationalities Democratic Party (SNDP)
Tigyit coal and power project, 106
Tin Aye, 165, 166
Tin Htut, 204

Tin Maung Than, 33
Top White Tiger Company, 111
trade, 8, 9
trafficking *see* drug trafficking; people trafficking
True, Jacqui, 70, 73

U

UNICEF, 122
Union Election Commission (UEC), 140, 144, 145, 147, 154, 156, 164–8, 225
　international assistance to, 169–71
　members, 174
　similar institutions, 164–5
　see also elections (2015)
Union Pa-O National Organization (UPNO), 99, 101, 108, 114, 115n9
Union Parliament *see* Hluttaw
Union Peace Conference (2016), 155
Union Peacemaking Central Committee, 31, 205
Union Peacemaking Working Committee, 31, 32, 33, 41, 44n6, 205
Union Political Dialogue Joint Committee, 155
Union Solidarity and Development Association (USDA), 114n7
Union Solidarity and Development Party (USDP), 5, 101, 140–1
　as Buddhist alternative to NLD, 190–2
　charitable welfare initiatives, 321
　CSOs and, 106
　elections (2010), 12, 111, 115n7, 165, 181
　elections (2015), 112, 152, 168
　elections (2015) in Rakhine State, 178, 181, 185–94
　government, 5, 12–13, 189–90
　patronage of Buddhism, 324
unions, 232
United Kingdom, 169
United Nationalities Alliance, 167
United Nationalities Federal Council, 35
United Nations Committee on the Rights of the Child, 123
United Nations Convention on the Rights of the Child, 235
United States of America
　anti-Muslim sentiment, 287–8, 294, 295–6, 297
United Wa State Army (UWSA), 7, 10, 11, 35–6
　census and, 148
　elections (2015) and, 146
unity and benevolence, 253–6
Unlawful Associations Act (1908), 39–41, 42
USAID, 169

V

Vahu Development Institute, 30
Van Thio, Henry, 6
village tract system, 108–11, 113
violence
　material basis for, 68, 73–4, 81–2, 83, 84
　nonpolitical response to conflict, 354–5
　against Rohingya *see* Rohingya
　use of force for a cause (survey results), 278–9
　against women, 71, 73–4, 79–82
　see also Buddhist–Muslim violence; communal violence; political violence; sexual violence
Volunteer Service Overseas, 102

W

Wa people, 10, 40 *see also* United Wa State Army
Wa Self-Administered Division (SAD), 146, 148
war, 7–11 *see also* ceasefire agreements with EAGs; Kachin conflict; peace talks and agreements (2011–15); violence
Ware, Anthony
   chapter by, 17, 47–65
   referenced, 139, 360–1
warlords *see* frontier strongmen
wealth (enrichment), 7, 8, 60 *see also* ceasefire capitalism
Weber, Max, 354
welfare groups, 315–16, 327, 360
   Buddhist-imbued services in Taungoo, 317–21
   political and social activism, 321–3
Wells, Tamas
   chapter by, 14, 18, 245–60
   referenced, 307n23, 326, 359, 360
Welsh, Bridget
   chapter by, 18, 261–83
   referenced, 11, 54, 360, 361
White Tiger Party *see* Shan Nationalities Democratic Party (SNDP)
Wirathu (preacher) *see* Ashin Wirathu
women
   ethnic nationalism and, 71–2, 76, 80, 82, 83–5
   exclusion from leadership roles, 70, 72–3, 75, 78–80, 83
   exclusion from peace talks, 77, 79
   gender equality indicators, 76
   inequality of, 68, 69–70, 73–6, 83, 361
   leaders (as anomalies), 85n1
   physical security of, 76, 80–2
   seen as "needing protection", 71–2, 77, 79
   structural inequalities and, 69–70
   studies with a gender perspective, 72
   support for Kachin conflict *see under* Kachin Independence Army
   traditional roles, 77–8, 80, 81
   as victims, 67
   violence against, 71, 73–4, 79–82
   see also female soldiers
Wong Pak Nun, 94, 101, 103
World Economic Forum, 5
Wunna Maung Lwin, 303
Wunna, U, 254

Y

Yang, Olive, 85n1
Yangon School of Political Science, 263
Yawnghwe, Samara, 95
youth
   CSOs and, 102, 104–5, 113
Yue, Ricky
   chapter by, 17, 91–119
   referenced, 127, 226
Yuval-Davis, Nira, 71

CPSIA information can be obtained
at www.ICGtesting.com
Printed in the USA
LVOW13*1038050617
536968LV00010B/95/P